AF248951

Gender and Modern Irish Drama

Drama and Performance Studies
Timothy Wiles, general editor
Volume 14 in series

Gender and Modern Irish Drama

Susan Cannon Harris

This book is a publication of

Indiana University Press
601 North Morton Street
Bloomington, Indiana 47404-3797 USA

http://iupress.indiana.edu

Telephone orders 800-842-6796
Fax orders 812-855-7931
Orders by e-mail iuporder@indiana.edu

The paper used in this publication meets the minimum requirements of American National Standard for Information Sciences—Permanence of Paper for Printed Library Materials, ANSI Z39.48-1984.

Manufactured in the United States of America

Library of Congress Cataloging-in-Publication Data

Harris, Susan Cannon, date
Gender and modern Irish drama / Susan Cannon Harris.
p. cm. — (Drama and performance studies ; v. 14)
Includes bibliographical references and index.
ISBN 0-253-34117-5
1. English drama—Irish authors—History and criticism. 2. Women and literature—Ireland—History—20th century. 3. Feminism and literature—Ireland—History—20th century. 4. Yeats, W. B. (William Butler), 1865–1939—Dramatic works. 5. Yeats, W. B. (William Butler), 1865–1939—Characters—Women. 6. English drama—20th century—History and criticism. 7. Body, Human, in literature. 8. Ireland—In literature. 9. Sex role in literature. 10. Women in literature. I. Title. II. Series.
PR8795.W65 H37 2002
822'.91209352042'09417—dc21

2001006882

1 2 3 4 5 07 06 05 04 03 02

For Liz and Barbara

Contents

Acknowledgments

This book has deep roots, and owes much to many people. First and foremost, I must thank Elizabeth Butler Cullingford and Barbara Harlow, who have guided me through every stage of this project and without whom this book would not have become what it is. Through their scholarship and in the classroom, they taught me most of what I needed to know in order to write this book, and their generosity as mentors has been invaluable to me. This book would have been equally impossible without Ann Cvetkovich, whose work has greatly influenced my approach to gender and the body. I would also like to thank Charlotte Canning and Oscar Brockett for helping me make this a book about theater as well as a book about drama.

All of my colleagues at the Keough Institute for Irish Studies at Notre Dame, especially Seamus Deane, Chris Fox, and Luke Gibbons, have helped create an environment that provides both the intellectual stimulation and the institutional support necessary to do this kind of work; and I thank them, along with Kevin Whelan and the Keough Notre Dame Center in Dublin, for all of the help they have given me in the later stages of this project. I am also grateful for the friendship and feedback of all the colleagues who have read or heard parts of this work at various stages, including, but not necessarily limited to, David Alvarez, Margot Backus, Bret Benjamin, Fran Buntman, Katie Conrad, Nancy Curtin, Aimee Ellis, Salah Hassan, Zjaleh Hajibashi, Mary Harvan, Katie Kane, Vera Kreilkamp, Rachel Jennings, Ed Madden, Joey Slaughter, Sandy Soto, Karen Steele, and Jenny Wenzel. I would particularly like to thank Mary Trotter for her help in revising the manuscript, especially in terms of my use of performance theory.

Writing may be difficult, but publishing is harder; and I owe special thanks to all those who helped make this manuscript a book. Many of my colleagues in the English department at the University of Notre Dame generously invested their time and effort in helping me place the book; I am indebted especially to Barbara Green, Glenn Hendler, Cyraina Johnson-Rouiller, Kathy Psomiades, Chris Vanden Bossche, and Ewa Ziarek. I am also deeply grateful to Steve Watt for his advice and for the interest he has taken in my work. Most of all I thank Robert Sloan and Kendra Stokes at Indiana University Press for supporting the project and for their help in preparing the manuscript, and Elizabeth Yoder for copyediting.

Archival research for this project was made possible in part by support from the Institute for Scholarship in the Liberal Arts in the College of Arts and Letters at the University of Notre Dame. Part of chapter 2 is adapted from an article that first appeared in 1996 in the journal *Modern Drama,* published by the University of Toronto Press. Another part of chapter 2 was published as "More Than a Morbid, Unhealthy Mind: Public Health and the *Playboy* Riots" in *A Century of Irish Drama: Widening the Stage,* edited by Stephen Watt, Eileen Morgan, and Shakir Mustafa, published by Indiana University Press. A shorter version of chapter 5 appeared in 1998 in *Eire-Ireland: An Interdisciplinary Journal of Irish Studies,* published by the Irish-American Cultural Institute. I thank the University of Toronto Press, Indiana University Press, and the Irish-American Cultural Institute, respectively, for permission to include that work here.

I also want to thank some people whose contributions may be less easily documented. As always, my thanks go to Victor Luftig and Weldon Thornton, who first turned me on to Irish studies and whose teaching and scholarship continue to inspire me. All of my friends outside of academia deserve special recognition for seeing me through this. And above all, I am profoundly grateful for the lifetime of support and love my parents, John and Elin Harris; my sister Lynn; and my brother John have given me. Finally, I would like to thank my partner, Liza Reynolds. It was thanks to her that I acquired the knowledge of ancient literature that informs chapter 2, and her work on Ovid's *Metamorphoses* helped me wrestle with the questions raised in chapter 5. But more than that, she has always believed in me and in this book, and her faith has kept me going at times when nothing else would. For all of her support at the best and worst of times, and for her genuine enthusiasm for this project, I can never thank her enough.

Abbreviations

CP	*The Complete Plays of J. M. Synge*
EI	*Essays and Introductions*
LSO	*Letters of Sean O'Casey*
PSP	*Plays, Stories, Poems*
PWS	*Political Writings and Speeches*
SP	*Selected Plays of Sean O'Casey*
VPl	*Variorum Plays of W. B. Yeats*

Gender and
Modern Irish Drama

Introduction: Bodies and Blood

In February of 1980, republican women prisoners in Armagh responded to an increase in harassment and brutality on the part of the prison authorities by organizing a dirty protest. It was a strategy that had already been used by their male comrades in Long Kesh, where IRA members had refused to wear prison uniforms, take showers, or use the toilets, instead disposing of their bodily wastes by emptying them onto the cell floors or spreading them on the cell walls.[1] The Long Kesh protest was slow to receive media attention, partly because it was hard for those who had never been subjected to prison discipline to see bodily functions as a vehicle for political protest.[2] The protest in Armagh Prison proved even more "horrifying and incomprehensible"—not only to the press and the public, but to the "republican men who tried hard to dissuade the women from their protest" (Aretxaga 127). Brenda, one of the strikers, described her brother's reaction in an interview with anthropologist Begona Aretxaga:

> They didn't want us on dirty protest because of our periods. They didn't say that; they said that we were women, that we were different. But we knew it was because of our periods. These were men who had killed, had been imprisoned and they couldn't say the word 'period'! (qtd. in Aretxaga 127)

Aretxaga agrees that what made the women's protest unspeakable was "the appearance of menstruation in the political field"; commentators who could bring themselves to read urine and feces as political speech gave up in "disgust" when confronted with menstrual blood (127). As the "unspeakable sign of sexual difference," menstrual blood cannot be incorporated into the vocabulary of protest; it must be kept "outside representation" (127). Its "excess of signification" is so explosive that it cannot be incorporated into "existing discourse"—even a discourse that has come to grips with other unspeakable excretions—"without disrupting it" (128).

As Aretxaga argues, the prisoners' use of menstrual blood was a gender-specific response to a gender-specific problem—the "sexualized violence" to which they had been subjected by the male guards who performed the unannounced search that triggered the protest (128). The fact that this gesture proved unreadable even within the republican movement is, in one sense, surprising; from its earliest beginnings republican discourse relied on blood as a symbol, especially when deployed in the context of imperial violence. The Irish republic from which the IRA takes its name was consecrated in 1916 by the blood shed by Padraig Pearse, James Connolly, and the other leaders of the Easter Rising. It would seem that the Armagh prisoners' protest should have been *more* effective than the Long Kesh one, simply because as menstruating women they had access to this powerful symbol.

But at the same time, the fact that the Armagh protest has been ignored or dismissed is not at all surprising. As "Brenda" knows—as your own reaction to her story may be informing you right now—there is a vast difference between the blood of the sacrificial martyr and the blood coming from these women's bodies. One cleanses; the other stains. One promises rebirth; the other negates that possibility. Blood, which in the martyr's case marks his release from the limited corporeal world into the realm of ideal and abstraction, marks the menstruating woman as mortal, embodied, gendered, tied by her cycle to a temporally bound existence. The Armagh protest's reception illustrates the relationship between the meaning of blood and the meaning of the body, between national politics and sexual politics.

This book is about that relationship—how it developed, why it matters, and what it means, both for the playwrights whose work I read and for the men and women who still contend with the consequences of the four critical decades that encompassed the development of the Irish National Theater and the creation of the Irish Free State. The book focuses on the work of the Abbey Theater's most prominent playwrights—W. B. Yeats, J. M. Synge, and Sean O'Casey. The historical boundaries are the premiere of Yeats's 1899 *The Countess Cathleen* and the writing of his last play, *The Death of Cuchulain,* in 1939. This period covers the conflicts that led to the birth of the modern Irish state; it also encompasses the development of major trends in medical science that transformed conceptions of gender, sexuality, and the body itself. Thus, it offers a unique opportunity to study the relationship between political violence, literary production, and the construction of national and sexual identities.

Blood

Drama has long been recognized as a genre preoccupied with sacrifice; the idea of theater as a rite leading up to the immolation of a protagonist whose suffering purges the audience is as old as Aristotle and as new as Artaud.[3] And sacrifice was an important motif in Irish literature throughout the Irish literary revival. The cult of blood-sacrifice reached its high point, perhaps, in the rhetoric of Pearse and the 1916 Easter Uprising; but even now the symbology of ritual sacrifice retains enormous power for modern audiences and provides a literary model that writers and readers alike return to again and again in their attempts to understand or represent Ireland and Irish history.

But although the presumed Irish fascination with sacrifice has been heavily analyzed and critiqued, the fact that the martyr is marked as male and the great Other that receives the blood of the sacrifice (whether she is Hibernia, the bog, the Virgin, or the Shan Van Vocht) is marked as female has been taken for granted by many who write, or write on, Irish drama. The blood that Pearse envisioned washing the fields of Ireland was blood let from male bodies; and the literary tradition that grappled with the consequences of the Rising has, even in its critiques, largely remained faithful to that aspect of his vision. Within the confines of that tradition, women are not symbolically eligible for the role of sacrificial victim, and playwrights are reluctant to allow them to fill it.[4]

The reaction to the Armagh dirty protest suggests that this insistence on a male martyr is not arbitrary. When it proceeds from a female body, blood becomes "dirty" through its association with sexuality; it means not redemption but menstruation or defloration. Both of these events, closely tied to woman's reproductive function, mark her body as irredeemably material and therefore resistant to idealization. The female victim's body does not disappear behind her transfigured image; it remains present, solid, weighted down with the burden of corporeality and stained with sex and gender.

The sacrificial story that gets played out in nationalist Irish drama requires a male victim whose body can be more easily translated. It requires, also, a female counterpart—the mother/wife/lover who accepts the sacrifice and whose body can then fulfill the more "natural" role of transforming that death into a rebirth. One of the foundational premises of this study is that the sacrificial paradigm was popular among Irish nationalist audiences in part because it enforced those gender roles.

The fact that these gender roles are so widely taken for granted has to do with two long-established critical trends from which this analysis must and will depart. The first is the tendency to explain both the omnipresence of sacrificial imagery and the reiteration of traditional gender roles in modern Irish literature almost exclusively in terms of the power of the Catholic Church. From that point of view, all of the questions I am about to take on have a very simple answer: representations of sex, gender, and sacrifice are the way they are because Catholic dogma and iconography have made Christ and the Virgin Mary the only culturally acceptable role models available to Irish men and women. The all-pervasive power of the Catholic Church inexorably forces Irish men and women into these positions and therefore requires them to continually recreate not only the crucifixion but also the pietà.

It is undeniable that Catholicism had, and continues to have, remarkably intense effects on Irish culture. However, to treat Catholicism as if it were the sole and sufficient explanation for the phenomena this project investigates would be to assign it an almost magically privileged position—to imply that the Catholic Church's power in Ireland (and especially over Irish women) is self-generated and self-sustaining, supernaturally independent of political, economic, or historical conditions. Similarly, to assume that Irish nationalists responded to sacrificial imagery uncritically and unthinkingly simply because it echoed Catholic iconography is to accept stereotypical constructions of the Catholic Irish as superstitious, idolatrous, and easily manipulated. If we do not want to fall into either or both of these traps, then instead of merely observing the persistence of Catholic ideas and images in this literature, we must ask *why* those ideas and images are so persistent. Instead of allowing the influence of Catholicism to tautologically explain itself, we must ask what material conditions allowed Catholicism in twentieth-century Ireland to develop both its peculiarly distinctive features and its remarkable cultural authority.

It is precisely because I want to ask those questions that I must challenge a second cherished critical paradigm: the anthropological understanding of drama that has become so important to theater studies. Most contemporary treatments of sacrificial drama are grounded in the idea that drama itself is a primal sacrificial rite—an idea that reaches back to the ancient Greek model but is also derived from more recent work done by European anthropologists on "primitive" cultures. Since this contemporary conception of drama-as-ritual entered theater studies during the 1960s via the work of figures like Richard Schechner and Victor Turner, it is based on an anthropological model now forty years out of date; and although anthropology itself has gone on to acknowledge and interrogate its original imperial biases, anthropological readings of theater continue to look backward rather than forward. While the universalizing anthropological model promoted by Schechner can help us understand contemporary playwrights who have been influenced by it, it is fundamentally inadequate for my purposes because it dismisses and denies the material effects of imperial domination on colonized cultures—exactly the effects that I will argue shaped the production and reception of modern Irish drama.

The most influential anthropologists of sacrifice—James Frazer, Henri Hubert and Marcel Mauss, Rene Girard—were motivated by a "search for ultimate origins," which might be admittedly "futile" (James 2) but which nevertheless discouraged them and their followers from asking questions about how imperial interventions may have affected the development of a "primitive" culture's ritual practice or European understandings of it. Mary Karen Dahl shows, in the introduction to her 1987 study of political violence in contemporary drama, how literary criticism can perpetuate that omission: "Following Frye's lead, I assume that anthropological evidence offers the least mediated view of the explicit structure of sacrifice. My first task, then, is to sketch an outline of the rite in order to expose those formulas that playwrights consciously or unconsciously combine and recombine" (3). But since anthropology as a discipline first emerged in the context of European imperialism, the "view" provided by this "evidence" must be very heavily mediated—especially since Dahl is getting it, not from her contemporaries, but from Northrop Frye and his predecessors. Hubert and Mauss, whom Dahl adopts as her "guides to ritual practice" (4), published their most influential contribution—a comparative study of Hindu and Hebrew rituals—in a French journal in 1898. Because it was Britain's expansion into India that exposed Hindu practices to the European gaze, however, the lens through which Hubert and Mauss are studying India is not transparent.

Gayatri Spivak demonstrates in her foundational essay "Can The Subaltern Speak?" that once an indigenous cultural practice enters imperial discourse its meaning is transformed and, ultimately, overdetermined. Her paradigmatic example, in fact, is a Hindu sacrificial practice—the custom of *sati,* or the self-immolation of the widow on the pyre of her husband. Hubert and Mauss never credit the British raj with having any influence on the practices they discuss or on the knowledge that has been made available to them—any more than the Oxford scholar E. O. James, in his 1933 discussion of human sacrifice among the Aztecs, ever wonders whether the fact that human sacrifice appears to become more prevalent at the time of European contact might have anything to do with the fact that the Aztec empire is fighting for its life against a technologically superior foreign power.

By failing to recognize or understand that kind of mediation, literary scholars who adopt the anthropological model adopt the assumptions that go with it; and adopting those assumptions makes it impossible to do certain kinds of work. By treating sacrifice as a universal practice that all human cultures have performed from time immemorial and that represents a link to our pre-rational, pre-literate, pre-industrial past, we reinscribe a self-serving developmental model that locates Europe and the West at the end of history while keeping the Third World frozen at the beginning of time. In the process, we limit our own understanding of how and why sacrifice works on the modern stage.

Once one accepts sacrifice as the result of primal human urges that cannot be significantly affected by historical and geopolitical change, certain questions must go unasked. For instance, neither Dahl nor her "guides to ritual practice" ask why these sacrifices are always performed by men on male victims, because the gendering of sacrifice is so foundational to the anthropological paradigm as to be invisible. The association of women with pollution and defilement, like the association of idealized Woman with the earth and fertility, is such a naturalized and necessary element of this understanding of "primitive" ritual that it cannot be called into question.[5]

What I want to suggest is that at least in modern Irish drama, this ordering of the ritual universe reflects, not a "primitive" phenomenon, but a complex of preoccupations that are very much conditioned by modernity. It is my contention that the model of sacrifice described by European anthropologists is in part a fantasy whose contours are determined by the anxieties, desires, and motivations wrapped up in the imperial project. Thus, the fact that Yeats's deployment of sacrifice in *Cathleen ni Houlihan* does conform to the model sketched out by Hubert and Mauss is not proof that Yeats has tapped into a universal and pre-colonial sacrificial past but rather proof that Yeats shares their fantasies. Similarly, the enormous power that *Cathleen ni Houlihan* exerted over its audiences derived not so much from the collective unconscious as from the fact that the play affirms an interpretation of Ireland's history (and a correlating vision of Ireland's future) that had already become central to Irish nationalism.

This shift in perspective allows for a more complex, critical, and useful discussion of the nature and function of sacrificial drama in the Irish context. For example, E. O. James's 1933 *Origins of Sacrifice* explains blood sacrifice in terms of the "primitive" belief that blood was "the life-stream *par excellence*":

> From this primary observation other deductions would easily follow: (a) that blood was the essence of life; and (b) by the primitive law of association, any substance resembling blood, like red ochre, had a similar significance and potency. Therefore (c) blood, or its equivalent, being the vehicle of life and consciousness, was employed as a revivifying agent. (22)

But James does not need to go to Neolithic cave paintings for an example of faith in blood as "a revivifying agent." He might, for instance, flip through back issues of the *Dublin Evening Mail* and find this advertisement for Veno's Seaweed Tonic:

> BLOOD IS LIFE. LET IT BE PURE. Blotches, pimples on the face and body, scrofula, sores, itching and redness of the skin, tetter and eczema are symptoms which indicate impure blood and skin diseases. If your blood is pure your skin will be clear and healthy-looking; the direct cause of skin eruption is found in the blood. Purify the blood and you purify and clear the skin. (26 January 1905, 5)

It is possible, of course, that this advertisement simply represents the persistence of ancient beliefs about blood. But it is also possible that James's description of this primitive belief, like Veno's advertisement, draws on a contemporary medical understanding of blood as a vehicle for debility, disease, and degeneration. If we accept that possibility, we also accept the possibility that this understanding of what blood means may be determined, not by our primitive past, but by that quintessentially modern phenomenon, medical science. And an investigation into the genesis and development of the medical view of the human body—one that takes into account the partnership between modern medicine and the modern European empire—may help answer some very puzzling questions about how and why blood functions as it does on the Irish stage.

I would argue, then, that if we refuse to complicate the anthropological model of sacrifice, this chapter of literary history remains—like the Armagh dirty protest—fundamentally unreadable. Although the use of sacrifice by the Abbey playwrights corresponds broadly to the accepted anthropological model (sacrifice involves expiation, redemption, and regeneration; the victim is male, while that which is sacrificed *to* or *for* is female), that model cannot help us understand what happens to the victim's body. Consider, for instance, William Beers's meditations on the enduring power of the spectacle of human sacrifice:

> A human being is drugged and held over a wedge-shaped monolith while an Aztec priest, using an obsidian knife, slices open the victim's abdomen, just below the rib cage, thrusts his hand into the incision up into the chest cavity, and rips out the still-beating heart. . . . This sacrifice business is a subject to which we keep returning because it affects us so viscerally, and intellectual rationalization—the so-called logic of sacrifice—never fully satisfies. Like others I too have been lured by the darker existential question of what motivates men to do what they do. Why do they make things bleed and die in the name of the sacred? (10)

But the image Beers paints in such lurid colors is precisely the image that does *not* appear on the Irish stage during this period—at least not without exciting vigorous protest. Not only is Michael's death in *Cathleen ni Houlihan* not represented, but it is not allowed to happen within the time frame of the play. Even Synge, whose impolite insistence on bringing dead and dying bodies onto his stage gave grievous offense to his audiences, makes both of Christy's "murder" attempts take place off stage. And after having Minnie's death in *Shadow of a Gunman* reported from offstage and killing off *Juno and the Paycock*'s Johnny between scenes, O'Casey stages Bessie Burgess's death in *The Plough and the Stars*—a play that was immediately blasted by republicans as a betrayal of the sacrificed martyrs of the Easter

1916 uprising. Sacrificial drama worked for nationalists only when it did *not* allow the victims to "bleed and die" on stage. Understanding the medical view of the body and how gender and sexuality were transformed by that process of medicalization can help us understand why Irish audiences insisted that the sacrificed body remain hidden.

But taking a more materialist and historicist approach to sacrifice also changes our understanding of the political struggle taking place outside the theater. The second half of Beers's divagation, in which the "visceral" power of the sacrificial spectacle resists and negates the power of the kind of "intellectual" analysis in which I make bold to engage, hints at how the anthropological understanding of sacrifice shapes readings of contemporary political conflict. It is clear that in Beers's view "what motivates men" to sacrifice each other is a psychological drive much deeper than anything that could be explained in material or rational terms. When this understanding of sacrifice is applied to twentieth-century Irish history, it produces readings like Padraig O'Malley's 1990 *Biting at the Grave,* which represents the 1981 H-block hunger strike as a ritual repetition of the Easter Rising:

> You could outline it like a story: a chosen few, the elite of the elite, resolve to take matters into their own hands, prepared to sacrifice their lives to achieve through the shedding of blood what they cannot achieve through physical force. . . . The story, of course, had been written. It was history, old stuff, part of the national mythology. (5)

O'Malley asserts that the strike proves that "we are our own oppressors" (5). And indeed, if one accepts the anthropological view of sacrifice as the expression of innate, atavistic, primal urges, this is the only conclusion to which one can come.

In contrast, David Beresford's history of the same hunger strike reads sacrificial imagery as a strategic means to a definite political end—the defeat of Britain's criminalization policy. The IRA communications that Beresford cites reveal that the organizers and the strikers were aware of the importance of martyrology as a form of propaganda and routinely made cold-blooded calculations about how to get the maximum political effect from each death. The power of sacrificial symbolism supports the strikers as they fast and maintains the pressure on England, but it is not proffered as the *explanation* of the strike.

The difference between these two analyses is not merely academic. The O'Malley reading concludes that the Irish can and must end their own oppression by unilaterally refusing to die for Ireland. In Beresford's reading, Thatcher's policies are held responsible for the shape of Irish sacrificial politics, and therefore any solution to the problem of sacrificial violence must involve England. The anthropological model of sacrifice thus allows commentators to erase imperial violence and to represent political conflict in Ireland as self-perpetuating.

Being interested primarily in how the mythology of sacrificial martyrdom functioned—and functions—as a normative force, I have chosen to focus on canonical playwrights: W. B. Yeats, whose early work helped establish the sacrificial tradition that he later revolted against; J. M. Synge, whose burlesque of that tradition incited one of the century's most notorious theater riots; and Sean O'Casey, whose attack on sacrificial mythology resonated (at least initially) with an audience growing impatient and disillusioned with sacrificial violence after four years of living in its midst. The exception is Padraig Pearse, who many would argue is neither canonical nor a playwright. Slight as his dramatic output was, Pearse's writing is absolutely central to this project. I have devoted a chapter to him because his career provides a particularly illuminating illustration of how it was possible, through representations of sacrificial patriotism, to subvert imperial constructions of the Irish subject by reshaping conceptions of gender and sexuality.

Pearse's claim that bloodshed was "a cleansing and a sanctifying thing" and that "the nation which regards [bloodshed] as the final horror has lost its manhood" (*Political Writings and Speeches* 99) is one of the more frequently cited instances of republican sacrificial rhetoric. Pearse was not the first or the last to associate violence and masculinity or to insist that one becomes an Irish man only by shedding blood. Margaret Thatcher demonstrated how powerful that conception of Irish masculinity was and is when she asked if the H-Block hunger strikers were out "to prove their virility" (Beresford 212). As Ann R. Jones and Peter Stallybrass argue in "Dismantling Irena," Thatcher's comment is part of a British strategy that dates back to Spenser's *View of the Present State of Ireland,* in which Spenser develops a vision of the Irish as hypermasculine and hyperviolent, "barbarically/heroically resistant to all change," in order to "justify his own insistence that the English must be more Scythian than the Irish, pursuing a policy of terror" (161). Thatcher's strategic naiveté, like her refusal to refer to the strikers as anything other than "men of violence," demonstrates that the connection between sacrificial martyrdom and gender identity is implicated in, and in part a product of, Britain's attempt to control Ireland and the Irish by constructing them.

Pearse's masculinist rhetoric has implications not only for the men it addresses but also for the women it ignores. Since without the implied rebirth the death loses its power, women are written into the sacrificial narrative in order to make the bloodshed not only sanctifying but also procreative. The paradigmatic example is Yeats and Gregory's dramatization of the myth of sovereignty in *Cathleen ni Houlihan,* in which Michael's decision to die in the 1798 rebellion transforms Cathleen from a barren hag into a young, potentially fertile woman with "the walk of a queen" (*VPl* 231). This is not to say that the female figures involved in sacrificial drama necessarily literalize that regeneration by giving birth; Cathleen, in fact, will never conceive a child because her mythological role requires her to remain sexually inaccessible. But as spiritualized and untouchable as Cathleen is, the image of her female body is necessary in order to turn Michael's death into a sexual consummation and to make it bear symbolic fruit. The fact that Cathleen persuades Michael to choose allegorical fertility over the opportunity for literal procreation that his marriage with Delia would provide indicates that one of the purposes of sacrifice is to rewrite the story of how the Irish subject is produced—to reject the mortal Irish mother in favor of a symbolic one whose body, unlike that of her pedestrian counterparts, is inviolable and who can therefore provide the Irish subject with a clean genealogy and an uncomplicated pedigree. It was the intense investment in that image of the ideal and inviolable female body that made nationalist audiences so sensitive to representations of Irish women. And although that investment derives from a shared belief in a naturalized and "primitive" association between women and the fertile earth, it also derives from the very modern mythos constructed and promoted by medical science.

Bodies

The Irish literary renaissance took place during the period in which science became the dominant narrative of Western culture and medicine the accepted authority on the human body. My analysis is indebted here, obviously, to Michel Foucault, but also to a generation of feminist theorists, postcolonial scholars, and medical historians who were inspired by that work to investigate the network of power relations that medicine constructs. Central to all this work—and a foundational premise of my own study—is the understanding that because medical science is so successful in defining, constructing, and controlling the human body, it becomes a phenomenally effective means of enforcing political and social control. And medicine becomes especially powerful, and therefore especially problematic, when it is practiced on a population that is being subjected to more visible and identifiable forms of oppression.

Feminist theory has long recognized the role that scientific discourse plays in defining and enforcing gender norms—and specifically in creating a pathological, endangered female body on which the medical establishment then has the right, power, and duty to operate. In colonized locations, as David Arnold, Sheldon Watts, and others have demonstrated, medical constructions not only of the body but also of disease, epidemic, and contagion provide ideological, institutional, and structural support for the colonial administration's attempts to exploit indigenous populations and the colonized landscape. All three forms of power—science, Empire, patriarchy—came together in the Irish medical establishment; and its operations—especially on the bodies of Irish women—played a crucial role in forming the conceptions of masculinity, femininity, health, disease, and fertility that affected both the plays produced by Yeats, Synge, Pearse, and O'Casey and their reception by nationalist audiences.

At first glance, the relationship between Irish nationalism and orthodox medicine appears to be clearly antagonistic. Turn-of-the-century Irish nationalist writing explicitly identifies state-sponsored medicine as an imperial tool and attempts to inspire resistance to it. But that same nationalist movement tacitly accepts medical constructions of the body—in part because they are indissociable from constructions of masculinity and femininity in which the nationalist movement is heavily invested. Irish nationalism thus accepts the medical view of the body but accepts it uneasily and anxiously. I argue that the nationalist audience saw Yeats, Synge, and (by the time of *The Plough and the Stars*) O'Casey as complicit in imperial science's attempt to control the Irish body, and that this was one reason controversies about representations of "Irish life" so consistently focused on gender and sexuality. Before I make that argument, however, I need to explain what I mean by the term "imperial science," and why it is a valid descriptor of orthodox medical practice in twentieth-century Ireland.

Medicine as the Western world understands it was first established in Ireland during the seventeenth and eighteenth centuries. England and continental Europe experienced the medical revolution at around the same time. The difference is that in Ireland modern medicine was imported by a colonizing elite. Whatever the native Irish had developed in the way of a medical tradition, it was not incorporated into the colonial medical establishment. Writing in the *Dublin Journal of Medical Science* in 1884, Macalister laments that "the numerous medical manuscripts" in Irish collected at the Royal Irish Academy have not even been translated (3). Before the existence in Ireland of universities and teaching hospitals, Ireland's practitioners were primarily educated in England or Scotland. Major institutions like the Royal College of Physicians of Ireland and the Royal College of Surgeons of Ireland were modeled on similar institutions in England, and both the profession and its members were strongly identified with metropolitan culture. Financially, intellectually, and ideologically, the medical profession in Ireland looked to England for inspiration.

The mere fact that in Ireland medicine was initially an Anglo-Irish institution would not necessarily make it complicit in the imperial project; after all, drama was a British import too. However, it becomes clear long before the twentieth century that in Ireland medicine and colonial administration are involved in a symbiotic relationship, relying on and supporting each other so that the term "body politic" starts to become something both more and less than a metaphor. In the preface to Sir William Petty's 1672 *Political Anatomy of Ireland,* for instance, the distinction between Ireland's allegorized political body and the bodies of individual Irish subjects becomes slippery:

> It is as reasonable that as anatomy is the best foundation of the one [medicine], so also of the other [politics], and that to practice upon the [body] politick without knowing the symmetry, fabrick, and proportion of it is as casual as the practice of old women and empirics.
>
> Furthermore, as students in medicine practice their inquiries upon cheap and common animals, and such whose actions they are best acquainted with, and where there is the least confusion and perplexion of parts, I have chosen Ireland as such a political animal, who is scarce 20 years old, where the intrigue of state is not very complicate, and with which I have been conversant from an embrion. (qtd. in Macalister 8)

Petty's identification of Ireland as the kind of "cheap and common animal" ideally suited for the dissecting table is an early rehearsal of one of the staples of imperial rhetoric: the construction of the colonial subject as subhuman. In this context, the comparison suggests that one effect of this rhetoric would be to make Irish bodies available to "students of medicine" as subjects upon whom it is easy to "practice." Thus, the creation of the colonial subject produces a pool of experimental subjects. Imperial power provides the Anglo-Irish scientific establishment with the bodies it needs; medical science returns the favor by constructing those bodies according to the designs of the colonial administration.

As Mary Poovey shows in *A History of the Modern Fact,* Petty—who came to Ireland in 1652 as the official physician of Cromwell's invading army—has reasons for choosing Ireland as a subject that have nothing to do with cheapness, availability, or simplicity of structure; his political writings were motivated at the most basic level by his own economic interests (Poovey 125–26). In fact, Poovey identifies Petty's writings on Ireland as a critical stage in the production of the modern fact—an "objective" unit of knowledge whose apparent impartiality made it "attractive to governments seeking to strengthen their national and international positions" (93)—and argues that Petty served as "the critical link between natural philosophy and the promotion of systematic sciences of wealth and society" (94). His authority as a physician helped him serve as "a literal go-between" through whom the principles of natural philosophy could be applied to political questions (94). In his career we see medical knowledge crossing disciplinary boundaries to exert its power over the Irish landscape and the Irish economy.[6] Petty's fusion of medical with political authority allowed him to create a theoretical model that could "establish the 'value of people,'" making it possible for the colonial government to define "the 'value' of human beings . . . in monetary, not religious or ethical, terms" (Poovey 131). The major discursive consequence of this conjunction of scientific authority and "royal power," Poovey maintains, was the creation of the abstractions on which modern political economy relies—putatively objective but ideologically inflected concepts such as "'national wealth' or 'the population'" (137). Petty's work thus ultimately generates the received economic ideas about the relationship between the size and makeup of Ireland's population and its economic health that would so heavily influence the ideologies espoused by Irish nationalists during the early twentieth century.[7]

Petty's use of the anatomy metaphor, then, supports Poovey's claim that science became valuable as a political tool precisely because of its ability to produce an *apparent* objectivity that could conceal ideological motivations and that would therefore become one of imperial discourse's most useful fictions.[8] The anatomy metaphor enables Petty to claim that his decision to operate on Ireland is a purely pragmatic one made in the interests of science, and it allows him to represent his endeavor as a disinterested attempt to uncover a body of factual truths. Precisely because scientific knowledge was constructed as free of ideological content or bias, it became a particularly effective vehicle for imperial policies.

Within Petty's text, of course, power and knowledge function only at the discursive level. But his development of the metaphor suggests that the overlap between the categories of "experimental subject" and "colonial subject" could easily have material consequences. In fact, Petty's choice of Ireland as a dissection subject was prophetic. Before the Anatomy Act of 1832 made it easier to obtain human cadavers through legitimate channels, British medical institutions were supplied by body-snatchers or "resurrection-men," who surreptitiously exhumed and then sold recently buried corpses. Although grave robbing was a documented phenomenon in England and Scotland, Irish graves supplied a disproportionate number of these illegal cadavers.

According to Irish medical historian Dr. John Fleetwood, Irish newspapers reflect public concern about body-snatching as early as 1732 (33). What made the Irish situation distinctive was the existence of an export trade to London and Edinburgh which was "well-organized and carried on quite openly" (66). Dublin became such an important source of cheap bodies that by the 1820s the cadaver trade was recognized—albeit with a certain amount of disgust and horror—as "a major branch of Irish commerce" (67). Writing in 1829 in the *Lancet,* "Erinensis" identifies the cadaver trade as Ireland's major contribution to Western medicine: "The most accomplished [body snatchers] have . . . diffused our scientific reputation as widely among the civilized nations, as our Dublin Hospital Reports" (qtd. in Fleetwood 67).

The cadaver trade is more than a gruesome footnote to the history of Irish medicine. It is a classic illustration of the partnership between imperial policy and scientific progress and of the effect of that "progress" on Irish bodies. Thanks to Britain's efforts to keep Ireland in an economically dependent position, the human body has become another natural resource to be sold on the cheap. It is England's prerogative to process those bodies into scientific knowledge, which will then be redistributed through the Anglo-Irish medical establishment. The cadaver trade is a historical analogue to the hypothetical baby-eating scheme advanced by the crazed narrator of Jonathan Swift's 1729 *A Modest Proposal*—an indication that in eighteenth-century Ireland imperial policies have reached their logical, if revolting, conclusion, and the human body has become the currency of a cannibalistic economy.

Underdevelopment alone, however, could not have produced this bizarre form of exploitation. If the cadaver trade owes its existence to Ireland's artificially engineered poverty, it is also dependent on the presence in Ireland of medical institutions engaged in training Irish doctors. Grave robbing was most prevalent in and around Dublin, where the major medical institutions were located. The cadaver trade could only have been produced by imperialism and science operating in concert: the imperial administration creates the necessary economic climate, and science provides the local demand. It is also something that could only have happened in Ireland, which, unlike England's other colonies, was close enough to make a trade in this highly perishable commodity practical.

The cadaver trade shows, among other things, that Ireland's unique position in the Empire affected its relationship to orthodox medicine—and that the relationship Petty articulated between political and medical forms of power/knowledge had serious consequences for the "cheap and common animals" he promised to rhetorically dissect. If the Irish were not there to see these purloined bodies opened on British dissecting tables, they did see the desecrated graves and smell the decomposing corpses that were often packed in the cargo holds of passenger ships going back and forth to London and Edinburgh. By the beginning of the nineteenth century, the trade had become such an open secret in Dublin that its practitioners sometimes "left naked bodies on the public road while awaiting transport" (Fleetwood 69). Fleetwood documents burial customs that developed in order to make loved ones' graves harder to rob; it is my contention that the effects of this kind of power were and are much wider-reaching. The cadaver trade furnished generations of British doctors with a more detailed map of the human anatomy. What the Irish learned from the cadaver trade was that their bodies were not safe.

By the early twentieth century the cadaver trade could only have been a very faint memory. But medicine was still operating on living Irish bodies, and the effects were still visible—and, I argue, *more* visible on female bodies than on male ones. That excessive visibility results partly from a Western tradition that insists on a dichotomy between the finite, corporeal, imperfect body and the infinite, immaterial, perfectible psyche, identifying femininity with "the unreason associated with the body" (Grosz 4). But in Ireland that effect is intensified by a history of colonial intervention that has rendered Irish women's bodies disproportionately vulnerable to imperial science.

Birth

The way Irish audiences and Irish playwrights constructed or read images of Irish women is influenced by a history that Ireland shares with other colonized locations. It is also the product of specific circumstances that both link Ireland with, and differentiate it from, these other cases. Ireland's "postcoloniality" is famously (and appropriately) contested. Ireland was the subject of England's first serious experiment with imperial rule, but opinion is divided on the question of how that experiment can be meaningfully related to what happened later on in Asia, Africa, and the Americas.[9] For instance, a persuasive and growing body of scholarship documents Britain's attempt to produce and maintain a racial distinction between the English and the Irish; however, this distinction collapsed earlier and more completely than the racial distinctions produced by the European conquests in other locations.[10] Ireland's relationship to its imperial other is thus necessarily significantly different from that obtaining in, say, India or Nigeria.

Yeats's insistence on recruiting female fertility in the service of nationalist drama therefore represents both a standard pattern of nationalist discourse and this more local history. Benedict Anderson argues in *Imagined Communities* that nationalist movements are able to inspire "love, and often profoundly self-sacrificing love" (141) by mobilizing the "vocabulary of kinship" (143) in the service of the idea of the nation. The family narrative is useful in that it presents "nation-ness" as an essential quality that cannot be disavowed—a "natural" attribute like "skin-colour, gender, parentage and birth-era" (143)—thus making an abstract idea concrete, fixed and human enough to inspire acts of devotion and sacrifice. Anderson does not explore the consequences for women of nationalism's use of the family narrative, but others have.

As Norma Alarcon's discussion of the mythology of Malinche and the virgin of Guadeloupe demonstrates, an insistence on "maternity" as the "primary cultural function" of women, who remain "bound to a double reproduction . . . that of [their] people and [their] culture" (113), is not a phenomenon peculiar to Irish nationalism. That "double reproduction" becomes important—and thus women become ever more tightly bound to it—for a number of nationalist movements dealing with the aftermath of colonial rule. Radhakrishnan discusses this phenomenon in "Nationalism, Gender, and Narrative," arguing that postcolonial nationalisms equate control over the nation with control over the bodies of its female subjects because this enables them to resolve conflicted ideas about progress and modernity. By "internaliz[ing] rather than problematiz[ing] the Western blueprint in the name of progress, modernization, industrialization, and internationalism," and accepting the assumption that for Third World nations "'being themselves' and 'becoming modern nations'" can only be mutually exclusive activities, these nationalist movements develop a "schizophrenic" model of identity (Radhakrishnan 85–86). Narratives of national and political development remain "hostage to the Enlightenment identity of the West," while histories of the private and personal are reconstructed according to idealized conceptions of pre-colonial culture. The individual woman's experience of imperialism is denied so that the female body can become the container of an unspoiled "essentialist indigeny" (86) that must be protected from the contamination of development. A "schizophrenic" desire to fulfill the expectations of the Western developmental narrative while retaining a distinct national identity is naturalized by dividing it along gender lines: the male world of technology and politics progresses into modernity, while women are confined to the static domestic realm.

In the terms of Alarcon's model, the colonized woman's role as conservator of that "essentialist indigeny" is predicated on woman's function as the bearer of children. That function, of course, underwrites almost all constructions of femininity; but for populations that have been subjected to colonial rule, its importance becomes particularly intense. The threat of sexual intercourse between colonizer and colonized produces, in the imperial imagination, nightmares about miscegenation. For the colonized subject, it can become a powerful symbol of unchosen and intimate contact with a hostile alien culture. Thus, Malinche's double role as Cortez's translator and his lover identifies the destruction of the national language and culture with the sexual contact that allowed the Spanish invader to pollute the Aztec bloodline. She becomes useful because her story allows a complex problem to be recast in simple terms: if Malinche had not sold her body, the nation would not have been sold with it. The moral of Malinche's story, as Alarcon dissects it, is that modern Chicanas can repair their sister's blunder by refusing her transgressions, allowing their sexual behavior to be regulated by the Chicano movement and (not incidentally) by Chicano men.

The already overloaded significance of the colonized woman's reproductive function becomes more complicated when imperial rule leads to direct interference with human reproduction. The consequences become clearest in a case like that of post-independence India, where, during the 1960s and 1970s, a central government dominated by urban elites crafted a family planning policy that subjected impoverished rural populations to surgical sterilization on a grand scale.[11] Once reproductive medicine has been used as a coercive tool, reproductive choices become overdetermined; practices like birth control, sterilization, and abortion are no longer available to be "chosen" by women on whom they have been involuntarily inflicted. If there is a masculinist bias in reproductive medicine, India's history suggests an imperial bias as well.[12]

Because obstetric medicine was practiced by men on women, there was a built-in power differential between doctor and patient that enabled obstetric medicine to "catch and keep" (Murphy-Lawless 45) the body it worked on—to constitute that body according to its own specifications, to make the truth about what its needs, defects, and weaknesses were. The Irish example is distinct, however, in that the specialty of obstetric medicine assumed greater importance both within the medical community and within Irish society than it had in other colonized locations. Because the most highly visible form of medical practice was one that operated exclusively on women, the anxieties associated with medical progress came to be associated more closely with the female body.

The prominence of obstetric medicine in Ireland owes something to temporal coincidence: most historians identify the first half of the eighteenth century—which also happened to be the period during which Ireland's settler class was working most successfully to establish a distinct cultural, economic, and political identity for Anglo-

Ireland—as the crucial period for the development of obstetric science. Since obstetrics was a new specialty, the fledgling Irish medical community could hope to distinguish itself on what was a comparatively level playing field. As soon as obstetric medicine began to develop in the British Isles, Ireland was on the cutting edge. The first book on midwifery to be published in English by a man-midwife was James Wolveridge's 1670 *Speculum Matricis: Or, the Irish Midwives' Hand-Maid;* the first significant English-language textbook was produced in 1742 by the Irish doctor Fielding Ould; and the Lying-in Hospital (later to become the Rotunda Hospital), founded in 1745 in Dublin, was the first maternity hospital established in the British Isles. Since then, "hundreds of textbooks and thousands of articles have marked out a distinctive Irish contribution to obstetrics" (Murphy-Lawless 25).

The history of obstetrics in Ireland, with its long list of firsts, seems to subvert the "federation" structure that Macleod identifies as characteristic of scientific progress within the British Empire: instead of getting its marching orders from England, the Rotunda pioneers innovations that are exported to England.[13] Put in a broader context, however, Ireland's prominence in the field of obstetrics becomes very much a function of its peripheral status. Obstetric medicine is attractive to Irish doctors as a new field in which they can gain the specialized expertise that will establish Dublin as a medical center on a par with London and Edinburgh; but it is available to them because of the same combination of circumstances that produced the cadaver export trade.

Irish medicine in the eighteenth century cannot compete with England in terms of institutional prestige. What it does have that English medicine does not is easy access to a large population of "cheap and common animals." If Irish medical practitioners cannot set the pace at the theoretical end, they *can* trade on practical experience. For instance, an 1843 contributor to the *Dublin Medical Journal* speaks proudly of Dublin as "a school of practical medicine" where "the clinical student . . . learns the great art of mental combination—of grasping *all* the phenomena of a case, be they physical or vital, or having reference to time, and of thinking justly upon them. In this way his *medical mind* is formed, the one thing needful to the good physician, and which no course of reading, no multiplication of lectures, can ever create" (Graves 125).

If the author sounds defensive, it is with good reason. Materialist as it eventually became, the medical establishment was initially disdainful of practical knowledge—a contempt registered by Petty in his dismissal of the "casual practice" of "old women and empirics." But if in other specialties the prestige rested with the theoretician rather than the clinician, in obstetrics that hierarchy was reversed.

In the literature on midwifery, practical knowledge is privileged at the expense of theory, which is uncomfortably reminiscent of the "superstitions" guiding midwives' practices. In 1742 Dublin man-midwife Fielding Ould distinguishes his treatise from the ill-conceived "schemes" of his predecessors, who "never made use of a Compass, but in their Closet" (ix). The English obstetrician William Smellie, in the introduction to his influential 1764 treatise on midwifery, avers that he has "industriously avoided all theory" (iii), since it is "of little service towards . . . improving the practice of midwifery" (xxxix). In the preface to their 1848 *Observations on Midwifery,* McClintock and Hardy—Irish doctors attached to Dublin's Rotunda Hospital—note that "our main, indeed, we might almost say, exclusive object, was to be as *practical* as possible, avoiding all speculative or unprofitable questions" (vi).

This identification of midwifery as peculiarly "practical" made it an ideal specialty for Irish doctors, whose intellectual training might still be considered provincial. Ireland's prominence in this field became an important way for eighteenth-century Anglo-Ireland to argue for, and insist on, its right to be considered a distinct culture making an important and unique contribution to the British Commonwealth. Ould makes that argument by introducing his treatise with an explicit comparison between Ireland's political status and the status of obstetric medicine as a discipline:

> Nor is this Art, in any respect the meanest Province in the medicinal Common-wealth, but much on the contrary; as on it depends, not only the preservation of the Species, but the various Methods of relieving distressed Women, from extraordinary Pain and Torture, innumerable Disorders and Death, the consequence of bad Practice. (Ould 2)

Murphy-Lawless cites this passage as an example of the discursive process through which men-midwives constructed themselves as "the makers of a new science" that would save mothers from the "non-scientific, non-rational practices of midwives" (52). But this passage also indicates that in Ireland the attempt to establish dominion over the territory of childbirth was inseparable from the attempt on the part of the Anglo-Irish elite to raise Ireland's status within the "Common-wealth," whose structure provides Ould with his metaphor for the medical community. His phrasing reflects the indeterminate status of the Anglo-Irish: culturally and ideologically tied to England, Ould recognizes that he is nevertheless identified by English readers as a citizen, not of the mother country, but of its "meanest Province." By identifying his profession with Ireland, Ould can make his argument for the importance of obstetrics into an argument for the primacy of the "Province" within whose borders that science is flourishing.

Thus, while the history of reproductive medicine in Ireland is part of the gradual and pan-European appropriation of childbirth by the male-dominated orthodox medical profession, it also demonstrates that in Ireland that process had specifically imperialist implications. As Arnold argues, all modern medicine is to some extent "engaged in a colonizing process" in which a "quest for monopolistic rights over the human body" leads to invasive and interventionist practices; but although the practice of medicine in British colonial possessions has "precedents and parallels in nineteenth-century Europe," interventionist medicine takes "an exceptionally raw and accentuated form" when practiced in a colonial location and assumes a much greater role in "the cultural and political constitution" of the subject (9). Ireland's role as a leader in reproductive medicine intensifies the connection between the actual reproductive process and the production of Ireland that defines Alarcon's "double reproduction." Underneath the symbolism of regeneration and rebirth that made sacrifice a powerful trope was a conception of fertility that had been reconstructed according to the structures of obstetric thought—and that incorporated the obstetric reading of the female body.

Death

Putting Irish dramatists in this perspective highlights the previously hidden connection between the persistence of the sacrificial myth in Irish literature and political discourse and the gender politics that affected, through the operations of imperial science, Irish conceptions of the body in general and the female body in particular. This reading is important not only because it exposes the operations of a particular form of oppression, but because it reveals the denials and omissions on which the power of the sacrificial paradigm is founded. Among the most important of these is a repudiation of the female body that denies the history of pain and resistance to which the sacrificial narrative is supposedly faithful.

The idea of regeneration through blood sacrifice privileges the intangible rewards of death over the actual living body. Making what Pearse calls "the ultimate sacrifice" (*PWS* 66) requires the victim to decide to value a larger, as yet illusory goal above the immediate needs and desires of his own body. The conjunction of ritual violence and fertility helps participate in this process of disavowal by projecting corporeality and its attendant suffering onto the female body, leaving the male disembodied and therefore fundamentally unscathed. At the moment of death the martyr's body drops out of the narrative, and its pain is transferred to the female figure whose job it is to turn those death throes into birth pangs. This transformation, accomplished on the disembodied allegorical level in *Cathleen,* becomes more literal in post-partition drama as political allegiance becomes a source of cynicism and the sincerity with which Yeats and Gregory invested Cathleen has to find another home.

Feminist attempts to describe the creation of sexual difference through the production of gendered bodies are therefore crucial to this project because they offer a point from which to begin exploring the consequences of the sacrificial paradigm's rejection of that female body. I have, however, been careful not to proceed on the assumption that "sexual difference should be understood as more fundamental than other forms of difference" or that "other forms of difference might be *derived* from sexual difference" (J. Butler 167). On the contrary, what makes this strain of feminist theory so useful in this context is its description of the body as a point of "convergence" between narratives of gender, racial, class, and national identity—as the material evidence of the confluence of histories that produces the colonial subject. If the body is the record of the economic, cultural, and technological forces that have sustained imperialism and created the oppression that nationalism ostensibly resists, then the sacrificial narrative's rejection of that body at the moment of death reproduces imperial oppression. Transcending the body—as Michael does at the end of *Cathleen,* as Congal tries and fails to do at the end of *The Herne's Egg*—means leaving behind the marks of gender, race, class, sexuality, and history. By investing so heavily in the achievement of transcendence, sacrificial drama breaks faith with the condition it claims to represent and rejects the embodied Irish subject while valorizing an abstract, universal subjectivity.

By restoring that body to the narrative from which it has been dropped, I hope to increase our intellectual understanding of how we experience embodiment, how drama's representation of bodies on stage affects that experience, and how political pressures shape the literary, dramatic, and material production of gendered bodies. At the same time, I hope that this project might suggest different ways of imagining Ireland's future—not only its reproductive politics but also the national and international issues that hinge on them: Ireland's role in the European Community; its engagement with Western models of modernity and progress; its strategies for dealing with the effects of partition; and the continuing violence for which the sacrificial paradigm as it is usually understood is, finally, a misleading and inadequate explanation.

Chapter Summaries

Chapter 1, "Body and Soul: Yeats, the Famine, and the Two Cathleens," uses Yeats and Gregory's 1902 play *Cathleen ni Houlihan* to define the sacrificial paradigm I will be examining and to illustrate the connection between violence and fertility on which it depends. The massive popularity of this piece among Irish nationalists is partly due to its adherence to Irish nationalist literary and iconographic traditions of depicting Ireland as a beautiful woman in need of assistance. I assert that it is also a response to concerns about fertility and population growth that are part of the cultural legacy of the potato famines of the 1840s. Through a discussion of the 1899 controversy over *The Countess Cathleen* (read against the noncontroversy over Martyn's *The Heather Field,* produced at the same time by the same Irish Literary Theater), I suggest that Yeats develops *Cathleen ni Houlihan*'s sacrificial paradigm as a way of neutralizing the anxieties raised by *Countess Cathleen.* This argument is supported by a reading of Frank Hugh O'Donnell's published attack on *The Countess Cathleen,* in which O'Donnell's critique is explicated as an archetypal nationalist denial of the power of the physical body. To a nationalist movement concerned with restoring "pure" Irish culture and cleansing itself of the "taint" of outside influences, the fact that the body was vulnerable to imperial coercion—a vulnerability graphically demonstrated during the famines of the 1840s—made it a highly dangerous place. The rejection of *Countess Cathleen* was thus part of a broader attempt to reject that vulnerability by rejecting the feminized/pathologized

Celt as an identity position. Using the rhetoric produced about the Irish Literary Theater in the Gaelic League's organ *An Claidheamh Soluis,* I document the attempt to construct an alternative version of the Irish body: the vigorous, hypermasculine, athletic Gael, whose healthy virility is a rejection of the weaknesses associated with the effeminate Arnoldian Celt. The desire to reject the Countess Cathleen's vulnerable body thus contributes to a polarized construction of gender in which the masculine and the feminine are pushed farther apart in an attempt to protect the masculine subject position from that vulnerability.

The next chapter, "Under Siege: Blood, Borders, and the Body Politic," shows how Yeats's patronage of Synge led him to rethink earlier assumptions about the relationship between national politics and gender. The outcry over *In the Shadow of the Glen* indicated how invested Irish nationalism had become in a rigid and idealized construction of "Irish womanhood" and in the mythical peasant cottage as an untouchable space within which that ideal could be sealed. Yeats suggests in *On Baile's Strand* that nationalism can only become effective by giving up that masculine/feminine, public/private, political/domestic structure and accepting the more fluid model of gender represented by Cuchulain, Aoife, and the Young Man. The chapter closes with a reading of the riots that attended the production of Synge's *The Playboy of the Western World* as an expression of nationalist rage over Synge's violation of the boundary that nationalist discourse tried to erect between the Irish body and imperial control. Through an examination of the growing awareness of microbes, vaccination, and venereal disease evident in nationalist and mainstream publications, I argue that the panic evoked by the play's treatment of Irish women masks a deeper panic relating to Synge's representation of the Irish as a population already infiltrated by disease and debility.

The third chapter, "Excess of Love: Padraig Pearse and the Erotics of Sacrifice," investigates Padraig Pearse's masculinization of the sacrificial paradigm. Reading Pearse's plays and speeches alongside the writing of his republican colleagues, I argue that Britain's attempts to pathologize violence whenever it occurred in an Irish context led physical-force nationalists to naturalize militarism through appeals to Irish masculinity, and that this conflation of patriotism and masculinity eventually raised the specter of homoerotic desire. Pearse became the primary spokesman for the physical-force movement in part because he was so adept at drawing on the power of sexuality while containing it. While scholars who discuss Pearse's sexuality generally either insist on separating it from his political life or treat Pearse's political commitments as pretextual and his sexual desires as his "real" motivation, my analysis treats Pearse's political and sexual identities as coeval and inseparable. By incorporating his homoerotic desires into his political writing, Pearse was doing something his colleagues had been doing for years: enlisting sexual desire in the service of the republican cause. Pearse's exceptional successes depended on his ability to make the body of that male martyr disappear—to insist on a love object who, because he had died, was immaterial and therefore inaccessible. This made the sacrificial solution terribly expensive not only for Pearse but for the Volunteers, whose vision of Irish nationalism could never fully incorporate a critique of the material conditions produced by imperialism. Pearse's innovation thus intensified the conflict between republican and socialist revolutionary movements in Ireland. That conflict is the subject of chapter 4, "The Body of Truth: Sensationalism and Sacrifice in Sean O'Casey's Dublin Trilogy."

In that chapter, I argue that one of O'Casey's objectives as a "realistic" playwright was to rescue the disavowed and denied material body and represent the suffering that Pearsian rhetoric elided. His plays rely on the sensationalist traditions of melodrama, which seek to reproduce the physical sensations of its suffering characters in the bodies of the people in the audience. Because sensationalism is grounded in the naturalization of affect—the assumption that certain emotional bonds are biological imperatives that compel certain sensational responses—O'Casey's appeal to it allowed him to combat Pearsian nationalism by opposing an essentialized heterosexual and patriarchal model to the "artificial" homoeroticism structuring the republican universe. I argue that it was the opposition O'Casey set up between "natural" heterosexual attraction and a "perverse" obsession with martyrdom and martyrs that drove much of the reaction against *The Plough and the Stars.* Because it relied on an ideology that naturalized not only gender roles but also class hierarchies and social inequality, O'Casey's use of sensationalism reinforces the system he wants to overthrow, and his "realism" becomes a trap from which he has to escape.

The fifth chapter, "Misbirth of a Nation: Yeats and the Irish Free State," looks at changing attitudes toward female fertility as the truncated Irish state negotiates its entry into the modern European community. Sacrificial violence continues to haunt Yeats's later plays but in an increasingly stylized form. While this formal evolution is part of larger trends in European drama, it is also indicative of a more idiosyncratic desire to disembody drama, to complete the transformation of the body into symbol and icon. This desire is read in the context of Yeats's interest in eugenics and his association with the Blueshirts, a right-wing Irish political party with fascist tendencies. As Yeats's treatment of Attracta's rape indicates, his aesthetic practices deny the damage done to Attracta by the competing demands placed on her by Yeats's political ideologies. What *The Herne's Egg* demonstrates even more clearly is that in the end, the victim who is really being sacrificed is not Michael but Cathleen—who, bound to a double duty that she can now no longer discharge, is invaded, violated, and finally destroyed by the contradictory injunctions laid on her by Irish nationalism. The chapter ends with a reading of Yeats's final play, *The Death of Cuchulain,* which leads into a brief afterword suggesting some of the material consequences of the literary trends that this project investigates.

1
Body and Soul: Yeats, the Famine, and the Two Cathleens

THE FIRST PERFORMANCE OF *Cathleen ni Houlihan* ON APRIL 2, 1902, marked a number of other firsts. The production was the fruit of the fledgling national theater's first collaboration with an explicitly activist nationalist group, Inghinidhe na hEireann (Daughters of Ireland); it featured Maud Gonne's debut as an actress; and it was the first occasion on which a play produced and presumed to be authored by Yeats was received with unanimous enthusiasm by the nationalist press. By October of 1903, it was clear that many of these firsts might be destined to be lasts as well. *Cathleen* now stands out as anomalous amongst Yeats's dramatic works: its collaborative authorship, its enduring popularity with the same audiences who trashed *Shadow of the Glen* and rioted at *Playboy*, its uncharacteristically simple and melodramatic plot, and its embarrassingly transparent allegorical implications encourage scholars to treat it as an aberration, an isolated attempt to pander to a popular nationalism that Yeats abandoned when he saw the error of his ways.

But while Yeats never again produced anything quite like *Cathleen ni Houlihan*—and while, depending on whose account one believes, some, most, or all of this play was actually written by Lady Gregory—*Cathleen* is not as divorced from Yeats's other work as it might at first seem.[1] In fact, it marks a critical point at which Yeats's education in Irish politics began to reshape his conception of an Irish national theater. And while *Cathleen* was only the first stage through which that evolution passed, it was nevertheless tremendously significant. *Cathleen* was important, not simply because it influenced so many other Irish playwrights, but because it modeled strategies that could be used to allay the anxieties that would continue to drive nationalist politics. Five years before the protests sparked by Synge's *The Playboy of the Western World* demonstrated the lengths to which Irish nationalists would go to preserve their conception of Irish womanhood, the success of *Cathleen ni Houlihan* offered some hints as to why representations of Irish women should generate such anxiety—and how the story of blood-sacrifice could soothe it.

Precisely because its construction is so simple and its message so clear, *Cathleen* is an instructive illustration of the connection between nationalist hysteria about female sexuality and the nationalist love affair with the hero-martyr. The circumstances of its production are in this sense as important as the text itself. The fact that Maud Gonne incarnated Cathleen and that the play was produced under the auspices of a major women's nationalist organization rendered the strategies the play deploys more effective and suggested that the construction of gender symbolically established in *Cathleen ni Houlihan* could easily be—or, indeed, already had been—enforced on the actual Irish women who might otherwise threaten it.

As Cheryl Herr observes in her discussion of Irish political melodrama, *Cathleen ni Houlihan* only works in the context of a nationalist tradition that has already furnished the audience with the "ideological material" (Herr 18) they need in order to read it. For instance, thanks to the recent centennial celebration and at least two popular melodramas based on Wolfe Tone and the '98 rebellion, Yeats can assume that when he says the play is set "in a cottage near Killala, in 1798" its audience will fill in the political and historical significance. The conversation between Bridget and Peter about Michael's approaching marriage and what it will mean to the family draws on a different ideological context, this one related to the famines of the 1840s and their lingering aftereffects on Irish bodies, Irish fertility patterns, and Irish population growth. To understand what that context is and why Yeats makes it the background for a play celebrating patriotic self-sacrifice, it helps to go back to 1899 and *The Countess Cathleen,* Yeats's first attempt at a play with specifically nationalist content.

Despite its ahistorical setting, symbolist trappings, and preoccupation with the supernatural, *The Countess Cathleen* was recognized by its audiences as a commentary on the Great Famine of the 1840s. But although the play explicitly endorses one of the major arguments nationalists were making about the Famine—the contention that the British government exploited the potato blight in a deliberate effort to wipe out Irish resistance to imperial rule—it also sparked the first confrontation between the new national theater and its public. Yeats's play offered a critique of imperial coercion in the form of the demons who offer to buy the souls of the starving peasants, but he failed to protect his heroine from the demons' machinations—a failure that he recognized and rectified three years later in his second Cathleen.

Flesh and the Devil: The Countess Cathleen and the Demons' Bargain

The Irish nationalist community was never homogenous, and Irish nationalism never monolithic. When we speak of the "nationalist response" to a particular production, then, it is necessary to be specific about which nationalists are involved and what kind of nationalism they adhere to. Although any attempt to generalize is necessarily reductive, it is possible to identify distinct strains of nationalist ideology, espoused by distinct factions, that have influenced both the production and the reception of particular plays. For instance, the protests against Sean O'Casey's 1926 *The Plough and the Stars* were dominated by a group of women socialists who had strong emotional, ideological, and personal investments in the republican cause that clearly differentiated them from the more conservative nationalists who supported the Irish Free State.[2]

In the first years of the Irish Literary Theater, public response to the plays tended to reflect the concerns of a different strain of nationalism that was defined less by the republican objective than by the vision of a restored, purified, and idealized Irish culture. I will be using the term "Irish-Ireland" to refer to this strain of nationalism, whose major proponent was Arthur Griffith (editor of the influential newspaper *The United Irishman* and, later, one of the architects of Sinn Fein policy and the first Free State government). Irish-Ireland nationalism was characterized first and foremost by the belief that decolonization was most effectively achieved through de-Anglicization. The goals, strategies, and preoccupations of Irish-Irelanders were heavily influenced by, and in sympathy with, those of the Irish language movement. But the program of de-Anglicization was by no means limited to the restoration of Irish or the purging of corrupt foreign influences from Irish culture. It also had an important economic component, a patriotic version of protectionism that was foundational to the Irish-Ireland ideological paradigm.

After initially coexisting and cooperating, Griffith's Irish-Irelanders and Yeats's coterie soon found themselves locked in battle. There were a number of bones of contention: language (the Irish Literary Theatre, and later the Irish National Theatre Society, were English-language; the Gaelic League felt this disqualified their productions as "national" literature); religion (Yeats, Synge, Gregory, and O'Casey were Protestants; Irish-Irelanders tended to be Catholic); class (Gregory was part of the landowning Anglo-Protestant aristocracy; Irish-Irelanders generally were not); aesthetics (the Irish-Ireland audience expected naturalistic drama with "realistic" characters; the Abbey's major figures, with the exception of Sean O'Casey, were not interested in providing it); and competition (the Gaelic League produced its own Irish-language entertainments, including Irish-language drama).[3]

But the conflict also had to do with gender; and that fact had to do with conceptions about the human body, health, and illness that were influenced by imperial science. For centuries, Britain had been using constructions of gender and sexuality to help produce a version of Irishness that would suit Britain's needs, and resisting those constructions was a central part of the de-Anglicizing mission of Irish-Ireland.[4] That resistance, however, was almost entirely oppositional; instead of challenging the gender paradigms that supported disabling constructions of Irishness, the Irish-Ireland movement merely tried to reverse them, defining Ireland into the position of power, agency, and virtue. As a result, Irish-Irelandism was never able to change the terms of the debate, and it remained largely defined by the imperialist discourse against which it was reacting. The increasing cultural power of medical discourse played an important role in circumscribing and limiting those attempts at resistance.

As Marjorie Howes argues, the Arnoldian construction of the Celt as essentially feminine was inseparable from, and inflected by, "late nineteenth-century discourses on hysteria" that defined the same temperamental characteristics that distinguished the Celt—"sensitivity, romance, idealism . . . nervous instability, sexual pathology, [and] lack of 'balance, measure and patience'"—as both feminine and diseased (21). Frank Hugh O'Donnell's angry rejection of *The Countess Cathleen,* in which he identifies the play's heroine as the "demented female" hysteric constructed by Freud and his colleagues (262), shows how strongly that equation between neurosis and femininity had marked Celticism—and how passionately the Irish-Ireland community reacted against it. As would often happen, an imperialist construction of Irishness—in this case, the hysterical, effeminate, melancholic Celt—spawned a mirror image in nationalist discourse: the virile, healthy, hypermasculine Gael, whose manly vigor is in stark contrast to the oversensitive Celt's nervous prostration.

The polarization of the nationalist community that would lead to Gaelic Leaguers using Irish-language songs to disrupt productions of *The Playboy of the Western World* was conditioned by that rejection of Yeats's "Celticism" after the initial productions of the Irish Literary Theater in 1899. The main complaint voiced in the Gaelic League's organ, *An Claidheamh Soluis* (The Sword of Light), was always that an English-language movement should not call itself Irish or national. But the Gaelic movement rejects the Irish Literary Theater, not simply because it is English-language, but because it is tainted by that enervating Celticism. For instance, in "What Is Irish National Literature?" the editor mocks "the pleasant primrose paths of Anglo-Irish writing, with their dainty little bends and bowers, and their dear little gurgling rivulets of thought beside them" (248), using those belittling diminutives to project the effeminacy of "Celticism" onto the authors accused of promoting it. The primrose path is not only feminine but degenerate; these maligned "petty litterateur[s]" no longer "dare to think" and instead "prefer to vegetate," devolving into an unpleasant kind of weed whose "decaying stem" must be cut down by the phallic "sword" of the Gaelic movement (248–49). D. P. Moran's attack translates Celticism's neuropathology into physiological deterioration: the Irish Literary Theater is a "thing with no blood in it," an "anaemic sham" weak in body and in mind (261).

Conversely, the Oireachtas, an annual Irish-language cultural festival organized by the Gaelic League, is represented as producing virility, health, and strength:

> There is talk upon all sides of the vitality of the Gael, and of the resurgence of the Celt. The coming year or two will show whether the rally is a spasmodic effort before final extinction or whether it be real. It is altogether a question of the fibre of the men of the League, and especially of the men who are met at the third Oireachtas. Have they insight enough and grit enough to bend circumstances, and begin a new and successful chapter in the history of Ireland? ("The Third Oireachtas," 200)

This author's exclusive focus on the "men of the League" is eminently typical of *An Claidheamh Soluis*'s masculinist bias. What it also shows is that this lost Irish masculinity is closely associated with physical, moral, and mental health—"fibre," "grit," the "vitality" that is opposed here to the "spasmodic" final efforts of a vitiated and expiring culture. Like Moran, who contrasts the debility of the Irish Literary Theater with the robust health of the Oireachtas, Griffith hails the Third Oireachtas as the "visible and palpable proof" of a "sudden reaccession to manhood" that will not only wipe out this troubling effeminacy but also begin to cure the pernicious anemia of Anglo-Irishism:

> Ever since the attention of the Irish nation was diverted from the four shores of our country to the benches of Westminster the blood of the people has been thinning, until it became under the chilling blast of the Union of Hearts the most colourless serum that ever pulsed through a nation's body. . . . Today the cure is not nearly complete; but the heart of Erin—the true, fierce, heart that lived down Aughrim and Limerick, the Penal Days and Ninety-Eight, that seemed smothered in the blood of Emmet, but resurgent with Young Ireland and the Fenian Men—that heart is again throbbing. ("The Third Oireachtas," 200)

We find the battle lines drawn early, then. On the Anglo-Irish side, affectation, effeminacy, neurosis, disease; on the side of the Gaelic League, the "vigorous, sinewy, strong-minded manhood" (Griffith 18 March 1899: 1) in which masculinity, health, power, and cultural and linguistic purity combine. But just as—as Howes argues—Yeats's eventual rejection of his own Celticism represents a concession to imperial models of Irishness and gender identity, the Gaelic League's self-definition as the antidote to the poison of Anglo-Irish culture was a crucial and damaging acceptance of the Empire's terms.

Irish-Irelanders, by accepting so many of the basic premises of imperial science (femininity is pathology, virility equals health, impurity is equivalent to disease), not only ensured that the Abbey Theater would be falling out with the nationalist community for decades to come but also allowed itself to be confined and constrained within the limits of imperial discourse. The Oireachtas—the "visible, tangible proof" of that Irish Ireland's rebirth—were held in the Round Room of the Rotunda Hospital, an equally visible, tangible, and material indication that the health and integrity of the Irish body and the Irish birth process were still very much endangered by imperial discourse and practice. The same discursive framework that set up the Oireachtas as a sign of the healthy and natural "development" of Irish-language culture from its unformed "protoplasm" (Griffith 20 May 1899: 1) into a "great body of national sentiment" ("Third

Oireachtas") complete with throbbing heart and manly sinews also propped up the imperial administration. The movement's use of medical discourse, like its use of that institutional space, would come at a price. Looking closer at the first battle between Yeats and Irish-Ireland—the controversy surrounding the initial production of *The Countess Cathleen* in 1899—begins to give us an idea of what that price entailed.

There were any number of things that any Irish nationalist might easily not like about *The Countess Cathleen.* As Adrian Frazier points out, the play confirms the worst stereotypes the Protestant aristocracy held about the Catholic peasantry: they are venal, greedy, crafty, cowardly, and superstitious.[5] The play affirms class hierarchies so enthusiastically as to suggest that they are recognized in the other world as well as this one; the plot depends on the fact that the Countess Cathleen's soul is worth several thousand times more than the most highly rated peasant soul. Along with Frazier, Elizabeth Butler Cullingford, and James Flannery, Marjorie Howes points out the play's clear, if coded reference to the Great Famine of the 1840s, arguing that the "famine setting" made the insult infinitely worse by using "nationalist thematics usually associated with criticism of the grim social reality created by the exploitative tenantry system as the setting for the play's central affirmation" (47) of that system. Given the rich tapestry of offense that *The Countess Cathleen* spread out before its aggrieved audience, it is surprising that the actual protests coalesced around the comparatively technical question of whether the play's resolution was heretical.

The charge of heresy derived from two basic affronts to Catholic sensibilities: a scene in which a Catholic peasant frustrated by the Blessed Virgin Mary's refusal to intercede on behalf of her starving faithful destroys a shrine to her, and the heroine's final redemption.[6] In the play, the Countess Cathleen, a good-hearted but sheltered and naive aristocrat, sells her soul to the devil so she can give the money to the peasants and thus prevent them from selling their own souls in order to buy food. She dies very shortly thereafter and is taken up to heaven in spite of her bargain. An angel appears to explain that the Countess's bargain with the demons is void because she sold her soul for altruistic rather than selfish reasons. The rationale with which the angel justifies the Countess's apotheosis—"The Light of Lights / Looks always on the motive, not the deed" (*VPl* 167)—was found by Yeats's critics to be inconsistent with Catholic teaching and became the focus of a debate that involved Cardinal Logue and that culminated in an opening-night protest organized by a group of Catholic university students.

The protests against the play's heretical ending appear to have upstaged criticisms about its class politics or its representation of the Famine. Lady Gregory, in retrospect, considers the *Countess* brouhaha "not a very real" (28) controversy and attributes it to bad blood between Yeats and Frank Hugh O'Donnell, author of the two major anti-*Countess* tracts. Even Arthur Griffith, at the height of his post-*Shadow* dudgeon, dismissed *The Countess Cathleen*'s opponents as "dishonest," "ignorant," or both (Griffith 18 April 1903: 1), and as motivated by narrow-minded sectarianism rather than legitimate nationalist scruples. As Lady Gregory suggests, however, the anger sparked by the Countess's redemption cannot be explained entirely on doctrinal grounds; before production Yeats and Gregory submitted the play to Catholic readers who failed to be offended by it (25–27).

If we resist explaining this controversy purely in terms of F. H. O'Donnell's personal problems with Yeats or dismissing it as a knee-jerk reaction on the part of the Catholic nationalist bloc to the condemnation of Cardinal Logue, it appears as the earliest example of a pattern that would often be repeated in the early decades of the Irish National Theater. The nationalist community's substantive objections to a play's political content would, again and again, be transmuted into a reductive and "hysterical" outcry over the behavior of its female characters. If we read the heresy controversy as being about gender and the body as well as about religion, *The Countess Cathleen* has much to say about how representations of Irish women came to be a matter of such intense concern to nationalist audiences. As a parable about the spirit's susceptibility to the suffering of the body, *The Countess Cathleen* contradicts nationalist assertions of the absolute incorruptibility of the Irish character in the face of British economic and military oppression. Worse, as the story of a woman who saves her people by sacrificing her soul, it disables one of the main strategies nationalism used to back up those assertions—the idealization of the Irish woman. Although, as Howes demonstrates, the Countess is descended from a long line of idealized female representations of Ireland, "the common practice of representing Ireland as a woman forms an important site of ambivalence and conflict in Irish national discourses" (45). Not all Cathleens are created equal. As Yeats was to discover, the ideal he incarnated in his Countess was very much at odds with the idealized Irish woman that O'Donnell, and later Griffith, would come to insist upon.

O'Donnell, in the letters that he eventually published as the pamphlet "Souls for Gold: Pseudo-Celtic Drama in Dublin," was the first to publicly denounce the Countess's apotheosis as "blasphemous" (262). He was also the first to demonstrate that these dogmatic objections arose from a more fundamental rejection of Yeats's depiction of the Great Famine's effect on the Irish peasantry. O'Donnell makes it clear early on that what is really eating him is the sight of "the Catholic peasantry of an Irish district, being pressed by famine, hasten[ing] to sell their souls to the devil for the means of purchasing food" (261). Denouncing such a story as "utterly alien to all our national traditions" (261), O'Donnell spends most of his time restating the claim that this plot is not part of Irish history or culture and that if Yeats wants to preach his "loathsome doctrine that faith and conscience can be bartered for a full belly and a full purse . . . he has no right to lay the scene in Ireland" (264).

The first of many hints that O'Donnell may be protesting too much is the barb that closes his opening paragraph: "I could understand such a theme being welcome at a souper meeting at Exeter Hall" (261). This and other references to the "soul-selling and soup-buying" (262) peasants show O'Donnell making the same inference that Frazier and Howes do: that although Yeats originally set *The Countess Cathleen* in the sixteenth century (by 1899 he had altered this to "in old times"), its real reference is to the potato famines of the late 1840s. But although O'Donnell's ranting might easily persuade us to dismiss "Souls for Gold" as an act of sectarian spite, the "mythology of souperism" (Howes 48) he invokes also involved more material concerns.

By O'Donnell's time that sinister Protestant with his bowl of soup had become a metaphor for the network of economic and bureaucratic institutions that turned a natural disaster into an opportunity to consolidate imperial power. Stories collected after the Famine depict public works administrators, landlords, and educators (Poirteir 168, 169, 172) collaborating with proselytizing Protestants in their efforts to lure Catholics away from the fold. *The Countess Cathleen* participates in this tradition. Yeats, although preserving the religious connotations of souperism by making his tempters supernatural and demonic, also directly alludes to the secular forces that supported this project by making them capitalists (Frazier 16). Asked why they do not give alms to the poor instead of trading with them, one of the demons responds, "We know the evils of mere charity, / and would devise a more considered way" (*VPl* 41). The merchants evidently hold the views of the 1847 Poor Law Commissioners, whose report warns against the "evils of endeavouring to give relief" (qtd. in Killen 85) without demanding labor in return, and they share the same obsession with preserving ideal market conditions and avoiding anything that might "stifle private enterprise" (Kinealy 46) that was used to justify the British government's manipulative and ineffective attempts at famine relief.

Yeats's characterization of the demons as capitalists taking advantage of a natural disaster in order to despoil the Irish population of whatever they might still possess was perfectly in tune with the prevailing nationalist interpretation of the Famine, anticipating arguments that Arthur Griffith would later use in "The 'Economics' of Famine." In fact, Griffith borrows Yeats's metaphor, charging that Anglo-Irish landlords "acted the part of demons" ("'Economics'" 5), serving as minions to the British government, a.k.a. "His Britannic Majesty" ("Constitutionalism" 3). Griffith's insistence that the crisis of 1845–50 was an "artificial famine" deliberately created by British policy ("'Economics'" 5) is heavily informed by propagandistic concerns, but more recent and more rigorous scholarship supports his contention that the starvation and suffering that accompanied the potato blight were, if not caused, at least exacerbated both by the preexisting economic system established by colonialism and by British famine relief policies.[7] Thus, when Yeats puts two deal-making demons on stage and has them mouth the tenets of laissez-faire capitalism, he is concurring with the reading of the Famine as a state-orchestrated disaster—an important concession that might well have persuaded nationalist audiences to embrace his heroine despite her connections to the "demons" Griffith denounces.

However, Yeats's treatment of the play's peasant characters undoes all that work—and not simply because it is condescending and arrogant or because his depiction of peasants as soupers is historically inaccurate (Frazier 8–9). When O'Donnell protests that Yeats's peasants are not Irish, he is not simply arguing that "real" Irish Catholics would never convert under pressure. He is claiming that the invincible Irish spirit is invulnerable to the kind of state coercion that was linked to souperism and that no matter how powerful the material forces that are brought to bear on the Irish subject may be, imperial control cannot fundamentally alter Irish behavior or change Irish culture. In order to make that argument, however, O'Donnell has to deny considerable historical and material evidence that shows that the Famine and British policy relating to it certainly did change Irish behavior and Irish culture. And it is partly because Yeats dramatizes that evidence in *Countess Cathleen* that the play offends O'Donnell's conception of Irishness.

It seems strange to talk about *Countess Cathleen* as history, populated as it is with supernatural beings and allegorical figures; and indeed, this play is very far from being a documentary. But the voluminous mists of myth and legend do swirl around small bits of concrete history—details that evoke specific memories of the Famine. Maire tells Shemus that the only food they have left is "a bag half full of meal" (*VPl* 11), suggesting the notoriously inedible Indian meal that was distributed by the government; their neighbor has died with "her mouth . . . green with dock and dandelion" (*VPl* 29), an emblematic image of starvation common to much post-Famine folklore.[8] A more obscure reference, but one that was evidently clear to O'Donnell, is the Second Merchant's story of transforming himself into a pig and killing Father John, the local priest.

O'Donnell singles this passage out as especially worthy of contempt: "Good old Father John, in spite of his prayers and his breviary, killed by the devil in the shape of a brown pig! How Irish! How exquisitely Celtic!" (264). The pig is a touchy subject in this context, since during the nineteenth century the Irish custom of housing a pig inside the cabin was used by the English media to dehumanize the Irish and assimilate them to animals. But the image of a pig killing an Irish man who is too weak to fight him off also evokes eyewitness reports of the Famine, which often dwelt on sensational details involving miserable deaths and revolting desecrations. Father John's story bears some resemblance, for instance, to the one told in this piece appearing in the *Vindicator* in January 1847:

> HORRIBLE!—An inquest was held on the 12th instant, upon the body of Thomas M'Manus, of Kilmactranny—verdict. "Deceased came to his death by hunger and cold." . . . We copy the evidence of Thomas Burrows, Esq., M.D.—"Examined the body of Thomas M'Manus; both the legs, as far as the buttocks, appeared to have been eaten off by a pig; is of opinion his death was caused by hunger and cold." There was not a particle of food found in the deceased's stomach or intestines. Those who saw the body were of opinion, from the agonized expression of M'Manus's countenance, that he was *alive* when the pig attacked him. (qtd. in Killen 99)

Stories of animals attacking and eating famine victims either before or after death were widespread enough to give O'Donnell some justification for fearing that this kind of detail was already seen as "exquisitely Celtic" by a world whose perception of Ireland had been affected by coverage of the Famine.[9] Underlying O'Donnell's quarrel about accuracy is a desire to repress the evidence, in all its horror and grotesquerie, of the disastrous effect the Famine had on those starving Irish bodies. It was clearer during the Famine than at any other time just how vulnerable the Irish body could become to imperial rule, and stories like that of Thomas M'Manus show how inevitably that vulnerability translated into demoralization, despair, and defeat.

Frazier's contention that *The Countess Cathleen* is unfair because Irish peasants did not in fact abjure Catholicism en masse during the Famine thus misses, in one sense, the point. O'Donnell's revulsion is sparked as much by the pious Father John's starvation-accelerated death as it is by Shemus's hunger-inspired apostasy. What O'Donnell is denying, when he argues that stories like Father Jack's are "utterly alien to our national traditions," is the power of the body—the physical need that could reduce an Irish peasant to the point where resistance was impossible; where he would trade his faith for soup, would become easy prey for a pig, would crowd with a thousand others into a fever-ridden workhouse, would stain his mouth with grass. O'Donnell has to deny that power because it is through the body that the Irish "soul"—which as Howes points out is a political as well as a spiritual entity—is corrupted.[10] The story of the souper—like the story of the Great Famine—represents the starving body as the point at which economic manipulation translated into cultural disintegration, the crucible in which material pressures dissolved intangible commitments. The body is what renders the "Irish national character" vulnerable to imperial coercion, what makes imperial intervention inescapable and cultural pollution unavoidable.

O'Donnell was not the only critic of *The Countess Cathleen* who wished that power away. Maurice Joy, writing what is actually a defense of Yeats in the *United Irishman,* is equally bothered by the suggestion that Irish peasants might succumb to the demands of the body, claiming that if *Countess* were intended as "an historical representation of the Irish character under stress, we should be justified in objecting to it as a fallacy disproved by historical truth" (3). To the Irish-Ireland movement, which would become increasingly concerned with restoring "pure" Irish culture and cleansing itself of the "taint" of outside influences, the body's vulnerability made it a highly dangerous place: the focus of all imperial efforts at corruption and perversion, a site on which the evidence of Irish susceptibility to British power was forever inscribed.

The Countess Cathleen's sacrifice is problematic, then, because it is the final proof of the fact that Yeats's play has inverted the accepted relationship between materialism and idealism. Instead of sacrificing the body in order to keep the soul uncorrupted, the Countess willingly puts her soul at the mercy of the imperial demons in hopes of keeping life in the bodies of her tenants. Although motivated in part by concern for their spiritual welfare, the Countess is conceding what O'Donnell refuses to admit: that for ordinary humanity, the needs of the body take precedence over the health of the soul. Altruistic though her sacrifice may be, it is profoundly antithetical to the "souls for gold tradition" (Howes 58) whereby the Irish nationalist's first duty is to be prepared to suffer any form of physical hardship rather than compromise or betray his political ideals. Simply by considering these "soul-selling and soup-buying peasants" worthy of compassion, the Countess is violating that tradition.

But if it is the body itself that O'Donnell, Joy, and the play's other critics are denying, why does O'Donnell read the Countess's final redemption as compounding the insult rather than expunging it? After all, the angel's assertion that God judges based on the intention rather than the deed reaffirms the primacy of the intangible and immaterial, treating the Countess's heartfelt desire to help her tenants as more important than the act of converting her soul into ready cash. By rejecting this explanation as heretical, O'Donnell denies Yeats the authority to wipe the Countess's slate clean, insisting on holding her to her bargain. For him, as for the other protestors, her decision had to be irredeemable; Yeats could not be allowed to create a moral universe in which it was possible for his heroine to sell herself and get away with it.

To understand O'Donnell's refusal to accept the Countess's redemption, we must remember that the Countess combines two roles that nationalist tradition used gender to separate. The Countess Cathleen is both an allegorical personification of Ireland and a sacrificial martyr. By allowing her to be redeemed, Yeats confers on the Countess the martyr's usual reward—although her body dies, her transfigured soul lives on, eternally glorified both above and below. But he is also casting Countess into a role normally reserved for male characters. By reading *The Countess Cathleen* in conjunction with Edward Martyn's *The Heather Field*—in which Martyn follows convention by separating the feminized ideal from the masculine idealist who worships her—we can come to a clearer understanding of why that role was reserved for men and why Yeats's audiences refused to allow the Countess Cathleen to join the pantheon of sacrificial martyrs.

There but for Grace: Gender and Materialism in *The Heather Field*

Fortunately for Edward Martyn, Irish-Irelanders did not transfer the hostility that *The Countess Cathleen* evoked to his play *The Heather Field,* which opened the following day under the auspices of the same Irish Literary Theater. Critical response to the play varied, but although not everyone shared George Moore's opinion that Martyn was the next Shakespeare, the play "immediately eclips[ed] Yeats's play in popularity," giving Martyn his "only enduring theatrical triumph" (Eakin and Case, xii). There is, of course, an obvious explanation for the difference in reception: the sectarian rancor that Yeats's play excited could not possibly have become an issue for Martyn's. *The Heather Field* engages spiritual questions but not in an explicitly religious framework: all of Martyn's characters are presumed to be Protestant, and Martyn himself was Catholic. But if, as we have seen, the heresy argument is driven by a more fundamental anxiety about Irish vulnerability to imperial control, the obvious explanation becomes inadequate. If Martyn's play—which was in some ways politically heretical if not theologically heretical—was better received than Yeats's, that has much to do with the fact that in *The Heather Field* the relationship between the material and the ideal worlds is properly constructed—because it is properly gendered.

There are, certainly, well-marked formal differences that would lead audiences to respond to these plays differently. *The Countess Cathleen* is indebted to the French Symbolist movement, whereas *The Heather Field* translates Ibsen's methods and preoccupations from Norway to Ireland. Martyn also made the decision not to represent Irish Catholics or Irish peasants on stage, which meant no one could complain about their portrayal. But there are also some important similarities that ought to have adversely affected Martyn's reception. For instance, as Trotter notes, both plays "evoke the Irish Literary Theatre notion of an elite nationalism" that was created by "the leisured artist/intellectual" and then imposed on the "common person" (15). Different as Yeats's symbolism and Martyn's Ibsenism were, both the *Irish Times* reviewer and Griffith lumped them together as high-flown artistic constructs that were obscure to the "Average Man" (Griffith 13 May 1899:2). The *Times* critic finds exactly the same formal flaws in *The Heather Field* that he found in *The Countess Cathleen:* both are "mystical and exalted" to an incomprehensible degree; both have "stilted" dialogue; neither has any "action" to speak of or provides a "convincing" representation of Irish life; and, with the exception of Kit, the elfin young son of Martyn's protagonist, neither play includes believable or sympathetic characters.[11]

In fact, the formal differences that are so obvious to literary critics have tended to obscure some striking correspondences in terms of these plays' thematic content. As Trotter points out, "both plays emphasize the conflicts between the imaginary life and material concerns" (16). Griffith's comment on *The Heather Field*'s premiere shows that Martyn succeeded in getting that point through the head of at least one "Average Man": Griffith confesses himself somewhat at a loss as to "what it all meant" but suggests tentatively that the play is about "the impossibility of reconciling the Real and the Ideal" (13 May 1899: 2). As in *The Countess Cathleen,* the central character of *The Heather Field* is a landowner whose approach to estate management is romantic, extravagant, and highly impractical. Both of these idealistic main characters are betrayed and destroyed by materialistic villains. Each character is given an androgynous sidekick who shares the protagonist's vision and professes unconditional love for his doomed companion (Aleel in *The Countess Cathleen,* Kit in *The Heather Field*). And each protagonist is afforded an apotheosis that compensates for the apparent victory of the material world—the Countess Cathleen is assumed into heaven, while Tyrrell is transported into a fantasy world of eternal youth and possibility in which his dreams will no longer be frustrated by reality.

Seen from this perspective, the question of why the response to *The Heather Field* was so much more positive becomes more interesting. Since, as Moore points out, the play depends on the audience's sympathizing with Carden Tyrrell, Martyn should have faced some of the problems Yeats encountered when he located the moral and spiritual center of his dramatic universe in a representative of the Anglo-Irish landlord class. At best, he was courting the indifference of a public in whose image Carden Tyrrell was not created; at worst, he was repeating Yeats's insult by locating worth and virtue in the landlord while treating the tenants as too insignificant to represent. Tyrrell's claim to the audience's sympathy ought to be undermined by his complete disregard for his tenants' welfare: by Act III, Tyrrell has evicted his tenants because they cannot pay the rents he has to charge in order to subsidize the heather field. And if Catholics objected to the idea that the Irish peasant was capable of robbery, adultery, or blasphemy, should they not also have been troubled by the fact that when Tyrell's tenants finally are mentioned, it is only because they are threatening to murder him?[12]

If Yeats was asking for trouble by trying to force his audience to accept his valuation of the Countess's soul, then Martyn should be in dire straits once he asks an audience to identify with Carden Tyrrell. Yet Tyrrell's decision to evict—a point of contention that is far less obscure than the doctrinal problems raised by the Countess's redemption—never comes up in responses to *The Heather Field*. Martyn's play passes muster because Martyn does not commit the *real* heresy for which Yeats is being pilloried—the failure to protect the ideal from the real. Martyn is not called to account for his other heresies because he follows the strategies of representation that allow the idealistic protagonist's moral victory to cancel out his material defeat. And perhaps the most important of these strategies is Martyn's decision to make that protagonist male.

Tyrrell's particular brand of idealism is not easily understood by the play's other characters. This is partly because, as the *Times* reviewer is relentless in pointing out, Tyrrell's visionary rhetoric is deflated by the extreme banality of the objects on which his obsession is focused ("Irish Literary Theatre" 10 May 1899: 5). In fact, Tyrrell's "dreams" are eminently materialistic: he wants to turn some waste property on his estate—the eponymous heather field—into profitable pastureland. He has almost accomplished this task when the play begins, but the reclamation effort has flooded some of his other lands, and he has applied for a Board of Works loan that will allow him to start draining the runoff. Everyone else in the play—with the exception of the innocent Kit—is bent on preventing him from taking out that loan. His estranged wife Grace goes so far as to attempt to have Tyrrell certified as insane. Tyrrell's friend and fellow-landlord Barry Ussher foils this plot; but in Act III things have nevertheless taken a turn for the worse, and Tyrrell ultimately realizes that the success of the heather field is the only thing standing between him and ruin. He is thus dismayed to discover that heather has started to grow in the field again and it will soon be worthless once more. The shock unhinges Tyrrell, who abandons reality in favor of a delusionary world based on his nostalgic fantasies.

If we put aside Moore and Griffith for a moment and take a look at the play, it is hard to see exactly how Tyrrell's quest to reclaim the heather field comes to be constructed as an idealistic crusade. Tyrrell frankly admits that he is doing it for the money: "A fortune is to be made by such work" (*Heather Field* 221). Even his irrational determination to take out the disastrous loan could be read as more grasping than quixotic: "It was absolutely necessary to obtain this further loan unless the value of the previous one was to be destroyed" (223). Likewise, there is no question of his being motivated by an idealistic concern for his tenants. The heather field will be rented out to other landlords who need pasture for their cattle, and Tyrrell is critical of Ussher's decision to lower his own rents. The chief and indeed only virtue of his scheme is that if it is successful, "[Tyrell's] income must be greatly increased" (223). And yet somehow Tyrrell is constructed—by the other characters as well as by Moore, Griffith, and the reviewers—as an idealistic dreamer rather than a greedy capitalist.

The fact that none of Martyn's critics challenge Tyrrell's claim to the title of "idealist" testifies to Martyn's success in manipulating familiar dramatic and ideological structures so that despite his clearly expressed materialistic motivations, Tyrrell is built into the idealist's position. That position is defined almost entirely by two things: Tyrrell's mystical connection to the land he wants to reclaim, and the opposition between Tyrrell and his wife Grace. Tyrrell is given a number of opportunities to express his love for the field and his joy in the reclamation work:

> Yes—the great mountain field out there . . . that it was my ideal to bring to fruitfulness. There I awaken to true life indeed, as I stand looking over the Atlantic; and sea winds sweep against my feet the young grass in its matchless Irish green that gleams a golden green in the Autumn sun to-day. There I am haunted by those departed joys of my youth—again and again. (227–28)

Tyrrell's love affair with the land, which he hopes will bring it to "fruitfulness," is in stark contrast to his barren and deadlocked relationship with Grace, who is jealous of her husband's "infatuation with that mountain" (245). In Tyrrell's mind, at least, it is his intercourse with the heather field that will prove "creative" and will work the "magic" that will "change the face" of Ireland (245–46).

Tyrrell is idealized, first and foremost, by an attachment to the land itself, which allows the language of romantic love to transfigure his otherwise worldly obsessions. Martyn insists on the romance analogy, making it clear that Tyrrell has transferred his affections from Grace to the heather field. Before he became obsessed with grazing and drainage, Tyrrell's idealism was focused on his beautiful fiancée, but familiarity quickly bred contempt:

> Ah, Miles, I have simply found [Grace] to be absolutely different from what I once imagined her. I was very young then, very inexperienced. I longed for sympathy, and thought it was easy to find. I idealised women in those days. I believed that they were idealists. Ah, that was my fatal error. (225)

Grace's beauty is mere "sham," whereas the heather field offers Tyrrell communion with the "truly beautiful" (225). In fact, Tyrrell turns to the heather field precisely in order to compensate for the failure of his marriage with Grace: having been "forced" into marriage and the "drudgery" of farming, Tyrrell cannot find "contentment" until he hits on "the master-thought of the heather field," where he "return[s] to [his] youth's ideals" as he communes with the "magic in those mountain breezes" (246).

If the heather field assumes everything Tyrrell formerly invested in his idealized vision of women, Grace comes to incarnate everything Tyrrell hates and despises about the material world. Tyrrell blames the fact that Grace was "never in sympathy with [his] ideas" (232) for his present difficulties. His friend Ussher agrees, telling Miles that Grace was too "prosy" for an "ethereal" nature like Tyrrell's, and reading his obsession with the heather field as a "revolt" against Grace's attempt to domesticate him (220). This opposition between the "simple, barren prose" of Grace's outlook and Tyrrell's "ideal," "imaginative," visionary spirit is the conflict that drives the play. While Tyrrell complains about her lack of "sympathy," Grace harps on the danger of ruin and the necessity of being "economical" (232). And although Tyrrell's troubles are caused by a host of material forces that work their will off stage, Grace is Tyrrell's only visible adversary. It is because Grace's materialism is so flagrantly advertised and the opposition between her and Tyrrell so clearly defined that Tyrrell can be an idealist. We know that Grace is the *real* materialist, and we know that Tyrrell is Grace's mortal enemy.

Tyrrell's idealism is thus dependent on the construction of Grace as materialistic, and that construction is itself utterly conditioned by Martyn's deployment of gender norms. Grace's materialism is distinct from and opposed to Tyrrell's because it is feminine—deriving, not from masculinized traits like ambition or the desire to discover and conquer, but from her position as a female dependent. Grace is a gold-digger; Ussher accuses her of "marrying [Tyrrell] for his means and his position" (219). She is a social climber, willing to sacrifice her husband's happiness in order to "shape [his] life altogether after . . . that of Lady Shrule" (225). When she plots her husband's downfall, she uses her responsibilities as mother and homemaker to justify her actions: she characterizes her attempt to have Tyrrell committed as one of "the measures I have decided upon for the security of the child's interests and mine" (248). Yoked to other particularly unpleasant and stereotypically feminine traits—a taste for manipulation and intrigue, a tendency to nag, and a belief that marriage gives her the right to reshape her husband according to her own desires—the material concerns Grace expresses are demonized along with her, just as Tyrrell's are idealized through their association with Tyrrell's more spiritual, intellectual, manly qualities.

Martyn's play functions, then, because of the overwhelming cultural power that supports Tyrrell's assertion that "the true idealist can only be a man" (225). The *ideal* may be feminine or feminized—like the heather field and the magical voices that sing to Tyrrell while he works in it—but this is precisely because the *idealist* who loves her must be masculine. What *The Heather Field* suggests is that in order to be an idealist, the hero needs not just that feminine ethereal beloved but her loathed corporeal counterpart—the flesh-and-blood woman against whose vulgar materialism the hero revolts. To revise Tyrrell's phrase, a man can only be a true idealist *because* materialism has been defined as the essential and foundational characteristic of femininity. It is that conflation of femininity and materiality that marks Grace's greed and selfishness so strongly that it can completely obscure Tyrrell's. Martyn's hero becomes idealistic by virtue of those two defining gendered relationships—the doomed heterosexual romance between the cultivator and the potentially "fruitful" land of Ireland, and the polar opposition between the high-minded husband and his venal and spiteful wife. The fact that Martyn follows the tradition of gendering idealism and materialism is the *only* thing that makes Tyrrell look like an idealist—and therefore the *only* thing that makes this conflict work.

The power of this paradigm explains why Martyn was able to sell Tyrrell to his audiences as an idealist sacrificed to the demands of the worldly Grace; it also helps explain why Yeats failed to sell the Countess Cathleen as a sacrificial hero. When the Countess Cathleen decides that it is more important for her tenants to eat than for her soul to go to heaven, she is in one sense obeying the rules of gender construction: like Grace, she decides that material well-being is more important than any abstract promise of future glory. But Yeats also tries to work *against* those rules by constructing Cathleen as an idealist who is motivated by an abstract love for her tenants—a love based, not on any personal or material connection to them, but on her absorption in the same kind of "dreams" about Ireland that transfigure Tyrrell's obsession with the heather field. Yeats is allowed to work with the prevailing paradigm—the Countess Cathleen is condemned for having committed the sin of materialism—but not against it. Unlike Martyn, he is not allowed to rescue his protagonist from the material consequences of her actions. Because as a mortal woman she is still charged with the burden of corporeality that Grace carries, the Countess Cathleen is denied transcendence. Tyrrell can escape the material consequences of his actions by withdrawing into a utopian dream world; but when Yeats tries to bring the Countess into heaven, her femininity resists translation, and she is left stranded in the physical world—female, material, and therefore culpable. Yeats's resolution is "heretical," then, not just because it violates Catholic doctrines, but because it violates audience expectations about gender roles.

Making idealism masculine and materiality feminine is of course not a phenomenon specific to Irish literature. But as the success of *The Heather Field*—and of Yeats's later play *Cathleen ni Houlihan*—suggests, that paradigm was particularly useful to Irish nationalists because of the (apparently) absolute and stable separation it effects between the material and the ideal. The assumed stability of gender difference preserves the position of pure idealism—as, in *The Heather Field,* Tyrrell's idealist status is preserved despite dialogue that reveals his materialistic desires. That position is necessarily then reserved exclusively for the male figure, whose claim to idealism is protected by the presence of a more clearly and crassly corporeal female counterpart. (Men are idealists because women are not; Tyrrell cannot be a materialist because he cannot be Grace.) This allows the idealist to triumph no matter what happens in the material world, because the triumph of idealism is defined precisely as a refusal to concede to or be tainted by materialism. Tyrrell wins, not by reclaiming the heather field, but by choosing his alternative reality—in which, significantly, he decides that he is not married to Grace and never will be—instead of giving in to Grace and withdrawing his loan application.

When gender difference is not used to structure separation between the real and the ideal, things get much messier. In *The Countess Cathleen,* the distinction between real and ideal collapses not so much because of what the Countess Cathleen does as because of her mere existence as a figure in whom the two categories become intertwined. The peasants' souls are separable from their bodies—they sell them off without feeling a thing. The Countess Cathleen, however, dies as soon as she makes the demon's bargain, showing that for her the two entities are fused and one cannot survive the loss of the other. Because she is both a mortal woman and an iconic figure in the tradition of Fair Erin, Hibernia, and the Shan Van Vocht, the Countess blurs the line between material and ideal existence; her corporeal body is inseparable from the "idealized set of beauties and virtues" (Howes 56) that it represents. By conflating these two roles, Countess Cathleen makes the ideal mortal and therefore vulnerable. Because in her, body and soul cannot be separated, one cannot be shielded from the dangers inherent in the other.

O'Donnell's attack on *The Countess Cathleen* gives some indication of how and why Irish nationalists became so invested in maintaining a complete and stable opposition between the spiritual and the material. What *The Heather Field* shows is that it is partly in order to preserve that opposition that Irish Ireland rose up in anger when Irish playwrights challenged prevailing gender norms—since any challenge to the rigidity of gender difference endangered that separation. If Irish nationalists want to believe that the Irish man cannot be corrupted or tainted by material pressures, then they need to protect him from the needs of his body; and in order to do that, they need to project corporeality, materialism, and vulnerability onto the female Other, preserving the male subject position for idealism and invulnerability. O'Donnell's nationalism cannot incorporate the Countess Cathleen, but it absolutely needs Grace.

Grace is especially useful because she is also a member of the Anglo-Irish ascendancy and can therefore be demonized with impunity. Unlike Synge's more dangerous women—Nora Burke, Pegeen Mike—Grace belongs to what Griffith identifies as the demon class, which allows Martyn to treat her and the dangerous power she represents with the proper contempt. Thanks to the amount of agency that her ascendancy position confers on her, Grace becomes the *agent* of materialism rather than its victim. This is demonstrated most clearly through her attempt to have Tyrrell committed at the end of Act II, as she invokes the specific and sinister power represented by the two doctors.

The antagonistic relationship between the philosophy of scientific materialism that drives the British-identified medical establishment and the idealism that animates Tyrrell is perhaps best displayed in this exchange between Tyrrell and Dr. Dowling:

> TYRRELL: Yes; was [the reclamation project] not a discovery? And what contentment it brought after the previous life-drudgery. I felt like returning to my youth's ideals in that free mountain air. Oh! There is magic in those mountain breezes!
>
> DOWLING: All I know, sir, is that the Faculty consider sea air blowing over a mountain bog to be the finest remedy in the world for bile or dyspepsia. (246)

Tyrrell's sensibilities are highly offended by Dowling's reduction of his "ethereal mountain breeze" to a remedy for intestinal complaints (246). But through these doctors and the medical establishment whose authority Dowling has just quoted, scientific materialism has the power to do more than hurt Tyrrell's feelings. These doctors are in Tyrrell's home for the purpose of determining whether he needs to be committed to a lunatic asylum. Their power over him is created by a "conspiracy" between the colonial administration, which grants these doctors the authority to identify Tyrrell as a public health threat, and Grace, who is unscrupulous enough to exploit it.

It is through Grace that medical science enters *The Heather Field* as a threat—both to the welfare of the protagonist and to the survival of the world of ideals whose standard he carries. Ussher articulates some of the broader implications of that threat when he tries to talk Roche out of his diagnosis:

> [Tyrrell's] work may or may not be practical. Who knows? Personally I agree with you in thinking it is not. Still, that is no plea for trying to deprive him of his liberty and rights. If it were, I fear that many, and those too in responsible positions, might have their freedom of action endangered. It is only common-place and unimaginative people who consider the poetic and original temperament to be a mark of madness. (249)

It is not hard to read through Ussher's defense of the poetic temperament to a defense of Irish nationalism. In much nationalist rhetoric—particularly in that of the Gaelic League—the cause of Irish freedom is persistently defined *against* the "practical," as an idealistic crusade nationalists carry out, not because they expect tangible rewards, but because they are inspired by love for an ideal they may never achieve. If Tyrrell's irrational attachment to his idiosyncratic project is enough to make him certifiable, how much more vulnerable does the nationalist community become to the power of a medical establishment that refuses to separate sanity from pragmatism? If the voices Tyrrell hears in the heather field are mere dementia-induced delusions, then so are the voices that lead a figure like Joan of Arc to embark on the highly impractical project of national liberation.

The closing scene of Act II is an early and particularly concrete illustration of the danger that the ascendancy of scientific materialism represented for the Irish nationalist movement. The same mystical and overpowering love for the land that animates the Irish patriot now becomes the justification for Tyrrell's diagnosis and committal. The belief that Ireland has a metaphysical as well as a material existence, represented in Tyrrell's insistence on the untranslatable "beautiful meaning" of the voices that he hears singing to him in the heather field, is transformed by scientific materialism into a disease that renders the victim a danger to himself and others. The transformation of that magical breeze into a cure for dyspepsia reduces Ireland from nationality to geography—from a spiritual entity to a place that can be possessed, bought, and sold by whoever has enough material might. Tyrrell's transition from idealism to clinical insanity shows that by exerting the intangible power of discourse, the advocates of scientific materialism can destroy both the nationalist cause and the nationalist hero.

But if this subplot shows why Irish nationalists would have good reason to see the medical establishment and its practitioners as natural—and powerful—enemies, it also indicates serious anxieties about the medical establishment's relationship with the Irish woman. Grace is the character who puts Tyrrell at the mercy of these doctors, and it is Grace who explicitly labels Tyrrell's vision a "hallucination" (246). When Roche expresses "reservations" about Tyrrell's commitability, Grace trades on her position as wife and mother: "If he is not restrained he will surely bring the child and me to irreparable ruin" (248). Her final action is a desperate appeal to Roche's responsibility as a representative of a paternalistic system to defend the interests of a helpless mother and child: "Oh, Doctor Roche, we are in your hands. Our fate lies upon your decision. I implore you not to fail us" (250–51). Without Grace's interference, Tyrrell would never have been brought to the attention of the Commission for Lunacy, and Dowling and Roche would never have had the opportunity to exercise their diagnostic powers on him. It is only through the collaboration of his material and materialistic female counterpart that the idealistic protagonist becomes vulnerable to this form of state control.

Imperial science, in other words, hurts the Irish man *through* the Irish woman. Medicine operates on the female body; the woman who owns that body then operates on her idealistic counterpart. The burden of vulnerability can be projected onto the Irish woman's body; but it cannot be contained there. In fact, her materiality and corporeality ultimately make her *more* threatening as a weapon that the forces of British materialism use against the idealistic Irish patriot—and that threat becomes more sinister once the illusion of agency is removed. Grace at least can choose whether or not to expose her husband to the Commission on Lunacy. The Gaelic/Catholic Irish women who were practiced on by Anglo-Irish doctors could not choose not to expose themselves, their wombs, and the Irish reproductive process to imperial intervention. The strategy of projection and disavowal solves some very important problems; but it creates a number of others.

Yeats's denouement strikes his critics as "blasphemous," then, in part because it represents the Irish woman's special vulnerability to material pressures—and represents it as unchosen and unavoidable. Unlike Grace, the Countess Cathleen is both virtuous and violable—susceptible not because she is weak and venal but because she has to be. Protected as she is from the worst vagaries of the Famine, the Countess still cannot avoid making the demons' bargain. The only way for her to save either the souls or the bodies of the starving peasants around her is to agree to make herself as vulnerable as they are and to allow the system of coercion represented by the two merchants to destroy her as it has destroyed them. The Countess responds to physical suffering, albeit that of others rather than her own; and playing on that vulnerability, the merchants are able to extract her soul just as they extracted the others'.

One of Yeats's mistakes, then, was in evoking the anxieties relating to imperial control and its effect on the Irish body. By setting the play in Famine times and making his sacrificial heroine female, he engaged fears about the violability and vulnerability of the body but did not assuage them. The other mistakes that *Countess Cathleen*'s critics cite—the play's uncritical and disingenuous celebration of aristocratic values, its unflattering portrait of the Irish peasant's spiritual character, its insistence on putting a higher price on the Countess's soul—proved resistant to critique. They are preserved and, as

Howes argues, even intensified in the play's subsequent revisions (50–55). But one thing Yeats does do when he revises *The Countess Cathleen* is delete or rewrite virtually every passage O'Donnell singles out in "Souls for Gold."[13] Yeats, for all his righteous anger, appears to have taken O'Donnell's attack to heart. This is evident from *Cathleen ni Houlihan,* in which he once again engages anxieties about famine, fertility, and vulnerability but corrects his mistake by making the sacrificial protagonist male—and giving his audiences a very different Cathleen.

And We Going to Be Married Tomorrow: Making War, Not Love

The plot of *Cathleen ni Houlihan* is much simpler than that of *The Countess Cathleen.* On the eve of the French landing at Killala that signaled the beginning of the ill-fated 1798 uprising organized by the United Irishmen under Wolfe Tone, Michael, the son of a prosperous peasant family, encounters a mysterious old woman who identifies herself as Cathleen, daughter of Houlihan. Her words win Michael's heart, despite the fact that she makes it perfectly clear that anyone who really wishes to serve her must be prepared to die young. After she leaves, Michael, over the protestations of his mother, Bridget, and his fiancée, Delia, charges off to join the French and the United Irishmen in the battle, where he will die. Bridget asks her younger son if he saw the old woman leaving the house, and he responds, "I did not, but I saw a young woman, and she had the walk of a queen" (*VPl* 231).

Contemporary responses to the 1902 premiere of *Cathleen ni Houlihan* indicate that audiences had little trouble understanding the play's message. "Kathleen, in reality, represents Ireland," wrote the *Irish Times* reviewer, echoed by the *Daily Express* (qtd. in Coleman 132). If Cathleen was instantly recognizable, the *Freeman's Journal* found Bridget to be an equally familiar face: "The two old peasants who discuss their son's approaching marriage have their counterparts in hundreds of homes in Ireland" (qtd. in Coleman 131). Yeats made doubly sure he would be understood by providing a summary in the *United Irishman* before the premiere:

> I have described a household preparing for the wedding of the son of the house. Everyone expects some good thing from the wedding. The

> bridegroom is thinking of his bride, the father of the fortune which will make them all more prosperous, and the mother of a plan of turning this prosperity to account by making her youngest son a priest. . . . Into this household comes Kathleen ni Houlihan herself, and the bridegroom leaves his bride and all the hopes come to nothing. It is the perpetual struggle of the cause of Ireland and every other ideal cause against private hopes and dreams—against all that we mean when we say the world. (*VPl* 234)

As important as Cathleen is, from Yeats's point of view the play's dramatic impact is dependent on the contrast between her and her surroundings. The sharply defined conflict between "the terrible claims of Mother Ireland and the protective response of a biological mother" (Cullingford, *Gender and History,* 67) is what makes *Cathleen* work as drama.

Aside from making the conflict more dramatic, setting up this polar opposition between Cathleen and Bridget allows Yeats to handle some of the issues he raised in *The Countess Cathleen* without getting burned. By constructing two diametrically opposed versions of femininity, Yeats offers his audience the solution that *Countess* does not hold out: he dramatizes, through the mortal and materialistic Bridget, the effects of imperial control on fertility and population growth; but through Michael's interactions with the supernatural and immortal Cathleen, he suggests a way of protecting the Irish woman's body from violation and routing the foreign influences that threaten to destroy it.

Yeats's synopsis stresses the economic benefits the Gillane family expects to reap from the marriage, as does the play's opening dialogue. Peter, Michael's father, is concerned with Delia's dowry more than anything else (*VPl* 216–17), and much of the laughter the play evoked in its first audiences stemmed from Peter's comic venality: "You are the best woman in Ireland, but money is good too" (*VPl* 218).[14] The fortune is important primarily because it will allow the family to do two things that in post-Famine Ireland became increasingly difficult: extend the size of the farm, and find living situations for all of the family's grown children. Both of these issues relate to land-use problems, arising from the colonial tenant system and exacerbated by the Famine, that had serious implications for sexual and reproductive behavior in Ireland.

When Peter mentions that his youngest son Patrick will have trouble finding a wife "with no place of his own" (220), it is clear that he intends to leave his entire holding to Michael, the first son, instead of dividing it between them. Although the scene of the play is technically 1798, this line identifies the Gillanes as a post-Famine family. The change in inheritance custom from subdivision to primogeniture was motivated by long-term economic pressures that increased the minimum acceptable size of a holding, but the Famine was the catalyst that forced the conversion.[15] Without the potato it was impossible for a family to survive on very small holdings.[16] Evictions carried out during the Famine and a general shift from grains to livestock as the major cash crop helped wipe out the "cottiers" (Poirteir 1) who had lived on these plots and increased the pressure on those farmers who survived to consolidate rather than subdivide.

As Kennedy's analysis of demographic trends in nineteenth-century Ireland indicates, the Famine produced "a great change . . . in the proportion of Irish persons willing to postpone marriage," which was followed by "a sudden rise between 1851 and 1861" in permanent celibacy among Irish women that continued to increase until the beginning of the twentieth century (143). With the destruction of the subsistence farming system, the "desired minimum standard of living" in rural Ireland necessarily rose; and since marriage, unless both partners had their own farms, would decrease that standard and force the same patch of ground to support more people, Irish men and women "who might have married. . . .were increasingly unwilling to do so" (150). Instead, they opted to emigrate, work their holdings alone, or attach themselves to a relative's household (150). Combined with the shift to the "stem-family" system that Kennedy and O Grada describe, under which at most two children of any family could be expected to "marry locally," the Famine-accelerated rise in acceptable holding size meant that for significant portions of the Irish population, marriage would happen late or not at all, and that "some siblings . . . [would] never become part of the legitimate child-bearing population" (Kennedy 152).

Bridget appears to appreciate this trend, since she is already planning to get Patrick into the priesthood; before he reaches puberty, he is destined for permanent celibacy. Bridget is also well aware that the fact that Michael has managed to find a "nice comely girl" (219) who will also bring in enough money to allow the family to take over the ten-acre farm of Jamsie Dempsey is a real piece of luck. As Kennedy points out, few families looking to marry off their sons in post-Famine Ireland "found what they were looking for: a relatively young woman in the immediate neighborhood who was already in sole control of perhaps as much land as the family already held"

(150). Had Delia not been available and moneyed, or had Jamsie Dempsey not died at a convenient time, Michael's fate might well have been to live single on his parents' farm until their deaths.

Postponed marriage and permanent celibacy helped decrease the growth of the Irish population; they also, Kennedy argues, contributed to the "strong emphasis on the dangers and sinfulness of sex among single persons" that characterized social mores (15). When a large portion of the population is required not only to remain single but to avoid having children (which would decrease the standard of living on a holding as much as marrying would), premarital sex becomes a serious economic problem. The colonial history that produced the subsistence farming system, the Famine, and the resulting readjustment in land use thus produced demographic trends that affected the Irish family and Irish sexual behavior, especially that of the women who were at risk of having these unsupportable children. Bridget, who consigns Patrick to childlessness in order to preserve the farm for Michael, is doing her best to solve a problem with roots that go back to the penal laws and beyond. But her solution, like the Countess Cathleen's, is problematic for a nationalist movement becoming increasingly concerned with the size of its population.

That concern derives from a specific reading of the Famine that, though it did not originate with Arthur Griffith, was at this time being widely disseminated by him in *United Irishman.* Griffith saw the Famine as a deliberate attempt at genocide. He devotes three columns of the December 6, 1902 issue of *United Irishman* to refuting the claim that "the so-called Famine of '47 and the decrease of population that followed on its heels" can be attributed "to the normal working-out of economic law" (5). Griffith sees the decrease in the Irish population after the Famine, not as a Malthusian adjustment, but as part of Britain's "plan for the extermination of the Nationalist population" ("'Economics'" 5). He concludes by inveighing against emigration, agreeing that "should the population diminish it must mean a serious loss to all classes" because "it is the intellectually and physically strong who are fleeing the country," leaving behind "a large residue of the intellectually and physically infirm and weak" ("'Economics'" 5).

Griffith would develop this argument in more detail in *How Ireland has 'Prospered' Under English Rule,* in which he blames the British government and the Famine for the fact that "eleven million six hundred and ten thousand of the Irish race have disappeared somewhere in the past seventy years" (7). He goes to great lengths to prove that Ireland's drop in population is anomalous among the nations of "modern Europe," even those ruled under other colonial regimes (8) and that this drop has been "managed" by England: to retain control, "it has been necessary to the English government in Ireland to destroy more than one-third of the men of Ulster and Leinster, and more than half of the men of Munster and Connacht" (10). Throughout the argument, numbers are implicitly equated with strength: if Ireland only had within its borders "the children who should form the extra 11,610,000 on our soil today" who are "citizens of other countries" instead, it would be able to take its place among the nations of the world (7).

The famine period represents for nationalists, then, the single most blatant—and successful—attempt on the part of the British government to check the growth of the Irish population. Yeats's audiences would have been more aware of that argument and more sympathetic to it in 1899 and 1902 than they might have been ten or twenty years earlier. In the years 1897 and 1898 partial famines recurred in the west of Ireland; and one of the nationalists who agitated on behalf of the stricken tenants was Maud Gonne, who was the inspiration for *The Countess Cathleen* and the first to portray Cathleen ni Houlihan.

Although Griffith may have formulated the most explicit statement of this anxiety, the general interest among *United Irishman* authors during 1902–1903 in slowing the rate of emigration and building up Irish industry in an effort to give Irish youth an incentive to stay in the country demonstrates that he was not the only nationalist who attached enormous importance to the demographic effects of the Famine or who felt that raising the rate of population growth was an important step toward independence.[17] Reacting to the Famine and other perceived imperial manipulations of the Irish birth process, Irish-Irelanders, during the period of the Irish National Theater's genesis, were becoming increasingly invested in manipulating it themselves.

As Bridget's dilemma illustrates, however, this population problem is complex and intractable, being connected as it is to almost every aspect of Ireland's economic and political history. As indicated by Griffith's increasingly frustrated advocacy of projects that might work to repair the population decrease—reforestation, reclaiming bog land, support of Irish industries—the domestic efforts nationalists were making to restore Ireland's economy and population were progressing slowly at best. Similarly, in *Cathleen ni Houlihan* Bridget's management of a partial economic solution—Michael's marriage to Delia—will not by itself solve the larger problems that have infiltrated the Gillane household; even a relatively prosperous peasant family making an advantageous match for their oldest child must give up any hopes of seeing their second marry and reproduce. Yeats solves the problem for her—and thus for his nationalist audience—by providing Michael with another bride who offers him the chance to make Ireland fertile and free through one dramatic act of sacrifice. Michael's death at Killala is a symbolic solution to the problem of Irish fertility, one that can do more to resolve it than any efforts in the domestic sphere. What sex alone cannot do, violence will.

The Old Woman, having lost her land, her house, and her chance to bear children, incarnates the damage done to Ireland by imperial interference. When Peter mistakes her for "the widow Casey that was put out of her holding at Kilglass" (*VPl* 223), he is recognizing the Old Woman's function as a symbol of what has happened to Irish peasants and the land they live on. At the same time, as Bridget realizes, "she is not" what she seems (223); the withered and infirm body that has been turned by "strangers" (222) onto the roads to wander destitute and alone is merely a disguise that temporarily conceals an immortal, untouchable essence. Even before her transformation, the Old Woman makes it clear that her material body is an illusion to whose demands she need not respond. She refuses offers of food and of money, just as in the past she refused to "set out the bed for any" (226) of her lovers. Her dialogue uses agricultural and economic metaphors, but it is quite clear that these *are* metaphors and that her concern is not for any literal "green fields" (223) but for the abstract ideal they represent. Put-upon and distressed as she is, the Old Woman is beyond the reach of the material world—temporarily dispossessed, but fundamentally invulnerable and inviolable.

This aspect of Cathleen would have been even more apparent in performance than it is from the text. Everyone in that theater would have known who Maud Gonne was and recognized her under the Old Woman's costume. What Yeats called the "weird power" (qtd. in Coleman 130) of her performance depended, as Fay asserted, partly on audiences seeing this "beautiful tall woman with her great masses of golden hair" (qtd. in Coleman 127) through the veil of stage artifice that created her age and infirmity. Gonne's celebrity as a nationalist activist would have made audiences aware that underneath the stage Cathleen was a "real" Cathleen who would eventually drop the disguise and assume her true and radiant form.

Because she is immortal and supernatural, this Cathleen, unlike her predecessor, will not have to make the demons' bargain. By rejecting the power of the material world, she renders herself proof against imperial manipulation, wearing the signs of oppression but remaining finally unchanged by them. And since Cathleen "represents Ireland," she offers O'Donnell what he wanted: an Ireland that can resist any form of pressure the Empire is able to apply. If she represents Ireland, however, she does so by representing Irish women, and by representing them as being just as invulnerable as she is. Neither the temptations of materialism nor the machinations of free-market capitalism can touch this Cathleen. Although the same economic conditions that will be forcing Patrick into the priesthood have apparently withered her and rendered her literally infertile, she can still give birth to the nation.

But that birth necessarily becomes a metaphysical process, since the price of her invulnerability is inaccessibility. She cannot afford to "set out the bed" for her lovers because to represent herself as sexually attainable is to suggest that she might also be violable. To be capable of physical sexuality and literal fertility she would have to inhabit a material body that would make her vulnerable to the kind of intervention that entrapped the Countess Cathleen. Because she is beyond the reach of the material world, Michael can only touch Cathleen by entering the supernatural plane she inhabits; and he can only do that through death. Unfortunately for Michael, but happily for nationalist audiences, tradition furnishes Yeats with a model that transforms Michael's death into the metaphysical union that will allow Cathleen to resume the vitality and fertility that has been taken from her.

As Cullingford argues in *Gender and History in Yeats's Love Poetry*, the plot of *Cathleen* is informed by Celtic mythology that has been "modified . . . considerably" (57) by Yeats to suit his purposes. The play "resurrect[s] the tradition of human sacrifice to the goddess," familiar to contemporary readers through Seamus Heaney's bog poems, "in which sexuality is conflated with violent death as the blood of the young male victim sinks into the receiving earth" (57). Combining this with "the myth of sovereignty" (66), in which a young man's marriage to an old hag magically rejuvenates her, Yeats casts Michael's death as a sexual union that transforms Cathleen from a dispossessed and homeless old woman to a young girl with "the walk of a queen" (*VPl* 231).

This paradigm depends, of course, on an identification of the Irish woman with the Irish landscape—one that, as Cullingford demonstrates, has its precedent in Celtic mythology but that is given new and vigorous existence in nineteenth-century nationalist art and literature. What Yeats's use here of the myth of sovereignty suggests is that this identification was powerful partly because it fuses different but related anxieties deriving from the Famine by conflating agricultural productivity with female fertility. Without the implications added by the sovereignty myth, the earth goddess who receives the blood of the sacrifice primarily represents the outraged soil of Ireland, still wounded by the blight, the evictions, the clearances, and the short-sighted land-use policies of its imperial possessors. When Yeats brings in the sovereignty myth by using Cathleen's body to represent the change from barrenness to fertility and by casting Michael's sacrifice in terms of a romantic/sexual attachment to a woman who becomes Delia's rival, he makes Cathleen also represent Irish women, charged with the responsibility of producing healthy Irish children but hindered from doing so. Bridget's problem indicates a connection between the health of the Irish agricultural economy and the fertility of the Irish population. By donning the guise of both chthonic and human infertility, Cathleen offers the hero an opportunity to cure one by curing the other.

The promise of fertility that this rejuvenated Cathleen holds out is not, of course, literal. She produces not actual children but the nation itself; and she does it by demanding blood, not sex. The message of *Cathleen,* then, is that violent rebellion—successful or otherwise—will solve on the ideal plane what cannot be resolved in the material one. It will restore the Irish woman to her intact, untouched, and glorious state; and by so doing, it will cure the infertility that Britain has inflicted on Ireland. It makes the argument that will become familiar in both Griffith's and Gonne's writings in the *United Irishman*—that if Ireland can secure political independence, the demographic problems (and their economic causes) with which Bridget is struggling will finally end once and for all.

Cathleen becomes as popular as it does, not simply because it taps into a Celtic tradition of glorifying self-sacrifice and heroic failure, but because it shows its audience *why* that futile sacrifice is useful. Representing not only the potentially fertile Irish landscape but also the potentially fertile Irish woman, *Cathleen ni Houlihan* translates the hero's failure—his bloody death on the battlefield—into a kind of success in the domestic arena that nationalists had not yet achieved through economic and cultural resistance. This Cathleen turns death into life by allowing Michael's sacrifice to restore her—and, by association, Irish womanhood and Irish fertility—to her "true" and pristine condition. The two operations are indissociable: without her participation, Yeats cannot use the metaphor of fertility to render Michael's sacrifice regenerative; and without Michael's death, Yeats cannot use the myth of sovereignty to restore Cathleen. Cathleen's magic will glorify Michael; Michael's passion will transfigure Cathleen.

Cathleen ni Houlihan thus solves a number of the problems that *Countess Cathleen* raised, including the problem of vulnerability to the body's demands. Not only is Cathleen herself used to render Irish women fundamentally invulnerable, but by committing his own body to destruction on the battlefield, Michael demonstrates that the true patriot is able to transcend material concerns and make what Pearse will call "the ultimate sacrifice." By choosing death over survival, Michael demonstrates that the world of physical suffering holds no terrors for him and that, although the stranger can and will destroy his mortal body, death can have no influence over his Irish soul, nor can it interfere with the metaphysical union that will fructify Cathleen.

In order to become part of this solution, Michael is forced to abandon the material world represented by Bridget and Delia; he chooses Cathleen's promise of metaphysical fertility over the literal promise represented by his young bride. The resounding ratification of this choice helped make *Cathleen* dear to the hearts of nationalists. As Coleman points out, the ending of the published version, in which Michael breaks out of Delia's embrace and "rushes out" past his tearful fiancée toward his destiny, represents a change from the directions recorded in the original promptbook, which calls for Michael to "[put] Delia gently from him" before exiting (129). Coleman suggests this change was at the suggestion of Griffith, who felt that showing Michael to be "under compulsion from an irresistible power" would help underscore the play's patriotic message (129). *Cathleen* justifies the hero's flight from domestic responsibility and its attendant frustrations by presenting violent sacrifice as not only the right choice but the only choice Michael can make—the one answer to all the questions raised by both *Cathleens.*

One thing *Cathleen* does, then, is ratify, mystify, and calcify the opposition we saw in *The Heather Field* between the material/domestic world embodied by the mortal woman (Bridget) and the visionary world represented by the feminine ideal (Cathleen). And, as in *The Heather Field,* it is clear that the Irish man *really* belongs to the idealized world of Cathleen—just as it is clear that the mortal woman is structurally prevented from following him there. Cathleen may be able to slough her battered body and assume her ideal form, but neither of the mortal women in this play will; both, in fact, will have entirely new material problems to contend with. Michael, by leaping into death and the arms of Cathleen, will avoid having to play any long-term part in the resolution of his family's economic problems. According to the paradigm set up in *Cathleen,* the role of the male patriot is to make the blood sacrifice that will symbolically regenerate Ireland, while the job of doing the work that will give material reality to this regeneration falls to the women. This division of labor is reified in the text of the play itself—as Pethica argues, Yeats conceived the play's overall structure, claimed authorship, and took the credit for *Cathleen,* but evidence suggests that at the very least Lady Gregory wrote the dialogue for the Gillane family, while Yeats probably took charge of writing Cathleen (9). The symbolic sacrifice and the structure in which it is embedded is his work; the realization of the concrete details of that economic and material context is hers.

The effect of this division of labor is visible in the columns of the *United Irishman,* in which Irish women are increasingly held responsible for resolving any number of material and cultural problems in Ireland, from emigration to economic depression, to widespread "denationalisation," or lack of proper nationalist feeling, among the Irish men they marry and the Irish children they bear. At the same time, they are charged with using their bodies to represent an ideal Ireland and to keep the image of Cathleen alive. Perhaps the most literal example of the effect the imposition of this double duty had on Irish women is Maud Gonne, who incarnated the first Cathleen and whose post-*Cathleen* writing testifies to the play's lingering influence on her conception of what a patriotic Irish woman's responsibilities were. Other less-celebrated contributors to the *United Irishman* demonstrate the more wide-ranging effects, for Irish women and Irish nationalism, of a sacrificial paradigm that makes female fertility the key metaphor for Irish liberation.

In the Shadow of Cathleen

The role Maud Gonne played in establishing *Cathleen*'s sacrificial plot as a dominant paradigm in nationalist thought points out some of the paradoxes on which the power of that plot is based. As we have seen, her physical presence under the Old Woman's costume helped make one of the play's central points—that the Old Woman's apparently withered body is not "real" but is a shell concealing an uncorrupted essence. But while that inner essence is conceptualized as spiritual and incorporeal, it is represented to the audience via their perception of Maud Gonne's actual body. Literally seeing Gonne on stage dramatically increased the affective power of the idea she represented, as the writer reviewing the performance for the *Daily Express* recognized when he faulted Yeats for "not closing his play with Kathleen as herself—rejuvenated" (qtd. in Coleman 132). Like many in the audience, no doubt, this reviewer felt cheated for not having been treated to the vision that *Cathleen* primes its audience to expect—Maud Gonne's appearance "as herself." Maire Nic Shiubhlaigh, who took over the role, explains why Gonne's presence made such a difference and why the logic of that production would seem to insist on staging that final transformation: "She was the very personification of the figure she portrayed on stage" (qtd. in Margaret Ward, 56–57). Fay puts the matter more bluntly in his account: "Miss Gonne was in fact what Kathleen ni Houlihan was in symbol" (qtd. in Coleman 127).

Fay's phrasing is a succinct statement of a complicated problem of representation. He recognizes Cathleen, as did everyone else who saw her, as a female figure personifying a free and glorified Ireland—an idealized vision that could not yet exist in reality. At the same time, he claims that it *does* exist in reality—"in fact"—in the person of Maud Gonne, a woman Irish nationalist renowned for her beauty as well as the strength of her commitment to the cause. For the nationalist movement as well as for the cast of *Cathleen,* Gonne is useful because she can embody what is by definition immaterial and turn an abstract ideal into concrete lived experience.

The "weird power" of her performance thus derives from a strange kind of homeopathy in which her female body is displayed on stage as a way of displacing the image of another, more problematic female body. By giving a shape and a voice to the ideal Ireland, she renders it as "real" as the material and more imperfect Ireland represented by Bridget, while her incorruptible body replaces the violated bodies of Irish women who, like the first Cathleen or like Bridget, have been operated on by imperial coercion. Her female form must remain concrete so that it can be perceived as real and at the same time be idealized enough to keep Cathleen recognizably otherworldly and spiritual. Instead of having an inner spiritual soul and an outer mortal shell, Gonne becomes a single entity in which ideal and real fuse, interior and exterior meld; and her physical body is identified absolutely with, and cannot be distinguished from, the spiritual essence animating it.

In order to bring Cathleen to life, then, Gonne (like the Countess Cathleen before her) has to agree to *be* what she is representing—to remake herself in the shape of the national ideal and to make her "real" identity the visible "fact" that proves the existence and viability of this incorruptible, invulnerable, translated, and glorified vision of Irishness. It is her peculiar ability to do so—to become the flesh-and-blood proof of the purity and invincibility of the Irish spirit—that makes Gonne critical to the initial success of *Cathleen.* In turn, the *Daily Express* suggests that one of the useful things about *Cathleen* is its ability to compel Gonne to keep on doing this: "Miss Gonne seems to have at last struck her vocation" (qtd. in Coleman 132). Her persona is "well suited to a rather doleful part"; and although it may be "out of place in politics," her self-dramatization is "all right in connection with the footlights" (qtd. in Coleman 132). *Cathleen,* this reviewer suggests, is the perfect context and containment field for a woman of Gonne's particular talents.[18]

Gonne's role in the production and reception of *Cathleen* suggests that the play's success is dependent on its ability not only to recruit Irish men for the role of Michael, but to recruit Irish women for the doubled-but-single role of Cathleen. The paradigm works only if women can be convinced to embody the ideal, to turn themselves into the hard evidence of an illusory spiritual essence. And it is this task—transforming their female and/or maternal bodies into that ideal vision of a purified, glorified Ireland—that both Gonne and Mary Butler exhort the female readership of the *United Irishman* to accomplish. Gonne's "Ireland and the Children" is a particularly explicit statement of the demand that *Cathleen*'s sacrificial paradigm makes on Irish women; Butler's "Womanhood and Nationhood" series demonstrates the breadth of that paradigm's influence on nationalist attitudes about gender.

Gonne begins her piece—published in June of 1902, two months after *Cathleen*'s premiere—by recreating in prose the image she had so recently incarnated on stage:

> Though our sacred mother, Ireland, sits with the chains of tyranny weighing down her delicate white hands, though her dress is the torn and ragged one of misfortune, though the stranger has taken from her her golden crown of sovereignty, she yet wears the bright flower-crown of her children. . . . [I]t is the only shining glory left the Kathleen ni Houlihan. ("Ireland and the Children" 3)

Here she once again presents Cathleen as superficially conquered but inwardly invincible—the "chains of tyranny" have stilled but not mutilated or bruised her "delicate white hands," and beneath that "torn and ragged" dress is an unquenchable source of power—the fertility that will continue, despite the "stranger's" efforts, to maintain the "bright flower-crown of her children." Gonne thus explicitly identifies that unconquerable spiritual essence with fertility—it is through continuing to produce the children who will make up that "bright flower-crown" that Cathleen retains her "shining glory" and her hope of restoration.

Gonne argues here that the best way to "fight for the spirituality of our nation against the hideous materialism which England represents" is to ensure that the "flower-crown of Ireland's children glows with radiant living light, and fresh baby faces replace those" that disappear ("Ireland and the Children" 3). The ideal, incorruptible Ireland is presented as dependent on the actual Irish woman's ability and desire to continue using her body to produce Irish children whose "small hands must also help to uphold the National banner." This ability is threatened by the efforts of the "stranger," who in his efforts "to destroy the flower-crown . . . brought the blight of famine often upon our land," and by emigration, which is "robbing Ireland of her flowers" (3).

Gonne's self-conscious invocation of "Kathleen ni Houlihan" and repeated use of crown imagery derived from the sovereignty myth show how effectively the play identified Ireland's spiritual welfare with the fertility of its women. To rejuvenate Cathleen, the male patriot must shed his heart's blood on the battlefield; but unless the female patriot is willing to shed her own blood, tears, and sweat in childbirth, regeneration will remain impossible. And from this specific connection between female fertility and the ransom of "our holy Motherland"—not just from England but from "brutal materialism, the world, the flesh and the devil" ("Ireland and the Children" 3)—derives a broader conviction that the health of Ireland as a nation is dependent on the woman's ability to keep not only her own body but also the domestic sphere within which *Cathleen*'s paradigm traps it pure, untainted, and beyond the reach of external corrupting influences.

Mary Butler's five-part "Womanhood and Nationhood" series, which ran in the *United Irishman* some months after *Cathleen*'s premiere, shows some of the wider consequences of the argument Gonne makes in "Ireland and the Children." Butler clearly understands the opposition Yeats created in *Cathleen* between the materialistic, mortal Irish woman and the spiritualized, immortal one, and the position into which that split has put the female Irish patriot. "There are two Irelands, the ideal and the real," she states in her final article; and "to strive to bring the real into harmony with the ideal is the aim which we must set before us" (31 January 1903: 6). "We," it becomes clear, refers not to Irish people in general but to Irish women, since the primary way she and her readers will be reconciling these opposed entities is by reinventing the Irish home—using their literal function as housekeepers to turn the Irish home into "the nursery of patriots; the source and centre of national life, the origin of national well-being, the inspiration of national greatness" (31 January 1903: 6). As Butler argues, this will entail not only actually bearing children and exposing them to nationalist culture but also creating a material environment that fosters national feeling and supports the Irish economy:

> The ideal Irish home—how one loves to picture it in one's mind! There is no air of pretentiousness about it, but everything in it is good of its kind, and is genuine. There is no shoddy, no make-believe, no pretence or imitation. . . . The clothes worn by the household, the furniture of the house, the pictures on the walls, the language spoken, the songs sung, the books read, are all of native origin. Irish hands and heads have fashioned them, and they are suited, in consequence, to be used and enjoyed by Irish people. (31 January 1903: 6)

Presiding over the home, the Irish woman becomes responsible for preserving cultural authenticity ("no make-believe"), cultural purity ("all of native origin"), and nationalist feeling by turning her domestic space into a hermetic and impenetrable fortress of Irishness. She will accomplish this partly through education, but it is equally important that she construct this space using Irish-made materials. The Irish woman's responsibility as a homemaker entails a responsibility as consumer; and as numerous contributors to the *United Irishman* demonstrate, this logic threatens to make the Irish woman responsible not just for the biological reproduction of Ireland but for its economic production as well.

By "shoddy," Butler means a category of English-made textiles that, at least according to the nationalist writers who took up the cause of the Irish textile industry, were less durable but cheaper than Irish-made fabrics. In inveighing against "the peasant or artisan's wife or daughter, who spends her spare pence on . . . third-rate imitations of

'Southhaven' fashions" (24 January 1903: 6), Butler predicts an argument that will be made periodically in the columns of the *United Irishman* by writers who blame the weakness of the Irish textile industry on the Irish woman's frivolous preference for cheap, trendy, imported materials. "For England's share in the destruction of the woollen trade we have no concern; to English legislation we need look for no redress," states 'Brigid' in April of 1903; "the revival of the trade lies in the hands of Irishwomen" (5). Two years later the argument is so familiar that "Lasairfhiona Ni Shamhraidhin" begins her piece on "Irish Shoddy" by taking it as read that "the thoughtless vanity of our fellow-countrywomen is responsible for much that is evil in the industrial condition of Ireland" (11 February 1905: 6). 'Brigid' makes it clear that using Irish dress materials is the Irish woman's version of the supreme sacrifice that Michael makes: "The support may call for sacrifice. Well, if the united efforts of the Irishwomen helped to keep even a dozen good, earnest, worthy men in Ireland, the sacrifice would not be in vain" (5). This summarizes the connection between the call for supporting "Irish-made" materials and the population problem—by strengthening Irish industry and creating jobs, women will encourage men to stay in the country, stemming emigration and increasing the population of single men, which will ultimately lead to higher marriage and childbirth rates.

The writers who make this argument attribute the Irish woman's failure to buy Irish-made to her desire to remain "in fashion," an assumption that links national prosperity to female sexual behavior. Charged with the responsibility of keeping up Ireland's population by supporting industry and stemming emigration, Irish women are accused of shirking this duty in order to make themselves more attractive. What they are asked to "sacrifice" by buying Irish materials is the pleasure of flirtation, of putting themselves on display, of engaging in behavior that has a sexual aspect but will not contribute directly to the solution of the population problem—behavior that is seen, for that reason, as dangerous.

Inghinidhe na hEireann, under Gonne's influence, shared this vision of the Irish woman's patriotic duty. One of the main objectives stated in the society's charter was "to support and popularize Irish manufactures," which each member pledged to do by "using as far as possible Irish-made goods in her household and dress" (qtd. in Trotter 86–87). Although this campaign on behalf of Irish dress materials is grounded in pragmatism (textiles being one of Ireland's major industries), it soon begins to accrete less material connotations, as this item from a 1903 *United Irishman* indicates:

> The first annual report of the Cork Branch of Inghinidhe na hEireann is an encouraging one. The branch was founded on St. Patrick's Day, 1902, by Miss Gonne: "The idea of such an organisation as ours," says the report, "which aims at making Irish women take their rightful place in the work of Ireland's freedom and nationality, was a new one in Cork. . . . By wearing the costumes of our grandmothers, those dear old hooded-cloaks, we developed a quality much needed in both our country men and women—initiative—and faced what is hard for a woman to face—the idea of being thought 'out of the fashion.' But Inghinidhe na hEireann will yet make fashions of their own." (Griffith 18 April 1903: 1)

Along with the familiar rhetoric about teaching "little ones" to honor and revere their motherland, this report demonstrates Inghinidhe na hEireann's acceptance of the idea that Irish women's vanity was a significant obstacle to Irish economic prosperity.

What we see emerging after *Cathleen* in the nationalist press, then, is a growing sense that the integrity and purity of the domestic sphere and the female body at its center is necessary for all forms of national security—whether cultural, economic, or demographic—and that the job of maintaining that integrity falls to the Irish woman, who must regulate not only her sexual behavior but a host of other desires and preferences in order to render herself proof against outside intervention. All these concerns are reiterated in Mary Butler's rhetoric of the hearthstone, in which she blames Ireland's trouble on the fact that "hearths are being quenched in Ireland by the thousand, and scarcely any are being lit" (17 January 1903: 6). Connecting emigration, the weakness of Irish industry, and "denationalisation" to the Irish woman's failure to recreate the ideal Irish home, Butler agrees that the male patriot's efforts at self-sacrifice are worthless unless they are paralleled by the woman patriot: it is useless for "the men [to go] on preaching patriotism from the platform" if "the women [go] on destroying the very foundations of nationality at the hearthstone" (24 January 1903: 6). At the same time, by defining this home explicitly as the "place where mothers dwell" (17 January 1903: 6), she excludes the male patriot from it. This "nucleus of a nation" (17 January 1903: 6) is left entirely in the charge of its female members, whose primary weapon in the struggle against imperialism will be their fertility.

At the same time, as Butler's acknowledgment of the gap between the ideal and the real home points out, this conception of nationalism requires Irish women to be in two places at once—in Cathleen's, incarnating the Irish spirit and inspiring the male patriot's sacrifice, and in Bridget's, trying to build in the material world the actual domestic space (and providing the literal womb) in which this ideal will have to take physical shape. And, as *Cathleen* makes evident, these two places are so widely sundered that passage from one to the other can only occur through death—specifically, the death of the male sacrificial martyr, which transforms the material, injured, imperfect, and exhausted Irish maternal body into the immortal, incorruptible, fertile Cathleen.

For Irish nationalism, then, the *Cathleen* paradigm means that the male hero's sacrificial death remains an indispensable element of any proposed solution for Ireland's domestic problems. For Irish women, it means that their function as guardians of the untainted essence of Irish identity will be equally indispensable and that they will be called upon to exercise it—by maintaining their own sexual purity, by conceiving and bearing Irish children within the confines of the ideal Irish family, and by preserving the domestic interior as an inviolable shrine to national identity—with increasing regularity.

Cathleen thus helps set the stage for *In The Shadow of the Glen,* in which Synge's dramatization of a woman who refuses that function outrages the *United Irishman*'s contributors. That controversy, in turn, has its effect on Yeats's understanding of the relationship between gender identity and Irish national identity and leads to his reworking of *Cathleen*'s paradigm in *On Baile's Strand,* in which he suggests that Butler's gospel of the hearthstone, by insisting on an absolute separation between private and public versions of nationalist activism, valorizes and promotes a kind of sacrificial violence that may do very little to solve Ireland's domestic problems.

2
Under Siege:
Blood, Borders, and the Body Politic

If *Cathleen ni Houlihan* INAUGURATED A BRIEF ROMANCE BETWEEN Yeats and the nationalist public, the honeymoon didn't last long. The premiere of J. M. Synge's *In the Shadow of the Glen* sparked a confrontation between Yeats and the Abbey coterie on one side and Griffith and the nationalist press on the other that would finally burst into flame at the premiere of *The Playboy of the Western World* in 1907. In both cases, Griffith's anti-Synge crusade was motivated by concerns connected with the economic, cultural, and biological health of Ireland and the Irish, which were expressed as a defense of the sexual purity of Irish women. As the Irish became more aware of the power of medical discourse and the presence of the British public health establishment, concern about the susceptibility of the Irish body to disease and to imperial medicine became more widespread and intense, and the sacrificial paradigm established in *Cathleen ni Houlihan* became an even more attractive solution to the problem of vulnerability. Synge and Yeats developed their critiques of the sacrificial paradigm at a moment when nationalists were increasingly interested in following *Cathleen*'s lead and protecting Irish cultural and economic strength by locating it in the body of the invulnerable Irish woman. Although *On Baile's Strand* and *The Playboy of the Western World* make their critiques in very different terms, both playwrights start from the same assumption—that the purity Griffith and the nationalists are defending is an impossible and unrecoverable thing.

After wrestling with Griffith over *Shadow* in 1903 and again in 1905, Yeats produced in 1906 a revised version of *On Baile's Strand* in which he revealed and critiqued the connection between the valorization of blood-sacrifice and the adherence to traditional gender roles that was implicit in *Cathleen*. Suggesting that Conchubar's desire to protect his kingdom by sealing off borders enforces a restrictive and reductive conception of gender, the revised *On Baile's Strand* blames that desire for the death of Cuchulain's son and implies that by clinging to the vision of a pure Ireland enclosed by impermeable borders, Irish nationalists are forcing a futile repetition of the same sacrificial plot. A year later *Cathleen*'s fusion of bloodshed and sexual potency is satirized in the figure of Christy, the Playboy of the Western World, whose supposed "savagery" (*Complete Plays* 42) renders him irresistibly attractive to the women of Pegeen's village. But audiences who accepted Yeats's half-regretful critique of his own paradigm in *On Baile's Strand* were far less willing to stand for Synge's burlesque of it.

Playboy's send-up of the sacrificial paradigm is not offensive to its audiences merely because it presents nationalist violence as homicidal rather than suicidal, or even because it literalizes the sexual connotations that remain symbolic in *Cathleen*. From Griffith's perspective the play is also dangerous because it attacks the purity, not just of Irish culture or even of the Irish character, but of the Irish body itself. Synge mounts his attack on the sacrificial narrative's sex/violence connection by invoking the discourse of infection, filth, and degeneracy mobilized by the eugenics movement in England—a vocabulary that is circulating throughout Synge's career in both nationalist and antinationalist discourse. In a climate in which both British imperialists and Irish nationalists are using venereal disease as evidence of the unfitness of their adversaries, Synge's insinuation of sexual promiscuity among the Irish peasantry translates easily into an insinuation of racial degeneracy. And at a time when nationalists are coming to see their own bodies as under siege—threatened by a medical establishment bent on infecting them with the disease that will give the state an excuse to operate on them—his suggestion that the Irish body is anything other than healthy reads like an invitation to intervention.

In addition, Synge's self-constructed status as an anthropologist and the claims for authenticity that he initially makes about both plays leave him open to the charge of collusion—of participating in imperial science's attempt to construct the Irish subject as diseased, degenerate, and depraved. Griffith accuses Synge of exactly that when he claims that *Shadow* proves Synge knows as little about Ireland and the Irish as "any Englishman who has ever yet dissected us for the enlightenment of his countrymen" (17 October 1903:1). The complaint against *The Playboy* is that Synge is both unrealistic and too realistic—inaccurate in his depiction of "Irish life" but driven by materialism to find in the Irish peasant all the disease that imperial science has told him to look for.

In the Shadow of the Glen contains many of the elements that Synge would later combine in *Playboy*—a young woman dissatisfied with her marital options, a rival stranger who talks his way into her favor, an isolated rural setting, and a corpse that isn't dead. Without the catalyst of violence, the controversy failed to produce a *Playboy*-class explosion, but Griffith's attack on *Shadow* was another stage of Yeats's political education. After this experience, Yeats reversed the change that produced *Cathleen ni Houlihan* and defended Synge's critique of *Cathleen*'s paradigm by staging his own.

Closing Our Ports: Petronius and Protectionism

As we have seen, nationalist writing produced after *Cathleen* recognized—and enthusiastically reproduced—the play's dual and polarized version of femininity, exhorting women both to incarnate the ideal spiritual Ireland and to devote themselves completely to the maintenance of the Irish home—to play either Cathleen or Bridget, or both if they can manage it. As *Cathleen*'s structure indicates, however, Mary Butler's vision of bridging the gap between the real and the ideal is extraordinarily difficult to realize as long as *Cathleen*'s conception of femininity is in place. Reviewing *Cathleen*'s premiere, the *Freeman's Journal* expressed some disappointment that Bridget and Peter were not allowed to feel Cathleen's power or to make Michael's sacrifice. This never happens because under the conditions that allow this play to operate, such a resolution would be impossible. As long as the material and spiritual worlds are kept separate, irreconcilable, and opposite—which is necessary if Michael's struggle between his patriotic duty and his concrete responsibilities is to be affecting as drama—Bridget, as the genius of the domestic world, can never enter the one represented by Cathleen. It is precisely because the female figures are fixed immovably to their separate spheres that Michael is forced to make the sacrifice that is the only bridge between them.

What becomes apparent in Griffith's response to *Shadow* is that this identification of materiality with the home and the home with the Irish woman is an attempt to ensure the purity of Irish culture by enclosing it in a protected space that cannot be infiltrated—the body of the invincibly chaste Irish woman. Her moral and physical incorruptibility stand for the impenetrability of the home in which she is installed. Material and concrete, but at the same time thoroughly Irish, this ideal home defies imperial power, showing that, despite its greater military and economic strength, Britain is not capable of changing the physical reality of Ireland—that instead of being the point of entry for imperial contamination and corruption, the physical world and the corporeal body can function as a shield. And it is because the *Cathleen*-inspired paradigm and the discursive power that supports it force the Irish woman into this role that Griffith is unwilling to believe, not just that Nora would go away with the tramp, but that Synge's play could have been based on an Irish source.

Possibly the most frequently cited statement from the *Shadow* controversy is Griffith's assertion that "Irishwomen are the most virtuous in the world" (24 October 1903: 2). This chivalric defense of the Irishwoman's honor forms the unfortunate rhetorical climax of a response to Yeats's "The Irish National Theatre and Three Sorts of Ignorance." It marked the beginning of what was to become an ongoing fight over whether *Shadow* was based, as Synge and Yeats claimed, on a folk tale Synge heard in the Aran Islands, or, as Griffith claimed, on the story of the widow of Ephesus, which appears in Petronius's *The Satyricon.*[1] In Petronius's story, a woman who is in the process of starving herself to death at the tomb of her recently deceased husband meets a soldier who is in the cemetery guarding the crosses to make sure that none of the victims' relatives try to steal and bury the bodies.[2] The widow is initially inconsolable, but as a result of the soldier's attentions she eventually cheers up and becomes his lover. While the soldier is thus occupied, the body of one of the criminals is stolen. To save the soldier from being put to death when his superiors discover the empty cross, the woman suggests that he nail up her dead husband in the missing body's place.[3]

Comparing this with the plot of *Shadow,* it is easy to see why Yeats appears so baffled by Griffith's claim. In *Shadow,* a tramp arrives at a lonely farmhouse where Nora is sitting up with the body of her dead husband Dan. During their initial conversation we find out that Dan was much older than Nora, that she neither feels nor pretends to feel any particular sorrow over his loss, and that Nora's life with him has been one of disappointment, loneliness, and barrenness. When she leaves to meet a young male friend, Dan reveals to the tramp that he is playing dead in order to trap Nora into giving him proof of her infidelity. When Nora returns with Michael, Dan eventually leaps back to life and orders Nora out of the house. The tramp offers to go with her, Nora accepts, and they depart together, leaving Dan and Michael to end their quarrel over a drink. As Yeats suggests, the claim that the play is a rewriting of the Ephesus story would seem to indicate either unfamiliarity with the classical text or willful desire to misread.[4]

Despite the problems with the analogy, however, Griffith refused to abandon it. He spontaneously returned to it in 1905, at which point it becomes easier to see what is at stake in all this pedantic bickering. If we subtract the sniping about who knows Petronius better, what remains is Griffith's reassertion of his 1903 argument:

> Mr. Synge's Nora Burke is not an Irish Norah Burke—his play is not a work of genius—Irish or otherwise—it is a foul echo from degenerate Greece. His absurd ignorance of the Irish peasant is shown in every line of the play. Mr. Yeats never heard an Irish tramp in Wicklow or elsewhere address a peasant-woman as "Lady of the House," nor did he, Mr. Synge or any other human being, ever meet in Ireland a peasant-woman of the type of Norah Burke—a woman void of all conception of morality, decency and religion. She is a Greek—a Greek of Greece's most debased period and to dress her in an Irish costume and call her Irish is not only not art, but it is an insult to the women of Ireland. (28 January 1905: 1)

As Yeats points out, Griffith has dropped his earlier charge that the story was "imported" by hedge-schoolmasters and is working to establish a direct line between Synge's play and "degenerate Greece" that does not pass through Ireland.[5]

By arguing that Nora is Greek and not Irish, Griffith intends to make it clear not only that Irish women would never adopt "degenerate" continental ways but also that "real" Irish tradition does not, cannot include or incorporate material from other European cultures—despite the fact that this makes his argument much harder to construct. When Synge provides him with the source story, which is clearly much closer to the plot of *Shadow* than the Ephesus anecdote, Griffith's logical next move (assuming his primary goal is defending the chastity of Irish women) would be to argue that the Aran Islands story is simply a recasting of some foreign folktale that has been brought to the islands and retold, and whose real inspiration is some other country's amoral womenfolk. Instead, Griffith claims that in fact the Aran Islands story is not at all like *Shadow*, since in the folktale the wife is merely "callous," while in Synge's play she is a "strumpet" (4 February 1905: 1). He is forced into this position because to prove that Irishwomen are virtuous would be a Pyrrhic victory if he had to do it by conceding that Irish peasant culture had been contaminated by foreign narratives. Thus, at the risk of looking ridiculous, he persists in his folly—because the pure Irish woman is worthless as an icon if there is no pure Irish culture for her to embody.

The Ephesus story thus appears to be not context but pretext, introduced primarily for the purpose of challenging the "Irishness" of the national theater that Yeats is presently establishing. But if this is Griffith's main objective, there are grounds on which he could have raised a much sturdier argument. He could, for instance, have pointed out that both Yeats and Synge had spent a significant amount of time in Paris, or that the playwrights championed so far by the Irish Literary Theatre had all shown clear evidence of prolonged exposure to European dramatic movements. Instead of raising these solid and reasonable points, however, Griffith continues to attack the Irishness of Synge's universe by attacking the Irishness of Synge's Nora. Griffith's extraordinary fidelity to what is by now clearly a losing argument is generally explained in terms of his own pigheadedness. While admitting that this pigheadedness can explain much, I would suggest that Griffith's obsession with his two widows is also a product of his obsession with Ireland's economic health, and that he focuses on Nora and the widow of Ephesus because the female body has become a particularly compelling metaphor for the kind of economic self-sufficiency that he saw as a necessary condition of Irish independence.

Other contributions to these issues of the *United Irishman* reveal that Griffith's conflation of female sexual purity with cultural purity is attached to yet a third kind of purity, this one economic. As we have seen, the Irish dress materials controversy provides the most explicit illustration of this triangular reasoning: by sacrificing her desire to remain in fashion and buying Irish-made materials, the Irish woman (1) supports Irish industry by drying up the import market and keeping British goods out, (2) revives Irish culture by wearing traditional Irish forms of dress, and (3) renounces frivolous and flirtatious behavior. By conflating economic prosperity with female modesty and thrift, these authors were participating in a long tradition with roots in eighteenth-century Anglo-Irish writing. Perhaps the most famous early example is Jonathan Swift's 1729 *A Modest Pro-*

posal, in which the narrator singles out for attack "several plump young Girls in this Town, who, without one single Groat to their Fortunes . . . appear at a *Play house,* and *Assemblies* in foreign Fineries" and suggests that "curing the Expensiveness of Pride, Vanity, Idleness, and Gaming in our Women" might do much to strengthen the Irish economy (147, 149). This tradition—which is visible in the *United Irishman* in the relentless focus on women's apparel, to the relative exclusion of men's clothing or other forms of consumption—helps to both explain and support Griffith's intense investment in the sexual chastity of the Irish woman.

The sudden rash of articles exhorting Irish women to use only Irish dressmaking materials is undoubtedly related to the rise of Inginidhe na hEireann, all of whose members were dedicated to the cause and many of whom appear to have contributed pieces on the subject to the *United Irishman.*[6] Dressmaking first becomes a common topic in the early months of 1903, culminating in "Brigid's" April 6 article. Thereafter it drops out of sight, only to resurface in February of 1905 in the same issue of the *United Irishman* during which the argument over Petronius's role in the genesis of *Shadow* is at its most acrimonious.[7] Both the *Shadow* controversies thus take place in the context of a campaign on behalf of economic protectionism. In January of 1905, just as the source controversy is being reawakened, Griffith stresses the necessity of boycotting imports and buying Irish:

> Like England herself, who at one time rejected the silk and woollen manufactures of the East Indies and was content with her own inferior goods for the sake of promoting her domestic industry—like America, whose sons at first depended on English wares to supply the want of home manufactures, but later prided themselves on being worse clothed that they might learn how to make better stuffs—so must patriotic Irishmen and Irishwomen voluntarily determine for a period to use nothing but the manufactures of Ireland—even if inferior—since the nation can only thus be indemnified for the compulsion to which it must yield, and by forcing the foreigners out of the markets revive the national prosperity. (21 January 1905: 1)

The inclusiveness of this appeal to "Irishmen and Irishwomen" is later belied by the number of pieces focusing specifically on dressmaking, in which authors like "Lasairfhiona Ni Shamhraidhin" chastise the average Irishwoman for being unwilling to "sacrifice the petty pleasure of acquiring a new dress which she fondly believes to be 'becoming' for any national duty whatever" (11 February 1905: 6).[8]

Elsewhere, the same author makes it clear that the success of any economic campaign depends on Irish women:

> They are the treasurers of the nation; it is they who disburse the weekly wage of Ireland, and through their ignorance and conservatism most of this money finds its way into the clutches of the enemy, while the children of these same women find their way to Cove. We export flesh and blood and import all else. Would we could close our ports! ("A Paper for Irishwomen" 6)

Since the author has already identified herself as a woman, it is unclear whether the "our" in that last sentence refers to the Irish in general or to Irish women. "Lasairfhiona Ni Shamhraidhin" thus captures in a single image the logic that led Griffith to choose his particular and bizarre method of condemning *Shadow.* By closing her ports—rendering herself both physically and psychically proof against the blandishments either of English fashions or the men who encourage her to adopt them—the Irish woman closes Ireland's ports, not only excluding foreign cultural influences but also keeping out economic competition and keeping *in* the children who are in danger of emigrating.

The chaste body of the virtuous Irish woman stands for both the economically independent Ireland, with its closed ports and thriving native industries, and the culturally pure Ireland, whose citizens would never dream of abandoning traditional Irish dress or of reading a decadent Roman novel. In the chastity of the "real" Nora Burke, Griffith is defending an Irish Ireland, one capable of culturally educating, economically supporting, and retaining within its borders all of its children. But, as "Lasairfhiona Ni Shamhraidhin" demonstrates, the maintenance of the home, as the actual space in which this Ireland has to be constructed, is just as important as the preservation of chastity. And it is because *Shadow* not only opens up Nora's ports but also breaks her out of that home that Griffith finds it particularly threatening.

In Griffith's Ireland, apparently, "men and women marry lacking love, and live mostly in a dull level of amity. Sometimes . . . the woman lives in bitterness—sometimes she dies of a broken heart—but she does not go away with the Tramp" (17 October 1903: 1). From the tenor of the rest of the debate, it would seem that the main problem with this scenario is the Tramp, but Griffith's rejection of the Aran Islands story as a possible source suggests that what may really be bothering him is the going away. The significant difference between the folktale and Synge's plot is that in the source story the wife and her young man go into the bedroom to have their tryst, where the husband walks in on them and attacks the young man. We never hear what happens afterward, but the fact that blood "spurted up into the gallery" indicates that this may be a story that includes not only adultery but also murder.[9] In *Shadow,* Nora and Michael never get the chance to commit adultery, and instead of attacking Michael, Dan forces Nora out onto the roads.[10] Since the source story is clearer about the wife's infidelity than *Shadow* is, it would seem that for Griffith what separates the "callous" woman of the folktale from the "strumpet" of the play is not sexual incontinence but the act of leaving home.

What she is betraying, then, by leaving with the Tramp is not just Dan, but her responsibility as homemaker—her sacrificial duty, which is not only to bear and rear children but also to preserve the peasant cottage in which they grow up as a repository of all that is Irish. And if the Irish peasant's cottage actually contains women like Nora—women who are not content to sacrifice their personal desires and "live in bitterness" while defending the Irish home against external influences—this leads to the inescapable conclusion that either Irishwomen are not as virtuous as Griffith thinks they are or that foreign corruption has penetrated to the hearthstone. If Synge's play is based on a story he heard in the Aran Islands, then either women like Nora do and did exist even in the heart of the Gaeltacht, or the "Irish" culture that has been putatively preserved intact in the peasant heartland has been exposed to, and has incorporated, foreign traditions.

Because this argument about the integrity of the home is disguised as one about Synge's methodology, neither Synge nor Yeats ever points out that Griffith's critique is based on a misreading. Griffith writes as if Nora leaves the home of her own free will in order that she may gratify her own depraved cravings. In fact, Nora has no choice. She is put out of the house by Dan, who warns her to "walk out through that door . . . and let you not be passing this way if it's hungry you are, or wanting a bed" (*CP* 116). Michael makes it clear that he has no intention of sheltering her. Unlike Ibsen's Nora, of whom Griffith is probably thinking, Synge's heroine is not making a revolutionary decision; she is accepting what she knows will be a harsh fate and is not deceived by the Tramp's eloquence into believing otherwise. "I'm thinking it's myself will be wheezing that time with lying down under the heavens when the night is cold," she says in answer to his rhapsody on life on the open road, "but you've a fine bit of talk, stranger, and it's with yourself I'll go" (117–18). In *Shadow* we have, not a New Woman in the heart of Ireland, but something perhaps even more troubling—the suggestion that the task of preserving the Irish home may be an impossible one and that even women willing to attempt it may not be able to do it.

In fact, *Shadow* suggests that Nora's departure is caused not so much by her own willfulness as by the same economic pressures that acted on the Gillane family. A "hard woman to please" (*CP* 112), Nora nevertheless marries Dan because he is the only man in the vicinity who can provide for her economically: "What way would I live, and I an old woman, if I didn't marry a man with a bit of a farm, and cows on it, and sheep on the back hills?" (112). They have no children, and from Nora's wistful description of Mary Brien's growing family it seems that this is not her choice. Her remark that he was "always cold, every day since I knew him . . . and every night" (102) suggests that Dan's age has rendered him impotent. Synge's Michael brings up marriage in the same context that we saw it emerge in *Cathleen*—Nora is counting the money that would be her dowry, and Michael is making plans for Nora's land (113–14). Economic reality has forced Nora into a marriage that is sterile; it has also made her an object of interest for a young man like Michael, who needs to increase the size of his holding and who seems as interested in her assets as in her personal charms.

Thus, even before the Tramp arrives, Nora's home has already been shaped by imperialism and its economic effects, which ultimately play a larger part in forcing the offensive ending than Nora's own choices do.[11] If Nora is a "bad wife" (*CP* 108), the play suggests that it would be impossible for her to be a good one under these conditions; she cannot nurture the children of a man who cannot beget them. If Mary Butler's hearthstone is the example of the hermetic Irish home, Nora lives in a home that is already broken. Her final departure is not so much an act of resistance as one of resignation, one that she makes unwillingly and from which she expects little good to come, either for herself or for Dan: "What is it you'll have now but a black life, Daniel Burke; and it's not long, I'm telling you, till you'll be lying again under that sheet, and you dead surely" (118).

Shadow is threatening, then, not only because it challenges prevailing conceptions about female sexuality, but because it threatens the concepts to which that chastity had become attached. It refuses to honor the fiction of the protected domestic space from which foreign influence and imperial manipulation can be excluded. Yeats's revised *On Baile's Strand* suggests that after seeing the source argument go around a second time in 1905, Yeats finally recognized what was at stake and responded to Griffith's argument by dramatizing the tragic result of a nationalism that clings to that fiction.

Blow the Witches Out: Boundaries in *Baile's Strand*

Griffith's first attack on *Shadow* demonstrated not only his hostility to Synge's vision of Irish womanhood, but his continuing fidelity to Yeats's vision of it as articulated through Cathleen ni Houlihan: "If [the Irish Literary Theatre] substitutes 'Cathleen ni Houlihan' by the Widow of Ephesus, we are as certain it will pass and leave not a wrack behind" (17 October 1903:1). Indeed, anti-*Shadow* sentiment may have been intensified by the fact that it first appeared on the same bill as a revival of *Cathleen*—and that Maire Nic Shiubhlaigh played the female lead in both plays.[12] If the contrast was unintentional then, Yeats probably knew what he was doing by putting *Cathleen* and *On Baile's Strand* on the same bill when the Abbey Theatre opened in 1904. As the first play on the program, *On Baile's Strand* represented what patrons of the Abbey could look forward to, while *Cathleen ni Houlihan* reminded them of what they had been getting. That juxtaposition invited the audience to contrast what Joseph Holloway called the "red-hot patriotic sentiment" (17) of *Cathleen* with the more complicated treatment of nationalism in *On Baile's Strand* and to recognize the formal innovations that marked *On Baile's Strand* as the first product of Yeats's "search for a new mode of presentation" (Good 12). It also offered evidence of a more subtle transition intimately related to the other two—a change in Yeats's conception of gender and of its relationship to sacrifice.

Yeats moves from an unqualified endorsement of self-sacrifice for Ireland in *Cathleen* to a position in *On Baile's Strand* that questions the very possibility of dying "for Ireland" in a meaningful way. At the same time, he breaks the formal ties to earlier popular drama that are evident in *Cathleen* as he searches for a new dramatic idiom that will be more congenial to "the deeper thoughts and emotions of Ireland" (Gregory 20). Not coincidentally, the rigid distinction established in *Cathleen* between the mortal women who claim the hero for the family and the supernatural woman to whom he rightfully owes allegiance is also challenged in *On Baile's Strand.* Using female figures to articulate a strategy of mediation between the supernatural and the mortal worlds rather than to reiterate their disjunction, Yeats questions *Cathleen*'s celebration of sacrifice in the name of Ireland by complicating its double vision of woman as either a supernatural force propelling man toward heroic self-immolation or a wife/mother intent on trapping him in materialism. Just as *On Baile's Strand*'s tragic resolution mitigates against attempts to read the Young Man's death as regenerative or productive, the play's approach to female characterization asks its audience to abandon the rhetoric of the hearthstone and the kind of nationalism it supports.

Embryonic versions of Aoife and the chorus were helping Yeats do this even in *On Baile's Strand* as it was originally performed in 1904. This reading, however, will concentrate on the revised text, published in 1906 after Yeats's second engagement with Griffith and his consequent reappraisal of the dangers of Griffith's argument. Writing to John O'Leary after the first round in 1903, Yeats mentions that he thinks "Arthur Griffith has behaved handsomely." But by round two he realizes the implications of Griffith's attack: "The story that Synge had taken a plot from Petronius and pretended that it was Irish was calculated to do a great deal of mischief" (*Letters* 448). Yeats emerges convinced that if this insistence on the absolute purity of the Irish woman and her home is allowed to go unchallenged, nationalism will lose its capacity to adapt to new conditions and deal with new forms of conflict. To make his play's challenge more explicit, Yeats expands the role of the female chorus, revises dialogue to give Aoife a more consistent symbolic function, and foregrounds the importance of the oath not only by adding a scene in which it is ritually solemnized, but by basing Conchubar's appeal to Cuchulain explicitly on the sanctity of the hearth and the necessity of protecting the domestic sphere.

In *On Baile's Strand,* as in *Cathleen,* the main conflict is cast in terms of a battle between Conchubar's mortal, material kingdom and the supernatural realm represented by the "Shape-Changers" over the soul of the hero. But the polarities appear to be reversed—as far as Conchubar and the Young Kings are concerned, at least, Cuchulain's duty as a patriot is to defend home and family, while his attraction to the Shape-Changers is dangerous and subversive. In addition, Yeats introduces Aoife as a character whose femininity allows her to exist between both worlds, part of each but belonging to neither. The feminization of the occult reflected in the construction of Cathleen remains a constant in Yeats's drama (Cullingford, *Gender and History* 41). But while in *Cathleen* Yeats's renovation of Irish goddess mythology reinforces traditional constructions of gender in the mortal world, *On Baile's Strand* begins to capitalize on some of the "revolutionary" potential that Cullingford sees in Yeats's goddess figures (36). Instead of confining the transformative power of the goddess to the occult realm and keeping the mortal world safe for "big, strong, manly" heroes and their "good, kind, motherly" women (Holloway 27), Yeats disrupts gender in the mortal domain by introducing female figures who belong to both worlds.

Formally, *On Baile's Strand* is considered part of the first stage in Yeats's progress toward "modernity" (Worth 152). Even the version performed in 1904, which did not include the alienating masks for the Fool and Blind Man or the oath ceremony, demonstrated some of these changes. Holloway comments on the "novel staging" and on the "amber coloured draperies" that were part of Yeats's first experiment with non-naturalistic lighting.[13] But despite this consensus on the formal innovations of *On Baile's Strand,* Yeats scholars tend to assume that the gender construction evident in *Cathleen* is reproduced unchanged in the later play. Readings stress the incompatibility of the feminized occult and the masculinized world of political responsibility, citing Cuchulain's description of love as "a brief forgiveness between opposites" (*VPl* 489) as proof that the conflict between Aoife and Cuchulain presents "the division of the sexes as an illustration of the fragmentation of primal unity" (Hassett 90) between spiritual and material. This imposes on *On Baile's Strand* the same two versions of femininity offered in *Cathleen:* "the conservative female of 'threshold and hearthstone,'" who subscribes to patriarchal ideas about her patriotic and feminine duty, fights Aoife, the "wild female," who represents the occult Shape-Changers (Moore, *Masks of Love and Death* 105). Cuchulain is supposedly presented, like Michael, with a choice between domestic bliss with wife and child, and a seductive but dangerous otherworld full of "witches and deceiving sirens" (Good 20), the difference being that it is the rejection of domesticity that jeopardizes the new nation.

In assuming that the universe of *On Baile's Strand* is constructed according to the same premises as the universe of *Cathleen,* these critics have perhaps been unduly influenced by Conchubar, who spends much of the play trying to convince Cuchulain that this is the case. Exhorting Cuchulain to take the oath, he pleads his desire to " leave / A strong and settled country to my children" (*VPl* 479), linking national security with the preservation of the family; later, he attributes the Young Kings' insistence on the oath to their status as "settled men" (493). He consecrates the swords to the service of "the threshold and the hearthstone" (499) and insists that Cuchulain balks only "because [he has] no children of [his] own" (483). As Conchubar uses the domestic, mortal wife/mother to represent all that is material, constructive, and desirable, he uses the Shape-Changer, who represents "the will of woman at its wildest" (495), to symbolize all that is occult, disruptive, and endangering. Like Griffith, he equates the preservation of the home with the preservation of the nation, and he defines the conflict between the nation and its enemies in terms of a battle between the good woman who stays home and the bad one who lurks outside.

It becomes clear as the plot unfolds, however, that Conchubar's conflation of polity and family is strategic and that his definition of the conflict is disingenuous. Conchubar's kingdom is threatened, not by the Shape-Changers, but by Aoife, the leader of a hostile foreign power; and in light of the number of readings that assume that she and the Shape-Changers are interchangeable, it is worth pointing out that Yeats deliberately informs us that Aoife is not one of them.[14] Cuchulain rejects Conchubar's suggestion that he "should have overtaken on the hills / Some daughter of the air" with the line "I am not blasphemous" (485), implying that however attractive he finds Shape-Changers, he has never had the audacity to proposition one. Since he has clearly been Aoife's lover, this draws a distinction between them and her. Aoife is dangerous precisely because her "turbulent" (487) spirit, "stone-pale cheek" (485), and beauty identify her with the "pale windy people" (522), but her "wild body" (487) is female and mortal. She is neither Cathleen nor Bridget, but a hybrid whose existence threatens the structures that safeguard Conchubar's kingdom.

Aoife's indefinite position on the continuum of mortality threatens the separation of the feminized occult and the world of kings and counselors that Conchubar wants to keep inviolably masculine. As a warrior-queen she also challenges his attempt to enlist all mortal women in the service of threshold and hearthstone. The threat that she poses to these two crucial distinctions—the one between the occult and the material worlds, and the one between private and public spheres—is figured as androgyny, which separates her from the hyperfeminized Shape-Changers and which Conchubar's descriptions of her attempt to elide. Although Cuchulain later calls her fierce, he reacts indignantly to Conchubar's calling Aoife a "fierce woman of the camp" (487), because in Conchubar's mouth it is an attempt to masculinize her. Cuchulain attributes the epithet to Conchubar's over-long dalliance "among the spinning-wheels" (487) and the pleasures of wifely submission, deriding the poverty of his conception of femininity and linking it to his investment in the ideal of domesticity. Cuchulain's description of Aoife puts equal stress on her "laughing, turbulent head" and her "grave eyes / Full of good counsel" (487), implying that she is both as disruptive as the Shape-Changers and as staid as Conchubar's Old Kings. This mingling of elements that Conchubar wants to separate is what, to Cuchulain, endows her with "all beauty" and makes her "so fitted to give birth to kings" (487).

Cuchulain's praise reminds Conchubar that despite her hatred, Aoife is a perfect match for him and that Cuchulain is a danger "within these walls" (489) for the same reasons that Aoife is dangerous outside them. Although the "wildness of [his] blood" (481) and his "burning heart" (491) make him valuable, they also testify to his connection with the feminized occult, rendering him androgynous like her. His "turbulence" (493), the "fancy" that "runs as it were a swallow on the wind" (489), his dancing, and his reluctance to be "oath-bound" (495) are all qualities associated with the feminine Shape-Changers. Cuchulain and Aoife represent the same danger: in them, gender ceases to be a structure that separates the supernatural from the material and instead allows one to merge with the other. Cuchulain's special status in this community derives from his refusal to respect boundaries; he is a hero because he is willing and able to cross borders.

The real conflict in *On Baile's Strand*, then, is not between the occult and the material worlds, or between the "conservative female of 'threshold and hearthstone'" and the Shape-Changers, but between Cuchulain—who values indeterminacy, spontaneity, and the freedom to defy structure and blur distinction—and Conchubar, whose definition of a prosperous kingdom is based on Griffith's model: a pure Ireland sealed inside a domestic space guarded from within by the women who produce it and from without by the men who defend it against the invading powers of the occult world. Thus, the play's real climax is not the battle between Cuchulain and his son, but the scene in which Conchubar attempts to defend his realm against what Cuchulain and Aoife represent by devising a ritual that will enforce the separation of the occult and material worlds by repolarizing femininity.

Conchubar's oath ritual is a play within a play—an attempt to turn his hall into a theatrical space that enacts the separation of the material domestic world and the occult foreign one. As Hannah Scolnicov argues, the disposition of a play's female figures—in Conchubar's case, the three women who make up the chorus—is crucial to the maintenance of the distinction between "seen and unseen spaces" that is "an inherent elementary structure" of drama (6). Stable gender distinctions preserve the barrier between inside and outdoors; since gender is "spatially defined in relation to the inside and the outside of the house" (6), it is stabilized when female characters are kept inside the house and becomes indeterminate when they are allowed to move between spaces.[15] By choreographing the fire ritual, Conchubar hopes to separate the domestic interior from the supernatural otherworld by fixing the members of the chorus—the only women who are visible to Conchubar's audience of Young Kings—inside the house where they belong.

According to Conchubar, the purpose of the fire ritual is to create an inviolate space from which occult influences are excluded:

> The holders of the fire
> Shall purify the thresholds of the house
> With waving fire, and shut the outer door,
> According to the custom; and sing rhyme
> That has come down from the old law-makers
> To blow the witches out. Considering
> That the wild will of man could be oath-bound,
> But that a woman's could not, they bid us sing
> Against the will of woman at its wildest
> In the Shape-Changers that run upon the wind. (493–95)

Conchubar wants to project what he fears onto a supernatural female figure who can then be driven out by the mortal women of the chorus who "shut the outer door" (493) on their occult mirror-image. When that door shuts, these women will themselves be reclaimed for the domestic interior, and their allegiance to "threshold and hearthstone" (493) confirmed. Passage from the otherworld to the material world will be blocked as Woman is fixed in her proper places: outside on the wind or inside at the hearth.

If successful, the fire ritual would be an excellent defense against Aoife, who could find no home at either of these extremes and would therefore be unable to exist within Conchubar's kingdom. It would thus argue that Conchubar is right in investing so much in the preservation of the home and that protecting the domestic interior is the best way to defend the nation against a foreign threat. But however carefully Conchubar orchestrates the ritual, and however neatly the song sung by the chorus reiterates the split between the mortal women who safeguard domestic tranquility and "the Shape-Changers who can put / Ruin on a great king's house" (495), the oath does not serve its purpose; the ritual is subverted by the women who perform it. Their activity realizes on stage, not a safely circumscribed domestic femininity, but the ambiguous definition of gender associated with Aoife.

Yeats subordinates the language of the song to the visual symbolism of the ritual, which sends a message different from the one in Conchubar's script. The reader, who has access only to the words, understands the song as a charm sung by devotees of the hearth against the "women none can kiss and thrive." However, Yeats's stage directions stipulate that these verses are "all but drown[ed]" (*VPl* 495) by the dialogue that overlays them, so that what the audience actually reads is not the verbal proscription of the occult femme fatale, but the spectacle of two human women with their hands full of fire bringing magic from the outer world into the supposedly protected hall. The third woman stands watch at the outer door, a visual reminder of the permeability of the border Conchubar wants to seal off. By declining either to enter the charmed domestic circle or disappear into exile, she changes the construction of Conchubar's theatrical space, undermines his attempt to contain women within it, and undoes the opposition the ritual is designed to create. Instead of exorcising supernatural power from the domestic space, the women of the chorus dissolve the barriers between them.

These women are not, as Conchubar wants them to be, "female pillars of society" preserving the mortal community from "dark forces which, if allowed to gain the upper hand, will surely tear the community apart" (Moore, *Masks of Love and Death* 114). Instead, in them the feminine-occult and feminine-domestic intermingle; they occupy a new position that does not exist in the universe of *Cathleen ni Houlihan* and that Conchubar does not want to exist within his borders. In their hands the ritual celebrates integration, a rapprochement of the occult and material worlds that might mitigate the antagonism between them and obviate the need for sacrifices like the one Michael made.

In this light, the appearance of the Young Man is not, as Moore claims, evidence of "the essential failure of the women's magic" (*Masks of Love and Death* 115). The chorus's ministrations conjure up on the doorstep "the only person who could attach [Cuchulain's] heroism to domestic affection" (Nathan 110). This is the Young Man, Cuchulain and Aoife's son, who, like the female chorus, is a mediator, a figure through whom Cuchulain's "turbulence" can be incorporated into Conchubar's nation rather than suppressed or banished. To Conchubar the Young Man, the representative of an enemy nation can only be a threat to the integrity of his kingdom and his sovereignty; but to Cuchulain, whose conceptions of nation and patriotism are more idiosyncratic, he is something else. Cuchulain's remarks about the Young Man's resemblance to Aoife are not included solely for the sake of dramatic irony; they present him as a possible solution, a way to bring what Aoife represents inside the boundaries of the kingdom without destroying it.

Like Aoife, the Young Man sports the "stone-pale" (504) complexion that bespeaks his affinity with the pallid women of the wind. Cuchulain is attracted to him because he has "a hot heart and a cold eye" (505), uniting the passion associated with the otherworld and the pragmatism linked with the guardians of the material one. Cuchulain assumes that the Young Man can negotiate the passages between the two worlds as easily as he does and will take the same pleasure in serving as a link between hall and hearthstone and the "wood and water . . . where the Shape-Changers of the morning come" (505–506). His potential as an intermediary figure is marked once again by androgyny; his body is masculine, but his "head is like a woman's head" (508).

The Young Man's incorporation into the national community, then, would symbolize its rejection of Conchubar's definition of gender identity and its acceptance of the interplay between the occult and the domestic. If Conchubar's Young Kings allow him to become one of them, that signals an openness to outside influence—or at the very least an acceptance of the fact that borders are necessarily porous. Cuchulain supports this view of the limitations of Griffithian nationalism by hinting that accepting the Young Man might break the cycle of war, death, and reprisal that is the real threat to Conchubar's kingdom (489). Cuchulain's vision of their future at first draws the Young Man into that cycle: "He would avenge me / When I have withstood for the last time the men / Whose fathers, brothers, sons and friends I have killed / Upholding Conchubar" (510). But he ends by suggesting a different outcome: "I'd need no avenger" (510). Though unable to conceive of a world without battles, Cuchulain does sense that the Young Man offers another future, one in which Aoife is not an enemy but an ally and in which oscillation between extremes—spirit and matter, male and female, love and hatred—is not the only pattern of human existence.

The friendship between Cuchulain and the Young Man, and his resultant incorporation into the kingdom, is thus offered as an alternative resolution, one appropriate to a kind of political conflict more complex than the one dramatized in *Cathleen.* Conchubar and his men are given the chance to leave behind the reductive model of nationalist commitment depicted in the earlier play and upheld by Conchubar's insistence that the Young Man must not "go unfought" (507). *On Baile's Strand* dramatizes the inadequacy of simple readiness to fight and die for the ideal of Ireland; personal bravery and self-sacrifice will not, by themselves, protect the kingdom. It also emphasizes, through Conchubar's double concern with protecting his borders and preserving his home, the connection between this sacrificial patriotism and the adherence to traditional gender roles that underwrites nationalist investment in the Irish home. Cuchulain's offer of friendship is presented as a stage in the necessary evolution of nationalism, a move away from the ethic of martyrdom toward accepting a more pragmatic definition of patriotism.

To Conchubar, however, the Young Man merely represents the threat Aoife poses to his universe: "He has come hither not in his own name / But in Queen Aoife's" (506). Like his indeterminate mother, the Young Man as an intermediary figure threatens the artificial separations that Conchubar wants to preserve; his androgyny makes him an embodiment of Aoife's unfixed, unclassifiable version of gender. Conchubar, desperate for a way to banish this disruptive influence and reassert the definition of gender celebrated in the language of the ritual, asserts his power over this threatening force by naming it.

When Conchubar claims that Cuchulain's refusal to fight proves that "some witch of the air has troubled [his] mind" (508), Cuchulain protests, "No witchcraft. His head is like a woman's head / I had a fancy for" (508). He does not yet realize that the boy's resemblance to Aoife is exactly what Conchubar means by "witchcraft." Witchcraft is Conchubar's term for the undoing of the structures that enforce rigid gender definitions, the introduction of the third position, the recovery of mobility, the act of mediation. Witchcraft makes it possible for men to resemble women, for women to leave the hearth, for mortals to encounter the occult without being violently ripped from the human world, for the occult to enter the mortal world with results other than the immediate destruction of the hero. Witchcraft is that troubling power exercised by women like Aoife, who defy Conchubar's gender paradigm and in whom femininity becomes a site of interchange between the material and ideal worlds and a threat to the integrity of the domestic sphere. Witchcraft is the flexibility and indeterminacy that must, according to Yeats, characterize nationalist thought if it is to be either honest or effective.

The kings rephrase Cuchulain's rebuttal as a confirmation: "Some witch has worked upon your mind. . . . The head of that young man seemed like a woman's / You'd had a fancy for" (512). Cuchulain now understands Conchubar's accusation of witchcraft as an attempt to demonize the mediating influence the Young Man represents. Cuchulain can either accept Conchubar's definition of the kingdom and its subjects and ratify his name for what Aoife represents or insist that Conchubar is wrong, that "the winds are innocent," (509) and that the Young Man and Aoife are possibilities that need to be included in any construction of a successful political community. Unable to make that gesture, Cuchulain agrees once again to "be obedient in all things / To Conchubar" (499) by accepting his terms: "Yes, witchcraft, witchcraft! Witches of the air!" (512).

Cuchulain's capitulation shuts down the possibilities the Young Man's entrance opened up. It also collapses the space in which Aoife and the women who represent her subject position on stage exist. The moment Cuchulain chases the Young Man out of the hall, the women of the chorus abruptly become the witches Conchubar wants to detect. Their sudden resemblance to the weird sisters of *Macbeth* is triggered by Cuchulain's repeated citation of one of Macbeth's soliloquies—"Out, out!" (513). Conchubar enforces his definition; the mortal woman who crosses the line between the hearth and the outside world becomes the witch whose relationship to the community is always suspect and who is dislodged from her intermediate position and merged with the purely occult Shape-Changers (who are also "witches"). The possibility of negotiating the space between "the will of woman at its wildest" and the will of woman at its most submissive evaporates; Aoife is ejected from Conchubar's kingdom.

Like the Young Man, the witches must now leave the hall; but on their way out, "they stop for a moment upon the threshold and wail" (514). Their cry is intended for Cuchulain, but it is also a lament for the loss of their former identity, for the foreclosing of the third option and the end of their role as mediators. Their almost-keen, like their *Macbeth*-style prophecy, links the destruction of Cuchulain's house with the reassertion of the gender roles that operated in *Cathleen ni Houlihan*. By returning to the gender politics of the earlier play, Conchubar has forced a return to old conflicts and old solutions and has sacrificed the Young Man on the same pyre that claimed Michael. The resolution of *On Baile's Strand* vindicates the "witches" and the pessimism of their prediction; the damage is done, not by the "pale windy people," but by Conchubar's attempt to exclude them (522). This is not a battle "full of glory and heart-uplifting pride" (522); Cuchulain's unnamed son will not be "remembered forever" (299). The Young Man's murder accomplishes only the extinction of a promising future and the expulsion of the women who could have brought it into being.

A Morbid, Unhealthy Mind: Disease, Degeneracy, and the *Playboy*

In *On Baile's Strand,* then, Yeats presents the male martyr's sacrifice as the price of Griffith's insistence on impossibly impermeable borders that enclose an impossibly pure Ireland, and he dramatizes through Conchubar's rhetoric how utterly dependent that vision is on a conception of gender that confines women either to the home or to the realms of perdition inhabited by the Shape-Changers. By couching this critique in myth and legend, Yeats renders it obscure enough to pass muster with the Abbey's audiences; and by keeping Aoife offstage, he avoids dramatizing his challenge to nationalist ideas of gender decorum as explicitly as *Shadow* did. However, when Synge attacks the same ideas about purity, he sets his play in the present day and the "real" world, making a claim for authenticity that *On Baile's Strand* never makes. Despite Synge's claims that he never intended the play as a representation of Irish life, his preface and his attempts to justify both this play and *Shadow* based on his experience as an anthropologist in the Aran Islands send a different message.

While contemporary nationalist readings of *Playboy* tend (to put it mildly) toward the reductive, they are also responses to what they see as Synge's own reductionism—his insistence on a materialist point of view in which the body usurps the place of the soul. If apparently trivial details like the word "shift" take on exaggerated and surreal importance during the *Playboy* controversy, that is partly because *Playboy* seems to dispense with allegory and symbolism and instead define purity in the most narrow and concrete terms possible—returning it from the realm of myth and legend to that of the corporeal body.[16] And though the anti-*Playboy* hysteria focused on the female body (specifically, the perceived sexual incontinence of Pegeen Mike and the other characters who swoon over Christy), it is my contention that this outcry masks deeper anxieties that referred specifically to the health and purity of the *male* Irish body.

In arguing that these anxieties may have been at stake in the public reaction to *Playboy,* I am not trying to suggest that the objections voiced more explicitly by Synge's critics—that Synge's portrait of Irish peasant life was inaccurate, that his language was a crude and inaccurate representation of Irish peasant speech, that his female characters were unrealistically and unflatteringly wanton—were not real, or that *Playboy*'s detractors were making a conscious effort to disguise the "true" source of their discontent by focusing on irrelevant details. In fact, the more obscure issues I am about to discuss have everything to do with the main problem that is repeatedly raised in anti-*Playboy* critiques—the fact that Synge is claiming to reproduce an accurate portrait of Irish life while at the same time manifestly doing something else. On one level, Griffith and his fellow-protestors understand quite clearly what is at stake in *Playboy* and realize that, given his portrayal, Synge's claim to be representing the "real" Ireland can only hurt the cause of Irish nationalism.

What I am arguing is that the question of accuracy becomes as important as it does in part because Griffith and company read Synge's portrait of the west of Ireland as evidence that he is complicit with the imperial medical establishment, with whose machinations they are by 1907 already familiar. Because Synge's treatment of the human body seems to them to coincide with eugenist constructions of the Irish as a degenerating race, to admit that his portrait was accurate would be to agree that the story British medicine has been trying to tell about Ireland and the Irish is right. This is a point that Griffith correctly realized Ireland could not afford to concede. In the environment created by Edwardian medicine, any admission of biological weakness became an admission of unfitness and an invitation to invasion.

Although they never become explicit, anxieties about the health of the Irish race, and particularly of the Irish male, are already visible in the *Shadow* controversy. Griffith's attempt to ensure the chastity of Nora and the integrity of her home explains why he needs to find a foreign source for Synge's play; but it cannot explain why he should choose one as utterly inappropriate as the story of the Widow of Ephesus. Put in the context of the medical discourse from which *Playboy's* critics will draw, his choice begins to make more sense. Griffith repeatedly applies the epithet "degenerate" to Petronius, his novel, and his putative Greek sources. His use of the term signals that he has accepted the identification of sexual incontinence and racial deterioration that is a first principle of eugenist science. Rather than accept the claim he believes Synge is making—that the Irish are sliding into degeneracy by way of sexuality—Griffith traces those elements of Synge's plot back to the late Roman Empire, a time and place that still define "degenerate" for students of Western civilization.

At the same time, his fixation on the Ephesus story suggests that whatever their other divergences, the two plots share enough common points to make them look like analogues to Griffith. The only thing that connects these stories is that both center around a widow who takes a new lover instead of mourning her husband—and whose infidelity is expressed through a disrespect for the husband's body. The most striking aspect of the Ephesus story is its resolution, in which the widow's decomposing husband is hauled up onto the cross to replace the missing criminal. Similarly, the primary distinctive feature of *Shadow* is the fact that all the action takes place in the presence of what Nora believes is her husband's corpse. But if this is what bothers Griffith, why does he seem so much less offended by the Aran Islands story, in which the wife actually has sex with her lover while she thinks her husband is lying dead in the front room?

Synge first diverges from the source plot late in the play, when Nora explains to Michael why she *doesn't* want to marry him:

> Why would I marry you, Mike Dara? You'll be getting old and I'll be getting old, and in a little while, I'm telling you, you'll be sitting up in your bed—the way himself was sitting—with a shake in your face, and your teeth falling, and the white hair sticking out round you like an old bush where sheep do be leaping a gap.
>
> *Dan Burke sits up noiselessly from under the sheet, with his hand to his face. His white hair is sticking out round his head. Nora goes on slowly without hearing him.*
>
> It's a pitiful thing to be getting old, but it's a queer thing surely. It's a queer thing to see an old man sitting up there in his bed with no teeth in him, and a rough word in his mouth, and his chin the way it would take the bark from the edge of an oak board you'd have building a door . . . God forgive me, Michael Dara, we'll all be getting old, but it's a queer thing surely. (*CP* 114)

Dan is brought back to irate life, not by Nora's infidelity, but by her mockery, which he turns against her: "Walk out now, Nora Burke, and it's soon you'll be getting old with that life, I'm telling you; it's soon your teeth'll be falling and your head'll be the like of a bush where sheep do be leaping a gap" (115). Just as the widow of Ephesus, instead of allowing her husband's body to disintegrate in the privacy of its family mausoleum, drags it into public view and displays it on the cross, Nora betrays Dan by describing his aging body—a body that in her words appears to have started rotting even before death.

The right thing to do, for both widows, would have been to cooperate with the fiction of the male body's incorporeality. Instead of proving to all and sundry that the male body can be as real, as corrupted, and as disgusting as any female body, their duties compel them to preside over that body's disappearance into a grave that closes seamlessly and never reopens. What connects the widow of Ephesus and the widow of Wicklow is their refusal to keep that grave closed and that body invisible. Nora is faulted not just for breaking the home, for dallying with Michael, and for taking up with the Tramp, but for bringing this talking corpse back from the dead. And it is this sacrilege—the display on stage of the decaying male body—that will make *Playboy*'s revision of the sacrificial paradigm so threatening.[17]

Blood Is Life: Pestilence and Pollution in the Dublin Press

While the arguments used by both mainstream and nationalist critics to condemn *The Playboy of the Western World* vary slightly, detractors are consistent in citing a few key offenses: (1) Synge's insinuation that Irish women find parricide sexually exciting, (2) his use of "coarse" language, (3) his implication that Irish men are violent and that Irish people are lawless, and (4) his general misrepresentation of Irish life. They are also consistent in their expressions of revulsion and horror. Griffith's review brands Synge a "moral degenerate" ("The Abbey Theatre" 2); Holloway speaks of his "morbid and unhealthy mind" (81); Maire Nic Shiubhlaigh recalls the performance as emphasizing the "nastiness" of the individual characters (81); Pearse charges Synge with propounding "corrupt morality" and calls *Playboy* a "revolt against sane and sweet ideals" (qtd. in Kiberd, *Synge and the Irish Language,* 252); the play is characterized in the *Freeman's Journal* as "sordid, squalid and repulsive" (qtd. in Kiely 164). Synge's defenders satirize this consistency: the author of "Mr. Synge's Secret" in the

Dublin Evening Mail ironically characterizes the protesters as the "advocates of delicacy and purity" (2), while "P.M.E.K." in "A Plea for the Playboy" points out the absurdity of "a people supposed to possess a firmly-established character for purity of language and morals" defending this character by rioting (3).

In the discourse surrounding both the play and the riots, there is a universal concern with purity and decency on the one hand, and filth and degeneracy on the other. If, for modern readers, it is difficult to understand why *Playboy* should be considered "filthy," that is not simply because standards of sexual decency have changed since 1907. The kind of sexual license supposedly evident in Synge's choice of language was associated in the public mind with disease through a rhetoric of degeneration being put forward as part of the eugenics movement in medicine and public health. That rhetoric had already claimed words like "morbid," "degenerate," and "squalid."[18] Without that context, it is hard to see why Synge's play was condemned in these terms or why his "morbid" outlook should have become a specifically nationalist problem. If *Shadow* attacked the idea of pure Irishness by breaking up the Irish home within which it is enshrined, Griffith and others saw *Playboy* as mounting the same attack but collaborating with imperial medicine to target the sanctum sanctorum—the body itself. And while the protesters explicitly focused their attention on Synge's failure to respect the privacy of the Irish woman's body, they were perhaps more troubled by his dissection and display of the Irish man's body.

The public health movement that supported eugenist medicine during the first decade of the twentieth century began with panic over the health of the male body. Fears of racial degeneration first became news in Britain as a result of problems that the British Army encountered when it tried to recruit for the Boer War.[19] Once large numbers of potential recruits had to be disqualified for failing to meet physical fitness requirements, the fear that the British race was in decline led to increased governmental support for eugenist medicine, whose premises and tactics seemed to promise a return to racial fitness—and by implication the right and the ability to conquer and control other races.

In 1907 the Eugenics Education Society was formed, and through its efforts eugenics became the accepted theoretical basis of orthodox medical practice. Starting from the premise that heredity determined not only physical but also moral and intellectual fitness, eugenist medicine stressed the need to control reproductive practices and ensure that the fit procreated and the unfit did not. To prove their central premise, eugenicists produced research designed to show that disability and disease were inherited characteristics and that intellectual ability and poverty itself were linked to biological and inheritable characteristics.[20]

Along with this emphasis on heredity went the doctrine of differential fertility, a contemporary variation on Malthusian themes that posited that the poor were inherently more fertile than the rich and that if allowed to procreate at will they would eventually form the bulk of the population, while the numbers of the rich withered away. Since, according to eugenist doctrine, poverty and debility were synonymous, the result of this "fertility gap" was racial deterioration as the ranks of the "defective" swelled while those of the healthy dwindled.[21] At the same time, advances in microscope technology made it possible to identify microorganisms, a development that "created a widespread sense of psychological unease about the sinister invisible undercurrents of modern urban living" (Harris 55). Linked to "fears about degeneracy and physical deterioration" fueled by eugenics, this paranoia about germs became an "Edwardian obsession with 'cleanliness'" (55) that focused not only on physical hygiene—sanitation, disease control, vaccination—but on "racial hygiene" (236), which involved cleaning up the British gene pool by discouraging diseased or "defective" individuals from reproducing.

The emphasis on heredity meant that sexuality became not only a moral problem but a physical liability as well—misdirected sexual energy led to pathogenic unions that produced unfit children and accelerated degeneracy. Private sexual practices thus became a matter of public health; the fear of racial degeneration through irresponsible breeding attached itself to microbe-related paranoia and emerged as a crusade against venereal disease. Armstrong's analysis of early-twentieth-century British public health discourse argues that venereal disease scares were "invented" (18), along with other public health crises, for the purpose of allowing greater surveillance and disciplinary control over the British working class; thus, syphilis became a greater danger as a discursive construct than it was as a disease. As this 1909 report on the urban poor indicates, venereal disease became both the cause and symptom of debility among the underclass:

> I am convinced that the greater majority of children born in the poorest districts (slum) are tainted with syphilis. . . . They are mostly feeble

> in body and mind, possess no inhibitory power, and readily give way to the vices by which they are surrounded. It is from this class that paupers and criminals are made. (qtd. in Mazumdar 32)

Venereal disease serves as the link between moral and physical decay, simultaneously identifying both with the marginalized underclass.

Thus, in Edwardian Britain "'purity' and 'pollution' . . . were no mere anthropological abstractions" (Harris 55)—they were part of the framework of modern medicine, which sought to ensure racial purity (both biologically and morally) through the elimination of pathological agents. Whether these agents were microbes or people who were presumed to carry them, the British government believed it had a compelling interest in attacking and suppressing them in an effort to restore the health of the race and thus of the Empire. Accepting the premise that, as George Newman puts it in his pamphlet *The Health of the State,* "the physical health and fitness of the people is the primary asset of the British Empire" (qtd. in Harris 60), the state threw its weight behind a program of public health measures that, while ostensibly designed to control the spread of disease and degeneration, also attempted to regulate sexual practices and to infiltrate and reconstruct individual bodies. And, as Harris suggests, "latent fears about the global eclipse of higher races by lower ones" (235) translated the classist bias of eugenics into a racist one that identified colonized populations as unfit and therefore as legitimate targets for intervention.

As both the mainstream and nationalist presses demonstrate, Ireland was as firmly in the grip of antigerm paranoia and as concerned about infection and degeneration as England was. The difference between the mainstream presentation of disease, as illustrated in the *Irish Times* and the *Dublin Evening Mail,* and the nationalist approach modeled in *Sinn Fein,* is an awareness on the part of Griffith and company of the imperialist uses of both the rhetoric of disease and the practice of public health. Despite this, Griffith accepts the basic principles of eugenics, as illustrated by his attempt to prove that the Irish are more racially pure and physically fit—an argument that requires him to accept the eugenist view of sexuality as a potential vector of racial degeneration and thus to see *Playboy* as a deliberate attack on the health of the Irish race.

Concurrent with the rise of Synge at the Abbey, there was growing concern on the part of the *Dublin Evening Mail*'s readership with medical matters and with infection and debility in particular. Five days before *Shadow*'s premiere, the *Mail* ran an article entitled "Microbes and Their Doings: The Curious Tricks They Play," which introduced its readers to Edwardian germ paranoia:

> Of the chemical activity of microbes, what we know is as nothing in comparison with what it may be. Every species, every race, every variety of microbe, is charged with a special function. . . . Some species have this power in a marked degree, which is distinguished as virulence. They are called pathogenic microbes, which means capable of causing illness. Each species of this microbe produces a particular kind of disease. (7)

With subheadings like "Places Where They Lurk" and "The Hostile Microbe Everywhere," this article is typical of the alarmist attitude toward infectious disease taken by this newspaper. It also shows paranoia about germs translating into a more general anxiety about the permeability of the body's boundaries:

> The hostile microbe is in fact everywhere—within and without us, seeking, we might say, what it may devour. All the natural cavities of the body—the nose, the mouth, and the digestive tube—having exterior openings are seeded with microbes brought from without by air or food, and afterwards multiplied. (7)

Since the vagina does not appear on this list of dangerous orifices, the passage appears to refer to a male body. Even without this most dangerous port of entry, the male body is porous, vulnerable, and susceptible to foreign invasion—as endangered and under siege as the female body could be.[22]

The *Irish Times,* Dublin's major conservative publication, was less addicted to lurid descriptions of hostile microbes but no less interested in promoting public health. Along with its regular medical coverage, the *Times* ran a number of letters from the editor about medical topics, including an instructive missive submitted by Anthony Roche, professor of public health and lecturer on "Sanitary Science" at St. Patrick's College, which gives some indication of the extent to which concerns about germs and infection have penetrated the Irish public mind. Although he laments that "of the three Medical Schools in Dublin, that of the Catholic University alone gives a complete course of lectures in Public Health," he finds this strange, given that the Royal University of Ireland requires a "complete course on Public Health" and that "the medical profession and the press are almost daily impressing on the public and the authorities the importance of sanitary science in elementary schools" (Roche 8). While the zealous Roche finds this inadequate, his letter illustrates the extent to which hygiene had become part of the medical curriculum. Roche's piece also illustrates the transmission pattern that germ paranoia followed: the letter accompanies a clipping from *The Lancet,* the journal of the British Medical Association, "on the teaching of Public Health in Medical Schools" (Roche 8).

The *Mail*'s advertisers capitalized on this paranoia, incorporating the vocabulary of purity and corruption into their copy. Often ads for patent medicines focused on the need to cleanse the bloodstream of unwanted pollutants. For instance, in 1905 Veno's Seaweed Tonic attracted its prospective buyers' attention with the header "BLOOD IS LIFE. LET IT BE PURE":

> Blotches, pimples on the face and body, scrofula, sores, itching and redness of the skin, tetter and eczema are symptoms which indicate impure blood and skin diseases. If your blood is pure your skin will be clear and healthy-looking; the direct cause of skin eruption is found in the blood. Purify the blood and you purify and clear the skin. (26 January 1905: 5)

And the *Irish Times* trumpeted the virtues of Clarke's Blood Mixture:

> ECZEMA, SCROFULA, ULCERS, SORES OF ALL KINDS, and all diseases arising from impurities in the blood such as Rheumatism, Glandular Swellings, Skin Diseases, Eruptions, Boils, &c should test the value of CLARKE'S BLOOD MIXTURE. It is certainly the finest Blood purifier ever discovered, and will cleanse the Blood from all impurities, from whatever cause arising. (27 January 1904: 4)

If the good people at Clarke's and Veno's claimed that corruption worked from the inside out, the copywriters at Zam-Buk Skin Rub were equally certain that it worked from the outside in:

> A tiny pimple on the face is usually attended to, because of the disfigurement it causes; but if the same kind of trouble manifests itself on back or chest, it is too often neglected—with dire results. Taking root in the unnoticed little sore, skin disease gets a firm hold on the tissue, and increasing irritation eventually compels attention to what may be by this time a mass of eruptions, a discharging ulcer that will eat deep into the flesh, or an obstinate poisoned wound. (4 January 1907: 5)

HIDDEN
SKIN TROUBLES.

Figure 1.
Advertisement for Zam-Buk Skin Rub. Detail.
Dublin Evening Mail,
January 4, 1907, page 5.

Although the text claims that men and women alike suffer from the heartbreak of skin disease, the graphic that accompanies it shows a man standing in front of a mirror searching for lesions or blemishes (Fig. 1).[23] Thus, the integrity and purity of the male body is specifically at stake. That body's surface, the skin, becomes both the symptom and the cause of corruption at the heart: through the body's porous surface the hostile microbe seeps into the bloodstream and poisons the well.

Nor was the hostile microbe the only potential agent of corruption. Almost anything that entered the body could become a pollutant, at least according to the makers of Dr. Butler's Tonic Digestive Pills, who warned prospective clients that "YOUR FOOD IS POISON!": "If [food is] not digested, fermentation and decomposition are set up in the Stomach and Intestine. Poisonous gases and effete products get into the blood, vitiating the whole system" (*Dublin Evening Mail* 2 January 1907: 2).Once the connection between superficial and internal pollution is established, it becomes necessary to attack corruption aggressively and invasively, even if the only evidence of such a pollution is a topical skin infection. These advertisements, then, used their audience's fear of foreign substances to convince them to consume their medicine—effectively playing on their paranoia about infiltration and pollution to get them to allow patent medicines to infiltrate and pollute them.

This tactic repeats in the commercial realm what was already happening in the medical profession, which promoted fear of infection in an effort to make intrusive public health measures more palatable to the public. The *Mail*'s medical correspondent, in an article on cancer, shows how the fear of infectious disease could be used to justify invasive treatment:

> An infant a few months old, born of healthy parents, is found to have a mass of internal cancer. A woman, struck on the breast, has the disease at that very point where she was struck. A sore on the lip, fretted for years with a clay pipe, becomes malignant. A group of cottages round a village-green seems to be haunted by the disease. What theory will cover all these cases? ("Study of Cancer")

The author does not know, but he is sure of one thing: " We must not dream of trying, for the present, to get away from the surgeon." The cancer patient who "must not dream of trying" to avoid the surgeon's knife stands for his society, which must not dream of resisting the medical establishment's regulation of its habits and behavior. As the *Mail*'s columns document, during this decade the state-sponsored medical establishment was increasingly involved in regulating public life, from instituting quarantine procedures during epidemic outbreaks, to directing public sanitation projects, to establishing sanatoria and lunatic asylums.[24] And, as various contributors to *Sinn Fein* (Ourselves Alone) would later point out, it was also instituting a program of compulsory vaccination, which would require participants to allow a doctor to inject a foreign substance directly into their bloodstream.

The *Irish Times* supported the *Mail*'s claims about the necessity of increased government intervention, making up in harshness what it lacked in sensationalism. The *Times* coverage, especially the material submitted by readers, is much clearer than is the *Mail* about the connection between controlling disease and controlling the people infected with it. An article on "How Smallpox Is Spread," for instance, makes it clear that state workers have an important duty as public health officials (5). In this piece, smallpox is spread through a combination of two factors: an indigent vagrant who "import[s]" the disease to the towns he passes through, and a lackadaisical government that fails to deprive him of his mobility. The *Irish Times* readership appears to have embraced both the notion that disease spreads from the poor upward and the idea that the only thing that would protect them from contagion was the colonial administration. In January of 1907, for instance, the editors printed a letter from a reader signing himself Marcus Tertius Moses encouraging, nay, imploring "the State" to "declare its fatherhood and save its people" by institutionalizing victims of tuberculosis:

> Tuberculosis is declared by the best medical authorities to be a very infectious disease, and particularly so amongst our poorer brethren, who have not the means of isolating the afflicted member effectually, and whose training is not such as to have perfect precautions against the dissemination of the germs. (6)

Moses' plan for state control of TB is breathtaking in its comprehensiveness: early-stage sufferers should be put in state-run sanatoria; those in the "advanced stages" should be "removed to homes or asylums"; those who are infected but can still function will be herded into "a colony for keeping them at work or exercise . . . and for having a general supervision over them." TB patients should be handled at a "special dispensary" where doctors could monitor "when a patient was leaving the sanatorium or colony" and "note the treatment, investigate the state of the dwelling, the risk of infection to others"; and the state should use all its power to "compel the poor sufferers to submit to treatment" (6).

If Moses' use of the vocabulary of imperial control ("colony," "asylum," "compel," "submit") is striking, so is the response submitted by one Thomas Hewson, who "agree[s] with Mr. Moses that this is a case for Imperial legislation" but advocates sending the afflicted into exile (8). According to Hewson, who supports state intervention in disease control but objects to having his taxes pay for it, the recent health panic has rendered Dublin "over-hospitaled" (8). In other words, along with the rise in state concern there has been a noticeable increase in state-funded institutions.

What emerges from the pages of the *Mail* and the *Times,* then, is the idea that the body—this time the male body as much as the female one—is endangered as never before, beset and besieged by invisible agents bent on corrupting and finally destroying it. If one eludes the "hostile microbe" at home, one still runs the risk of infiltration and infection during one of the "Deadly Tram Rides" against which the *Mail* warns its readers in January of 1907, in an article suggesting that tuberculosis, rheumatism, and sciatica are being spread by microbes that fester in the "Dangerous Cushions" upon which passengers sit ("Deadly Tram Rides" 2). While the *Mail*'s use of the language of invasion, pollution, and corruption is generally unselfconscious, in the hands of writers with a more highly developed nationalist consciousness, this sense of being threatened by foreign bodies that would get under the skin and into the blood became a description of imperial power over the Irish subject—a power exercised literally through public health projects like vaccination, and metaphorically through the medical establishment's use of the rhetoric of degeneracy on the Irish subject.

In this context, then, it is not surprising that the meaning of sacrifice shifts and that blood becomes a symbol, not simply of the purity of the martyr's intention, but of the purity of his biological organism—a purity that is constantly jeopardized and that must be jealously guarded. This sense of embattlement led to increased vigilance over the body's borders—and, inevitably, increased attention to sexuality. Venereal disease, once it corrupted the bloodstream of the individual, would poison the lifeblood of the race itself. For nationalists who were already concerned with defending their bodies against imperial science, sex became a matter of national security.

Our Bodies, Our Selves: Sinn Fein *and Imperial Science*

As we have seen, the period leading up to *Playboy* was one of increased public interest in health issues, of increased concern about the permeability of the body's boundaries and the vulnerability of the bloodstream to pollution and corruption, and of increased state efforts to protect the health of the British race by instituting Empire-wide public health measures. While the *Dublin Evening Mail*'s—and, even more so, the *Irish Times*'s—coverage of these efforts was sympathetic to the state's fears and supportive of the medical establishment, the contributors and correspondents published in *Sinn Fein* (the 1907 reincarnation of *United Irishman,* still under Griffith's direction) were not. While their resistance to British public health measures bespeaks an understanding of the power of imperial medicine and the threat that medical practices posed to the Irish body, it also indicates a fundamental acceptance of the theoretical principles of eugenist science. As a result, outrage that might have been used to challenge the medical establishment's attempts to "breed out" genetic liabilities was instead marshaled in defense of Irish racial and biological purity against a playwright whose work appeared to attack it.

As early as 1903, writing in the *United Irishman* indicates an awareness of both the increasing authority of medical discourse and its antinationalist potential. Writing under the pseudonym "Irial," socialist playwright Fred Ryan takes issue with Yeats's depiction, in *Where There Is Nothing,* of nationalist fervor:

> Paul Ruttledge [is] a picture of the man who is a rebel by temperament. . . . In the play, of course, Paul Ruttledge is a madman; that is to say, his abnormality is so striking as to be what we generally class as insane. . . . Paul is certainly not mentally sound. That, perhaps, is the defect of the play as a presentation of the average innovating temperament. (3)

Ryan is concerned because Ruttledge's extremism renders his nationalism vulnerable to diagnosis and therefore dismissal. His use of medicalized terms ("abnormality," "Hysteria," "class as insane") indicates that he reads Paul's madness, not as divinely inspired lunacy or the idiosyncrasy of genius, but rather as the result of an unfortunate "temperament[al]" predisposition toward mental instability. If Paul Ruttledge can indeed be "class[ed] as insane," his political commitment becomes a disease, one that eugenics links with hereditary unfitness. The play exposes Irish nationalism to the clinical gaze and allows patriotism to be reduced to pathology.

As Eglinton points out in his response, however, in order to make this critique, Ryan must accept the premises of current scientific thought:

> This, as it seems to me, is what those scientists do who think they shall become wise by much counting, and if it is "mediaeval" to tax Lombroso with incapacity to understand the real greatness of Shelley, for instance, because he prefers to think of him as an "abnormal subject" rather than as a mind of extraordinary reach, subtlety and power, I am sorry that modern thinking should be content to leave common sense in the keeping of the dark ages. (2)

Eglinton's invocation of Lombroso—a criminologist and a major proponent of an especially crude formulation of biological determinism—indicates that he lumps Ryan in with the Victorian proto-eugenists who attempted to explain all forms of "deviant" behavior in terms of physiology. Ryan, he suggests, reads Paul Ruttledge's "madness" as pathological only because he has been converted to this dangerously reductive "modern thinking." Eglinton is aware of the threat posed by scientific discourse, which threatens to reduce any intellectual, political, or cultural phenomenon to a function of biology, to brand literature as "'degenerate' intellectual rubbish" (2) and writers as "abnormal subjects."

By 1907 that discursive threat has become more concrete; Griffith's publication defends the Irish, not just against medical discourse, but against medical practice. During the weeks leading up to *Playboy's* premiere—January and early February 1907—compulsory vaccination was a hot topic in *Sinn Fein.* Even after the major players—F. O hUiathne and Mrs. A. S. Hunter, a Scottish nationalist—had laid out the arguments against vaccination, a letter from "An Irish Doctor" defending the law generated so many irate responses that Griffith did not have space to print them all. All of these arguments use the same basic premise: vaccination pollutes the bloodstream without conferring any health benefit, and by compelling the Irish to submit to this the British government is deliberately trying to poison the Irish race. The fact that under the terms of the vaccination law there was a "conscientious objector" clause in effect for England and Wales but not for Scotland and Ireland supported this view of vaccination as a coercive tool designed more for Britain's subjected Celtic populations than for use at home in the metropolis.

For readers at the beginning of the twenty-first century, it is easy enough to see the vaccination controversy as pure paranoia. I do not want to suggest, by taking the antivaccination argument seriously, that the British medical authorities who wanted to institute compulsory vaccination believed that it would adversely affect Irish public health. Nor, indeed, am I suggesting that vaccination is somehow evil in itself simply because it has been associated with repressive public health measures.[25] But just as eighteenth-century distrust of Jenner and his pioneering vaccinators makes sense, given how painful, ineffective, and fatal most forms of eighteenth-century medical treatment were, uneasiness about compulsory vaccination makes sense in the Irish context. Having already experienced the effects of this partnership between the colonial government and modern medicine, Irish nationalists were reasoning from experience when they suggested that accepting compulsory vaccination might have unfortunate consequences.

Hunter is unambiguous in her choice of language: vaccination, a plot hatched by "an English quack doctor," has now become a deliberate attempt to "sow corruption in the blood of the people"; it is nothing more than "compulsory rottenness" inflicted on a helpless population for the sole and express purpose of "polluting the pure Irish blood" (1). Hunter's argument demonstrates that Griffith is not alone in conflating economic health, the integrity of the home, and the purity of the body:

> But, seeing you advocate the boycotting of all foreign commodities, you may as well boycott this 'pure rottenness' from the English pharmacopoeia—with your fine climate, and with the inheritance of health still due from clean living progenitors, you could easily get quit of the English 'rottenness' by living on your own home-grown products and educating your people on the advantages of cleanly . . . and healthy homes. (1)

Would we could close our ports. As it does in imperialist discourse, so in this strain of nationalist discourse the individual body becomes the body politic, and the body's borders stand for the nation's. Violating the body's borders violates national sovereignty, and protecting that sovereignty becomes synonymous with policing the body's boundaries.

The dire effects of this "rottenness" are laid out in more graphic detail by F. O hUiathne, who describes the process by which the vaccine is produced:

> The fluid is taken in a vessel, "purified," skin, hair, scabs, etc. removed, and after various processes glycerine is added, and "pure calf-lymph" is ready for distribution to the dispensary doctors, who will impregnate the blood of our children—the children we are rebuilding a nation for. . . . We can never hope for a virile, healthy race, when the life stream is so early polluted with an animal excrescence. (3)

The equation of health with virility suggests that from the nationalist perspective the target of this vaccination plot is the body of the male patriot; Britain is attempting to enfeeble Irish men in order to render them incapable of physical resistance. But here, as in the columns and advertisements of the *Daily Mail*, the Empire's attack on the male body's boundaries is presented in terms of a physical health risk, whereas its effect on the female body is depicted in terms of moral decay. Hunter encapsulates the distinction when she charges that vaccination will "suck out the virility from our men and the morality of our women" (1).

As in British medical discourse, the link between moral and physical decay in the antivaccination argument is venereal disease, specifically syphilis:

> Lately we have detected the abnormal percentage of disease in the British Army, and have used it to our advantage, and let us trust dissuaded many a pure-minded young Gael from sacrificing his life for the sake of "the Empire." But the Anti-Vaccination Society which is formidable on the other side, has pointed out that many experts regard vaccination and syphilis as identical, notably Professors Hutchison and Crooksbank. The Army is vaccinated and re-vaccinated subject to the caprice of the Medical Department, and it seems plain they receive successive doses in an attenuated form of the above dread affliction. May not this be the cause of the early loss of the teeth, a syphilitic symptom, in those countries where cow-pox, or "calf-lymph," is so extensively used? (3)

O hUiathne's logic shows how unerringly panic about the permeability of the body returns to the question of sexual continence. However ridiculous it seems to us to equate the smallpox virus with the spirochete responsible for syphilis, eugenist science's rhetoric of pollution and degeneration rendered this analogy plausible in the realm of discourse if not in the realm of biology. Both syphilis and vaccine are acquired through a breach of the body's boundaries. Both are conceived of as polluting the bloodstream, tainting both individual and racial purity. Both are believed to corrupt the body into which they are introduced. Both are "foreign-imported diseases": vaccination is brought to Ireland by the British public health system, and syphilis is brought in by the British Army, which Griffith claims is "rife with loathsome diseases, the result of personal immorality." As a result, the moral rot associated with syphilis attaches to the physical debility associated with vaccination; and just as refusal to be vaccinated preserves the subject against both infectious and venereal disease, chastity becomes a prophylactic against not only sin but sickness—a barrier against the onslaught of syphilis but also against the more insidious germs being injected into the Irish bloodstream via the British doctor's needle.

But Hunter's formulation about the virility of men and the morality of women indicates that while this anxiety about the purity of the body is focused on the *male* patriot, the fear of moral contagion into which it translates is easily projected onto the *female* patriot's body, from which the threat of racial deterioration is presumed to emanate. For instance, W. E. Fay's "A Note on National Games," which appeared in *Sinn Fein* during the vaccination controversy, argues that the rehabilitation of the male body through Irish sport should be one of nationalism's objectives: "We cannot overrate the value, physical, moral, and mental, of outdoor games, so the more of them we play the better" (4). Griffith shared this view, judging by the amount of space his paper devoted to sporting events. It is clear, however, that Irish men and Irish women will be playing different sports:

> If there is one fact more than another which the study of physiology and psychology has emphasised, it is the intimate and inseparable connection that exists (in this life) between soul and body. The Greeks saw this connection clearly, and sent their women to look upon beautiful statues before child-birth, in order that their children might be beautiful. (Fay 4)[26]

While the male patriot keeps himself in fighting trim by playing rugby and hurling, the female patriot does her part by producing beautiful children. The corruption or decay of her body is important, not so much in and of itself, but because it will be transmitted to the children who are the nation's future. According to eugenist theory, it is in the mother's body that disease is turned into degeneration—that syphilis engenders birth defects, that promiscuity produces disabled children, that moral turpitude translates into racial deterioration. For her, then, bodily purity becomes almost exclusively a matter of sexual purity; her duty is to protect the race by protecting herself from venereal disease through abstinence and, after marriage, fidelity. The anxiety with which male nationalists contemplate the infiltration and pollution of their own bodies by a hostile foreign power is displaced onto the Irish woman's body and emerges as concern over her ability to close her ports—to protect her body from corruption by refusing sexual contact and thus refusing to accelerate racial deterioration.

The vaccination controversy shows that Griffith and his cohorts identified disease itself as an imperial weapon used to destroy the strength and purity of the Irish race and that they conflated—inaccurately, in this case—imperial medicine and the diseases that medicine attempts to control. At the same time, Griffith shows in "The Immorality of the British Army" that he knows that the *discourse* of disease can be an equally powerful weapon. Citing the fact that Patrick Lagan has been prosecuted for circulating statistics about venereal disease in the British army, Griffith suggests that the accusation of disease is dangerous enough to prompt the British authorities to make it "a new crime" (2). He then uses the charge that the British Army has the highest per capita rate of venereal disease in Europe to prove that "the British army is the most immoral army in civilisation," and therefore unfit to be enforcing the dictates of an empire that justifies its colonial project on the grounds that it is bringing civilization to untutored peoples (2).

By using venereal disease in this way, however, Griffith is accepting the equation of disease with "personal immorality" ("Immorality" 2); and although the British Army is perhaps too tempting a target to pass up, seizing the moral high ground is a costly maneuver because it allows imperial medicine to define the terms of the conflict. Eglinton's suggestion that the eugenist model of degeneracy might be flawed is foreclosed, and the only question becomes whether it is the British or the Irish who are more unfit. Under these conditions, the charge of degeneracy that Griffith sees Synge making in *Playboy* becomes as dangerous as the threat of actual disease represented by the doctor's needle.

A Fine Husband This: Playboy *as Eugenist Parable*

In this context, then, it is not surprising that Griffith's coterie should be suspicious of a play whose central premise is "the fighting of the women of the West for the hand of a parricide because he is a parricide" ("Abbey Theatre" 2). That Irish women should fight over anyone is bad enough; sexual desire threatens to lead to sexual intercourse, which opens Ireland's ports to disease. But the fact that they are competing for the attentions of a man whose distinguishing characteristic is a tendency toward homicidal violence is even more problematic. It suggests, not simply that Irish women share the amorality that supposedly accompanies sexual incontinence, but that the sacrificial paradigm that Griffith and others praised so highly in *Cathleen* is itself a eugenist parable—a "gallous story" (*CP* 77) disguising some dirty facts about Irish physical and moral debility.

This is the attitude clearly taken by "P.M.E.K.," author of "A Plea for the Playboy," the only pro-Synge article published in *Sinn Fein.* Arguing that the play's detractors are, so to speak, protesting too much, he claims that the riots prove that "we have really no saintliness, no morals whatsoever, and we must keep shouting that we have, to make up for it" (3). "P.M.E.K." assumes that this lack of "morals" is both the cause and symptom of an epidemic of physical debility that marks the Irish as a deteriorating race:

> [Pegeen's community] is . . . a handful of men and women, a fragment of a once strong and healthy race of which the existing male representatives are, Shawn Keogh, a poor craven, weak in body and brain, and

> Philly O'Cullen; Jimmy Jarrell and Michael James, none of them much better. (3)

This degeneracy, already far advanced, could be cured by exactly what Griffith and company are most horrified by—the Irish woman's sexual attraction to an Irish murderer:

"A fine husband this, for a spirited girl, but better than none, thinks she, and is ready to put up with him till Christy Mahon arrives, strong, well-favoured, and courageous; has he not laid his father low with a lick of a spade, and Pegeen exalts him to a hero" (3). Her attraction to Christy is described as "a healthy girl's admiration for a strong man" (3), that strength having (supposedly) been demonstrated by his willingness and ability to murder his father. Thus, a complicated plot is boiled down to a story about the survival of the fittest, and *Playboy* becomes a cautionary tale about the importance of eugenics: Pegeen recognizes the right breeding partner, but is unable to fly in the face of public disapproval and therefore rejects him for one of the weaklings in the village, which is "the whole tragedy of the play" (3).

"P.M.E.K." is echoing the argument put forward a week earlier in the columns of *The Irish Times* by P. D. Kenny, who wrote drama criticism under the pseudonym "Pat" (Holloway 277) and who seems to have been even more forcibly struck by the play's eugenist moral. Labeling Shaneen Keogh a "half idiot" who "has not enough intelligence to love" this "lively peasant girl," Kenny describes Pegeen's dilemma in strikingly Darwinian terms:

> Why is "Pegeen" prepared to marry [Shaun]? "God made him; therefore, let him pass for a man," and in all his unfitness, he is the fittest available! Why? Because the fit ones have fled. He remains because of his cowardice and idiotcy in a region where fear is the first of the virtues, and where the survival of the unfittest is the established law of life. (9)

Christy, on the other hand, is "a real, live man," superior to Shaun because poor Shaun is too craven "even to kill his father" (9). Pegeen chooses Christy "instinctively and immediately," her hormones evidently having recognized the advent of a suitable mate.

The eugenist reading of *Playboy* was thus produced on both sides of the political divide—in the nationalist *Sinn Fein* and in the conservative *Irish Times.* It is also obliquely endorsed by Synge himself in a letter to the editor of the *Irish Times:* "'Pat', I am glad to notice, has seen some of [the *Playboy*'s messages] in his own way" (31 January

1907: 5). Synge goes on to hope that other reviewers may find more in the play, but he appears to see Kenny's reading as legitimate rather than wrong-minded. And indeed, there is support for his reading in *Playboy*—enough certainly to indicate that Synge was aware of, and playing with, the connections being made in medical discourse between disease, degeneracy, and sexual immorality.

Pegeen, teasing Shawn about his papal dispensation, describes her community as stocked with what eugenicists would call "defectives": "If I was him I wouldn't bother with this place where you'll meet none but Red Linahan, has a squint in his eye, and Patcheen is lame in his heel, or the mad Mulrannies were driven from California and they lost in their wits. We're a queer lot" (*CP* 9). There has been a falling-off, since Pegeen sighs for the heroes of yore: "Where now will you meet the like of Daneen Sullivan knocked the eye from a peeler, or Marcus Quin, God rest him, got six months for maiming ewes?" (9) And when Michael James gives his blessing to Pegeen and Christy, he justifies it in eugenist terms:

> It's many would be in dread to bring your like into their house for to end them, maybe, with a sudden end; but I'm a decent man of Ireland, and I liefer face the grave untimely and I seeing a score of grandsons growing up gallant little swearers by the name of God, than go peopling my bedside with puny weeds the like of what you'd breed, I'm thinking, out of Shaneen Keogh. (71)

Michael James, like the rest of Pegeen's fellow villagers, sees Christy's parricide as proof of his virility, assuming that Christy's purported strength and the "savagery" of his anger make him worthy to be numbered among the dead-and-gone local heroes—a specimen of manhood the like of which is now rarely seen. The fact that Christy wins the games and sports in Act III seems to support the villagers' assumption—violence and virility go hand in hand, and a lad "with the great savagery to destroy [his] da" (42) is exactly the kind of individual that a "spirited girl" like Pegeen should be selecting as her mate.

However, the use of the word "savagery" offers a different answer to the question Stephen Tifft poses, which is why "the notion of rising up in violent retribution against a tyrannical father" should "seem outrageous to nationalists who themselves paid lip-service, at least, to the Fenian revolutionaries of former days" (315). Tifft, like other modern commentators, suggests that Christy's rebellion is an allegory of nationalist struggle.[27] "H.S.D.," reviewing the play for the *Dublin Evening Mail*, suggests the same: "Perhaps, it is an allegory, and the parricide represents some kind of nation-killer" (2). He adds, however, that "if it is an allegory it is too obscure for me" (2). If "H.S.D." cannot appreciate the parallel between parricide and nation-killing, the context in which Synge constructed that allegory explains why.

The title of "H.S.D."'s review—"A Dramatic Freak"—reminds readers that in this climate, a parricide is seen not so much as an allegory for nationalist violence as the expression of some moral, mental, or biological defect—an atavistic "savagery" that healthy humans are supposed to have outgrown. Thus, if Michael James and Pegeen see Christy's supposed violent tendencies as proof of a healthy and laudable virility, they can also be read as indicative of insanity or hereditary degeneracy. These conflicting interpretations illustrate the double bind in which eugenist medicine puts any population that British medicine can classify as degenerate. On the one hand, it suggests that an enfeebled, effete race desperately needs an infusion of health and virility; on the other, it reads the violence that indicates virility as proof that this race is either trapped in primitivism, or prone to insanity and disease, or both. *Playboy* seems to be reading Christy's imaginary violence both as eugenic and dysgenic—something that produces Christy's physical prowess but is also linked to physical and mental disease.

Playboy connects violence and insanity through the character of Old Mahon, Christy's father. Christy's description of him stresses his irrational fits of anger, his drinking, and his violent outbursts: "And he after drinking for weeks, rising up in the red dawn, or before it maybe, and going out into the yard as naked as an ash-tree in the moon of May, and shying clods against the visage of the stars till he'd put the fear of death into the banbhs and the screeching sows" (25). Christy mentions that Mahon has been more than once been "locked in the asylums for battering peelers or assaulting men" (25), which suggests that the authorities read his violence as a symptom of mania. Mahon admits to having hallucinations and to having been studied as a psychiatric case once before: "There I was one time, screeching in a straightened waistcoat, with seven doctors writing out my sayings in a printed book" (62).

The kind of "savagery" Christy has presumably demonstrated—the kind that he may have inherited from his father—is associated here with mental illness rather than revolutionary fervor. The fact that insanity was not only seen as a marker of degeneracy but often attributed to a family history of syphilis makes the insult worse—Mahon and Christy can be read as evidence of moral decline as well as intellectual and physical deterioration in the Irish population. While later commentators are free to read Christy's story as an Oedipal allegory, for contemporary nationalists the equation of parricidal and revolutionary violence was an extremely dangerous and damaging one—and one that Synge seems to be insisting on in Act I. The great men of yore that Pegeen cites as evidence of her village's degeneracy are perpetrators of patriotic violence: Daneen Sullivan attacked a British policeman; Marcus Quin participated in agrarian violence.[28] When the men try to guess what Christy has done, they assume that if it is not theft or rape it must be political protest in one form or another: "Maybe the land was grabbed from him, and he did what any decent man would do." "Was it bailiffs? . . . Agents? . . . Landlords?" "Maybe he went fighting for the Boers, the like of the man beyond, was judged to be hanged, quartered, and drawn" (16–17). Once they learn the story, Christy's listeners decide that parricide qualifies him as a defender of Ireland and the home: "The peelers is fearing him, and if you'd that lad in the house there isn't one of them would come smelling around." "If I'd that lad in the house, I wouldn't be fearing the loosed kharki cut-throats." (19).

The assimilation of Christy's presumed parricide into the category of patriotic violence brings with it both the sexual connotations—his implied virility, potency, and eugenic fitness—and the implication of insanity or feeble-mindedness, casting these other acts in a clinical light. This comparison between parricide and revolutionary violence can only be threatening to nationalists. Either this equation suggests that nationalism and insanity are the same thing, or it suggests that, when *Cathleen*'s audiences applaud Michael's decision to take up arms for Ireland, they are applauding not his patriotic fervor but the physical prowess of which the play makes it a signifier—a strength and virility important not so much because it will lay Britain low but because it will reverse the trend toward deterioration on which Ireland is embarked. *Playboy* thus appears to literalize what is symbolic in *Cathleen* and suggests that the male patriot will rejuvenate Cathleen, not by shedding his blood on the battlefield, but by impregnating Irish women, begetting children whose genetic material will represent an improvement over the current degraded stock and who will achieve the physical health and moral purity that is an impossible goal for the citizens of Pegeen's village.

This eugenist reading, by turning the sacrificial narrative into a story about racial redemption through better breeding, implies that in Synge's Ireland degeneration is already far advanced—that the

Irish have already been polluted by "foreign-borne diseases" and that the Irish body is already etiolated and corrupt. Kenny makes the implication explicit in his peroration on the significance of Shawn's character:

> We see in [Shawn] how the Irish race die out in Ireland, filling the lunatic asylums more full from a declining population, and selecting for continuance in the future the human specimens most calculated to bring the race lower and lower. "Shaneen" shows us why Ireland dies while the races around us prosper faster and faster. (9)

To read Pegeen's attraction to Christy as laudable is to accept Kenny's assessment of her alternatives, the idiots and lunatics with which rural Ireland is now riddled. Pegeen's choice is offensive to Griffith for the same reason it strikes Kenny as natural and right: she recognizes the murderer as a "real live man" because his local, law-abiding, and God-fearing competition is so woefully unfit and unworthy.

The kind of sexual prudery Synge's critics exhibit is thus related to more troubling anxieties about the health of the Irish race—a connection made clearer by the fact that it is not until after Old Mahon makes his appearance that the audience begins to find Synge's treatment of female sexuality offensive enough to protest.[29] Like Pegeen and the villagers, Synge's audiences revolted when confronted with the evidence Christy's story of violence represses—the decrepit male body whose debility Christy's virility is supposed to erase.

In Act II Mahon—who has been presumed dead up to now by everyone including Christy—walks into Pegeen's tavern and shows Widow Quin "his head in a mass of bandages and plaster" (48). Padraic Colum's account of the first production cites that entrance as the real catalyst for the initial protest: "That scene was too representational. There stood a man with a horribly bloodied bandage upon his head" (qtd. in Berrow 76). Colum's suggestion that it was actually the body of the father—and more specifically, the fact that his wounds were represented realistically—that the audience could not stand to watch supports the contention that the outcry over Synge's alleged slander on Irish womanhood masks an unspoken resistance to the message *Playboy* sent about the state of Irish manhood.

Mahon, who is the primary link between violence and insanity and who now appears on stage wounded, bloody, and infirm, unsettles the audience because he is living proof of Irish vulnerability; his body has been suborned from within by drink and disease, and breached from without by Christy's attack. His is a body under siege—and worse, a body that has already lost the battle—the body that, in "P.M.E.K."'s reading, must be banished and replaced by Christy's in order to stop the progressive deterioration of the Irish race and return it to its former purity. As he does in *Shadow,* Synge drags this corpse out of the void into which it is supposed to disappear and flaunts before his audience what the sacrificial narrative is designed to hide—the decrepit, polluted body that Christy's violence should have destroyed.

What *Playboy*'s detractors are perhaps reacting to when they castigate Pegeen and the women of her village for loving a parricide, then, is not their sexual license itself but their complicity in this eugenist narrative—their recognition of Christy as their righteous partner, not in spite of, but *because* of, his supposed destruction of this corrupted Irish body and the shedding of this tainted Irish blood. And if the play is described as "calumny gone raving mad" (qtd. in Kiely 167), the choice of insanity as a metaphor is perhaps not coincidental: the problem with *Playboy* is that a cherished myth has been transformed into a doctor's prescription, a cure for the mental and physical weakness that afflicts these Irish peasants. Depicting the Irish race as already in decline and in need of genetic redemption makes the play, as its critics constantly charge, "insulting" in the extreme; but as Griffith and the antivaccinists believe, under a colonial regime this particular insult leads to injury.

The antivaccinist contributors to *Sinn Fein* believed that the presence or threat of disease and infection in a subject population was already being used as an excuse for invasive procedures; the threat of contagious disease becomes a justification for injecting "rottenness" into the Irish bloodstream. Similarly, congenital disease, as a marker of racial unfitness, could be used to justify not only the colonization but the extirpation of a particular population. Griffith's attack on *Playboy* shows how the insinuation of degeneracy translates into an argument for extinction:

> The author . . . declares in the programme that "the central incident of the Playboy"—that is the fighting of the women of the West for the hand of a parricide because he is a parricide—"was suggested by an actual occurrence in the West." This is a definite statement, and if the author can sustain it, we shall regret that so vile a race should be permitted to exist. ("Abbey Theatre" 2)

Poor racial hygiene is grounds for extermination. From the antivaccinist perspective, a play that suggests the Irish are a race in decline is a play that offers them up as a target for state-sponsored eugenicists. And even the *Times*'s Kenny, while heartily endorsing the eugenist tenets he believes the play illustrates, responds to the message with a peculiarly intense discomfort:

> [Synge] has led our vision through the Abbey street stage into the heart of Connacht, and revealed to us there truly terrible truths, of our own making, which we dare not face for the present. The merciless accuracy of his revelation is more than we can bear. Our eyes tremble at it. The words chosen are, like the things they express, direct and dreadful, by themselves intolerable to conventional taste. . . . It is as if we looked in a mirror for the first time, and found ourselves hideous. We fear to face the thing. We shrink at the word for it. We scream. (9)

In other words, Kenny admits, the play represents Ireland as the monster England has long held it to be. Kenny may accept Synge's play because he believes the portrait is accurate, but even he regards this representation of "Irish life" with visceral horror and disgust.

Synge's attack on the purity and thus the fitness of the Irish body—through his dramatization of both Dan Burke and Old Mahon, through his suggestion that Irish women may be unwilling or unable to close their ports, through his mockery of the sacrificial paradigm (in which the blood shed is not the pure blood of the hero-nationalist but the tainted blood of his decrepit father, and in which the desired effect is not the symbolic liberation of Ireland but the literal production of healthier children)—coincides both with public anxiety about vulnerability to disease and with the nationalist concern over boundaries and the bloodstream that emerges as one of its variants. It also coincides with real efforts on the part of England to manipulate the behavior and makeup of the Irish race. Moreover, if compulsory vaccination was not necessarily the deep-laid plot Hunter and O hUiathne thought it was, the increasing institutionalization of the insane, warehousing of the sick, and promotion of "racial hygiene" provided plenty of justification for the general apprehension of which the antivaccination campaign was an expression. And it is for this reason that Griffith, Kenny, and "P.M.E.K." are all doing the *same* reading of *Playboy* as a eugenic parable about the relative unfitness of the Irish that uses sacrificial violence to propose a possible course of treatment.

A Gallous Story: Playboy *and the Power of Lying*

But when we look at the reading Griffith, Kenny, and "P.M.E.K." outline, we can see some of the contradictions and elisions that mark eugenist doctrine in general and the *Playboy* controversy in particular. The most important, perhaps, is that Kenny and "P.M.E.K.," in proposing Christy as Pegeen's naturally selected husband, overlook two major problems. One is that Mahon's obvious defects would, according to the laws of heredity, have to be passed down to Christy, which would make him an unlikely solution to the problem of degeneration. The other is that Christy has not actually *done* the deed that proves his fitness and virility. What turns Christy from a "dribbling idiot" into a "likely man" (*CP* 61) is not parricide but a story *about* parricide. If *Playboy,* as I am hardly the first person to argue, is about the power of language over reality,[30] then instead of validating eugenic practice, *Playboy* is demonstrating the power of eugenist *discourse.*

After all, Old Mahon's insanity is created by context—by the authorities who lock him up or the doctors who straightjacket him and write down his sayings. The Widow Quin's plot to convince everyone that Old Mahon is mad is a more extended illustration of the power of diagnosis. What convinces Mahon to accept Quin's diagnosis is Christy's transformation:

> WIDOW QUIN: You seen that you're mad. *Cheering outside.* Do you hear them cheering him in the zigzags of the road? Aren't you after saying that your son's a fool, and how would they be cheering a true idiot born?
>
> MAHON *getting distressed:* It's maybe out of reason that that man's himself. *Cheering again.* There's none surely will go cheering him. Oh, I'm raving with a madness that would fright the world! *He sits down with his hand to his head.* Here was one time I seen ten scarlet divils letting on they'd cork my spirit in a gallon can; and one time I seen rats as big as badgers sucking the lifeblood from the butt of my lug; but I never till this day confused that dribbling idiot with a likely man. I'm destroyed surely. (61)

Mahon assumes that he is mad because he accepts Quin's implication that if his son is "a true idiot born" this kind of transformation would have to be impossible—according to eugenist medicine, a "dribbling idiot" dribbles because of congenital weaknesses, and nothing can reverse that genetic damage. Rather than challenge the basic premise of eugenist science—that heredity determines mental and physical fitness—Mahon, with Quin's help, explains away this contradictory evidence by diagnosing himself as insane.

One thing medical discourse apparently has the power to do, then, is to silence opposition by pathologizing it. As Christy's transformation suggests, another thing it has the power to do is alter the subject to fit the diagnosis. When Widow Quin finds Christy, she mentions that he looks "fitter to be saying [his] catechism than slaying [his] da" (27); but by the time he has told his story to the village girls, he becomes the hero they want him to be. By assuming that violence equals virility, the village girls create not only his athletic prowess but also the implied sexual prowess that Griffith sees as the basis for their attraction to him. By accepting "P.M.E.K."'s reading of Christy as a eugenic hero who will redeem the Irish race, first through violence and then through sex, the villagers work the magic that unsettles Mahon and turns Christy into the Playboy of the Western World.

The plot of *Playboy* thus points out a contradiction in eugenist theory that reveals it for the lie that it is. Christy becomes the incarnation of racial fitness and virility only through a process of construction that according to eugenics ought to be impossible. Similarly, Old Mahon provides evidence of Irish racial deterioration only because he has been manipulated by outside forces—Christy's descriptions of him, the "seven doctors" who restrain and study him, and finally the Widow Quin's duplicity. The congenital debility of which he is supposed to be the symbol is actually constructed and imposed on him in front of the viewing audience. All the evidence for the eugenist reading that Griffith, Kenny, and "P.M.E.K." are doing is created *by* the sacrificial paradigm that links violence with reproduction, a link that in Christy's case sets in motion a process of transformation through description that eugenics argues can never happen. What *Playboy* proves is that the power of eugenics is built on a lie—and that eugenist science is valuable to its believers *as* a lie, as a tool that creates the reality it pretends to describe.

Realizing the power of that lie appears to liberate Christy and Mahon from it, although Pegeen and the villagers remain in its grasp. As Christy discovers to his grief in Act III, the villagers' admiration for him bears little relationship to his actual deeds; when he attacks his father in an effort to make his lie true, the villagers merely reverse his diagnosis from fit to defective: "He's going mad! . . . Run from the idiot!" (74) For Christy, however, realizing the gap between the story and the deed teaches him that what matters is not physical reality but who has the power to describe it. Christy refuses to abandon the role of hero-martyr, claiming it through his language even as he is tied up and dragged out: "If I've to face the gallows, I'll have a gay march down, I tell you, and shed the blood of some of you before I die" (78) When Mahon reappears, Christy corrects his earlier mistake by using language to enact the transformation that violence could not accomplish: "Go on now and I'll see you from this day stewing my oatmeal and washing my spuds, for I'm master of all fights from now" (80). Mahon appears not only to understand what Christy is doing but to accept and appreciate it: "Glory be to God! I am crazy again" (80). By "crazy," he means that he has once again witnessed the supposedly impossible transformation of Christy from a dribbling idiot into a likely man; but this time he embraces this "madness" as preferable to the perspective of the "sane" villagers who refuse to believe that Christy could be the hero they made him.

One or Two Words Only: Authenticity and the Aran Islands

Playboy can thus easily be read as anti-imperialist—a critique demonstrating, among other things, the damaging effects of imperial discourse on the Irish subjects to which it is applied and suggesting the sacrificial paradigm as a liberating lie. Nevertheless, the contemporary evidence shows that the play was read by both supporters and detractors as complicit in that discourse, an attempt to transform the mythic trope of sacrificial redemption into a diagnosis of degeneration and depravity. *Playboy* became an attack on the purity of the Irish body, a manifestation of disease either in Synge's own mind and body or in the bodies of Irish peasant men and women; or, from the most critical nationalist viewpoint, a deliberate attempt to poison Irish culture the same way the medical establishment attempted to poison the Irish bloodstream. Why were both Griffith and "P.M.E.K." unable to see the story and the lie for what they were or to read the play as subverting the power of materialism with the power of language?

An anecdote that Yeats tells after the fact in "J. M. Synge and the Ireland of his Time" may help answer that question. Discussing the protests that broke out at the premiere, Yeats recounts Synge's response:

> As I stood there watching, knowing well that I saw the dissolution of a school of patriotism that held sway over my youth, Synge came and stood beside me, and said, 'A young doctor has just told me that he can hardly keep himself from jumping on to a seat, and pointing out in that howling mob those whom he is treating for venereal disease.' (*Essays and Introductions* 312)

His point is that the protestors are hypocritical because their own behavior proves that Irish men, at least, are having sex out of wedlock. But for evidence of that hypocrisy, Synge turns to imperial science—the "young doctor" whose medical knowledge has been shaped by eugenics and whose diagnosis brands these rioters as moral and physical degenerates. And as eugenist science used venereal disease to link poverty, dirt, disease, and sex and thus to keep subject populations subjected by constructing them as unfit, in every sense, for anything else, Yeats here uses the venereal disease anecdote to denigrate the "howling mob" and argue that the riots were neurotic (*EI* 312). Thus, in this passage we see Synge and Yeats turning to British medicine as an authority—and, implicitly, making the statement that imperial science *does* have the power to tell the truth about the Irish.

The howling mob, of course, could neither hear Synge's young doctor nor read Yeats's apologia. But Synge's appeal to medical authority had a far more blatant parallel in Yeats's decision to call in the police and the courts. Synge's gratitude toward the doctor who helps discredit *Playboy*'s critics is symptomatic of the Abbey coterie's acceptance of some forms of imperial authority—a pattern of which Synge's audiences would have been aware if they had read the program. The reporter from the *Evening Mail* who interviewed Synge after the riots asked him whether he intended the play as a realistic representation of Irish life, to which Synge said no, "rather emphatically" ("I Don't Care A Rap" 2). Synge's critics can perhaps be forgiven for reading this denial as disingenuous. The preface to the play, which was printed in the program and quoted by Griffith in his critique, makes a very different statement about the relationship between his play and the Irish people:

> On the stage one must have reality. . . . In a good play every speech should be as fully flavoured as a nut or apple, and such speeches cannot be written by any one who works among people who have shut their lips on poetry. In Ireland, for a few years more, we have a popular imagination that is fiery, and magnificent, and tender; so that those of us who wish to write start with a chance that is not given to writers in

> places where the springtime of the local life has been forgotten, and the harvest is a memory only, and the straw has been turned to bricks. (*CP* 4)

Despite an ambivalence about the permanence or materiality of "reality" that is evident in almost all of his plays, Synge claims to have represented "reality" on stage; and more than that, he claims to have done it by capturing the "popular imagination" of Ireland. Since he identifies this reality so closely with the "fully flavoured" speech he is invested in reproducing, he substantiates his claim with his anthropological work:

> In writing "The Playboy of the Western World," as in my other plays, I have used one or two words only that I have not heard among the country people of Ireland, or spoken in my own nursery before I could read the newspapers. A certain number of the phrases I employ I have heard also from herds and fishermen along the coast from Kerry to Mayo or from beggar-women and ballad-singers near Dublin; and I am glad to acknowledge how much I owe to the folk-imagination of these fine people. (*CP* 3)

Anticipating, perhaps, the complaints of his audience, he justifies the plot the same way: "Anyone who has lived in real intimacy with the Irish peasantry will know that the wildest sayings and ideas in this play are tame indeed, compared with the fancies one may hear in any little hillside cabin in Geesala, or Carraroe, or Dingle Bay" (3).

Synge, by numbering himself among "those of us who know the people," constructs himself as an authority—staking his own claim for the right and power of telling the truth, of constructing the Irish subject, of representing the Irish not only to the rest of the world but to themselves. Though his purpose is clearly not simply mimetic, Synge does ground his entire philosophy of drama, as expressed in this preface, in the idea that, because he has lived with the Aran Islanders and learned their language, he now has access to a "reality" that is denied to others. He is as guilty as Griffith ever was of locating "Irishness" within a circumscribed, "pure" space, defined geographically for Synge rather than by the walls of the home, but just as embattled and just as sacred. And as *The Aran Islands* demonstrates, for all his "morbid" sensibilities, he is just as interested in finding in the heartland the purity that has disappeared from the outlying world.

Although his book documents the influence of the mainland and of Europe on Aran Islands culture, there is one last place in which

Synge finds unsullied and unadulterated Irishness: the body. Not only is he struck by the "strange beauty of the women" of the islands, but he observes, with an eye trained by eugenics, the health and vigor of the men:

> The absence of the heavy boot of Europe has preserved to these people the agile walk of the wild animal, while the general simplicity of their lives has given them many other points of physical perfection. Their way of life has never been acted on by anything much more artificial than the nests and burrows of the creatures that live round them, and they seem, in a certain sense, to approach more nearly to the finer types of our aristocracies—who are bred artificially to a natural ideal—than to the labourer or the citizen, as the wild horse resembles the thoroughbred rather than the hack or cart-horse. Tribes of the same natural development are, perhaps, frequent in half-civilized countries, but here a touch of the refinement of old societies is blended, with singular effect, among the qualities of the wild animal. (*Aran Islands* 48)

Here, then, are the Irish bodies that W. E. Fay, Griffith, O hUiathne, and A. S. Hunter are looking for—the healthy, unconstrained, uninfected, unpolluted bodies that the urban readers of the *Dublin Evening Mail* can never hope to maintain. But Synge defines this health in terms of the class system supported by eugenics—identifying fitness with "aristocracies" and unfitness with "the labourer." The gift of "physical perfection" comes at the price of language that assimilates the Aran Islander to "wild animal[s]," that identifies civilization with degeneration but equates the "natural ideal" with primitivism, that bestows health and virility with one hand and takes it away with the other.

The dangers of this approach become clearer when Synge tells the story that gave him the idea for *Playboy*. Although Synge refers to Lynchehaun in interviews, he also mentions a story from *The Aran Islands* that is much closer to *Playboy*'s plot. Indeed, the fact that Synge's protestors identified James Lynchehaun as the source for Christy is another illustration of the unarticulated connections they were making between violence, sexual misconduct, and insanity. Lynchehaun was concealed from the police by village girls after committing a crime, but his crime was not murder—he attacked a woman that he was reported to be sexually obsessed with, biting and maiming her. The bizarre details of his assault were familiar to readers of the Irish press, as was the story of his concealment and escape.

In Lynchehaun, violence is connected to both sexual incontinence and mental instability; and the protestors' insistence that Christy was Lynchehaun's equivalent indicates that they saw Christy's violence the same way.

The *Aran Islands* story, on the other hand, is the stuff of which nationalist legends might be made: a man who kills his father in a fit of anger flees to a neighboring town. He is hidden from the state authorities, who attempt to bribe a community that nonetheless proves "incorruptible" (96). But this story of Irish resistance to British authority becomes, in *The Aran Islands,* proof of the primitive, "tribal" nature of these islanders:

> This impulse to protect the criminal is universal in the west. It seems partly due to the association between justice and the hated English jurisdiction, but more directly to the primitive feeling of these people, who are never criminals yet always capable of crime, that a man will not do wrong unless he is under the influence of a passion which is as irresponsible as a storm on the sea. (96–97)

In other words, what looks like nationalism is "primitive feeling." For these people, violence can never be rational or strategic, but only the result of an "irresponsible" and ungovernable passion.

However hysterical the anti-*Playboy* voices became, then, it would seem that they were right about one thing: Synge's project is, in a sense, reductive. Translating "the association between justice and the hated English jurisdiction" into a putative "primitive feeling," Synge subordinates history and politics to a universalizing, essentialist vision of Irish culture; and instead of an act of resistance to British authority, the acceptance and concealment of a parricide becomes the expression of tribal feeling, a primal recognition of the irresistible strength of passion. Synge uses the language and paradigms of imperial science to accomplish this reduction—or, as Griffith would call it, dissection.

At the same time, *Playboy* is much more complex than Griffith or "P.M.E.K." realizes, or than Synge's own preface gives it credit for being. What disappears from the nationalist critique is the statement *Playboy* makes about the constructive, constitutive power of discourse—the relationship between what is perceived as "reality" and the language that is used to represent it. In the birth of *Playboy* from this story of impulsive violence and "incorruptible" community loyalty, we see the struggle in Synge's own mind between his desire to retain his idealizing view of the Aran Islanders and his awareness of the discourse of disease and degeneracy that was already fastening onto the Irish body.

Although modern commentators now agree that Synge suffered from Hodgkin's disease, during Synge's life and for many decades after his death his chronic ill health was attributed to tuberculosis, one of the contagious diseases that the *Dublin Evening Mail* warned its readers against. In either case, his undiagnosed "Glandular Swellings" would have made him part of the target audience for Clarke's Blood Mixture, Veno's Seaweed Tonic, and more reputable if not necessarily more helpful forms of medical intervention. As a man forever denied the health with which virility had become synonymous and accused of both representing and fomenting the decline of the Irish body, Synge experienced the power of medical science at the most intimate level. Between 1897 and his death in 1909, he was operated on several times for the removal of swollen glands; but although later Gogarty claimed to have diagnosed Synge's Hodgkin's disease just from looking at him when they met on a train in 1907, he also opined that Synge probably never knew what he was really dying of because "it was not a general practice at that time for a physician to tell a patient that he was not going to recover" (Greene and Stephens 17). While accepting its validity, Synge was perhaps aware of the limitations of medical science—not only of its inability to diagnose or cure his disease but also of its power to alter his own identity and others' perceptions of him and his work.

Given that many of Synge's later critics explain his "morbidity" in terms of his illness, it is hard not to read the ad hominem attacks made on Synge by his contemporaries—the accusations of degeneracy, morbidity, unhealthiness—as having some reference to his physical condition, which was deteriorating during the production of *Playboy*.[31] In Christy—the quiet, slight, delicate, physically weak hero who constructs out of words alone the virility and health that biology has apparently denied him—Synge both accepts and resists eugenist conceptions of disease and the body. He accepts, perhaps, the diagnosis but not the prognosis; the presence of disease but not its inevitable outcome. If biological purity remains an already lost cause, there is still the chance of redemption through reconstruction—not through the shedding of blood but through the telling of lies. Disease may have breached the borders and invaded the Irish body, but as long as Christy's command of language makes him "master of all fights," imperial science will not have the last word.

3

Excess of Love: Padraig Pearse and the Erotics of Sacrifice

ON EASTER MONDAY OF 1916, AN ARMED FORCE LED BY PADRAIG Pearse and James Connolly, made up of members of the republican Irish Volunteers and the socialist Irish Citizen Army, seized and occupied a number of positions in Dublin, proclaimed the establishment of an independent Irish republic, and held out against the British Army until their formal surrender a week later.[1] While the Easter Rising was not a military success—before the attack began it had already been sabotaged by the arrest of Roger Casement and organizational confusion—and did not initially have much popular support, public perception of the Rising and its leaders changed dramatically once the British Army executed Pearse, Connolly, and fourteen other men who had been involved in the rebellion.[2]

Following the public outcry over the executions, the Sinn Fein party fielded candidates in the 1917 parliamentary election who promised that if elected they would not take their seats in Westminster but would rather stay in Dublin and set up their own independent Irish parliament. When the election was over, Sinn Fein had gained a majority of the Irish seats. The Sinn Fein delegates set up their own government in Dublin, called the Dáil Éireann, and began trying to establish it as the legitimate government of Ireland. England, naturally, attempted to shut the Dáil down; and this led to a three-year guerilla war that finally ended with a truce in the winter of 1921. At a peace conference in England, a treaty was signed providing for the division of Ireland into two entities: the Irish Free State, which would be politically autonomous although still part of the Commonwealth; and Northern Ireland, which would remain under English administration. In 1922 the treaty was ratified by a majority in the Dáil. Immediately thereafter, a civil war broke out between those who saw partition as an acceptable outcome and accepted the legitimacy of the Free State government, and those who saw the treaty as a betrayal and the Free State as a poor substitute for the independent and unified Irish republic for which they had fought. The civil war ended with a cease fire in 1923, but republican opposition to partition did not.

The significance of the Rising in Irish history has long been a matter of dispute among historians, who debate the claim that it was the execution of Pearse and the Rising's other leaders that catalyzed this chain of events.[3] But Pearse's importance was undisputed by the soldiers who fought for Irish independence from 1918 to 1921. *An t-Oglach,* the official newspaper of the Irish Volunteer Army who carried on the war for independence, evokes Padraig Pearse and the other martyrs of 1916 at least once in every lead article. After the Irish civil war began, both the Free Staters who accepted the treaty and the republicans who rejected it based their claims to legitimacy on the proclamation that Pearse read from the balcony of the Post Office in 1916. It was certainly the conviction of the protesters who demonstrated against *The Plough and the Stars* ten years later that in making Easter 1916 the subject of satire and critique, O'Casey was striking at the foundation of Irish patriotism.

While, as in the *Playboy* controversy, anti-*Plough* arguments quickly coalesced around an apparently trivial violation of sexual decorum (in this case, O'Casey's inclusion of Rosie Redmond, a prostitute who plies her trade in the bar where Act II takes place), the protest was spearheaded, not by Griffith, but by the more persuasive and insightful Hannah Sheehy-Skeffington, a socialist and feminist who was careful to make it clear that she was protesting not O'Casey's immorality but the "derision and obloquy" (*Letters of Sean O'Casey* 168) to which he subjected the Rising and its participants.[4] At the same time, Sheehy-Skeffington detected, and O'Casey tacitly acknowledged, a connection between O'Casey's use of Rosie and his treatment of Pearse that is more important and more complicated than most interpretations of the play acknowledge. By juxtaposing Rosie's sales pitch with Pearse's oratory, O'Casey was not simply repeating the age-old comparison between politicians and whores; he was identifying the omissions and elisions that he believed characterized Pearse's strain of rhetoric and rendered it counterproductive—or, as *Plough* finally suggests, irresponsible and murderous.

Before we can fully understand O'Casey's critique—or, indeed, the uses to which Pearsian rhetoric is later put both in the arena of political protest and on the stage—we must arrive at a more sophisticated understanding of Pearse's version of sacrificial nationalism than the one that seems to prevail. Contemporary commentators are prone to summarizing Pearse's message by quoting one phrase from "The Coming Revolution": "Bloodshed is a cleansing and a sanctifying thing" (*PWS* 99). Removed from its context, this formula supports the arguments that then tend to follow, which interpret the focus on sacrifice and martyrdom in contemporary republican politics and propaganda as a more or less uncritical acceptance of Catholic symbolism and dogma: revolutionaries sanctify their dead brethren because they are already used to worshipping a male martyr, and this automatic reverence leads to a tragic repetition of the cycle of death and reprisal. The power of the sacrificial narrative springs from the power of the Catholic Church over the hearts and minds of its parishioners; and republican adherence to it both demonstrates and reinforces the essentially romantic, irrational, and sectarian premises of the movement.[5]

But although Pearse's use of sacrificial rhetoric in his speeches is indebted to Catholic symbolism and iconography, it is also influenced by a host of other factors that become invisible when his writing is lifted out of its original context. Restoring that context helps illustrate the conditions that created the Pearsian version of the sacrificial paradigm. Seen in its original environment, sacrificial nationalism is not an unmediated reflection of sectarian beliefs or a romantic flower of the morbid Celtic imagination.[6] It is a rhetorical strategy that developed in response to imperialist attempts to contain and neutralize physical-force resistance in Ireland. Pearse's rhetoric, and his death, became central to republican tradition because they offered a solution to an intractable problem—a solution that, although it certainly had its limitations, worked well enough to spark and sustain the three-year process of armed resistance and civil disobedience that eventually created the Irish Free State.

Pearse's plays and speeches preside over a crucial transformation of the sacrificial paradigm; it is in them that the focus shifts from the sufferings of Bridget and Cathleen to the passion of Michael as the male martyr becomes more central than the female figure for whom he sacrifices his life. This masculinization of sacrifice does involve a move from the pagan/Celtic version promulgated by Yeats—in which the trope of regeneration is paramount—to the Christian one, in which the martyr's blood is valuable primarily because it sanctifies the cause for which he dies and purifies the men who will take it up after him. Pearse's use of Catholic imagery has thus led commentators to explain the power of his rhetoric in religious and sectarian terms—an explanation that shapes not only contemporary perceptions of Pearse but also contemporary treatments of violence in Northern Ireland, for which Pearse's "unqualified glorification of blood-shedding" (Shaw 125) for the sake of the Irish Republic is often held responsible.[7] But it is also a logical development of trends we have seen at work in the *Playboy* riots—growing anxiety about the health of the Irish race, which is increasingly attached to the body of the Irish man—and an effect of the rise of the physical-force movement and its celebration of "Irish manhood." Both trends developed in response to what was, if not exactly a new problem, one that could now no longer be ignored: the threat of partition posed by the militant Unionist movement.

In republican publications like *Irish Freedom* and, later, the *Irish Volunteer*, contributors frequently defend their advocacy of physical force by pointing to the activities of militant Unionists and justify arming in terms of preserving the integrity of the Irish nation against this assault.[8] The Irish Volunteers, an Irish militia formed in September of 1913, were organized largely in response to the formation of the Ulster Volunteer Force, a militant Unionist organization dedicated to opposing Home Rule through violent rebellion. From its inception, the Irish Volunteers had as their goal the prevention of partition and the frustration of militant Unionism—a concern reflected in the first issues of the Volunteers' newspaper, which went to great lengths to present the Volunteers as a movement that would include Irishmen of all creeds, counties, and political affiliations.[9] If the threat posed by militant Unionism rendered physical force a more acceptable option for Irish nationalists and republicans, however, debate over the morality or practicality of physical-force rebellion also produced more internal division. Volunteer leadership was marked by tension between constitutionalists and physical-force advocates, and the organization finally split along that line in September 1914, when John Redmond declared his support for Britain as it entered World War I.[10] The constitutionalist faction then reorganized under Redmond as the National Volunteers, while the smaller physical-force faction remained the Irish Volunteers.

It is in hopes of resolving these two linked problems—how to preserve Ireland's integrity as a nation, and how to persuade moderate nationalists to embrace physical force—that the rhetoric of sacrifice is refined into the form associated with Padraig Pearse; and it is because these problems were so intractable that cleansing and sanctifying became such important functions. Pearse is being asked to do a job that centuries of British imperialist rhetoric have made difficult—to argue that violent resistance to British rule is not only necessary but righteous. The association between Irish violence and Irish criminality or pathology was, even before Pearse's time, tightened by British medical discourse to the point where an Irish republican arguing for the use of force as just or practical faced an insurmountable burden of proof. The sacrificial strain that came to dominate republican rhetoric of the time developed as a way out of this discursive bind. Its effectiveness was derived from, and limited by, its appeal to essentialist beliefs about gender and sexuality—in particular the construct of "virility," in which the concept of "health," as defined by medical discourse, becomes part of the Volunteer version of the ideal Irishman. But while in the hands of other rhetoricians this Irishman remained an ideal, abstract concept, in Pearse's work it took on flesh and blood and became real—almost.

Pearse's ability to keep the patriot's body almost real is what separates him from his equally sacrificially minded contemporaries and what has kept his rhetoric powerful even after his death. Of course, that death—the fact that he became the sacrificial hero he had exalted to his listeners—is part of his legacy. He is significant, not merely for showing his contemporaries how to use the martyr figure, but for providing them with a new martyr. We should not, however, allow the power of that narrative to obscure the fact that Pearse was only one of a number of republicans using sacrificial rhetoric to argue for physical-force rebellion, or the fact that the Easter 1916 Rising was not his handiwork alone. The shape that much of the scholarship on Pearse and the Rising has taken is a clear demonstration of the limitations of the rhetorical solution that Pearse developed—of what gets lost when the martyr is made central enough to eclipse the cause and when the radiance of the patriot's transfigured body obscures the material conditions that gave rise to the battle in which he fell. And it is this loss that O'Casey, whose loyalties are with the socialist James Connolly and the Irish Citizen Army rather than with Pearse and the Volunteers, will eventually try to restore in his treatments of Irish political violence a decade later.

Womanish Weakness and Prostrate Men: Masculinity and the Irish Volunteers

O'Casey's portrayal of Pearse in *The Plough and the Stars* is the final chapter in a history of antagonism between them that dates back to the transportation workers' strike of 1913 (Edwards 182). While Pearse was helping to organize the Irish Volunteers, O'Casey helped James Connolly revive the Irish Citizen Army, a militant socialist group that saw the Volunteers as "unsympathetic to the class struggle" (Edwards 207). Ruth Dudley Edwards credits O'Casey with single-handedly maintaining hostilities between the two organizations through his attacks in the *Irish Worker* (207). Certainly O'Casey's distrust of republican rhetoric was clearly and forcefully expressed in numerous articles, but it was to some extent shared by his comrades. In defense of his treatment of "Peace and the Gael" in *Plough,* O'Casey cited James Connolly's reaction to the same piece: "No, we do not think that the old heart of the earth needs to be warmed with the red wine of millions of lives. We think anyone who does is a blithering idiot. We are sick of such teaching" (qtd. in Edwards 245).

Connolly and O'Casey would have had plenty of time to grow sickened by this strain of republican discourse because Pearse was not the first to use it. In fact, the portion of "Peace and the Gael" that O'Casey inserts into Act II of *Plough* is strikingly reminiscent of the conclusion of "Not Peace but a Sword," a piece printed in *Irish Freedom* in September of 1911:

> Give us war, say we. War in our time, O Lord. Send the lightning of thy thunderbolts through the tyrant nations of Europe; let them rend and tear each other; to the end that the crucified nations shall have freedom and nobility at the last; and that the earth may purge itself from its sins in good red blood. ("Lucan" 5)[11]

Out of context, both this passage and "Peace and the Gael" are horrifying. This glorification of bloodshed for its own sake looks even more rabid to a modern audience than it would have to a public that had not yet watched the Great War fail to purge, cleanse, or warm the heart of anything whatsoever. But it is precisely because his more memorable lines are so frequently taken out of context that Pearse enjoys his reputation for gratuitous bloodthirstiness. The violence of this and much other republican rhetoric looks extreme and disproportionate when it is dissociated from the violence to which it responds—not only the increasingly violent strains of Unionist rhetoric and a pan-European advocacy of militarism coinciding with the buildup toward the Great War, but the more insidious violence inherent in imperialism.

In abstract and absolute terms, it is difficult to make the argument that war is better than peace; but as we have seen, for Ireland the Pax

Britannica translated into an assault on the Irish population—via famine, disease, eviction, and emigration—that is arguably as blatant and as damaging as more overt forms of warfare. "Lucan"'s "Not Peace but a Sword" takes that position, asserting that under imperial rule "peace" simply means that imperial powers have broader license to inflict their violence on the rest of the world:

> These and other vultures and tyrants, they want peace now; peace to rearrange at their option the map of Europe and Africa, to arrange concessions here, spheres of influence there, ports yonder; peace to crush down the smaller nations forever. Who calls for peace? Not Ireland, not Egypt, not India, not Poland, not any nation which is oppressed or capable of being oppressed by a more powerful neighbor. (5)

Making imperialist violence visible has always been a difficult business. By 1911 Britain had so successfully captured the discourse of rationality and enlightenment that logical argument alone could not persuade skeptics that the Empire was waging war on its colonial possessions.[12] "Types of Irishmen—The Imperialist," part of a series that ran at the same time in *Irish Freedom,* laments the fact that the Irish have fallen for Britain's paternalistic rhetoric and refuse to recognize the violence underpinning the Empire's "civilising" mission (Brennan 2). As "Lucan" realizes, once that violence recedes from view, his position becomes difficult because he is asking his readers to give up a status quo that involves a certain amount of prosperity and security in order to wage a dangerous battle for political freedom that may not translate directly into material benefits.

"Lucan" is thus forced to use other arguments to support his position, and it is here that we see the beginning of the trend that will ultimately produce Padraig Pearse. If "Lucan"'s audience cannot be persuaded via political arguments, perhaps it will respond when the problem is cast in more personal terms:

> Ireland has been maimed in war many a time, but it is in peace that she has been crucified. Peace has meant stagnation and degeneration and slavishness; war has meant activity and effort and achievement, courage and manhood. In war Irishmen have been shot and hanged and tortured, and her women have been starved and outraged; but in peace, for a century now, her men have been rotted mentally and physically, and sent out on the world to be hewers of wood and drawers of water, while strangers fattened in their places, and her women have been sent in thousands to walk the streets in the big cities of England and America. (5)

The way to make imperial violence visible, it seems, is to dramatize its effect on the Irish character—and in particular, to represent it as a threat to Irish masculinity. Peace reduces the colonial subject to "degeneration and slavishness," an unnatural condition he can throw off by claiming his "courage and manhood" through violent resistance ("Lucan" 5). "Peace" is a problem because it attacks the health and virility of the Irish male; it "rots" him both "mentally and physically" ("Lucan" 5). The fears about infection and degeneration that we have examined in reference to *Playboy* are brought back as an argument for breaking up the Empire by whatever means necessary. Home Rule is unacceptable and complete severance necessary because to remain part of the British Empire under any terms is to allow British degeneracy to infect the healthy Irish nation:

> England is an unclean nation. She is one of the most diseased nations in the world—socially, physically, and mentally. It is to this leper among the nations that our country is wed. . . . It is the clean strong good part of Ireland goes out of Ireland to mix with the scraps and parings of England in the British colonies. (Brennan 2)

Thus, "Lucan" ends his argument with an appeal to the reader's sense of himself not only as Irish, but as a man: "What of the living death of a poisonous and corrupting peace, when men grow timorous, and slavish, and materialistic, so that they do mean things, live meanly, and generally cumber the earth, men who might have died like men instead of living like hogs?" (5). In this piece we begin to see the transformation that will turn "Lucan"'s anti-imperialist declaration that "so long as one inch of territory is occupied by force . . . there ought not to be peace" (5) into Pearse's cry at the end of O'Donovan Rossa's graveside oration that "while Ireland holds these graves, Ireland unfree can never be at peace" (*PWS* 137).

The shift from exposing the violence of imperial "peace" to glorifying the sacrifices of the individual men who have fought to end it is accomplished through a number of intermediate steps, the most significant being the development of the complicated construct of Volunteer masculinity. The columns of the *Irish Volunteer*—the official newspaper of the Irish Volunteers, and the rhetorical heir to *Irish Freedom*—offer an illustration of how this transformation was accomplished and an explanation of why the male martyr became such an important symbol in republican rhetoric. The *Volunteer*'s obsession with virility is visible on the first page of each issue. Until its revamping in

Figure 2.
Front-page graphic of *The Irish Volunteer.* Detail.

1915, the front page of the *Irish Volunteer* always featured the same male figure.[13] Like most of the ballads printed in the *Volunteer*'s columns, this graphic is a paean to the Irish soldier, whose strength, courage, and single-minded dedication are the subject of tribute after tribute.

This ideal Volunteer is young, clean-shaven, broad-shouldered, and apparently pausing at the top of a rocky peak on which he is planting a flag (Fig. 2). At first glance he appears to be wearing only boots, breeches, and a bandoleer. Upon close inspection the outline of a breast pocket is visible on his well-defined left pectoral (the button on the pocket discreetly covers the nipple), but this is the only indication that he might be wearing a shirt. His breeches conform so closely to his thighs as to be well-nigh invisible except for the details of belt line and button fly. Next to one foot is the end of the flagpole he carries in his upraised right hand; next to the other foot, planted on the ledge below, is a crown of laurels and the butt of a rifle that extends diagonally upward through the space between his legs. His face is turned away from the flag to gaze dreamily into the distance as his dark hair waves in the breeze; his free hand grasps the barrel of the rifle at the level of his crotch.

The Freudian implications of the iconography are obvious. The rifle is already loaded with phallic significance; the fact that it juts out between the soldier's legs while his hand cradles it gently between his thighs is further evidence that in this case the cigar is not just a cigar. His body is turned so that his broad chest is displayed for the viewer, and his skin-tight clothing shows off his well-defined muscles. An image of sexual potency, he is at the same time the object of sexual desire, a man the male readership of the newspaper can narcissistically identify with while desiring.

But the same details that support this psychosexual reading can also be explained in terms of the political situation in which the editors of the *Irish Volunteer* found themselves. The rifle, for instance, is there to indicate that the Volunteers are a militia, not a political party; and it is also a defiant response to the arms embargo that Britain imposed on Ireland after the Volunteers began to organize. Similarly, the fact that the soldier's clothing is practically invisible could be the artist's attempt to avoid the vexed question of what the Volunteer uniform should look like—one that was not settled for some time as a result of conflict between those who saw the Volunteers' function as primarily symbolic and those who saw them as an actual army preparing for real war. His robust frame dramatizes the distinction Brennan draws between the clean and strong Irish and the degenerate and sick English, and his Greek-god good looks are a response to the caricatures of Irish men as hulking, misshapen simians that had become familiar sights in the pages of *Punch.*

To insist on the first reading as the only significant one would be to deny the history of occupation and resistance that appears in the second. But to refuse to read the sexuality invested in that figure is to leave a crucial element out of that history. Just as gender and sexuality cannot be considered independently of the historical and material forces that have constructed them, the history of Irish political struggle cannot be read without also reading the history of Irish sexuality. In fact, what the pages of the *Volunteer* show time and again is that republican rhetoric uses these two registers of meaning simultaneously, invoking one to reinforce the other. What this image says is that for the Volunteer, a rifle is as much a part of his self-image, identity, and gender as his genitals; he would no more think of giving it up than he would consider a future as a eunuch. Thus, the sexualization of the Volunteer and his rifle is not the unconscious expression of a libidinal impulse so much as a rhetorical strategy—a way of arguing that Irish patriotism is a beautiful thing and that it is natural for Irish men to be armed.

This image, then, does the same thing that the constant allusions to "Ireland's manhood" in the articles do: it uses supposedly universal conceptions of gender and sexuality to naturalize nationalist feeling in general and the willingness to bear arms in particular. By incorporating its definition of patriotism into its definition of masculinity, the *Irish Volunteer* seeks to make republicanism as essential as gender was thought to be—an integral part of every Irishman's human nature. To balk at taking up arms in defense of Ireland or to deny feeling nationalist sympathies is to fly in the face of good health. Nationalism becomes as much a part of the Irishman's organism as "an appetite for food" (Kittson 13), and militarism becomes indissociable from maleness.

The message that a man who will not consider taking up arms for Ireland is "less than a man" (Newman, "How National Degenerates Are Made" 9) is hammered home in every genre the *Irish Volunteer* published. The weekly "From the Outpost" column reminds recruits that "every man who has a spark of the Volunteer spirit loves a rifle" and that any reluctance to use one is simply a vestigial remnant of the "mean and womanish" spirit that Britain has deliberately fostered among Irish men in order to keep them docile (7 February 1914:1,

14 February 1914: 1).[14] As a way of fleshing out this equation between masculinity and patriotism, the Volunteer's duty to his cause (and his rifle) is described in terms of typical masculine roles and relationships. In "To the Trenches: The Mother Calls" we learn that to volunteer is to be a good son: "Is there a man amongst you who would not . . . shed the best blood in his veins to alleviate the sufferings of that dear mother—that dark-haired Rosaleen—so gentle and so enduring?" (Judge 13). Volunteering is a form of courtship; recruits are urged to "Come to your drills as if you were going to see your best girl—Clean shaven and with a hair-cut."[15] A good father must be a good patriot: "a man having in himself the power to found a family must also have in himself the power to defend a family" (Plunkett 4). Once armed, the Volunteer assumes his proper relationship as a man to the women around him, and "Sweetheart, sister, wife'll / Put on [his] trusty bandolier / To feed [his] trusty rifle!" (O hEaluigh 11).

This attempt to essentialize Volunteer nationalism is part of a larger effort to prove that the Volunteers are a representative movement. The body politic metaphor we have seen in British eugenist discourse is used in E. Creagh Kittson's "The Citizen and the State" to equate the Volunteers as an organization with the Irish people whose army they want to be:

> Soldiers and sailors will come out of the nation, and if the standard of manhood in the nation is low, the manhood of its fighters will be low, and when they go to fight they will be beaten. And the stability of the state depends . . . on the intelligence of the people, on the standards of honour and courage and diligence that prevail amongst them—all of which are elements of strength; for, an industrious nation will fortify itself by the honest acquisition of wealth . . . and a nation that cherishes high standards of honour will be free from the danger of its sons being corrupted by the enemy. (13)

Masculinity links "the safety of the state" with its "morally, intellectually, and physically fit" citizens, and keeps the Volunteers tied to the Irish people (13). By focusing on the "man" in the Irishman, Volunteer discourse also attempts to subordinate sectarian or political divisions to the putatively universal category of gender: "Nothing more absurd could be imagined than for one of these sets of invaders to try to arrogate to themselves the title of Irishmen and deny it to the others" (13).

The hope cherished by the *Irish Volunteer*'s editorialists and balladeers is that once they realize their common bond as men, the citizens of all thirty-two counties will awake to the realization that they are Irish and that therefore their natural place is in the ranks of the Volunteers. Essentializing the rifle as part of this "natural" Irish male identity allows republicans to turn Unionist militarism from a threat to national integrity into the hope of eventual reconciliation, as Landen argues in *Irish Freedom:*

> Even so, a hundred and thirty years ago, did they arm and organise to preserve Ireland in the British Empire . . . and behold arms turned them into men, and made them realise that they were Irishmen, and that the country which bred them, and supported them, and to which they owed allegiance, was Ireland, and not England or the British Empire. . . . Arm, then, Unionists of Ireland, and keep your powder dry! (5)

The power of essentialism helps explain the curious phenomenon of Irish republicans cheering on the efforts of a militant group dedicated to frustrating the republican agenda. Just as the connection between the rifle and masculinity allows republicans to justify their own use of force, it allows them to neutralize the threat of partition by incorporating Irish Unionists into their community of Irish men.

In their attempt to unite all Irishmen in allegiance to this archetypal vision of Irish masculinity, the *Volunteer*'s contributors strive to identify the ideal Volunteer *as* Ireland. The gesture visible in that iconic male figure on the front page is elaborated in Eamonn Ceannt's "The Volunteer Giant," which personifies the Volunteers as a baby, appropriately delivered in the Rotunda (the site of the Volunteers' first recruitment meeting), who will be nursed into manhood by its caretakers. This allows Ceannt to depict the growth of the movement as a natural and inevitable process—a process that produces not only freedom but also unity, as represented by the baby's growth into a toddler:

> Today, he sleeps. To-morrow he wakes up, a limb in Cork, a limb in Galway, one in Enniscorthy and another in Gorey. Now that he has begun to notice, what do you think but he's setting his eyes on Athlone and Sligo and Limerick and Strabane, and I declare he'll soon toddle from end to end of Ireland. (3)

By identifying Ireland with this allegorical baby, Ceannt renders it organic and indivisible—the North can no more split off from the rest of the country than one of the baby's arms could secede from his torso. And while at this stage the Volunteer Baby is still dependent and helpless, once he reaches manhood he will be able to liberate himself without having to be rescued by someone else.

Meanwhile, in the ballads that support the editorial arguments, we see the Cathleen paradigm—in which Ireland is a woman wrongfully possessed by a "stranger" who is routed when she mates with her true sexual partner—supplemented with a variation in which the sexual energy is aggressive rather than regenerative and is directed at the British invader. Developing the analogy between volunteering and masculinity, these ballads draw on sexual imagery to support the identification between the Irishman's masculinity and his rifle.[16] Seamus O hEaluigh's "Ode to a Rifle," for instance, describes the Volunteer's physical arousal as he handles his weapon: [17]

A rifle! at that very word
My blood boils up anew;
And every vein within me's stirred
As I the barrel view.

As I firmly grasp the polished stock
I swear that those who trifle
With freedom's barque as she nobly comes
Will feel the power of my rifle. (11)

"The Recruiting Sergeant" also treats the rifle like part of the recruit's body and advises him to use it to intimidate lesser and weaker men: when approached by a British Army recruiter, the Volunteer should "whip [his] rifle out / And send him scurrying home to England" (2). In "A Song for the Irish Militia" the power of the "soldier's sword" is contrasted with the prone posture of the "prostrate men" who are unable to rise from their submissive position until their more upright comrades have "sow[n] the seed" of patriotism in them (7).

Describing the relationship between British conqueror and Irish victim in terms of sexual dominance remains a powerful emotive tactic; but for a militant movement, the heterosexual version of the allegory has serious limitations. As long as Ireland is personified by a distressed maiden in the clutches of a male enemy, she must wait for a rescuer to intervene; she can never turn on her captor and become the aggressor. Casting both parties as male creates the possibility that the "prostrate men" will eventually rise and dominate their erstwhile masters—once they assert their masculinity by whipping out their rifles. It also capitalizes on the homophobic shame with which the hypothetical reader regards the sexually passive partner in any such exchange, urging him to move from the ranks of the "prostrate" and "slavish" men who accept colonial dominance into the company of those who can put the "soldier's sword" to its proper use.

While the ballads reinforce it on the symbolic level, the argument that antimilitarism means a loss of masculinity and a perversion of the Irishman's "true" sexual identity (in Kittson's words, that "a man is not fully a man until he holds the power of life and death" [13]) is developed in more detail in the signed articles, in which writers connect the fact that up till now "Irish manhood has forsaken the sword in favor of the pen" with a loss of both personal and national "vitality" (Judge 16). Newman provides the most explicit statement of this argument in his pieces on the "national degenerate," in which he castigates the anti-physical-force Redmondites as "the morbid symptoms of a grievous national disease":

> It is a sign of some serious physical complaints that the sufferer takes a joy in talking about the disease which is destroying his vitality; so, perhaps, on the same principle, the Irish National degenerate, poisoned by the microbe of the Saxon, takes a delight in considering the obvious cause of his illness. ("National Degeneration" 2)

Presenting Redmond as the pathogenic "agent" of this malady, Newman accuses England of infecting Ireland and creating the "less than [men]" ("How National Degenerates Are Made" 9) who make up the ranks of the nationally degenerate. That infection takes the form of sexual deviance, reflecting the contemporary view of homosexuality as a disease. Newman's free use of the term "degenerate," which echoes Brennan's liberal application of it to the British population, carries the same homophobic insinuations here that it does when it is applied three years later to Roger Casement after his diaries are circulated by the British government.[18] Working one side of the double discourse that we saw operating in *Playboy,* these writers present nationalist violence as the natural expression of a healthy and virile subject, a sign that the Irish man has rid himself and his body of British disease.

To render militancy healthful and manly, however, these writers must disable the second prong of that eugenist argument—the insistence that violence is an expression of barbarity, insanity, or depravity. As Jones and Stallybrass argue in their discussion of Spenser, presenting the Irish as hypermasculine and hyperaggressive was an effective way of justifying punitive and repressive measures against them long before eugenics allowed for more scientific rationalizations. The *Volunteer*'s staff is aware that the public is only too ready to read any attempt to use violence in the cause of Irish freedom as further evidence of the monstrous depravity of the Irish race. This anecdote from one of the "From the Outpost" columns shows that no attempt to construct the "fighting instinct" as a natural attribute of the "Irish race" was without peril:

> An esteemed correspondent writes enclosing a cutting from an Albany paper which states that the Irish Volunteers have carboys of vitriol to throw upon the troops passing through the streets . . . it is quite true . . . the vitriol is part of a horrible plan for indulging in cannibalism. It is well known in high places that the Volunteers are flesh eaters and the vitriol is to cook their human victims. Roast babies are known to be regarded as delectable by about 99.9 per cent of the rank and file, and all the leaders require a daily diet somewhat similar but still more shocking. (25 July 1914: 1)

Evoking Swift's "A Modest Proposal," this passage makes the point that the vitriol rumor participates in a long tradition of depicting the Irish as barbaric and using Irish violence, whatever its purposes, as evidence of Irish depravity.

As the *Irish Volunteer* argues, then, the difficulty of convincing Irish moderates that physical force is a legitimate option stems in part from British efforts to pathologize it.[19] Portraying Irish political violence as an internecine tribal conflict rather than a unified fight for independence was part of that strategy. "Ultach" warns readers against this in "Don't Play the Enemy's Game." Observing that, thanks to the British press, "the words Physical Force, in regard of Irishmen, like the word Agrarian . . . mean something desperately criminal, something far worse than burglary or even murder," he warns his readers that factionalism and schism will only make it easier for Britain and the rest of Europe to discount and dismiss Irish resistance:

> The anti-Irish party will then say, "Look at those Irish barbarians, that want self-government. See how they hate each other and are ready to destroy each other. In the name of civilisation, we must keep a grip on them and keep the peace between them." And the rest of the world will say "Quite right!" (8)

In order to counteract this tactic, the manly aggression with which the rifle-toting Volunteer is endowed has to be mitigated lest it be read as the kind of savage and self-defeating hatred that current opinion was ready to attribute to the Irish. Hatred for the oppressor has to be yoked with love for Ireland and the Irish, a love that will transcend division and unite all Irishmen in one cause against one enemy. Thus, the patriot-martyr begins to assume greater significance as a "type of ideal manhood" ("Patriot's Grave" 13) in whom virile aggression and a feminized capacity for love and suffering peacefully coexist.

Making the patriot-martyr the pinnacle of Irish masculinity forecloses the British attempt to criminalize and pathologize nationalist resistance by rooting it in selfless and suffering love rather than irrational and savage hatred. Summoning the Volunteers to action in "Now or Never," Liam de Roiste casts his closing argument in the terms of dominance and aggression we have seen in the ballads:

> NOW is the time to show what patriotism, what nationality, what love of freedom, what hope in the future of the race, what strength, what manhood is in the hearts of the young men of Ireland. If the men of Ireland fail now to profit by the opportunity given them, our nation will fall back again—back to the slave's place—scorned and derided by every heroic soul. NOW is the time to show our manhood—NOW or never! (7)

Before reaching this climax, however, de Roiste prepares the ground by showing that this attack will be motivated by love for Ireland and the Irish inspired by reverence for the martyred dead: "It has been preached to us that the dead who died for Ireland were young, foolish, vain enthusiasts. . . . But the olden faith is being preached anew and with vigour; the faith of self-sacrifice for the nation" (7).

The martyr is thus valued not only for his own sacrifice but for his ability to inspire the same love in the hearts of the Volunteers. In "Morality and Patriotism: How an Irishman should Feel," the Manchester Martyrs are described, again, in terms of their great love for their fellow-men:

> Here were men who loved Ireland indeed, and had served her in the measure of their humble opportunities and abilities, but who loved self so little as to gladly yield up their young lives on the altar of their country's freedom, and, in so doing, have served her as probably no others have since "lord Edward died, and Wolfe Tone (and Emmet) sunk serene." (10)

As a link in the great chain of martyrdom, the Manchester three—inspired by Edward, Tone, and Emmet—inspire ordinary Irishmen to emulate them: "We cannot all be heroes, but we can all be hero-worshippers" ("Morality" 10). At the same time, this great and universal love becomes a force for unity among all true Irishmen—a sentiment, latent even in Unionists and Home-Rulers, which will show them the true path to victory and freedom. The martyr thus helps make Kittson and Creagh's argument that the Volunteers represent all of Ireland.

This concern for unity was prompted not simply by the Ulster Volunteer Force, but by internal divisions within the Volunteers, the most traumatic being the split over the issue of British recruiting. Although martyr imagery is a staple of this genre throughout the *Irish Volunteer*'s run, appeals to the martyr's body and blood become more insistent in ballads that address the schism. Fidelity to the memory of the heroic dead and the "blood of martyrs" ("Steady, Volunteers" 15) is invoked in the service of national unity; to break ranks is to "dishonor the dead in their patriot graves" (Redmond 8). It is used to inspire the loyal; it is also used to excoriate and chastise those who would follow Redmond into the British Army. Defectors are characterized in "Seaghan O'Neil" as "slaves" who "would barter [the] dust" of the martyrs "to the foes of [their] life blood shed" (15). In "Forgive and Forget" it becomes "idle to talk of what might have been / Or to rant and croak of 'our martyred dead'" (3) once these defectors divide the Volunteers.[20]

What will keep the movement both from losing the moral high ground and from disintegrating under pressure, then, is the common love that all Irishmen are expected to share for their dead heroes—a love that will expand to include all fellow-Irishmen. Just as love for the martyred Christ translates, in the Christian tradition, into the Christian's love for his fellowmen, the patriot's reverence for the martyr will wipe out any enmity he may be cherishing for his Irish neighbors. "The Patriot's Grave" provides a clear example of how this logic works:

> This grave is a shrine for reverend hearts and hands that are undefiled;
> Its ashes are inspiration, it giveth us strength to bear,
> And sweepeth away dissension and reveth the will to dare! (13)

The martyred dead foster this purifying love by becoming perfect role models:

> He teaches the secret of manhood, the watchword of those who aspire
> That men must follow Freedom, though it leads through blood and fire!
> That sacrifice is the bitter draught that freemen still must quaff . . . (13)

The passive capacity for suffering is combined in the martyr with the willingness to unleash "blood and fire" in the nationalist cause, just as his recumbent posture in the grave is countered with the phallic image that opens the ballad: "Tear down the crape from the column!/ Let the shaft stand white and fair!" (13)

The same poem points out one of the problems that begins to trouble the *Irish Volunteer*'s contributors as their use of martyr imagery becomes more successful. In his desire to exalt the martyr, the poet subjugates all other forms of love and devotion to the patriot's love for his countrymen:

> Sweet is the love of a woman, and sweet is the kiss of a child;
> Sweet is the tender strength and the bravery of the mild;
> But sweeter than all, for embracing all, is the young life's peerless price—
> The young heart laid on the altar as a nation's sacrifice. (13)

This begins to suggest that instead of seeing patriotism as a means of fulfilling his prescribed role as a heterosexual male, the Irishman throws himself into this form of devotion *instead* of accepting the love of a woman or the kiss of a child. In other words, the recruit will go to his drill, not as if, but *instead of,* going to see his best girl. This redirection of the Volunteer's emotional and sexual energies toward his fellow men might succeed only too well and undermine the manhood this love is supposed to create. Degeneracy will reenter through the back door, and Irish masculinity will become pathological in a whole new way.

Thus, as the ability to feel and express ardent love for other men became central to the republican definition of Irish masculinity, it became vitally important to keep that love contained. As concerned as they were with rejecting the feminized passivity of the quiescent and conquered "slave," the Volunteers could not tolerate the prospect of a Volunteer's passionate devotion to the memory of Erin's dead mutating into—or being read as—passionate devotion to a brother Volunteer. It is in order to solve this problem that we see the *Volunteer* scrambling to include representations of patriotic *womanhood,* which heretofore has been grievously neglected (coverage of Cumann na mBan's activities is spotty at best). In 1914 the *Irish Volunteer* reprinted a piece by Terence MacSwiney on Wolfe Tone's wife that ran three years earlier in *Irish Freedom.* Originally this was part of a series called "Principles of Freedom" and was partly intended to counterbalance the risky brotherly-love rhetoric that imbues the earlier installments. In "Brothers and Enemies," for instance, MacSwiney imagines a hypothetical Unionist, republican, and moderate coming together in the service of a shared ideal:

> The sympathy that binds them is ardent, deep and enduring. Observe them come together. Note the warm hand grasp, the drawn face of one, a hard-worker; of another, the eye anxious for a brother hard pressed; of the third, the eye glistening for the ideal triumphant; of all, the intimate confidence, the encouragement and sacrifice, never a note of despair, but always the exultation of the Great Fight, and the promise of a great victory. (6)

The description is idealized, but these men are described in far more loving detail than the martyrs of the *Volunteer*'s ballads and have formed connections that are more emotionally and physically intimate than the patriot's generalized reverence for the martyr. Realizing, perhaps, the dangers of his own language, MacSwiney tries in "Irish Womanhood" to shift the Irishman's allegiance from the male patriot to the female one. He is surprisingly explicit about his motives:

> We have been saying in effect, if not in so many words, "For Ireland's sake, don't fall in love." We might as well say, "For Ireland's sake, don't let your blood circulate." It is impossible—even if it were possible, it would be hateful. The man and woman have a great and beautiful destiny to fulfill together; to substitute for it an unnatural way of life that can claim neither the seclusion of the cloister nor the dominion of the world is neither beautiful or great. (10)

In other words, unless the Irishman's fervid admiration of the "type of ideal manhood" represented by the male martyr can be redirected toward his female consort, there is a danger that nationalist sentiment will lead recruits into a "hateful" and "unnatural way of life" in which their "natural" heterosexual desires are supplanted by their attachment to Brother Ireland.

This fear is treated more lightheartedly in D. Holland's short story "O'Kelly's Bride," which details the adventures of a group of Irish nobles prior to their involvement in the 1641 rebellion.[21] The central characters are O'Kelly and his foster brother, Hugh Roe M'Moran; the main focus is not on their exploits in the 1641 rebellion but on their tender and beautiful love for each other, expressed in heartfelt terms by the normally laconic M'Moran:

> Am I not your foster-brother? Are you not the hereditary and chosen head of our clan? Were we not both suckled at the same faithful, virtuous breast, and rocked to sleep in the same oaken crib? Have we not

> had the same plays and sports from the time when we straddled a crooked stick, and played at baby soldiers, to the time when we learned to bestride a champing horse and tame his fiery temper? Have we, son of Owen, been ever twenty-four hours asunder? And am I not your sworn brother, sworn to die for you if need be? (12)

Fraternal as this language strives to make it, the relationship between the "almost womanly" O'Kelly and the "giant" M'Moran whose "fist would have felled an ox" (Holland 12) is also freighted with barely suppressed eroticism. O'Kelly blushes "like a maiden" upon being rebuked by M'Moran for marrying out of the tribe; M'Moran's face "flush[es] red-hot with pleasure" (Holland 12) when they make up. In fact, their affirmation of their foster-brotherly love for each other provokes some ironic commentary from one of their followers:

> "Soul within me! Cahir MacConn," exclaimed a merry-looking gallowglass in the front rank—a supple, wiry-looking fellow, with curling moustache and long flowing yellow hair, "What are the Thierna and Hugh Roe M'Moran up to? They are squeezing one another's hands to that extent that you would think they were going to kiss one another by and by. What is it at all?" (Holland 12)

The gallowglass's insinuation is refuted through triangulation—O'Kelly is engaged to Alice D'Alton, which gives M'Moran the chance to prove his devotion in an acceptable way by helping rescue her from the clutches of some drunken Puritans. But the danger represented by this patriotic brotherly love is not always so easily averted, because the insistent focus on masculinity in the *Irish Volunteer*'s rhetoric has rendered this third party—the female figure to whom this fervor can be deflected—progressively invisible. Since, without returning to the imagery of passivity and pacifism, Cathleen cannot be returned to her place in the paradigm, triangulation is not an option for the physical-force movement in the same way that it was for Yeats and cultural nationalists. Fortunately, Padraig Pearse was able to develop another solution—one that created some problems of its own.

From Abbot to King: The Transformation of Desire in the St. Enda's Plays

The manhood into which the Volunteer was initiated, then, required him both to profess certain forms of same-sex love and yet retain the attributes that were popularly supposed to characterize heterosexual masculinity—aggression, courage, indifference to physical pain, a hard and invulnerable body housing an unconquerable will and an incorruptible spirit. In a culture that held homosexuality and masculinity to be mutually incompatible, this feat could only be accomplished through sleight of hand—and it was Pearse's ability to perform this trick that made him such an effective spokesman for the physical-force movement. If the erotic aspect of this brotherly love can neither be purged nor contained, the only other option is redirection; and if female figures are not available, the next best thing is to direct it toward a male object who cannot possibly reciprocate it. And it is because Pearse has, through long experience, become adept at this form of sublimation, that he is able to make sacrificial rhetoric work so well for the Volunteers.

To understand why Pearse's oratory was so powerful, it will help to look at the plays that document the gradual emergence of the tropes that he later used to such great effect in his speeches. Even Pearse's best-known dramatic works—*The King, The Master,* and *The Singer*—have attracted little contemporary critical attention; and on purely aesthetic grounds it would be hard to argue that they deserve much.[22] To the reader expecting in-depth characterization, intricate plotting, convincing dialogue, or masterful stagecraft, they offer remarkably little. What they do offer is an illuminating and at times heartbreaking illustration of the process by which Pearse painfully transformed his forbidden desires into a passionate devotion to the ideal of Irish freedom—and of how those desires helped shape the form of the sacrificial narrative to which his successors would appeal. Like Pearse's political speeches, his sacrificial plays show how and why the story of the male martyr's self-sacrifice became so important to him. But while the speeches provide a better demonstration of the practical political uses of Pearse's solution to his personal struggle, the process of redirection that resolved it is much more clearly visible in the plays.

Before taking this argument further, it is unfortunately still necessary to explain that to claim that Pearse's political activism became an indirect outlet for his sexual desires is not the same thing as saying that the Easter Rising was just a morbid symptom of Pearse's own pathology. This confusion results from two erroneous assumptions that are depressingly common in Pearse scholarship: one, that Pearse *was* the Rising and vice versa; and two, that homosexual desire is inherently pathological and that therefore if we want to respect Pearse's sacrifice, we must either ignore/deny his sexuality or separate it completely from his political life.[23] Central as Pearse's image has become to the story of the Rising, he was not its sole instigator and executor; it was the culmination of a trend in republican politics that had been accelerating for years, as the columns of the *Irish Volunteer* demonstrate. As for the second and harder-dying assumption, it is true enough that in 1916 homosexuality was thoroughly pathologized; to have suggested then that Pearse felt the same desires that Casement's diaries recorded could only have had the effect of discrediting both him and the republican cause. But that climate of homophobia did not arise spontaneously out of some essential and unchanging "natural" human disgust for homosexuality; it was produced and maintained by cultural forces that were more powerful then than now, and one of them, certainly, was the public-health discourse that supported Britain's attempt to keep its grip on Ireland.[24] Eighty-five years later the power of that discourse has weakened enough to allow us to discuss Pearse's sexuality without maligning his character.

Nor does pointing out a relationship between Pearse's developing understanding of his own sexuality and his developing commitment to republicanism necessarily threaten "the integrity of Pearse's revolutionary motivation" (B. Murphy 41). To see sexuality as a taint from which the purity of Irish patriotism can and should be preserved is to refuse to understand not only Pearse, but republican politics in general. As we have seen, instead of separating politics from sexuality, Volunteer rhetoric went out of its way to conflate the two; and this was as much a response to conditions created by imperialist discourse and practice as it was the expression of individual desire. The *Volunteer*'s contributors clearly believed that it was possible, and in fact desirable, for recruits to transfer their emotional and sexual investments from other people to the cause of Irish freedom. These writers were not using politics as an excuse for sex, but rather using sex to strengthen and further their political agenda. Similarly, when Pearse infused his republican oratory with his own homoerotic desires, he was not just using republicanism as a cover for personal preoccupations. He was doing more successfully what his colleagues had done before him: using sacrificial imagery to enlist desire in the service of the republican cause. We can argue about whether Pearse was "actively" homosexual or not, we can argue about whether he recognized or understood his homoerotic desires, but we cannot pretend that Pearse was able to keep his sexuality separate from his politics any more than his heterosexual colleagues were.

At the same time, Pearse's use of the sacrificial paradigm is different from his predecessors'—in part because his desires were considered pathological and perverse. Indeed, the pressures that forced Pearse to undergo the process of disavowal and redirection that is legible in his writing have forced this denial to repeat itself in scholarly treatments of his life and work. Early biographers attempted to create a heterosexual romance for him, despite the lack of any supporting evidence. Later biographers, while they admit that there is no evidence that Pearse was ever involved in a heterosexual relationship, share an intense reluctance to suggest that he might have been a self-aware or practicing homosexual. This skittishness cannot entirely be ascribed to homophobia on their part. For one thing, there is too little documentary evidence available even to answer the question of whether he was sexually active. For another, insofar as Pearse can be said to have expressed sexual desire in his earlier writings, that desire seems to be directed at preadolescent boys, which means that suggesting Pearse recognized or acted on these desires looks very much like accusing him of pedophilia and/or child abuse. This obviously is a problem from a pro-republican standpoint, but it also creates difficulties for queer-positive scholars, since to identify Pearse as gay is to risk contributing to the unfortunate public tendency to equate homosexuality with pedophilia.

Faced with this dilemma, but unable to ignore the evidence, Ruth Dudley Edwards and Sean Farrell Moran take the same escape route: Pearse was sexually attracted to boys, but never realized that, and never acted on it. While this solution reeks of expediency, Edwards does make a valid case for it based on Pearse's early writing. She cites, for instance, a passage from one of Pearse's essays in Irish in which he describes his stay with a peasant family in the Gaeltacht:

> "If you only have two other beds," said I, "there will not be room for the five of you. You must put little Padraig in my bed."
>
> "God forbid," said Caitin, surprised. "Go up to bed quickly, Padraig."
>
> Padraig was on his way to the loft, but before he reached the ladder I told Cait that I wouldn't go to bed at all unless she let Padraig sleep with me.
>
> Although she was an obstinate woman, she had to yield to me. (qtd. in Edwards 54)

As Edwards points out, Pearse does not seem at any point to suspect that there is anything prurient about his desire to share a bed with little Padraig, despite the fact that little Padraig's mother clearly does. Similarly, Pearse published this poem during his tenure as headmaster of St. Enda's:

Little lad of the tricks,
Full well I know
That you have been in mischief:
Confess your fault truly.
I forgive you, child
Of the soft red mouth;
I will not condemn anyone
For a sin not understood.

Raise your comely head
Till I kiss your mouth:
If either of us is the better of that
I am the better of it.

There is a fragrance in your kiss
That I have not found yet
In the kisses of women
Or in the honey of their bodies. . . . (qtd. in Edwards 127)

According to Edwards, Pearse was completely oblivious to this poem's erotic overtones and was shocked and confused when friends took him aside to point them out (127). Had he been aware that "Little Lad" was erotic, her theory goes, he would hardly have published it in a public forum while he was working as the headmaster of a boys' school.

What I would suggest is that what Edwards calls Pearse's "innocence" (127) results, not from ignorance of his own desires, but from his constant struggle to transform them into something else. If we are willing to allow Pearse a certain amount of self-awareness, his fascination with the beauty and virtue of children can be read as the first stage of this transformation rather than an essential and innate neurosis—as a containment strategy that ultimately had to give way to less dangerous ways of coping with the impasse between his homosexual desires and his homophobic culture. Pearse's "obsession with boys," as Moran puts it, is thus not necessarily something that "obviously had its roots in his lack of maturity" or a "maladjustment in [Pearse's] personal development" that condemned him to a permanently "stunted sexuality" (123–24). Read from a less homophobic perspective, it has its roots just as obviously in the culturally constructed taboos that made it more acceptable for Pearse to wax rhapsodic on the beauty of children than to express or act on sexual desire toward adult men.[25]

Desire that would be dangerous if expressed toward an adult appeared safer and more acceptable if directed at children, because children were, according to the Victorian mores that still governed Pearse's world, too innocent and virginal to become sexual objects. As Morton Cohen argues in his discussion of Lewis Carroll, a "cult of childhood innocence" (12) was part and parcel of Victorian morality. Warned against expressing sexual desire toward adults, men like Dodgson instead invested their energy in children, whose innocence and purity theoretically turned this otherwise prurient desire into something beautiful and spiritual.[26] If, as Cohen claims, Victorians were used to looking at "drawings and paintings of unclothed, sexless children" (16) and thinking nothing of it, these bodies could appear "sexless" only because the presumption of childhood innocence was so strong that children supposedly could not arouse sexual desire, no matter how naked they were. Children were by definition not carnal; they were ideal "sprite[s] living an idyllic existence" (12) who could never descend to corporeality. The child was a safe object *because* he or she was presumed to be sexually inaccessible; Dodgson could cuddle, kiss, and take nude photographs of his girls without outraging either their parents or his own conscience *because* their innocence was presumed to be utterly invincible.

Similarly, Pearse is able to speak in the first issue of *An Macaomh*—the St. Enda's literary magazine, which was distributed to students, parents, and faculty—of his "great love of boys" without causing alarm because the passion of his interest is matched by a transparent and complete faith in their innocence and purity ("By Way of Comment" 7). And, just as Cohen concludes that there is no evidence in Dodgson's exhaustive self-documentation to indicate that he sexually abused his child friends, no evidence has yet been brought to light that suggests that Pearse acted out the fantasies implicit in his plays. In fact, I would argue, Pearse invested his desires in young boys for the same reason Dodgson invested his in young girls—*because* that would make his desires safe by making them impossible to act on.

Of course, as we know, children can be and are drawn into sexual relationships with adults, and innocence does not in fact confer inviolability. Realizing, perhaps, that youth alone would not keep his boys safe and his desire for them pure, Pearse reinforces that shield of innocence by drawing on Christian imagery and Irish mythology;

and it is here that we see sacrificial nationalism begin to do its work. For instance, in the 1909 issue of *An Macaomh,* Pearse describes his plans to produce a play based on Cuchulain's youth starring the St. Enda's boys:

> Frank Dowling will realise, in face and figure and manner, my own high ideal of the child Cuchulainn; that "small, dark, sad boy, comeliest of the boys of Mier," shy and modest in a boy's winning way, with a boy's aloofness and a boy's mystery, with a boy's grave earnestness broken ever and anon by a boy's irresponsible gaiety; a boy merely to all who looked upon him, and unsuspected for a hero save in his strange moments of exaltation, when the sevenfold splendours blazed in his eyes and the hero-light shone about his head. ("By Way of Comment" 16)

This, admittedly, is the young Cuchulain, with his death on the battlefield far ahead of him; but for that reason, this passage includes a number of dangerous moments. The romantic yearning underlying this description is only barely subtextual, and it is only safe because it is directed at the ideal "child Cuchulainn" rather than at Frank Dowling himself. Staging this version of his own "high ideal"—the fantasy in which his pathologized sexual desires are transformed into the acceptable and pure love of a teacher for his pupils or of an Irishman for a Celtic hero—is a risky business because the boy-hero remains alive and alluring. It becomes less dangerous when the narrative stretches to include the hero's death.

Thus, Pearse begins to dwell on the sacrificial aspects of the mythology he is using in order to render his boys even more untouchably and invincibly pure. His description of the St. Enda's philosophy leans on the ideal of death in a glorious cause to what one would expect, for the parents, would have been a somewhat alarming extent:

> We must be worthy of the tradition we seek to recreate and perpetuate in Eire, the knightly tradition of the macradh of Emain Macha, dead at the Ford "in the beauty of their boyhood"; the high tradition of Cuchulain, "better is short life with honour than long life with dishonour," "I care not though I were to live but one day and one night, if only my fame and my deeds live after me"; the noble tradition of the Fianna, "we, the Fianna, never told a lie, falsehood was never imputed to us," "strength in our hands, truth on our lips, and purity in our hearts"; the Christ-like tradition of Colm Cille, "if I were to die, it would be from excess of the love that I bear the Gael." It seems to me that with this appeal it will be an easy thing to teach Irish boys to be brave and un-

> selfish, truthful and pure; I am very certain that no other appeal will so stir their hearts or kindle their imaginations to heroic things. ("By Way of Comment" 1909: 9)

Pearse is sincere when he later argues that this focus on sacrifice is not purely "revolutionary propaganda"; it is his genuine attempt to inculcate in his students the "pure" and heroic spirit that will render them desire-proof. The only thing more innocent than a boy is a boy who dies young. In the words of Pearse's elegy for a student, once "so beautiful a spirit" is "[set] free from its prison" ("By Way of Comment" 1910: 17), the boy is permanently removed from the world of sexuality and desire attached to him ceases to be dangerous.

The St. Enda's plays, which Pearse wrote to be performed by the students, show how Pearse tried to use the sacrificial paradigm—here translated to involve children rather than adult martyrs—to transform desire that would otherwise be "degenerate" into an ennobling reverence and adoration. *An Ri,* or *The King,* performed first in 1912 and set in "an ancient monastery," is an allegory: the king of this unspecified realm, unable to win the battle he is fighting because he is sinful, comes to a monastery in the hopes of choosing a new, sinless king who can lead his host to victory. The monks, after concluding that none of them can help because "all that are men have sinned" (*PSP* 58), eventually choose the boy Giolla na Naomh, who wins the battle but dies in the process.

Giolla's main character trait is an unquestioning trust and love for male authority figures—a trust that from a practical perspective appears to be sadly misplaced. He accepts the task of leading the battle when the Abbot appeals to him: "O fosterling that I have nourished, if I ask this thing of you, will you not do it?" (*PSP* 59). Rather strangely, once Giolla responds to this plea, the Abbot then claims that this rush into battle is an expression of Giolla's own desires: "Did I not say that the young seek death? . . . The terrible, beautiful voice has spoken to this child. O herald of death, you shall be answered!" (59–60). The King, who initially refuses to accept Giolla's sacrifice—"No child shall die for me"—is finally prevailed upon, but he remains baffled by the Abbot's actions: "I do not understand your God" (60). The King comes, perhaps, to understand the Abbot's God more clearly during the next tableau, when Giolla is "stripped of his clothing" and carefully dressed in royal robes. After this, Giolla is given the King's sword, which Giolla draws for the Abbot's blessing: "A blessing on this sword! May it be hard to smite foes!" (60–62)

While presented—and apparently received—as a straight morality play, *An Ri* is also about the conflicted desires of the Abbot, who is keen to send Giolla to a glorious death on the battlefield but also grieves deeply for his loss: "King, I have given you the noblest jewel that was in my house. I loved yonder child" (63). When the Abbot delivers this line, Giolla is actually still alive; but what motivates the Abbot is his heartbroken knowledge that this love can only be expressed in the past tense. It is only once he knows Giolla is going to battle and not coming back that the Abbot can declare his love for him, which he does after dressing Giolla up with an adulthood he will never attain and girding him with a sword he is too young to wield. Significantly, however, Giolla's victorious sacrifice not only cures the Abbot's grief but allows the King, who until now has been confused and horrified by the Abbot's plan, to understand and share the Abbot's love. When Giolla's body is brought on stage, it is the King who finally acts out the Abbot's desires:

> THE ABBOT: (*lifting the sword from the bier*) Take the sword.
>
> THE KING: No, I will let him keep it. A King should sleep with a sword. This was a very valiant King. (*He takes the sword from the Abbot and lays it again upon the bier. He kneels.*) I do homage to thee, O dead King, O victorious child! I kiss thee, O white body, since it is thy purity that hath redeemed my people. (*He kisses the forehead of Giolla na Naomh.*) (67)

The King's speech is addressed, not to Giolla himself, but to his "white body"—a phrase that appears often enough in Pearse's writing to lay claim to the status of Homeric epithet. Thus, although Giolla is chosen because of his spiritual purity, it is the purity of his body that has "redeemed" his people—or perhaps more accurately, redeemed their desire for him. The stage directions for this scene say nothing about the body itself, but choreograph the other players; the bier is center stage, while a group of women keen around it. Given the emphasis placed in the St. Enda's productions on achieving a Yeatsian "aesthetic elegance" (Trotter 155)—and the fact that this play was performed by students for an audience consisting largely of their parents—it is unlikely that Giolla's wounds were represented in a graphic or realistic manner. The description of the body in the King's speech washes out any evidence of violence; it is a "white" blank. Thus, while Giolla's body is on display, his death is not; this is not Giolla's corpse so much as an idealized image of Giolla's departed spirit. Paradoxically, the King and Abbot address themselves to his immortal soul by interacting with the lifeless body it has left; and it is this paradox that makes that kiss possible. Laid out ceremonially on the bier, Giolla's body is now finally pure enough, inviolable enough, to receive this touch without being tainted; and the kiss itself, instead of marking the giver as a sinner, becomes the symbol of his obedience to God.

The strange status of Giolla's body—tangible but untouchable, lifeless but not dead, concrete but also ideal—is what makes that transformation possible; and this is a lesson that Pearse will bring to his political writing when his commitment to republicanism becomes more intense. Death purifies the body because the body can no longer be an agent of corruption once the spirit is gone. At the same time, if the body is allowed to *be* a body—the corporeal shell of what was previously a living being—any desire expressed toward it must necessarily be purely carnal—and therefore corrupt. Staging the scene this way—so that Giolla's corpse is represented by a body that is obviously still living, and on which there are no visible traces of the violence that separated it from his soul—means that what is on stage is in a sense neither body nor spirit but a third term, an image wavering between the two poles of this duality and inhabiting an ambiguous and strange space where that impossible kiss can happen.

Giolla is sacrificed, then, in order to stage this final scene. Ostensibly dying for the kingdom, he is also dying for the Abbot: the death that liberates the King's people from their enemies also saves the Abbot from a conflict he cannot otherwise resolve. If the political purpose of Giolla's sacrifice justifies the Abbot's decision, however, the love Giolla has for his mentor also sanctifies the King's cause. By substituting Giolla for the king, the Abbot is replacing the King's more worldly and therefore necessarily ambiguous and impure motives with Giolla's love and reverence. The King does not understand why this is necessary, but the *Irish Volunteer*'s contributors did: the only way to render violent resistance acceptable to the reading public was to put it in the hands of Thomas Davis's "righteous men," and the only thing that could make them disinterested and self-sacrificing enough to be righteous was love. *The King* thus provides perhaps the earliest indication of how Pearse's battle to subdue, redirect, and transform his desires would ultimately come to serve the aims of the republican movement.

When *The King* was performed in the Abbey a year later, Yeats and others, including Joseph Holloway, responded to it favorably.[27] The sacrificial narrative appears to have done its work, translating Pearse's desire into a form eminently acceptable to both the St. Enda's parents and more objective commentators. Of course, as Ruth Dudley Edwards points out, the play was performed in Irish, which for most of the audience would have rendered this subtext even more subtextual.[28] But for Pearse, it would seem that *The King* raised questions that he found difficult to answer and that the myth of the child-martyr was unable to resolve. *The Master,* written in 1915 and also performed by the St. Enda's boys, suggests that as his involvement in republican politics increased, Pearse moved closer to recognizing his desires, although no closer to accepting them. *The Singer,* written several months later, shows him embracing the more explicitly republican version of the sacrificial paradigm as a more effective way of redirecting those desires.

The Master is an allegory about faith, and the plot is even simpler than that of *The King.* Ciaran, a Christian missionary living in a cloister in Celtic Ireland, is confronted by king Daire, his foster-brother. Daire demands that Ciaran prove to him that Christianity is the truth by asking God for a sign. When Ciaran refuses, Daire threatens to kill his favorite pupil, Iollan Beag, if God does not send an angel to rescue him. Iollan calls on the archangel Michael, who appears. While Daire kneels to the angel, Ciaran dies. Pearse has thus revised the sacrificial narrative so that it is the desiring adult rather than the desired child who dies, and this change reflects what seems to be a growing sense of confusion and guilt related to his feelings for his students.

Despite his willingness to meet the king unarmed and to die for his faith if need be, Ciaran is troubled by doubt. Art mentions that Ciaran has been praying constantly for "a soul that was in danger" (*PSP* 71); the doubts to which Ciaran confesses in later asides indicate that this soul is probably his own. When he is alone with Iollan and Iollan declares that he would call on the angels of Heaven to help "the soul of any dear friend of mine" if it were "ever in peril," Ciaran responds, "The peril is near!" (90). Ostensibly this refers to his imminent confrontation with Daire, but Ciaran is clearly more worried about his own inner conflict: "The King I can meet unafraid, but who is not afraid of himself?" (92).

These doubts are expressed in terms of Ciaran's religious faith—"My spirit reaches out and finds Heaven empty" (89)—but that faith has been shaken by more than epistemological uncertainty. Maine, one of Ciaran's pupils, comments on the fact that Iollan seems to be Ciaran's favorite; when the other boys put this down to Iollan's "high, manly heart," Maine disagrees:

> MAINE: He has a beautiful white body, and therefore you all love him; aye, the Master and all. We have no woman here and so we make love to our little Iollan.
>
> RONAN: (laughing) Why, I thrashed him ere-yesterday for putting magories down my neck!
>
> MAINE: Men sometimes thrash their women, Ronan. It is one of the ways of loving. (73)

The connection between Ciaran's crisis of faith and his dawning realization of his own desire is underlined during Ciaran's lesson on church history. When Iollan defends Peter's primacy among the apostles, and specifically over Paul, Ciaran responds with the most poignant line of the play: "Paul said many hard things and many dark things. When you understand him, Iollan, you will like him" (80).

Among these hard, dark things are the passages from Corinthians and Romans in which Paul condemns homosexual activity. By defending Paul to his favorite pupil, Ciaran is doing his best to accept Paul's condemnation and obey his prohibition, and he is hinting that once Iollan has left the age of innocence he will be glad that Paul is there to stand between him and desire. In the end, however, Paul is not enough; Ciaran needs a more unequivocal demonstration of Heaven's might and power to keep him safe from himself. Although he tells Iollan that "if it were necessary . . . to save a soul that were in peril, we are taught that they would come in bodily presence, and that one could see them and speak to them" (89), the angels have not responded to Ciaran's call, and he meets Daire, not in confidence, but at the pitch of his despair: "I see that all my wayfaring has been in vain. A man may not escape from that which is in himself" (90).

What finally saves Ciaran is not his self-sacrificial bravery. Indeed, Daire treats Ciaran's offer the same way revisionists would later describe Pearse's sacrifice: as the last self-dramatizing gesture of a desperate man whose inner conflicts have put him in a position from which death is the only escape. "Men die for false things, for ridiculous things, for evil things. . . . Though you were to die here with joy and laughter you would not prove your cause a true one" (98). But Ciaran is saved from having to make that empty gesture by Michael, the archangel summoned by Iollan in answer to Daire's final challenge.

The fact that Iollan calls on Michael and not Gabriel or Uriel is not a coincidence. Michael is described in the stage directions as "a mighty warrior"; Daire addresses him as a "soldier," and Michael's speech lays heavy emphasis on his function as God's commander in chief: "I am he that hasteneth. I am he that rideth before the squadron. I am he that holdeth a shield over the retreat of man's host when Satan cometh in war. I am he that turneth and smiteth. I am he that is Captain of the Host of God" (99). Michael is not just an angel; he is a Volunteer. And it is the arrival of this incarnation of Irish virility that gives Ciaran the way out that he has been searching for. Ciaran dies proclaiming his vision of a battle to come: "The Seraphim and the Cherubim stand horsed. I hear the thunder of their coming. . . . O Splendour!" (100). The martial side of Volunteer masculinity has intervened to save the loving, self-sacrificing side; the soldier redeems the lover by gathering Ciaran into the ranks of the Host of God, where he will have no further need or desire for Iollan.

What we have at the end of *The Master,* then, is an image of what his involvement in the Volunteers and the Irish republican Brotherhood would mean to Pearse personally—the opportunity to once again redirect his desires toward a more acceptable goal, this time that of Irish freedom. By assuming the other side of patriotic masculinity—by becoming both the Abbot and the King, both Ciaran and Daire—Pearse saw a chance not only to use his desires in the service of the community, but to correct the problem his first attempt at redirection had created. As an initiate into Volunteer masculinity, Pearse was finally offered the chance to express love and desire for other adult men—a chance that *The Singer* shows him seizing with eagerness and no small measure of relief.

Written in the fall of 1915 when Pearse had already delivered his three famous orations on Wolfe Tone, Robert Emmet, and O'Donovan Rossa, *The Singer* was never performed during Pearse's lifetime. Partly, no doubt, this was because Pearse was busy with his political work, but partly it was also because it could not be performed by the St. Enda's boys: *The Singer* is unique among Pearse's plays in that it has no parts for children. The setting—a country village where an organized body of men is waiting for "the word" to rise up against "the Gall"—is generic, but it is also contemporary: mythic as this play strives to be, these men who meet at night, drill in secret, and are waiting for the word from the city are clearly Volunteers; and MacDara, the "singer" whose voice has a magical power to move the hearts and minds of his hearers, is just as clearly Pearse's imagination of his own role in the republican movement. Now that he has taken up this role, Pearse's alter ego can finally transform those problematic desires into a form so safe and contained that he can be reclaimed for heterosexuality through a romance with Sighle, who, aside from MacDara's mother, is the only female character in the play.

That recuperation is only possible, however, after MacDara has been banished from his community and has passed through a period of intense self-doubt, isolation, and despair from which he is finally rescued when he embraces politics. MacDara's old teacher notes that although MacDara was already filled with "love" and "wisdom" before his banishment, "exile has made him a better man"—he has found a use for his "terrible love" that will render it less troubling for his community and less destructive for MacDara (*PSP* 21). The story of MacDara's wanderings, as he tells it, is the story of his conversion from dreamer and poet to soldier and orator—a conversion that is simultaneous with, and inextricable from, his conversion from lover to fighter.

MacDara has struggled with, and finally overcome, the same doubts that almost claim Ciaran. Returning home, MacDara is able to appreciate Sighle's beauty, explaining that he never noticed it before because

> I thought that all beauty was in the heart, that beauty was a secret thing that could be seen only with the eyes of reverie, or in a dream of some unborn splendour. I had schooled myself to think physical beauty an unholy thing. I tried to keep my heart virginal; and sometimes in the street of a city when I have stopped to look at the white limbs of some beautiful child, and have felt the pain that the sight of great beauty brings, I have wished that I could blind my eyes so that I might shut out the sight of everything that tempted me. (26–27)

Here MacDara describes the same process that informs Pearse's statements of the St. Enda's educational philosophy and that drives the plots of the St. Enda's plays. Realizing on some level that his desires are "unholy," he attempts to keep his heart "virginal" by spiritualizing desire and directing it at the "heart" rather than the body. This in turn leads to his idealization of children, who he constructs as possessing a spiritual beauty expressed through a body that has not yet undergone the fall into duality. However, he soon feels the "pain" of knowledge—the understanding that the beauty of children *is* physical and that his desire for it is carnal—and a corresponding wish that he could avoid desire altogether by "shut[ting] out the sight of everything that tempted" him.

MacDara returns home knowing, however, that his struggle to keep himself "cold and chaste as the top of a high mountain" (27) is doomed to failure. After losing his job at a Catholic school, MacDara becomes a private tutor. In the midst of describing his two-year friendship with his sole pupil, a "winsome child," MacDara questions the idea that man can live by spirituality alone: "Aye, they say that to be busy with the things of the spirit is better than to be busy with the things of the body. But I am not sure, master. Can the Vision Beautiful alone content a man?" (30–31). But MacDara is able to save himself from insinuations like Maine's by casting his relationship to his pupil in maternal terms:

> Sometimes I think that to be a woman and to serve and suffer as women do is the highest thing. Perhaps that is why I felt it proud and wondrous to be a teacher, for a teacher does that. I gave to the little lad I taught the very flesh and blood and breath that were my life. I fed him on the milk of my kindness; I breathed into him my spirit. (31)

This speech, which reflects the "fostering" model of education that Pearse developed in his pedagogical writing, allows MacDara to have the physical connection with his pupil that he longs for without taking on the stigma of sexual desire. But MacDara can remain a man while assuming this feminine role only by copying the example of Christ, the prototypical male martyr. His maternal relationship with his pupil is described in terms of Christ's relationship with his followers; he nourishes them on his own "flesh and blood" and inspires them with his divine "spirit." For those who might miss the imagery, Pearse introduces the passage with an explicit comparison between MacDara and Christ: "The true teacher must suffer and do. He must break bread to the people: he must go into Gethsemane and toil up the steep of Golgotha" (31).

It is the Christian version of the sacrificial narrative, then, that allows MacDara to translate his desire for physical interaction with his pupil into this sanctioned form; he can only put himself in the mother's role by identifying with the martyr whose masculinity can comprehend that feminized capacity to "suffer and do" and whose sacrifice is life-sustaining and regenerative without being overtly sexualized. Significantly, however, MacDara identifies with Christ, not out of his own devout faith, but as a way of overcoming his doubts. MacDara's desire to take on the Christ role is an outgrowth, strangely, of his final failure to believe:

> Once, as I knelt by the cross of Kilgobbin, it became clear to me, with an awful clearness, that there was no God. Why pray after that? I burst into a fit of laughter at the folly of men in thinking that there is a God. I felt inclined to run through the villages and cry aloud, "People, it is all a mistake; there is no God." (33)

MacDara recovers from this state of despair, not by recovering his belief in God, but by acting out Christ's example. What the Christian sacrificial narrative offers him is not so much hope of eternal life in the hereafter as it is a way to transform his desires into something he can live with in the here and now.

Of course, living out the Christian sacrificial narrative does mean that MacDara will have to die; but from his point of view, this is not a drawback. For one thing, MacDara can now swear his undying love for Sighle without having to consummate it. He goes into battle without so much as a kiss goodbye: "I wanted to have your kiss on my lips, Sighle, as well as my mother's and Colm's. But I will deny myself that" (39). Thus, the role MacDara has assumed allows him to lay claim to heterosexual masculinity without performing it. More important, it allows him both to love and be loved by other men. As the Singer, MacDara inspires the same adoration in his adult listeners that he got from his pupil: "He has the voice of a silver trumpet, and words so beautiful they make the people cry" (16). When Maoilsheachlainn calls MacDara to "reveal yourself to the men that are waiting for your word," Diarmaid recognizes him as the Singer and immediately "goes up to MacDara and kisses his hand" (41). After Maire gives MacDara her blessing, all the other men come forward and do the same. Although in an earlier draft Sighle and Colm are the last to kiss MacDara's hand, Pearse revises this scene so that neither participates.[29] Aside from his mother's, the only kisses MacDara takes into battle with him are those of his male followers.

By offering himself as a sacrifice to the Gall, "as Christ hung naked before men on the tree" (44), MacDara is solving exactly the problem that we saw developing in the *Volunteer.* Having provoked with his oratory the emotional investment in the ideal of Irish freedom that will move "the people" to action, his willingness to die for them now transforms that emotion into a love that, because it is directed at a charismatic, handsome, living man, is more intense and powerful than an abstract reverence for Ireland's past and its long-lost martyrs. Because they know and love MacDara personally, "there's not a man that won't do his bidding" (22). As in *The King,* however, this love can only be expressed once it is certain that MacDara is going into battle. Because he is about to die, this love will never turn into the kind of desire MacDara has spent his life running away from. MacDara stimulates in the men of his town a love that will urge them to honor, and to repeat, his act of sacrifice and his dedication to the cause of Irish freedom but that can never become pathological because it is attached to a man who is already dead and therefore not available as a love object.

The Singer, then, is a clear statement of what the physical-force movement offered Pearse on a personal level: the opportunity to express love for other men without finding himself irrevocably consigned to the ranks of the degenerate and depraved. It is because *The Singer* references the Volunteers and the contemporary political situation instead of remaining in the mythic world of Celtic legend that Pearse is able to put himself in Giolla's place—to offer himself as the sacrifice in return for being allowed to transfer his desires from boys to men. The enthusiasm with which he embraced this solution, even though it would require his own death, says something about how insistent his desires were, how powerful were the prohibitions against them, and how disturbing it was to Pearse to realize that these desires were shaping his relationships with his students.

Pearse's political awakening, then, is clearly linked in these plays to his changing understanding of his own sexuality; and the version of the sacrificial paradigm that he develops here is what forges that link. At the same time, it would be reductive and inaccurate to infer from this connection that Pearse's politics were the pretext, while his sexuality was the "real" motivation for his activism. Indeed, what these plays and the trend we have been discussing in the *Irish Volunteer* show is that the two are coeval and inextricable. Pearse's interest in and love for Irish culture and his (admittedly romanticized) conception of the Irish people date back to the same adolescence in which his sexuality would have emerged; St. Enda's grew as much out of Pearse's desire to preserve the Gaelic language and Celtic culture as it did out of his "great love of boys"; his entrance into republican politics is a natural enough result of a life dedicated to protecting Irish spirituality from British materialism. The fact that sacrificial politics also offered him a means of living (and dying) with his sexuality demonstrates the extent to which Ireland's history of occupation and resistance has constructed the Irish experience of sexuality and desire.

In describing how Pearse's losing battle against his own fear and desire translates into his version of the sacrificial narrative, I am not trying to reduce Pearse's political commitment to suicidal self-hatred. What I am arguing is that in order to make the argument for revolution possible, republican writers had to redefine the concept of masculinity for Irish men; that this redefinition highlighted the instability and incoherence of sexual identity in a way that was profoundly disturbing; and that Pearse's experience with sublimating his own sexual desires translated into a version of the sacrificial paradigm that helped keep that construct of masculinity together. In the plays, the personal does threaten to overshadow the political; but in Pearse's much more influential political speeches, the balance is more equal. In fact, the power of his rhetoric derives from the fusion of personal desire and political ideology—his melding of personal and national liberation narratives, his belief that by freeing himself he would free Ireland. And it is this conflation—Pearse's application of the same process that transforms the Abbot into MacDara to the sacrificial narrative that was already emerging in Volunteer rhetoric—that allowed Pearse to solve the *Irish Volunteer*'s problem.

Love Him as a Man: The Patriot-Martyr Romance

What separates Pearse's work from that of the balladeers who sang the praises of Tone and Emmet or the writers who exhorted Volunteers to keep faith with their glorious dead is the strength of the passion that invests it—a passion that is not simply love for freedom in the abstract or of Ireland as a concept but that takes as its object an individual mortal man. While to other writers Tone, Emmet, and Davis remain names, stories, or symbols to be evoked in formulaic epithets, to Pearse they appear vividly real; and his speeches are animated with a desire to know them as themselves rather than as legends. Comparing Pearse on Robert Emmet, for instance, with an address on Robert Emmet given in March of 1911 in Belfast by John MacBride and reprinted in *Irish Freedom,* it is easy to see both what made Pearse distinctive and why he was a more compelling speaker. MacBride starts by stating that his motivation is "sympathy with the ideals of Emmet"; but he lets others give testimony about Emmet himself, quoting Washington Irving's coverage of Emmet's trial and one of Emmet's former students' memoirs. The bulk of his address is taken up with a detailed narrative of the actual rebellion for which Emmet was executed, in which he argues that the plot was foiled "by the lack of discipline, the disobedience, the drunkenness and the unpunctuality" of

Emmet's comrades. He closes with a perfunctory repetition of the sacrificial formula: "Emmet's epitaph must be written in letters of blood. Our martyrs shall not have died in vain" (2–3).

MacBride's approach, then, is to stress the military and martial side of the republican ideal of masculinity, focusing on the strategic details, inveighing against lack of discipline and moral strength, and closing with a promise of violence to come. Pearse takes the opposite approach, saying little about the attack except that it was a failure. It is in fact the failure that makes Emmet valuable:

> And yet he has left us a prouder memory than the memory of Brian victorious at Clontarf or of Owen Roe victorious at Benburb. It is the memory of a sacrifice Christ-like in its perfection. Dowered with all things splendid and sweet, he left all things and elected to die. (*PWS* 69)

This memory is "prouder" because it preserves the dual nature of that "ideal manhood" the martyr embodies: Emmet's patriotism may be "a terrible thing urging the generations to perilous bloody attempts," but it has "its root in all gentleness" (81). Patriotism is explained as love rather than anger, and Emmet's greatness lies in his ability to inspire this kind of love in other Irishmen: "Patriotism is in large part a memory of heroic dead men and a striving to accomplish some task left unfinished by them" (66).

So far, Pearse is simply picking up on the trends we have already seen in the *Irish Volunteer* and translating them into more explicitly Catholic and Christian terms: Emmet's sacrifice is, like Christ's, "a redemption"; and it purifies his memory, the men who follow after him, and "that deathless thing called Irish Nationality." What sets this speech apart is the focus on Emmet's person—both his indomitable spirit and the body from which it is taken. Pearse's description of Emmet at the moment of his death is as idealized as anything in the *Irish Volunteer,* but it is also invested with a personal and emotional freight that is not legible in more conventional treatments of Erin's great dead:

> In the great space of Thomas Street an immense silent crowd; in front of Saint Catherine's Church a gallows upon a platform; a young man climbs to it, quiet, serene, almost smiling, they say—ah, he was very brave; there is no cheer from the crowd, no groan; this man is to die for them, but no man dares to say aloud "God bless you, Robert Emmet." Dublin must one day wash out in blood the shameful memory of that quiescence. (70)

This passage is one of many retellings of a dream that Pearse described in *An Macaomh:*

> I dreamt that I saw a pupil of mine, one of our boys at St. Enda's, standing alone upon a platform above a mighty sea of people; and I understood that he was about to die for some august cause. . . . He looked extraordinarily proud and joyous, lifting his head with a smile almost of amusement . . . the great silent crowd regarded the boy with pity and wonder rather than with approval. . . . It would have been so easy to die before an applauding crowd or before a hostile crowd: but to die before that silent, unsympathetic crowd! (qtd. in Edwards 143)

In Pearse's dream, one of the boy's fellow-students embraces the martyr and puts a blindfold on him before he is executed; this gesture is the climax of the dream narrative, the moment of male-male contact that the dream engineers and that Pearse sees as ample "compensation to the boy that died for the indifference of the crowd" (qtd. in Edwards 143). In Emmet's story, however, that compensation is never given.

Pearse's use of his dream in this context thus changes the terms of the relationship between the martyr and his people—Emmet may still be a legend and a semi-divine figure, but he is also a man whose death is made bitter and lonely by the crowd's failure to make that gesture of "brotherly charity and loyalty" (qtd. in Edwards 143). Dublin's "shame" here is its failure to return his love for them. The image, to which Pearse returns later, of "that young figure, serene and smiling, climbing to the gallows above that sea of silent men in Thomas Street" just before his "comely head" is cut off and displayed to the crowd, brings Emmet to life in a way that MacBride's eulogy never does (*PWS* 82, 70). By presenting him as a living man about to be put to death rather than as a dead man who is already canonized, Pearse hopes to inspire in his listeners the love that these "silent" spectators failed to feel—the love that will prompt them to keep faith, not just with Emmet's ideals, but with Emmet himself.

It is the transformation of patriotism from a dutiful reverence for the great dead into a form of "communion" in which the living patriot is sanctified through the answering love that connects him with the spirit of the martyr that is Pearse's real innovation. The communion metaphor, which recurs in MacDara's description of his relationship to his pupil, is developed in more detail in Pearse's oration on Wolfe Tone, which was delivered at Tone's graveside in June of 1913 and printed in *Irish Freedom:*

> This man's soul was a burning flame, a flame so ardent, so generous, so pure, that to come into communion with it is to come unto a new baptism, unto a new regeneration and cleansing. If we who stand by this graveside could make ourselves at one with the heroic spirit that once inbreathed this clay, could in some way come into loving contact with it, possessing ourselves of something of its ardour, its valour, its purity, its tenderness, its gaiety, how good a thing it would be for us, how good a thing for Ireland; with what joyousness and strength should we set our faces towards the path that lies before us, bringing with us fresh life from this place of death, a new resurrection of patriotic grace in our souls! (*PWS* 56)

The sexual element of the Cathleen ni Houlihan trope is certainly at work here; but that regeneration has become a "resurrection" that happens through an intimate connection between two men—a "loving contact" between the martyr and the Irishman in which the living are transformed and revitalized by the consummation of this love between them and the "ardent" dead. The erotic aspect of this "communion" is made more evident when Pearse asks his audience not "to venerate [Tone] as a saint" but "to love him as a man," something Pearse certainly seems to be doing: "For myself, I would rather have known this man than any man of whom I have ever heard or ever read. . . . I have always loved the very name of Thomas Russell because Tone so loved him." (57–58)

Loving and ardent as he may be, Tone has also been dead for more than a hundred years; and as charged as Pearse's love lyric is, the "communion" he desires must remain spiritual rather than physical because its object no longer has a body. Pearse has thus solved the problem raised by the Volunteer construction of masculinity: instead of spreading to include other recruits, the Volunteer's erotic energy can be concentrated entirely on the martyr, who is human enough in Pearse's treatment to be invested with personal adoration. Because this love can never result in physical consummation, the Volunteer who loves Tone as a man cannot be accused of degeneracy or effeminacy. On the contrary, this form of same-sex love is spiritualized, pure, and transforming, and need never risk descending to corporeality. The Volunteer can experience self-sacrificing, compassionate, feminized love without risk to his own masculinity, which is reaffirmed through his dedication to armed struggle.

Pearse is able to promote this love while preserving the patriot's masculinity only because he has managed to hide the martyr's body—and hide it, paradoxically, in plain sight. Wolfe Tone, "as a man," is both there and not there—real enough to inspire Pearse's love and through it the love of his listeners, idealized enough to keep that love spiritual and sanctifying. Like Giolla's not-corpse, Tone's body exists in a third space where it is both and neither material nor ideal. This ambiguous space is difficult to maintain; and it is partly in order to keep it open that Pearse draws so heavily on Catholic symbolism. Commentators have typically explained Pearse's relentless Christ imagery in terms of his own religious faith, and certainly his personal familiarity with the Catholic mass and Catholic iconography would inevitably have influenced his writing. But just as MacDara compares himself to Christ because it will allow him to claim the relationship that he wants with his comrades, so Pearse draws on Catholic imagery, not as an unthinking reflex action, but because it will help him create a relationship between Tone and his listeners that will induce them to embrace the republican cause. Communion is a useful metaphor because the Eucharist, as it is celebrated in the Catholic mass, provides a model for exactly what Pearse needs to do to save Irish manhood from itself.

Insistence on the miracle of transubstantiation—whereby the wafers and wine consecrated during mass actually become the body and blood of Christ—is one of the major matters of doctrine that differentiates Catholicism from Protestant forms of Christianity. Worshippers in the Catholic Church believe that what they are eating is really the flesh and blood of Christ. In most other Christian services the communion ceremony is invested with symbolic rather than real significance; the bread and wine *represent* Christ's body and blood but do not actually *become* it. While this may seem to non-Catholics or non-Christians like it belongs in the angels-on-the-head-of-a-pin category of pointless dogmatic quibbles, it does make a significant difference in ritual practice and in the daily lives of practitioners; and Catholics of Pearse's generation would have understood and accepted the doctrine of transubstantiation.[30] Thus, for Catholics, mass provided a weekly opportunity to confront the same paradox that Pearse is replicating in his speeches. The ambiguous and conflicted status of Christ's body in Catholic ritual—present and absent, real and ideal, literal and symbolic—is also the status given to Tone's body: the body isn't really a body, and yet it is.

This, of course, is not the *only* reason Pearse keeps comparing Tone, Emmet, and Rossa to Christ; but it does help explain why those appeals should have been so powerful. Pearse was a Catholic speaking to a heavily Catholic movement, but to assume that republican audiences would respond to religious imagery simply because it was religious imagery is to reproduce the "mindless superstitious idolatry" stereotype that was and is a staple of Unionist propaganda. Pearse's Christ imagery works in part because it is able to solve the problems we have seen developing in the *Volunteer*—it allows his listeners to fall in love with another man and still preserve their own masculinity, to feel that brotherly love that will justify and safeguard the Volunteer project without worrying that it will make them "less than men."

Of course, in order for this solution to work, the man toward whom all this emotion is directed does have to be dead. For Pearse's version of transubstantiation, it is vital that the martyr leave the realm of corporeal existence and become the glorified, immortal, and radiant presence that Christ is. The purifying influence that "communion" with Tone has on the Volunteers is possible only after Tone has shed his blood for Ireland. And thus we finally arrive at that formula: "Bloodshed is a cleansing and a sanctifying thing, and a nation which regards it as the final horror has lost its manhood" (*PWS* 99). Pearse calls bloodshed "cleansing and sanctifying" for the same reason he praises Tone for putting "virility into the Catholic movement" or Emmet for inspiring Irish men to "draw the sword of Ireland"—because it creates the martyr whose love will counteract attempts to present revolutionary violence as barbaric and unreasoning, and who will, in turn, not only inspire but contain an answering love in the hearts of his followers (*PWS* 99, 59, 74). It is not bloodshed itself so much as Pearse's rhetorical use of it that "cleanses and sanctifies" the physical-force movement and preserves intact the unstable concept of masculinity that has become central to it.

Too Long a Sacrifice: Pearse's Legacy

As we have seen, holding that construct together was important not just for the self-images of individual Volunteers or their leaders, but because it allowed them to argue for both the right to arm and the universal brotherhood of Irishmen. Pearse's version of the sacrificial paradigm was useful in promoting both of these arguments, and Pearse himself became part of that paradigm when it was used after the Rising for the same purposes. The price of the Pearsian solution to the republican problem, however, is the same price that Pearse himself paid—the disappearance of the body, and what is attached to it, into that vague space from which it never emerges.

For Pearse, this meant a lifetime of disavowing and repudiating his own sexuality, sublimating it through his work in the service of Irish nationalism. For his listeners, it meant subscribing to a conception of Ireland that was idealized, oversimplified, and incapable of including a consciousness of the material obstacles standing in the way of the republican ideal. Through MacDara, Pearse may wax poetic on the subject of the "dumb, suffering people" (*PSP* 34), but his eleventh-hour realization that material poverty is one of the major evils of the imperial system he is trying to destroy comes too late to save his ideology, at least as far as O'Casey is concerned. Pearse's failure to acknowledge the importance of the economic effects of imperialism is a necessary corollary to the sacrificial ideal as he develops it. What drops out in that shift from "Lucan's" argument against imperial peace to Pearse's graveside orations, what disappears into limbo with Tone and Emmet, what is washed off the body of Giolla na Naomh, is the material effect of imperial violence—the record of suffering and violation written in the physical world. Giolla's "white body" bears no trace of its bloody death; Emmet's head remains "comely" even after it is severed from its body; Rossa's long years of pain and misery in captivity are eclipsed by the radiance of his "unconquered and unconquerable" (*PWS* 134) glorified spirit. This relentless idealization was, from a socialist standpoint, problematic even before the Rising. Afterwards, it becomes even more so as the ideal of sacrifice moves farther and farther away from the reality of political conflict. And it is that "idealisation" against which O'Casey will oppose his own sacrificial narrative.

But—as we will see—despite O'Casey's astuteness in recognizing the omissions at the center of the Pearsian narrative, he fails to repair them. O'Casey's attempt to bring back the body and to depict the suffering that he charges Pearse with betraying is undermined by his own fidelity to the same constructions of femininity and maternity that supported *Cathleen ni Houlihan.* Having elucidated the sexual politics of sacrifice, O'Casey attempts to solve them simply by straightening them out—redirecting the Irish man's ardor back toward the Irish woman. But because he cannot, in the end, see through the effect to its cause, he devises a solution that simply becomes part of the problem.

4
The Body of Truth: Sensationalism and Sacrifice in Sean O'Casey's Dublin Trilogy

> [A] talk with some of the young Republican women which I had after the disturbance enabled me to discover that the National tocsin of alarm was sounded because some of the tinsel of sham was shaken from the body of truth.
>
> —Sean O'Casey, letter to the *Irish Independent,* February 20, 1926

> Since receiving Mr. Yeats's police-protected 'apotheosis' Mr. O'Casey appears to take himself over-seriously, not sparing those of us who decline to bow the knee before his godhead.
>
> His play becomes 'the shaking of the tinsel of sham from the body of truth': an over-statement surely, for of the body of truth as portrayed in *The Plough and the Stars* one may only discern a leprous corpse.
>
> —Hannah Sheehy-Skeffington, "The Plough and the Stars: Reply to Mr. O'Casey," *Irish Independent,* February 23, 1926

Audiences who attended the first week of Sean O'Casey's *The Plough and the Stars* might well have left with a bad case of déjà vu. The protests that disrupted the second act of O'Casey's 1926 treatment of the Easter 1916 Rising, like the *Playboy* riots, were apparently triggered by a perceived slight on Irish womanhood. As he had in 1907, Yeats called in the police to prevent the protesters from disrupting the play; and as in 1907, he was roundly abused for doing so. Like Synge, O'Casey defended the controversial elements of his play on the grounds that they were authentic representations of Irish culture and that he was revealing the "truth" about Ireland and the Irish. It is thus not surprising that both O'Casey and Hannah Sheehy-Skeffington, the play's principal detractor, made the same comparison that Joseph Holloway made when he lamented that Dublin had "made a second *Playboy* of *The Plough and the Stars*" (254).

This time, however, the critique was less hysterical, more self-conscious, and more substantive, at least as articulated by Sheehy-Skeffington in her letters to the *Irish Independent.* Although she cites Griffith, she distances herself from him by explicitly stating that her disapproval is not "directed to the moral aspect of the play" (*Letters of Sean O'Casey* 167).[1] Instead, the protesters—all of whom, like Sheehy-Skeffington, have personal connections with the Easter 1916 Rising—condemn the play "on national grounds solely" (*LSO* 167). Sheehy-Skeffington explains the reasoning that remained latent and obscure in Griffith's criticism of *Playboy:* from a nationalist perspective, putting a prostitute on stage or showing the Volunteers bringing the tricolor into a pub is not offensive in and of itself, but it is offensive because it is part of a "reaction against idealisation" that drives O'Casey to push "realism" to the point of "morbid perversity" (*LSO* 168).

In the *Plough* controversy, then, we see that Dublin audiences have in fact learned something from the *Playboy* riots. Sheehy-Skeffington and her colleagues find O'Casey's violations of sexual decorum strategically useful but make an effort to keep them from obscuring the larger problem: "the realism of his representation of Dublin life" was clearly the real "locus of disagreement" (Watt 147). Sheehy-Skeffington's critique calls into question not only O'Casey's politics but also his dramatic idiom, the "realism" she reads as part of his political agenda. Instead of accepting the prevailing interpretation of O'Casey's Dublin dramas—that their value was in their ability to mimetically and transparently represent a "reality" to which Yeats and the Abbey's middle-class audiences would otherwise have no access—Sheehy-Skeffington accuses O'Casey of doctoring the photograph: given the chance, O'Casey "would point out not only the wart on Cromwell's nose, but . . . would add carbuncles and running sores" (*LSO* 168).

The point Sheehy-Skeffington makes—that neither O'Casey nor any other dramatist can claim to present an objective "reality" uninflected by subjectivity or ideology and that the "real world" of O'Casey's tenement dramas is as much a construct as is Yeats's mythological landscapes—was by and large lost on O'Casey's audiences. O'Donnell's review of *Shadow of a Gunman* in the *Evening Herald* identifies O'Casey as a documentary realist: "His photographs, for one really felt his men and women were but photographs, was [*sic*] nothing less than the work of genius" (qtd. in Hogan and Burnham 145). When P. S. O'Hegarty reviews *Gunman* for the *Irish Statesman* in 1924, this assessment is still current: "Mr. O'Casey records things as they were, but records them with that air of detachment and disillusionment which the historian aims at" (qtd. in Hogan and Burnham 146). Like O'Donnell, he uses the technology of reproduction to describe O'Casey's characterization: "It is a gramophone record of the Dublin accent and the Dublin tenement and the Dublin poor" (qtd. in Hogan and Burnham 147). Holloway echoes them, summarizing O'Casey's artistic strategy as an effort to coax audiences into swallowing the "bitter pill of fact" (236).

As the language of these reviews indicates, however, this assessment of O'Casey is not only inaccurate but also reductive, turning him into a recording lens or needle rather than a creative mind. Yeats demonstrates the more sinister implications of this understanding of O'Casey's "genius" in his letter to George O'Brien defending *The Plough and the Stars.* While rejecting O'Brien's principal demands, he agrees that the dialogue between Nora and Jack Clitheroe needs to be revised: "What is wrong is that O'Casey is there writing about people whom he does not know, people he has only read about" (*LSO* 146). Yeats assumes that unlike (for instance) Yeats himself, O'Casey is capable only of transcribing personal experience; when he uses imagination to create characters that he "does not know," O'Casey is in a false position. In other words, his value as an artist is absolutely identified in Yeats's mind with his status as native informant. The result was that in order to change as a dramatist, O'Casey had to break with the Abbey; their rejection of *The Silver Tassie,* his first serious experiment with expressionism, proved to him that Yeats and his coterie were unable or unwilling to see him as anything other than the recording eye of those early reviews.

O'Casey's credibility as a documentary realist is based on a phenomenon O'Casey deftly exploited in his early drama: an unrecognized essentialism that posited the experience of the working-class subject as an "objective" reality, an irreducible truth, the "pill of fact" whose bitter taste can no longer be obscured by the sugarcoating of artifice. As this chapter will argue, however, this essentialism ultimately limited O'Casey's ability to realize his ideological and artistic ambitions because, among other things, it kept him dependent on the models of gender identity that supported the narrative he was critiquing. Instead of denying the materiality of the body, as he argues that the Pearsian sacrificial model does, O'Casey attempts in his "realistic" plays to force his audiences to *confront* materiality and look at the "body of truth" (*LSO* 169). His use of the suffering body, both male and female, is part of his attempt to point out the gap between the material conditions of the Dublin poor and the ideal Ireland to which he believes the Volunteers and their ilk have pledged their allegiance. Like Marx, O'Casey uses "the body in pain" as "a *visible* and tangible site of exploitation or oppression" (Cvetkovich 167) that would otherwise remain obscured by the more dramatic spectacle of political violence. But if, as Cvetkovich argues, this use of the body is inevitably sensationalistic, the fact that O'Casey promoted himself as a realist eventually made this powerful strategy problematic.

The term "sensationalism," as I will be using it, derives from a particular genre of popular fiction that emerged in Victorian England during the 1860s. Sensationalist fiction was thought to be unduly preoccupied with the physical and emotional sensations of suffering characters and was designed to reproduce those sensations in the hearts and bodies of its readers. The theatrical equivalent of the Victorian "sensation novel" was the melodrama, in which a set of stock characters was run through a formulaic plot with the object of producing the maximum amount of pathos. As the genre developed, more importance began to be attached to the "sensation scene"—an elaborate tableau that aimed at representing, as lavishly and affectingly as possible, a particularly spectacular, perilous, and/or painful ordeal through which the hero or heroine had to struggle.[2] As Yeats noted, and as Stephen Watt's work demonstrates, O'Casey's early work clearly shows that he was indebted to the melodramas he saw at the Queen's Theater in his youth. Given this consensus, the decision taken by those early reviewers to treat the Dublin plays as "realistic" indicates that the distinction between realism and sensationalism was, at least in their minds, an unstable one.

As Watt argues in his treatment of popular theater in O'Casey's work, the tendency to treat sensationalism as realism and vice versa was something that Irish melodrama had already inculcated in Dublin audiences. Thanks to Boucicault and Whitbread, "to many Dubliners . . . history *was* melodrama—and melodrama was often the vehicle for a historically 'precise' account" (Watt 81). Audiences that were used to seeing historical fact conveyed to them as a sensationalist narrative—both on stage, where the 1798 or 1803 rebellions become tales of manly courage and feminine virtue and purity closed with "grossly sensationalistic executions" (Watt 86), and in equally sensationalist historical narratives that dwelt on the physical and sexual cruelty of the British forces—identified O'Casey's dramatic universe as objective "reality" despite its clear indebtedness to those melodramatic forms. Thus, his use of sensationalism in the service of socialism was from the beginning mislabeled as mimesis—an attempt to accurately reflect reality rather than to recreate it.

If we read these plays as sensationalistic rather than naturalistic, we gain a better understanding not only of the plays, but of the tremendous cultural power they wielded in 1920s Dublin. O'Casey's decision to focus on the suffering of the mother rather than the sacrifice of the son—a decision that makes his Dublin plays the most overt and aggressive attack on the sacrificial paradigm that nationalist audiences had yet seen—was in part influenced by melodramatic tradition, which made it easier for him to sensationalize the heroine's body than the hero's. Minnie Powell, Juno Boyle, and Bessie Burgess are useful to O'Casey because their bodies are *so* material that even the magical operations of sacrificial rhetoric cannot make them disappear, and thus O'Casey can use them to incarnate the realities that Irish sacrificial politics fail to address. Playing on the construction of the female body as the essential source of universal, "real" instincts like sexual attraction and maternal love, O'Casey seeks to devalue sacrificial politics by contrasting the artificial nature of political identity with the naturalized bonds between the male patriot and his female counterparts.

But precisely because it was promoted and accepted as "realism," O'Casey's use of the suffering body risked calcifying preexisting class prejudices by naturalizing imperial and capitalist oppression as part of "reality"—inevitable and unchangeable matters of fact. In O'Casey's case, this effect was amplified by the eagerness of an audience whose sense of the stability of "reality" was increasingly threatened as Ireland struggled through partition and civil war. The readiness with which O'Casey's "reality" was accepted as irreducible truth has its genesis not only in the "inequality of embodiedness" (Cvetkovich 188) that renders the working woman so rock-solidly material, but in growing nostalgia for the political certainties that disappeared with the 1922 treaty. O'Casey's heroines resist the erosive power of political violence, preserving in their bodies the essential Ireland that can no longer be located elsewhere. At least, that is, until *The Plough and the Stars.*

Investigating the influence of sensationalism on O'Casey's work will thus help explain why, when O'Casey brought "the body of truth" onto the Abbey stage in *Plough,* all Sheehy-Skeffington saw was "a leprous corpse." The radical shift in attitude toward *The Plough and the Stars* has traditionally been explained in terms of the subject matter. Audiences who had recently survived both the war of independence taking place during *Shadow* and the civil war that scars the Boyle family in *Juno* were relieved rather than outraged to see their own disillusionment reflected in O'Casey's treatment, but that same cynicism becomes a disloyal "pseudo-pacifist propaganda" ("The Insincerity of Sean O'Casey" 5) when applied to Pearse.[3]

But the reaction to *Plough* is also a reaction to a change in *how* O'Casey represents "reality." In his earlier plays O'Casey is allowed to attack the myth of the male martyr—the "shadow" of patriotic self-sacrifice and masculine virtue represented by the self-absorbed Donal Davoren and the melancholic Johnny Boyle—because he preserves its "substance" in female characters. In *The Plough and the Stars,* however, O'Casey deprives his audience of the redemptive power he has hitherto conserved in his female characters. Bessie dies for Nora, but dies cursing her own stupidity; and whereas in *Juno* Mary's baby will grow up under the tender care of its "two mothers" (*Selected Plays of Sean O'Casey* 154), *Plough* closes with the statement that Pearse's uprising has produced, not the birth of a nation, but its miscarriage.

Shadow of a Government: Republican Rhetoric vs. The Real World

In a letter to the *Irish Worker* on June 7, 1913, Sean O'Casey wrote:

> Workers for Ireland, let us help now to fertilize the seed sown by Padraig Mac Piarais by instant help and vigorous sympathy, that it may grow and bring forth fruit a hundred-fold to the glory of God and the honour of Ireland. Slaves, and worse than slaves, are we if it should be that this man's hope and this man's effort are as water spilled upon the ground. (*LSO* 27)

On February 21, 1914, he wrote this letter to the same paper:

> Not in the shouts of the deluded wage-slave Volunteers, but in the hunger-cry of the nation's poor is heard the voice of Ireland. (*LSO* 41)

It is difficult to believe, having read the Dublin trilogy, that O'Casey could ever have written the letter from which that first quotation was taken; it is equally astonishing that in a scant eight months O'Casey went from celebrating Pearse as a mighty progenitor sowing the seed from which "the honour of Ireland" would spring forth to lambasting the Volunteers as a snare spread before the feet of unwary workers. In October of 1913, O'Casey was still gamely trying to enlist the "Irish Irelanders" on the side of the workers; by January of 1914, he was urging readers of the *Irish Worker* to boycott the Volunteers. This sudden about-face makes sense only because this period also encompasses the transport workers' strike of 1913.

In mid-August of 1913, in response to the rising power of the Irish Transport and General Worker's Union (ITGWU), a prominent Dublin businessman named William Murphy began firing workers who had joined the union. The ITGWU responded by organizing a tramworkers' strike, which expanded as other unions joined in sympathy while other employers rallied behind Murphy. Although some Irish nationalists came out in support of the workers, Arthur Griffith was a significant exception; and neither Sinn Fein nor the Irish Revolutionary Brotherhood, the two most active nationalist organizations, publicly supported the strike. Police brutality was one of the employers' weapons, but the more devastating one turned out to be starvation. By remaining intransigent, availing themselves of scab labor, and refusing to negotiate, the employers wore down the union; and by the time the strike ended in December of 1913, it had brought its participants only poverty and hardship (O'Connor 84–89).

Before the strike, O'Casey's letters show him to be a vocal and enthusiastic proponent of cultural nationalism, belonging both to an Irish pipe band and to the Gaelic League, plugging a St. Enda's benefit in the *Irish Worker,* and defending the power and beauty of Irish history, legend, and culture in language that would have been quite at home in the pages of the *Irish Volunteer:*

> I am one of those who has entered into the labour of our fathers; one of those who declare—by the fame of our forefathers; by the murder of Red Hugh; by the anguished sighs of the Geraldine; by the blood-dripping wounds of Wolfe Tone; by the noble blood of Emmet; by the death-wasted bodies of the famine—that we will enter into our inheritance or we will fall one by one. Amen. (*LSO* 18)

Surprising as it is to see O'Casey using this rhetoric sincerely, this appropriation of the Pearsian paradigm was not unusual in the Irish labor movement. Fox's history of the Irish Citizen Army (ICA), a militia formed in 1913 for the purpose of protecting striking workers from the police, notes that Jim Larkin "continually appealed to the national revolutionary tradition" and that the *Irish Worker* ran "many articles glorifying the stand made by Tone and Emmet" (Fox 5–6). Examples can be found in the *Irish Worker* before, during, and after the strike of the tropes we have already seen in the *Volunteer*—from Christ comparisons ("You are as truly the liberators of the world today as were those twelve other working men who, long ago, threw up their jobs to follow the penniless Son of the Carpenter" [qtd. in Fox 37]), to ballads celebrating the manhood of the Union members ("Who fears to wear the blood-red badge / Upon his manly breast? / What scab obeys the vile command / Of Murphy and the rest?" [qtd. in Fox 34]), to the Pearsian resurrection paradigm ("A resurrection! Aye, out of the grave of the first Irishman murdered for protesting against Ireland's participation in this thrice-accursed war there will rise anew the Spirit of Irish Revolution" [Connolly, qtd. in Fox 99]).[4] James Connolly, leader of the Transport Workers' Union and editor of the *Irish Worker,* produced a peroration on O'Donovan Rossa that leans on the same opposition between British materialism and Irish idealism that had always underpinned the republican sacrificial paradigm:

> For slavery is a thing of the soul before it embodies itself in the material things of the world. I assert that before a nation can be reduced to slavery its soul must have been cowed, intimidated, or corrupted by the oppressor. . . . When the soul is conquered, the articulate expression of the voice of the nation loses its defiant accent and, taking on the colour of whining compromise, begins to plead for the body. (qtd. in Fox 123)

O'Casey concludes, after the 1913 strike, that inspiring though it may be, insistence on the power of the ideal over the demands of the real can only hurt the workers—that to maintain that the spirit can remain invincible while the body is trapped in poverty is to deny the conditions that make the workers' revolution necessary and allow nationalists to claim revolutionary status without doing anything about economic exploitation. This realization is spurred by what he sees as the betrayal of the strikers by the nationalist community, symbolized by Pearse's personal failure to support the cause:

> When the workers of Dublin were waging a life and death struggle to preserve some of the "liberties" which ought to be common to all Irishmen, this leader of democratic opinion consistently used the trams on every possible occasion, though the controller of the Dublin tramway system was the man who declared the workers could submit or starve. (*LSO* 41)

In this image O'Casey encapsulates the distinction he draws between socialist republicanism and the Volunteer version. While the strikers are willing to sacrifice their jobs, the leader of the Volunteers is not willing to sacrifice a tram ride. While capital brands its power violently on the bodies of the workers—through police beatings, through the starvation resulting from the loss of their incomes—the Volunteers refuse to put their bodies where their words are.

In O'Casey's battle with James McGowan over whether workers should join the Irish Volunteers, we see him developing the strategy that will reappear in his Dublin trilogy: identifying "reality" absolutely with the body of the suffering worker, and insisting on the primacy of that reality over the airy nothing of the "words—words—words" (*LSO* 34) that constitute Volunteer nationalism. The Volunteers' interest in uniforms becomes one of his favorite examples. Their fantasy of patriotic glory is punctured by O'Casey's presentation of the naked bodies of the Dublin poor:

> They will tempt money from you to deck you in uniforms of scarlet or grey, or green and gold, while they . . . cause you to forget the hundreds of your fellow-countrymen and country-women gliding through Dublin's streets naked and unashamed in sin, misery and want. (*LSO* 35)

He returns to the same image in a later article, drawing the contrast between the vainglorious posturing of the Volunteers and the concrete physicality of life in the tenements even more sharply:

> I challenge [the Volunteers] to tell us if it be prudent to excitedly discuss the colours and distinctions of Volunteer uniforms, to beg for money to gratify their craving for pomp and show, while in Dublin alone twenty thousand families are wriggling together like worms in a putrid mass in horror-filled one-room tenements. (*LSO* 41)

The assumption underlying both of these passages is that physical suffering must be a more compelling argument than any form of verbal rhetoric; that if the heroes of '98 testified against oppression with their blood, the heroes of 1913 have testified against it with their bodies; and that it is to the body of the starving striker rather than to the blood of the aristocratic martyr that the real Irish republican owes his allegiance. As far as O'Casey is concerned, the Volunteers are prevented from understanding this because they are aligned with the same capitalist interests that are oppressing the workers—a kind of collusion that destroys the Volunteer ideal of unity through martyrlove.

What develops in O'Casey's post-strike writing, then, is a conviction that the "voice of Ireland" is not the sacrificial rhetoric to which he had so recently contributed but an inarticulate "hunger-cry" that bursts spontaneous and unmediated from the bodies of "the nation's poor" (*LSO* 41). He counters the Volunteers' appeal to masculinity with his own version of essentialism, one in which the fundamental truth is not the Volunteer's identity as an Irish man but the Irish worker's experience of economic deprivation. *Shadow of a Gunman,* O'Casey's first successful attempt to bring that experience to the nationalist public, dramatizes the conflict between those competing essentialisms—the myth of the hypermasculine Volunteer versus the realities of Irish urban poverty.

It Takes One to Know One

Republican protests might have made *Plough* a second *Playboy,* but by rights it should have been the third. *Shadow of a Gunman,* the first play of O'Casey's produced at the Abbey, may take place in the slums of Dublin during the war for independence that lasted from 1918 to 1921, but it is still heavily influenced by Synge's plot. As in *Playboy,* the leading man is a bookish and shy poet-hero and an outsider who is welcomed into the community enthusiastically because it is believed that he has killed someone and is hiding from the police. As in *Playboy,* the story of his violent past makes him attractive to the local women. As in *Playboy,* the victim of his purported violence—here, the British government in the form of the Auxiliaries who raid the tenement—returns to expose the hero's fraud.[5] Like *Playboy, Shadow of a Gunman* is the story of a lie that takes on a life of its own and that eventually forces a confrontation between the killer-manqué and his invincible victim.

But whereas *Playboy* celebrates the transformative power of that lie, allowing Christy to become a hero, in *Shadow of a Gunman* Donal Davoren's attempt to pass himself off as an IRA gunman fails to transform anything.[6] Davoren and his roommate, Seumas Shields, allow Minnie to protect them by hiding the bombs left behind by Maguire (who actually *is* an IRA gunman). When she is arrested, neither intervenes, and she is shot and killed when the IRA ambushes the police lorry. Davoren's lie has the power to kill Minnie Powell, but it has no power to make out of Davoren anything more than the "poltroon and poet" (*SP* 67) he already was. More significantly, the lie has no power to transform the community into which Davoren has been accepted; it can only bring down the oppressive power of the imperial government on the heads of the people who are looking to Davoren for protection.

As hard as the play is on Davoren, however, *Gunman* assigns much of the responsibility for Minnie's death to the community, suggesting that Davoren's fraud is the creation of their collective need rather than of his personal vanity. Unlike *Playboy,* in which Christy is the first to tell the story of his parricide, *Gunman* has the myth originating with the neighbors, who decide that Davoren must be in the IRA long before the idea of pretending to be has occurred to him. Even at his most deliberately misleading, Davoren never lies outright: when Minnie calls him "a gunman on the run," he replies, "Maybe I am, and maybe I'm not"; and he later speaks in the third person about the life of "a gunman" without actually claiming that he has experienced it (*SP* 19–20). It is clear that the other characters are eager to believe this rumor with or without his collusion: Tommy Owens, Mrs. Henderson, Mr. Gallogher, and Mr. Grigson all treat him like a member of the IRA before he has the chance to confirm or deny their suspicions.

Act I raises the question, then, of why Davoren's neighbors should believe in his shadow identity despite his failure to give them any supporting evidence. *Gunman* offers an answer through its extended satire on the republican ideal of masculinity. Tommy Owens is the vehicle for the most direct attack; his conversation with Davoren reads like a collection of excerpts lifted at random from an issue of the *Irish Volunteer.* He clasps Davoren's hand to show the Irishman's love for his fellow Irishmen: "Two firm hands clasped together will all the power outbrave of the heartless English tyrant, the Saxon coward and knave. That's Tommy Owens' hand, Mr. Davoren, the hand of a man" (22). He then protests tearfully that he would "die for Ireland," castigates lesser men for not assuming their natural responsibilities ("Why isn't every man in Ireland out with the IRA?"), and contrasts Irish idealism with British materialism: "Who'd think o' dinner an' Ireland fightin' to be free?—not Tommy Owens, anyhow. It's only the Englishman who's always thinkin' of his belly" (23–24). It is clear that Tommy is protesting too much; and sure enough, it is Tommy's phenomenally indiscreet gossip that brings the Auxiliaries to the tenement.

But the contrast between Tommy's self-proclaimed masculine reticence and his liquor-inspired garrulity is only part of the irony. *Gunman's* depiction of Irish manhood is an attack, not just on the gap between word and deed, but on the strategy that creates that gap—the same strategy that underlies so much of the rhetoric we saw in the previous chapter. Tommy's behavior testifies to the success of the *Volunteer*'s efforts to make masculinity so inseparable from physical-force republicanism that Irish men can only perform masculinity by protesting their devotion to the republic. While failing to inculcate the virile qualities of the Volunteer in Tommy's heart, Volunteer rhetoric *has* convinced Tommy that others will recognize him as a man only if they also see him as a republican. And this, in fact, is why Tommy needs Davoren to be a gunman.

Tommy, described as physically "small and thin" and "anxious to be on familiar terms with those who he thinks are braver than he is himself" (21), is clearly concerned as much with affirming his own masculinity as with showing his republican credentials. He insists to Davoren that he is "a man, a man," using Davoren to establish his virility through the unspoken and mystical patriotic communion Pearse described: "Not a word, Minnie, not a word—Mr. Davoren understands me well, as man to man" (22). The gossip that attracts the Auxiliaries to the tenement is part of the same attempt to prove his own masculinity through his connection to other male patriots:

> I was in the Blue Lion this evening, an' who do you think was there, blowin' out av him, but that little blower, Tommy Owens; there he was tellin' everybody that *he* knew where there was bombs; that *he* had a friend that was a general in the IRA; that *he* could tell them what the Staff was thinkin' av doin'; that *he* could lay his hand on tons av revolvers; that they wasn't a mile from where he was livin', but that *he* knew his own know, an' would keep it to himself. (52–53; emphasis O'Casey's)

If Davoren's assumption of borrowed masculinity starts the wheels in motion, Tommy's belief that he cannot be an Irish man without also belonging to the ranks of Irish republicans is what ultimately forces the denouement.

With Tommy functioning as a general indictment of the Volunteer spirit, *Gunman* uses the Unionist Protestant Grigson to attack a more specific aspect of the Volunteer virility myth—the contention that manhood is a common, universal bond that transcends political divisions and that will unite Irish men on all sides of the national question. In his first appearance, Grigson gives every sign of having accepted the universality of Irish manhood, apparently vindicating the Volunteers' hope that Unionists and republicans would find themselves united in the brotherhood of the rifle. Grigson identifies with Davoren for the same reason Tommy Owens does—because it will allow him to claim the masculinity he fears he has lost. Already identified as an irresponsible alcoholic, Grigson makes his entrance too drunk to walk and covers the embarrassment of having to lean on his wife by repeating that he is "a man, mind you afraid av nothin'" (48). Casting about for evidence of this so-far-unsubstantiated assertion, Grigson seizes on Davoren so that he can display the telltale recognition of one real man for another: "Davoren! He's a man. Leave it there mate. . . . I don't know what you are or what you think but you're a man" (49). In order to use Davoren's supposed virility to shore up his own shaky claim to it, Grigson is indeed willing to overlook politics: "I'm an Orangeman, an' I'm not ashamed av it, an' I'm not afraid av it, but I can feel for a true man" (50).

Both Tommy Owens and Grigson, then, "recognize" Donal as a patriot-hero in the hopes that this recognition will function as proof of their own masculinity. By expressing toward him the supposedly essential and irresistible sympathy of one "true man" for another, they constitute themselves as the hero they believe him to be, appropriating a mythical manhood that will allow them to deny the evidence of their own failures in the "real" world. If Minnie's attraction to "the idea" is Davoren's motivation for playing along, it is the attraction of men like Tommy and Grigson that generates "the idea" in the first place—and the plot makes their attraction more culpable and more dangerous than Minnie's. Her devotion to her imaginary gunman is presented as the one passion genuine enough to prompt her to actual sacrifice. Although her love seems at first to be of a piece with Tommy and Grigson's adulation, the play actually pits these two forms of republican ardor against each other in a way that suggests that O'Casey has identified the central contradiction at the heart of republican masculinity and is, like Pearse, proposing a solution. Instead of urging Irishmen to shift their allegiance to the dead, *Gunman* proposes a return to "heteronormalcy" through Davoren and Minnie's romance.

Whereas in romantic comedy the obstruction in the path of true love is traditionally an overbearing father, a previous attachment, or a difference in social or economic status, in *Gunman* the two main impediments are (1) the lack of privacy that is an inescapable condition of tenement life, and (2) political violence. *Gunman* gets comic mileage out of the privacy problem; Davoren and Minnie's first kiss is interrupted by the entrance of Tommy Owens, and from then until the end of Act I, Minnie and Davoren are always on stage but are never alone together. Both of the conversations that keep Davoren and Minnie apart relate directly to his status as an IRA soldier: like *Cathleen ni Houlihan*'s Michael, Davoren is prevented from pursuing his attraction to a flesh-and-blood woman by his shadow responsibilities. But here that choice is made for the hero by his self-interested community, and choosing Cathleen over Delia is a tragic mistake.

Delia Strikes Back

The difference between Synge's realism and O'Casey's is epitomized by the way each handles his conclusion. Synge ends *Playboy* with Pegeen lamenting Christy's departure; O'Casey has his heroine "shot through the buzzom" (66). Just as O'Casey reintroduces specific and contemporary political content to Synge's universalized recasting of the Aran Islands story, he literalizes Pegeen's broken heart in Minnie's fatal chest wound. This use of Minnie's body to ratify Davoren's betrayal is the culmination of an identification *Gunman* develops between Minnie and the material reality that the republican movement has, in his opinion, deserted. It is obvious by the end of *Gunman* that Minnie is the play's only real locus of courage, loyalty, or conviction; but what is less clear is why Minnie should be appointed to this prestigious, if dangerous, position. Her characterization cannot be explained, as O'Casey's similar favoritism toward Juno Boyle and Bessie Burgess has been, in terms of "momism."[7] Minnie is not a mother. She is a young and attractive woman in whose body materiality almost becomes powerful enough to defeat the shadow of rhetoric.

Minnie's first entrance is prefaced by a description of her costume: "Her well-shaped figure—a rare thing in a city girl—is charmingly dressed in a brown tailor-made costume, her stocking and shoes are a darker brown tint than the costume, and all are crowned by a tam-o'-shanter of a rich blue tint" (15).This description indicates that her costume's purpose is to set off the only "well-shaped figure" on the stage. Her costume, like her figure, seems to depart from O'Casey's dramatic philosophy; her circumstances should have made her as lumpen as the other "city girls," just as they should have made it difficult for her to afford these clothes. But the fact that other characters comment on Minnie's dress suggests that her fashion sense is part of the dramatic universe rather than an expedient departure from it. Denouncing Minnie after her arrest, Mrs. Grigson blames her delinquency on her outfits: "With her fancy stockins, an' her pom-poms, an' her crepe de chine blouses! I knew she'd come to no good!" (63) This is a more focused version of Shields's criticism of Minnie: "Surely a man that has read Shelley couldn't be interested in an ignorant little bitch that thinks of nothin' but jazz dances, fox-trots, picture theatres an' dress" (39).

The opposition Shields sets up between Davoren's pretensions and Minnie's diversions reflects modernism's feminization of mass culture, through which masculinity is identified with art, the mind, and elitism while femininity is identified with product, the body, and commercialism. Shields's reprise of this theme is inflected by a specifically Irish concern: anxiety about the erosion of Irish culture and the Irish economy under the continued onslaught of British products. As we saw in the *United Irishman,* the dress-materials controversy helped identify the Irish woman's body even more closely with consumption and shifted the burden of responsibility for the Irish economy onto her by assigning her the task of buying and wearing sturdy Irish-made materials instead of cheap but fashionable "English shoddy." In *An Phoblacht* (The Republic), a republican newspaper that first appeared in 1925, two years after *Gunman*'s premiere, that argument is revived through its women's column, appearing alongside arguments against participating in non-Irish entertainments such as jazz dances and picture shows.[8]

Shields thus resurrects the old nationalist reproach against Irish women for failing to use their bodies to incarnate and preserve Irish Ireland. He concludes his diatribe by paraphrasing "Brigid's" castigation of women who refused to "sacrifice" the pleasure of dress: "I wouldn't care to have me life dependin' on brave little Minnie Powell—she wouldn't sacrifice a jazz dance to save it" (40). Shields, a disgruntled republican, has not extended his disillusionment with the cause to include nationalist constructions of Irish women. Instead, he projects the failures of sacrificial patriotism onto the female body, blaming violence on a transformed "Kathleen ni Houlihan," who is "a ragin' divil now," and whose bloodlust is linked to the kind of romantic infatuation he attributes to Minnie: "An' what ecstasy it ud give her if after a bit you were shot or hanged; she'd be able to go about then—like a good many more—singin', 'I do not mourn me darlin' lost, for he fell in his Jacket Green' (40). Minnie is still incarnating Cathleen, but Cathleen is now a sanguinary demon intent on causing men grievous bodily harm. As she was previously held responsible for the piecemeal destruction of the Irish economy, in the post-Rising disillusion the Irish woman is now also held responsible for political violence.

The fact that Shields is wrong about Minnie's sacrificial capacity argues that the materialism for which he denigrates her is not Ireland's undoing but perhaps its route to redemption. During Minnie's first scene with Davoren, she may repeat the republican clichés Tommy Owens spouts, but these speeches are offset by the power of her body, which by the end of the scene has almost reclaimed Davoren for (corpo)reality. Davoren can resist the appeal of *Volunteer*-caliber poetry, but he is as enamored of Shelley's universe as any Volunteer ever was of Dark Rosaleen, and his first interaction with Minnie shows him thoroughly mired in romantic universalities. Minnie's ability to turn Davoren's affections away from the archetypal figures of his favorite poets toward her own body is a model for the process of redemption that this play endorses, through which Irish women might finally save Irish politics.

Although Shields is demonized both by the stage directions, which cast him as a throwback to "primitive man" (4), and by Davoren, he is accorded a certain amount of intellectual authority. Davoren is irritated by Shields's habit of demystifying his literary allusions by identifying their sources, and he is even more irritated by Shields's disquisition on the artist's responsibility:

> I don't profess to know much about poetry. . . . I don't know much about the pearly glint of the morning dew, or the damask sweetness of the rare wild rose, or the subtle greenness of the serpent's eye—but I think a poet's claim to greatness depends upon his power to put passion in the common people. (37)

Shields's speech points out the irony of being a tenement romantic: morning dew, wild roses, and serpents are infrequently found in this environment; and if Davoren emulates his idols, he will produce literature that is illegible and irrelevant to those around him. Davoren rejects Shields's claim, but in fact by this time he has already shown himself susceptible to this argument when put forth by a different messenger.

After Donal quotes some poetry to her, Minnie assumes the woman in the poem must have been his girlfriend. He explains that literary conventions are not necessarily based on lived experience: "Oh, that—that was simply a poem I quoted about the Celandine, that might apply to any girl—to you, for instance" (18). This exchange deflates Davoren's romanticism by revealing its blindness. To Davoren, all beloveds are copies of the same archetype; and in the world of Shelley, Minnie would be indistinguishable from "any girl." Minnie puts Shields's argument against this kind of idealism in more concrete terms by using her own body:

> DAVOREN: Of course I like girls, Minnie, especially girls who can add to their charms by the way in which they dress, like you, for instance.
>
> MINNIE: Oh, now, you're on for coddin' me, Mr. Davoren.
>
> DAVOREN: No, really, Minnie, I'm not; you are a very charming little girl indeed.
>
> MINNIE: Then if I'm a charmin' little girl, you ought to be able to write a poem about me. (18)

Donal's attraction to Minnie, in other words, ought to persuade him to use his art to describe more immediate realities, and by so doing to put "passion" in at least one of the "common people." In this form, the argument seems to be working: when he begins to "become susceptible to the attractiveness of Minnie" (*SP* 19), he agrees to write a poem about her. While the pull of her body on his is responsible for his deception, it is also the only thing that can potentially involve him in the tenement life that he has until now been strenuously attempting to transcend.

Minnie's corporeal form and the sensations it produces in his thus displace romantic ideals, bringing Davoren back to earth. Davoren's opening monologue in Act II demonstrates that idealism is starting to lose its grip on him:

> "She makes all beautiful on which she smiles." Ah, Shelley, she couldn't make this thrice accursed room beautiful. Her beams of beauty only make its horrors more full of horrors still. There is an ugliness that can be made beautiful, and there is an ugliness that can only be destroyed, and this is part of that ugliness. (35)

Davoren is beginning to realize that he has encountered a reality that resists romantic transfiguration. In front of Shields, Davoren still denounces the materialism of "the people"—but Minnie's body has started to do its work.

Thus, Davoren's response to Minnie's body begins to pull him away from the idealism shared by his poetry and Tommy Owens's politics toward a more intimate engagement with his community and his surroundings—the attraction that proves that he "like[s] girls" (18) also attaches him to the material world. As part of that attraction, Minnie's costume is an argument against some of the assumptions underlying the dress-materials argument. Whether her outfit is Irish- or British-made does not matter; what matters is that she "thinks of dress . . . in the right way" (39). The "right way" to use her buying power is not necessarily to support Irish industry but to make her body attractive enough to keep Irish men interested in the real world.

What does not change, however, is the fundamental premise on which the dress-materials argument was built: the double duty assigned to the Irish woman of both embodying the material and representing the ideal Ireland. Even before the final scene, it is clear that Minnie's patriotism is "real" in a way that Tommy's is not, because it is naturalized through her body—rooted in her attraction to Davoren. She insists that sacrificial love can only spring out of an attraction between a real pair of (heterosexual) lovers: "No man ud lay down an' die for any but a sweetheart, not even for a wife" (19). She dutifully amends it later to "except for his country," but she is clearly more interested in Davoren's personal safety than in the republic's: "I wish it was all over, all the same. . . . You'll take care of yourself, won't you, won't you, Donal?" (20)

It is because her idealism is invested in a naturalized, heterosexual attraction to a living human being rather than an "unnatural" attraction to a dead martyr or a political construct that the play values it. Despite her romanticization of Davoren, Minnie's response to the actual crisis is specific and practical, and need not be read as sacrificial. It is, after all, not clear from the scene as written that Minnie still believes Davoren is a gunman when she hides the bombs. After having heard him discourse about throwing bombs "as casually as a schoolboy tosses a snowball," Minnie discovers him "almost fainting on the bed" (56) when she comes to alert them to the raid. Whether this spectacle undeceives Minnie is a question that has to be decided by the director or actress's interpretation. But it is definitely clear to her that once the Auxiliaries find the bombs, they will not care whether Davoren is or is not really in the IRA. Minnie is trying to save, not the Republic, but Davoren—and to do it, if possible, without harming anyone else. She hides the bombs in her room, not because she is eager to die for Ireland, but because she thinks that will be safer for everyone: "Maybe they won't search it; if they do aself, they won't harm a girl" (56). Her death is accidental rather than deliberate—during the ambush she tries to escape and is killed in the crossfire.

The difference between Minnie and the men is not so much that she is able to back up patriotic sentiment with actions as that the gap between word and deed is closed because her patriotism arises directly out of her emotional and physical sensations. She does not have to put her body where her words are because it is already there.

What Minnie's role suggests, then, is that O'Casey's "momism" may not be purely autobiographical, but instead it may be a variation on this basic identification between the female body and "reality." Just as Minnie's attraction to Davoren potentially reverses the damage done by Volunteer masculinist mythology by reclaiming Davoren for both the "real" world and heterosexuality, the slum mother can perform what Volunteer masculinity can only promise, denaturing political, sectarian, or ideological alliances as they are submerged in the all-encompassing bond between mother and son. If Minnie's nubile body is both the originator and object of a "natural," "real" attraction that can give the "unnatural" Volunteer attractions a run for their money, the maternal body is the only force that can compete for primacy with the ideological claims made on her children.

A Principle's a Principle: Civil War and the Battle for the Body

During the years that saw the Dublin trilogy produced, O'Casey's claim to be speaking for the Irish body was not without competition. In fact, his treatment in *Juno and the Paycock* of ideology—not only republican or Free State ideologies, but also those of organized labor—must be understood in the context of the war playing out in the streets and the rhetorical sniping that accompanied it. After the Dáil's acceptance of the 1922 treaty split both the republican movement and the IRA, the battle over actual power was accompanied by a propaganda battle over theoretical legitimacy. During the Irish civil war, in their eagerness to prove that they were the authentic representatives of the "real" Ireland, both sides appealed to the same arguments to support opposing claims, instigating what is presented in *Juno* as a collapse of meaning that renders all political rhetoric bankrupt. What is left after Irish politics self-destruct is the "real" world of bodily suffering. But the gendered dichotomy O'Casey establishes between Boyle's hypocrisy and Juno's authenticity—a dichotomy complicated by Johnny, who wavers unsteadily between them—has dangerous implications.

O'Casey's decision to locate authenticity in Juno's body rather than in Boyle's is underwritten, as we will see, by the melodramatic tradition from which the play arises. But it is also influenced by the unseemly squabbling taking place between republicans and Free Staters over who had rights to the body of the Irish man. *An t-Oglach,* the official newspaper of the Free State army, provides a useful demonstration of how and why this macabre conflict developed.

An t-Oglach, whose Irish title is probably best rendered in English as "The Volunteer," was originally founded in 1918 as the official paper of the Irish Republican Army.[9] When the that army split into the factions that fought the civil war, the portion of the army that stuck with the Free State took *An t-Oglach* with it. *An t-Oglach's* purpose had always been to provide rhetorical support for the activities of the army to which it was allied, and this function did not change after the treaty.[10] What did change was the difficulty of that mission. In 1918, *An t-Oglach* could base its claim to legitimacy on the simple fact that the Irish Volunteers were "an armed organisation of young Irishmen ready to shed their blood for Ireland's freedom" (Beaslai 1). But once it had competition from another armed organization of young Irishmen willing to die for the Republic, *An t-Oglach*'s publishers had cause to regret their assertion that a proven willingness to die for a cause is "the one argument that no lies or hypocrisy of the enemy can get over" (Beaslai 1).

This "one argument" became, paradoxically, more important as it got harder to make. Since the Rising, the republican movement had always based its legitimacy on two things: (1) that it was finishing the work of establishing the Republic proclaimed by Pearse in 1916, and (2) that it was carrying out the will of the Irish people as expressed through the parliamentary elections that returned the Sinn Fein candidates who formed the Dáil Éireann. After the split, the Free State government found itself unable to make either argument convincingly since the republicans who were fighting them could claim with equal validity that they were carrying out Pearse's program and since the Irish people could now no longer be considered a single constituency with a single and representable will. *An t-Oglach* continued to try to assert these claims, but fell back on a kind of argument-by-reiteration. In addition to citing Pearse as often as possible—his blessing is invoked on everything from the establishment of the Free State army to the playing of Gaelic sports—*An t-Oglach* also appealed to the language of democracy, casting the republicans as "Military Tyranny" or as a "Dictatorship," while claiming that the Free State army is "The People's Army."[11] Since the language of liberty was being used to justify the state army's attempt to put down a rebellion, this argument became at times downright Orwellian, as in this passage from February of 1922:

> It has been found necessary in some districts to proclaim martial law, and in others to take special measures to deal with the disturbers of the social order and the common weal. We feel sure that all Volunteers will show the same zeal and enthusiasm in the cause of preserving "the rights and liberties of all the citizens of Ireland" against lawless violence, intimidation and crime as they have shown in the past in their struggle for national freedom. ("Social Order" 1)

In other words, the Free State army has had to destroy Irish rights and liberties in order to save them. Whether a reader agrees or disagrees with the acceptance of the 1922 treaty or the attempt to quash the republican resistance, one thing is certainly apparent here: terms like "rights and liberties" and "national freedom" are starting to get a little slippery.

So, realizing the inadequacy of historical or political arguments, *An t-Oglach* fell back on the "one argument" that appeared to offer hope of success because it was based on something undeniably "real" —not the opinions of the living, but the bodies of the dead. Just as O'Casey dismisses Volunteer posturing as ephemeral in the face of the "hunger-cry of the nation's poor," *An t-Oglach* paints republican opposition to the treaty as an abstract quibble that pales to insignificance beside the body of the sacrificed Volunteer: "Blood and tears against formulas. How long will the Irregulars cling to their sterile choice?" ("Dublin Honours the Brave" 1). To the "fine phrases and speeches" ("The Army" 1) of the republicans, the Free State opposes the "heavy toll in life and blood" that "brought [Ireland] peace" ("Our Purpose" 1). Martyr figures are of course invoked during this argument; but because Tone, Pearse, and Connolly are now also available to the enemy as they were not during the war of independence, *An t-Oglach* relies heavily on the Free State army's own more recent martyrs. Once the Free State army has proved its willingness to die, its legitimacy is established through the sacrificial paradigm whose mystical operations need not be explicable and cannot be logically tested. Once Michael Collins dies in the service of the Free State, he has "sanctified the cause of the people with his blood" ("Carry On" 2); the more blood gets spilled, the more incontestable the Free State's claim to legitimacy becomes.

Or so it would, were it not for the fact that the republican army is also made up of sacrificially minded young Irishmen and therefore can also make that "one argument." Thus, the two sides find themselves locked in competition over who can offer the most evidence in support of this last remaining argument—and thus arises a situation in which the only "real" Irishman is a dead Irishman. By identifying legitimacy so closely with the body of the sacrificed patriot, *An t-Oglach* contributes to a political climate in which the dead are more valuable than the living, as evidenced by this piece, entitled "Desecration":

> The remains of Volunteer Patrick Greaney (21), who was killed at Gort by a bomb thrown by Irregulars, left Gort for Spiddal on Monday. The father and mother of the deceased Irish soldier, a priest and unarmed comrades made up the funeral party. At Craughwell Brigadier Callinan, Battn. Comdt. Rooney and two soldiers joined the cortege. Near Coshla, Athenry, the party were ambushed from both sides of the road and Comdt. Rooney, an Irish soldier with a splendid fighting record in the Liberation War, shot dead.
>
> There have been many wicked and cruel things done in Ireland during the past few months, but none so shameful and ignominious as this.
>
> The desecration of our dead is the blackest crime of all. (1)

An t-Oglach's identification of the martyr's body as the "one argument" for political legitimacy reaches its logical conclusion: the mistreatment of a preexisting Free State corpse is treated as a more heinous "crime" against Ireland than the creation of a new one.

By the time O'Casey set out to write *Juno,* then, both political movements had adopted the same strategy he used against the Volunteers in 1913. Each claimed to be representing the "real" Ireland by representing the body of the Irish martyr, the same way O'Casey used that body to authenticate his rendition of the "real" voice of Ireland. *Juno* is an attempt to take that authority back, to debunk Free State and republican claims to legitimacy by proving that *neither* is faithful to that body's pain. On the one hand, he pursues this agenda through the characterization of Johnny, through whom he attempts to let the male body speak for itself instead of being spoken for by one political group or another. As this attempt proves less than completely successful, thanks to the power of the narratives O'Casey is taking on, he deploys a different strategy through Johnny's mother, Juno: dramatizing the sufferings of the female body, which by and large are ignored or suppressed in sacrificial politics. But in establishing Juno's role as arbiter of the authentic, the "real" stuff of Ireland to which the mere "principles" of political ideology do not ultimately refer, O'Casey invokes Griffithian gender politics that work against his socialist agenda.

Sensationalizing Sacrifice

Gabriel Fallon, writing about *Juno* in his memoirs, professes himself baffled at O'Casey's insistence that *Juno* was a play "about a young man called Johnny Boyle" (qtd. in Harrington 502). It was Fallon's conviction that the play was about the young man's parents, Juno and "Captain" Jack Boyle.[12] The only vestige of this reported original intention is the subplot involving Johnny, Juno's only son, who is abducted and executed by his former republican comrades for having informed on a neighbor named Tancred. The play's famous ending seems to support Fallon's reading. In the penultimate scene, Juno learns from a neighbor that the police have found Johnny's body. After delivering her lament, Juno and the other women leave the stage. Instead of bringing down the curtain, however, O'Casey then brings on Juno's husband and his buddy Joxer, whose drunken, incoherent conversation is the play's final scene.

The juxtaposition of these two scenes, while baffling to some of O'Casey's contemporary reviewers, was immediately hailed by Fallon and others as the first positive proof that the Abbey had a genius on its hands. *Juno*'s ending is a blatant departure from the melodramatic conventions that, as Stephen Watt points out, O'Casey both borrows and undermines in his Dublin trilogy. At the same time, the ending indicates that O'Casey's subversion of the "dominant ideology" about Ireland and the Irish through his undermining of the "very devices which, on the popular stage, conveyed it" (Watt 149) has its limits. While this formal departure from melodrama does help O'Casey make his point about the failure of masculinist sacrificial rhetoric, it makes a dangerous argument about why that rhetoric fails.

As an example of O'Casey flouting melodramatic conventions, Watt cites the disappearance of the sensationalist execution scene that so often closed the nationalist melodrama: "O'Casey appropriates no extravagant tableaux from nineteenth-century historical drama to heighten his characters' deaths; in fact, we never see Minnie after she leaves Davoren's apartment" (179). Similarly, in *Juno,* Johnny Boyle is killed offstage between scenes. But the absence of this particular "sensation scene" does not mean that O'Casey has abandoned sensationalism as a strategy. In fact, what O'Casey is trying to do in *Juno* is to produce a treatment of Irish history that is *more* sensational than the sacrificial paradigm, and melodramatic conventions are valuable to him insofar as they help him do so. One of the arguments *Juno* makes is precisely that republican rhetoric denies the importance of sensation—the power of pain and the experience of the suffering body. While O'Casey does not stage Johnny Boyle's death, the presentation of his body on stage is an attempt to make political violence "sensational" to the audience—to "render suffering so palpable because so visible that the viewer will be convinced that an injustice is being done" (Cvetkovich 169).

Juno's opening scene demonstrates the problem O'Casey faced in his quest to make suffering sensational to his public. Mary, Juno's daughter and Johnny's sister, is reading a newspaper account of the death of Tancred, a republican who has been assassinated by the Free State. The newspaper account certainly seems sensationalist enough: "The full details are in it this mornin'; seven wounds he had—one entherin' the neck, with an exit wound beneath the left shoulder-blade; another in the left breast penethratin' the heart" (*SP* 72). As Mary's dispassionate reading indicates, Dubliners had already gotten "used to newspaper headlines" sensationalizing political violence as best they could (Hogan and Burnham 59); after three years of war with England, violence and its effects were more familiar to the Irish reading public than they had been during the Volunteers' heyday. Graphic and detailed as this description is, however, it lacks affective power. Although both of them know the victim, Mary and Juno are not particularly moved by the report. Their discussion of it does, however, provoke a response from Johnny: "Oh, quit that readin' for God's sake! Are yous losin' all your feelin's?" (72)

As "realistic" as this medical description of Tancred's body is, it fails to make Tancred's suffering as vivid or painful to its readers as it is to Johnny, who is lame in one hip and missing an arm as a result of his exposure to political violence. For the audience, Johnny functions primarily as a way of making that violence accessible by embodying its consequences. As Mary says, Johnny's wounds have left him "very sensitive" (72); many of Johnny's lines are cries of pain in one form or another, and he seems to respond somatically to intangible stimuli. He complains, for instance, that the noise from the upstairs apartment is "like thunderclaps in me brain" (75), and when his devotional candle blows out, he experiences it like a gunshot: "I'm afther feelin' a pain in me breast, like the tearin' by of a bullet!" (151)

While Mary and Juno, like O'Casey's audiences, are "losing their feelings" as a result of long exposure to this kind of violence (and this kind of reporting), Johnny's have become hyper-real, manifesting in physical symptoms extreme enough to become sensible to the audience. The most dramatic example of this process of sensationalization is during the party scene in Act II. Bentham, the British schoolteacher and theosophist who is courting Mary, offers this explanation of ghost stories:[13]

> Scientists are beginning to think that what we call ghosts are sometimes seen by persons of a certain nature. They say that sensational actions, such as the killing of a person, demand great energy, and that that energy lingers in the place where the action occurred. People may live in the place and see nothing, when someone may come along whose personality has some peculiar connection with the energy of the place, and, in a flash, the person sees the whole affair. (112–13)

What is speculation for Bentham soon becomes reality for Johnny, who moments later runs into the room with "his face pale, his lips twitching, his limbs trembling" (113) after having a vision of the dying Tancred:

> I seen him. . . . I seen Robbie Tancred kneelin' down before the statue . . . an' the red light shinin' on him . . . an' when I went in . . . he turned an' looked at me . . . an' I seen the wouns bleedin' in his breast. . . . Oh, why did he look at me like that? . . . It wasn't my fault that he was done in. (114)

What Johnny sees is an image that is obscured both in sacrificial rhetoric and in newspaper accounts: a living, suffering, bleeding body—no longer a hale and hearty Irish Volunteer but not yet an immortal martyr or a dissectable corpse. This vision provokes the physical sensations that the newspaper account could not when Johnny's agitation produces a sympathetic response in Mary: "Mother o' God, he made me heart lep!" (114)

Tancred's ghost is treated by the other characters as a figment of Johnny's superstitious imagination, and its placement (directly after Bentham's speech) strongly suggests that they are right. Thus, the play offers a "realistic" explanation for this visitation that otherwise comes straight out of the sensationalist tradition. But the ghost's unreality does not mean that its effect on Johnny is less pronounced or that its appearance does not affect his audiences on stage or in the theater. Here, then, we see O'Casey drawing on the sensationalist techniques of melodrama in order to render his "realism" more affectively powerful than the newspaper account with which the play opens, using Johnny to translate this imaginary vision into experienced sensation for the audience. If his sudden scream makes Mary's "heart lep," it also jolts the audience in their seats; the same theatergoers who listened without surprise or fear to the description of Tancred's dead body are startled by Johnny's scream into sharing his terror.

If Tancred's ghost, through Johnny's response to it, prevents the audience from taking refuge in either the newspaper's detachment or Bentham's pseudoscientific rationalization, his funeral undercuts the power of a different desensitizing rhetoric—the sacrificial narrative. Although several contemporary reviews single out Sarah Allgood's performance of Juno's lament for Johnny in Act III as the high point of the play, none of them seem to mention Mrs. Tancred's lament at the end of Act II, from which Juno is quoting verbatim. If audiences were less affected by Mrs. Tancred's grief, it was not simply because they had not met the victim. Tancred's death is appropriated by the play's republicans, who use it to support their claim to legitimacy; and the parallel O'Casey sets up between Tancred's death and Johnny's suggests to the audience that because it actually prevents them from experiencing the victim's pain or his family's loss, the sacrificial treatment that the republicans provide is a betrayal of Tancred's sacrifice.

Mrs. Tancred's neighbor, by offering her the standard sacrificial consolation, assimilates Tancred into the pantheon of martyrs: "He died a noble death, an' we'll bury him like a king" (122). Mrs. Tancred, unlike Juno, is "a very old woman" (121), and the epic sweep of her dialogue pushes her toward the realm of allegory; she becomes another Poor Old Woman lamenting a child who could be any Irish man:

> An' I'm told he was the leadher of the ambush where me nex' door neighbour, Mrs. Mannin', lost her Free State soldier son. An' now here's the two of us oul' women, standin' one on each side of a scales o' sorra, balanced be the bodies of our two dead darlin' sons. (122)

Although Mrs. Tancred's refusal to take pride or joy in her son's death differentiates her from Yeats's Cathleen, the impact of that refusal is limited by the frame that contains it. Mrs. Tancred's lament is part of a performance—the republican funeral that will later process down the street outside the apartment—and is flagged as a piece of theater by the presence of that audience of neighbors, by their citations of sacrificial rhetoric, by her own mourning garb, and by the other trappings that will accompany the procession. The overt theatricality of her lament, contained as it is within the spectacle of sacrifice, destroys the "reality effect" that Juno's lament will create and renders her grief less affecting.

Mrs. Tancred's effect on the audience is modeled in the Boyles' reaction to Tancred's funeral. Though Juno scoffs at Needle Nugent's appeal to "the Irish people's National regard for the dead" (126), she runs to the window with the rest of the characters (except, significantly, Johnny) to watch the funeral go by. The sacrificial narrative has turned Tancred's death, like his mother's lament, into a piece of theater—one that is entertaining rather than disturbing or painful:

> MRS. BOYLE: Here's the hearse, here's the hearse!
>
> BOYLE: There's t'oul mother walkin' behind the coffin.
>
> MRS. MADIGAN: You can hardly see the coffin with the wreaths.
>
> JOXER: Oh, it's a darlin' funeral, a daarlin' funeral!
>
> MRS. MADIGAN: We'd have a betther view from the street.
>
> BOYLE: Yes—this place ud give you a crick in your neck. [*They leave the room, and go down.*] (127)

Mrs. Tancred has now been reduced to the status of a prop in this production. The "Irish people's National regard for the dead" has rendered her lament emotionally impotent; it fails to have any lasting effect even on Juno. Instead, the wreaths, procession, and display of support have made Tancred's death a political pageant that may inspire awe or admiration but does not evoke sympathy or sorrow.

The ensuing scene between Johnny and the Mobilizer dramatizes the critique of sacrificial politics implicit in the funeral scene. Just as the spectators at Tancred's funeral are prevented by the ritualistic trappings from feeling for either Tancred or his mother, the Mobilizer's immersion in sacrificial politics has rendered him immune to the affective power of Johnny's suffering body.

> JOHNNY: [*passionately*] I won't go! Haven't I done enough for Ireland! I've lost me arm, an' me hip's desthroyed so that I'll never be able to walk right agen! Good God, haven't I done enough for Ireland?
>
> THE YOUNG MAN: Boyle, no man can do enough for Ireland! (128)

The logic of civil war politics denies Johnny any claim for sympathy or mercy because he is still alive. The Second Irregular makes this clear when Johnny is arrested at the end of Act III: to Johnny's final plea—"Look at me arm, I lost it for Ireland"—he replies, "Commandant Tancred lost his life for Ireland" (152). Johnny is not as "real" as Tancred because he is still living. The Irregulars refuse to be affected by anything less than martyrdom, demonstrating a callousness toward Johnny's physical and mental suffering that indicts the political movement with which they are identified.[14] The more successful the production has been at making Johnny's suffering sensible—the more sensational his performance is—the more damning that indictment becomes.

While Johnny is not an especially powerful textual presence—of all the Boyles he talks the least, and when reading the play it is easy to forget that he exists—a case can be made that Johnny is, in fact, what this play is really "about." Although he spends much of his time behind a curtain that separates his bed from the rest of the room, Johnny is always on stage (except for a few minutes at the beginning of Act III) until the Irregulars finally drag him off. Even when he is not speaking, his missing arm and limp serve as visible reminders of his internal suffering.[15]

It was, perhaps, through Johnny's suffering body that *Juno* really hooked its audiences. W. J. Lawrence, one of the play's initial reviewers, found "the haling to death of the crippled informer Johnny Boyle" one of those moments "so vivid in the light of recent experience that they transcend all theatricality and thrill me to the marrow like matters of personal suffering" (qtd. in Hogan 193). For Lawrence, at least, Johnny is what provokes that quintessential sensationalist response—he finds himself experiencing Johnny's death in his "marrow," and he shares his pain as if it is his own "personal suffering." It is also suggestive that, according to Fallon, O'Casey originally wrote a death scene for Johnny, which the directors cut (Harrington 502). This hints that O'Casey's decision to do away with the melodramatic execution may have had more to do with the restrictions he was working under than with a desire to avoid sensationalism.[16]

But even if O'Casey had staged the execution, it would have had to have been very different from the kind found in nationalist melodrama. The same sensitivity that allows Johnny to share his suffering with the audience also prevents him from going to his death with the quiet stoicism expected of the patriot-hero. The patriot-hero is never allowed to feel doubt, fear, or pain on his own behalf; any sorrow he expresses tends to refer to the suffering of his wife, sweetheart, children, loyal friends, or Ireland on his account rather than to his own imprisonment or demise. On the other hand, the villain—who in the Irish national melodrama is generally either a British solider or an Irish informer—can and does feel his own pain, and this weakness (expressed either as a desire for money, desire for the heroine, or simply fear of death and physical pain) becomes the motivation for his scurrilous actions. This manifestation of the ideal/material split means that all the traits we have seen in Johnny are associated in Irish melodrama with the villain:

> Craven process servers and barristers . . . appear routinely as informants and traitors to the Irish cause in Whitbread's historical dramas, typically claiming legal authority and the power of Dublin Castle in enforcing their self-interest. Beyond their cowardice, duplicity, and rhetorical enfeeblement, such characters are frequently effeminate or physically inferior to both comic and historically significant Irishmen. (Watt 69)

Johnny's disability, his sensitivity, his pleas for mercy, his relative taciturnity, and his obvious and consuming fear of death assign him, under the rules of melodrama, to the role of the villain. By making Johnny an informer, then, O'Casey is actually making an important concession to the logic of melodrama—and it is here that we see how the parameters of the melodramatic genre are shaping O'Casey's project even as he works to revise them. The generic conventions that associate materialism with villainy are still so strong that O'Casey can only make Johnny's pain sensible to the audience *by* making him a villain, preserving the same connection between carnality and treachery that created the cowardly, money-hungry, lecherous informers of Whitbread's melodramas.

Despite his other attempts to bend the rules of melodramatic characterization—Johnny has been a patriot-hero in the past, something that in a melodrama would be an unthinkable complication of the moral universe—O'Casey finds himself unable, when it comes to his male characters, to break that fundamental link between materialism and evildoing. This is borne out not only in Johnny's informing, but in his overall characterization: the sensitivity that makes Johnny valuable for O'Casey's project also makes him so self-absorbed that he has a hard time retaining the audience's sympathy. Johnny's narcissism is never more obvious than in the scene immediately before his arrest, during which his only response to the news that Mary is pregnant and has been abandoned by Bentham is to complain that he is now no longer the center of attention: "Not one o' yous, not one o' yous, have any thought for me!" (146).

By making this concession to melodramatic characterization, O'Casey gets himself into a dramatic bind. In order to prevent his audience from discounting once again the suffering body of truth, O'Casey must persuade them to sympathize with a character who, thanks to melodramatic precedent, is almost by definition unsympathetic. His solution is to follow Johnny's arrest with Juno's lament, ensuring that viewers who remain unmoved by the death of an informer will nonetheless be affected by his mother's grief. The success of O'Casey's sensationalism, then, depends absolutely on the power of Juno's final speech—a power that derives as much from the contrast with, as from the similarity between, this scene and Tancred's funeral. That power is also dependent on O'Casey's preservation of melodramatic convention as it relates to his female characters—especially the construction of Juno's and Mary's emotions (Juno's love for her children, Mary's attraction to Bentham) as "apparently natural as biological characteristics" (Cvetkovich 107).

Only a Poor Dead Son

While agreeing that O'Casey confers "goddess" status on Juno, Bernard Benstock points out that he has been careful to humanize her by giving her faults, which include "petty attitudes and parochially limited points of view" (66). Despite her working-class status, Juno shares bourgeois values that make her dismissive of Mary's labor politics and overly enthusiastic about the prospect of her marrying Bentham. While agreeing that Juno's politics are at variance with O'Casey's, I would argue that this false consciousness is not a deliberate attempt to make her flawed but an unavoidable side-effect of O'Casey's other strategies. Juno's rejection of Mary's politics is part of her status as the "body of truth"—the real thing of which ideology can only be a betrayal. Juno's dialogue makes it clear that her disdain for Mary's socialism is of a piece with her attitude toward Johnny's republicanism. Her equation of the two causes is underwritten by O'Casey, who makes Mary and Johnny cite the same motto to justify their actions: "A principle's a principle" (74, 99). *An t-Oglach*'s reproach to the republicans—that they are "killing the living of Ireland" for "an abstract political formula" ("Futility" 4)—resurfaces in Juno's criticism of Mary's activism.

O'Casey's apparently out-of-character refusal to differentiate between national politics and socialist policy makes more sense in light of civil war politics in Ireland. After the Treaty, the labor movement, as represented by the Transport Workers' Union, joined forces with the republicans. The logic behind this decision, as expressed by labor leader Jim Larkin at the time and later on by others in *An Phoblacht,* was that as long as Ireland was still attached to the British Empire, exploitation of the Irish workers would inevitably continue, and that therefore the workers' liberation would only be possible in a united republic. While O'Casey agrees that the Free State is very far from being the workers' utopia, he is also clearly skeptical of the labor-republican alliance, perhaps because it involves a return on the labor side to sacrificial rhetoric. Consider, for instance, the language of Larkin's declaration of support for the republican cause:

> We stand for the Dead. We entered into a compact with them when living. They did not fail us. We will not fail them. Connolly, Pearse, Clarke and our other comrades did not die for a phrase. . . . We will never in life, under any conditions, betray the Dead. . . . We will not willingly . . . join hand with the murderers of Connolly, Pears, Clarke, and our comrades who willing gave up their struggle in death. Yet in death they live. And we who are in life will never betray them. (qtd. in Fox 212)

If the logic behind the labor-republican alliance has its roots in an understanding of the relationship between imperialism and capitalism, its rhetorical expression obscures that understanding, invoking instead Pearsian fidelity to Erin's great dead. Juno's treatment of Johnny and Mary indicates that O'Casey sees the labor-republican connection as simply a further betrayal of the body of truth for the chimera of idealism. In both cases, the child's fidelity to ideology is opposed to the mother's anxiety over the family's actual survival: "Yis; an' when I go into oul' Murphy's to morrow, an' he gets to know that, instead o' payin' all, I'm goin' to borry more, what'll he say when I tell him a principle's a principle?" And later: "Ah, you lost your best principle when you lost your arm; them's the only sort o' principles any good to a workin' man" (*SP* 74–75, 99).

Juno's distrust of the labor movement is ratified by the characterization of Jerry Devine. O'Casey's authorial attitude toward him is made clear in the stage direction for his first entrance: "He is a type, becoming very common now in the Labour Movement, of a mind knowing enough to make the mass of his associates, who know less, a power, and too little to broaden that power for the benefit of all" (*SP* 76). Devine's actions bear this out; he fails both Mary and his organization by not going far enough. A professed atheist, he is still close enough to Father Farrell to use the Church's connections to wangle Captain Boyle a job opening; a principle may be a principle, but Devine is not above playing the system.[17] He is anxious to parlay his job as union secretary into upward mobility: "You an' I could live nice an' cosily on that; it would lift you out o' this place." (86). When Devine has the chance to win Mary back, he loses it through his fidelity to bourgeois sexual mores, proving that his "humanity is just as narrow as the humanity of the others" (149). Organized labor, as represented by Jerry, has become another bag of empty words, an organization interested only in perpetuating itself by appropriating power without changing power structures.

In *Juno*'s world, then, organized labor has been contaminated by sacrificial politics, rendered chimerical by the alchemy of republican rhetoric. Juno is offered as the material world's last faithful defender, the only character who refuses to help what is solid melt into air. But O'Casey runs into trouble when he guarantees that fidelity the same way the Volunteers tried to support their sacrificial politics—by naturalizing it through the innate, essential, "human" sentiments and inclinations associated with gender identity. Juno's connection to what is "real" is established and sold through O'Casey's appeal to the purported universality of maternal instinct.

As Cvetkovich argues, the "sensational power of a mother's separation from her children"—the tragic power to which so many of *Juno*'s early reviewers allude in their discussion of the play's climax—attests to, and is dependent on, "the force with which ideologies of maternity are taken for granted"; in other words, the unstated assumption that "nothing is more natural and inevitable than a mother's love" (112). In an attempt to break the connection between authenticity and the body of the slain political martyr—the connection that ensures, as Johnny says, that Ireland will "never be at peace" as long as each side has "a son left to pull the trigger" (*SP* 99)—O'Casey offers the only thing his audience is willing to accept as *more* authentic. "Ideologies of maternity" are so firmly entrenched that they can overwrite the sacrificial narrative: the body of the suffering mother, instead of the body of the dead son, becomes the last word in authenticity and undoes the power of political ideology.

While Juno repeats much of Mrs. Tancred's lament, she introduces one significant revision: "Maybe I didn't feel sorry enough for

Mrs. Tancred when her poor son was found as Johnny's been found now—because he was a Die-Hard! Ah, why didn't I remember then that he wasn't a Diehard or a Stater, but only a poor dead son!" (155). Juno's natural love for her son, which now extends to include Tancred, neutralizes the political divisions that have killed them both. Ideological affiliation melts away to reveal the only "real" Irish identity: what matters is that they are both poor dead sons of poor suffering mothers. Where the Volunteer vision of unity through masculinity fails, Juno's vision of unity through maternity succeeds: she repents her previous callousness toward Mrs. Tancred, who she had previously held responsible for her son's death because "she let the Die-hards make an open house o' the place" (124). Now Mrs. Tancred's political affiliation becomes irrelevant as Juno realizes the primacy of the bond that unites all mothers, which she then performs by repeating Mrs. Tancred's lament:

> It's well I remember all that she said—an' it's my turn to say it now: What was the pain I suffered, Johnny, bringin' you into the world to carry you to your cradle, to the pains I'll suffer carryin' you out o' the world to bring you to your grave! Mother o' God, Mother o' God, have pity on us all! Blessed Virgin, where were you when me darlin' son was riddled with bullets, when me darlin' son was riddled with bullets? Sacred Heart o' Jesus, take away our hearts o' stone, and give us hearts o' flesh! Take away this murdherin' hate, an' give us Thine own eternal love! (155)

As Juno's citation of Mrs. Tancred's words establishes the universality of the sentiment behind them, O'Casey suppresses the sacrificial accoutrements that accompanied Mrs. Tancred's lament, breaking her out of that confining frame. Because this scene takes place after the Boyles' furniture has been repossessed, Juno delivers her lament on an almost-empty stage; and instead of the crowd that attended Mrs. Tancred, the only spectators are Mrs. Madigan and Mary.[18] We know that Johnny will never have a republican funeral, and no one offers any consoling thoughts about Johnny's sacrifice for the good of the Republic. The fact that Johnny has been shot for informing precludes any rhetoric about his having died with honor. Even the invocation of the Virgin Mary, which suggests the same parallel between Christ and the fallen Irish hero that Pearse developed, is undercut when Juno accuses her of betraying her fellow-mothers: "Where were you when me darlin' son was riddled with bullets?" (155).

Here, then, is the vision of the "real" Ireland, the suffering that has been betrayed by Staters, Diehards, and trades unionists alike. Because the "naturalness of maternal affect" (Cvetkovich 113) is so resistant to challenge, it becomes the rock on which Irish identity can be rebuilt; and Juno's maternal body, dominating the almost-empty stage, embodies all that is finally irreducible and indestructible about Irishness—the body of truth that no ideological battle or political violence can make disappear. Suffering as she is, she is also triumphant, having rediscovered through the bonds of motherhood the strength that will allow her to protect Ireland's future in the form of Mary's unborn baby. Unlike Mrs. Tancred, who insists that she "won't be long afther" her son (122), Juno survives, driven by her "natural" desire to take care of Mary and her child. Unlike the rest of the Boyles, Juno sees past the stigma of illegitimacy to recognize Mary's baby as kin to her; and unlike Jerry Doyle, Juno is willing and able to rescue Bentham's victim. Mother love does what neither sacrificial nor labor politics can do.

It can only do this, however, by repeating some of the same statements that the sacrificial narrative makes about Irish gender identity—and, in the process, reproducing some of its omissions. The power of Juno's maternal love and her unswerving dedication to solving material problems and ensuring the family's material survival remain absolutely identified with her role as homemaker: "Who has kep' th' home together for the past few years—only me? An' who'll have to bear th' biggest part o' this throuble but me?" (146). It is exactly this "natural" feminine desire to keep the home together at all costs that engenders the bourgeois self-absorption that leads her to discount Mary's attempts at collective action because they adversely affect their individual family unit. Here, as in the nineteenth-century maternal melodramas that Cvetkovich analyzes, O'Casey's use of the "spectacle of the mother" means that *Juno* ultimately "represent[s] social problems as emotional problems" (112), transforming the larger forces of capitalist and imperial oppression into the conflict between Juno's maternal altruism and the Captain's flagrant selfishness. That final scene between Boyle and Joxer—the dissonant coda to Juno's closing lament—is another illustration of the trap into which O'Casey's use of essentialism is leading him.

Captain Boyle's Body

Just as Juno's maternal feelings are naturalized through her repetition of that universal lament, Mary's love for Bentham is presented as the kind of "natural and fatalistic force" (Cvetkovich 107) that sweeps the melodramatic heroine before it. Mary professes to love Bentham "with all my heart and soul" but against her better judgment: "Why, I don't know; I often thought to myself that he wasn't the man poor Jerry was, but I couldn't help loving him, all the same" (130). Her pregnancy testifies to the fact that, like Juno's mother love, Mary's attraction to Bentham has its source in her body as well as her heart and soul, and is in fact transforming that body through the pregnancy. Juno, Johnny, and Mary, different as their roles in the play are, have one thing in common: in them, feeling is made "real"—something that can oppose and supersede the self-subverting mirage of political ideology—through its incarnation in their bodies.

But using the body as the guarantee of authenticity is more problematic for O'Casey than it was for his nineteenth-century sensationalist predecessors, given the role that medical discourse has played in the maintenance of imperial ideology in Ireland. As we have seen, the rules governing melodramatic characterization—which demand that physical or emotional suffering be made the exclusive province of the heroine, while the hero is an idealized, bodiless superman—make it difficult for O'Casey to locate this authenticity in a male body, resulting in the ambivalent characterization of Johnny. But if he bent the rules for Johnny, O'Casey is in full compliance when he creates Captain Boyle, in whom materialism remains firmly associated with villainy—and whose body ultimately becomes the source of the Boyle family's downfall.

Like the petition subplot in *Gunman,* the will plot in *Juno* establishes an allegorical relationship between the male lead and the new Irish government.[19] One of Boyle's purposes is to dramatize the fundamental hypocrisy of political rhetoric as used at this period in Ireland, functioning as he does as a figure for the "new aristocracy" running the Free State government, with the will that Bentham makes out standing in for the Treaty.[20] O'Casey's dialogue makes the parallels fairly explicit. In Act I, before he gets the news of his inheritance, Boyle is in Volunteer mode, bragging to Joxer that "there's goin' to be issued a proclamation be me, establishin' an independent Republic, an' Juno'll have to take an oath of allegiance" (95). In Act II, Boyle's middle-class pretensions transform him, as Joxer says, into a "mastherpiece of the Free State counthry" (133), complete with a sudden interest in cultural nationalism and a corresponding dismissal of republicans and their concerns.[21] At the beginning of Act III, Boyle makes a show of supporting Irish industry by ordering a topcoat of "Irish frieze" (135); and in the last scene, after the will falls through and the family is destroyed, he tells Joxer, "If th' worst comes . . . to th' worse . . . I can join a . . . flyin' . . . column" (156) as an Irregular.

Thus, Boyle's final scene links his personal failure to the failure of Irish politics; and what this scene suggests is that both failures have their roots in the fundamental hypocrisy that characterizes Boyle—his refusal to acknowledge his own materialism even as he remains enslaved to it. The contrast developed in *Gunman* between idealistic patriotic rhetoric and the reality of physical existence is restated in this scene, during which Boyle is so drunk that he can hardly stand up, and his dialogue is halting and incoherent. It is at this point—when his body's dominion over his mind or spirit has never been more self-evident—that Boyle brings out his most explicitly sacrificial rhetoric, claiming to have "done . . . [his] . . . bit . . . in Easther Week" and witnessed a fellow-Volunteer's Ultimate Sacrifice:

> BOYLE [subsiding into a sitting posture on the floor]. Commandant Kelly died . . . in them . . . arms . . . Joxer . . . Tell me Volunteer Butties . . . says he . . . that . . . I died for . . . Irelan'! (156)

Sacrificial rhetoric appears for the last time in the mouth of a man who has demonstrated a proven inability to put the welfare of even his own family ahead of his own corporeal desires. Like Boyle's plan to join a flying column, this line suggests that sacrificial politics are not only the last refuge of the desperate, but a direct outgrowth of the kind of personal weakness with which *Juno* taxes Boyle.

Unlike the other three characters, Boyle is denied any claim to authenticity and is disqualified from using his body to render his experiences "real." In fact, the one occasion on which he does try to communicate his physical sufferings to an audience becomes the most devastating proof of his hypocrisy. Juno accuses him of intentionally shirking work by making up imaginary ailments: "If there was e'er a genuine job goin' you'd be dh'other way about—not able to life your arms with the pains in your legs!" (82). Boyle proves her right when, after declaring himself hale and hearty, he is suddenly seized by pains in his legs as soon as he hears about the job offer. He continues performing his "pain" as melodramatically as possible—"Nobody but meself knows the sufferin' I'm goin' through with the pains in these legs o' mine!" (85)—but no matter how extreme the performance becomes, it is never convincing. The Captain's "body in pain" cannot be made "real" to the audience because the audience has already been primed to interpret his suffering as an expedient fiction rather than an essential truth.

It is not my purpose to suggest that Captain Boyle may actually suffer from debilitating pains in the legs, but to point out that, given his characterization and his treatment by the rest of the cast, if Boyle *did* suffer any kind of actual physical pain there would be no way for him to convey that convincingly to the audience. He has been denied the opportunity to describe his own body, which has instead been assigned to anyone and everyone else. Boyle suggests that even Jerry Devine seems to think he "know[s] more about the pains in me legs than meself that has them" (85). Having demonstrated his willingness to lie about his own body (he claims not to have been drinking and not to want any breakfast, and is shortly proved wrong on both counts), he must now cede the right to determine what is "really" happening to his body to others. And since, aside from Jerry, the Captain is the play's only representative of the male Irish worker, those other narratives can now subvert the story that his body might otherwise tell about capitalist exploitation and make Boyle's body the cause and explanation of its own plight.

The only real effect of the phantom pains in Boyle's legs is that they prevent anyone from accepting social or historical explanations for his chronic unemployment. In front of the audience, Boyle is offered the opportunity to work and rejects it. The message *Juno* sends is that Boyle is unemployed because he is "naturally" bone-idle, not because Ireland's economy has been underdeveloped or because he is part of an underclass typically barred from holding any but the hardest and least remunerative jobs. Boyle's complaining about the physical demands of this kind of labor—"What ud happen if I had to carry a bag o' cement?" (92)—becomes self-justifying whining rather than a legitimate objection to capitalism's exploitation of the laborer's body. And with a eugenics-driven medical establishment out there only too willing to discover biological causes for social problems in the pathologized body of the Irish man, his alcoholism becomes another argument for blaming the Boyles' poverty on Boyle's body.

Constructed through turn-of-the-century medical rhetoric as a disease—a susceptibility that both has a biological cause and, paradoxically, can spread like a contagion—alcoholism later becomes a form of degeneracy associated through eugenics both with Britain's urban poor and with the Irish. Bringing Boyle and Joxer on in that final scene, then, and making that strong association between alcoholism and sacrificial rhetoric (both of which become more extreme here than ever before) offers the audience an explanation for the tragedies that have gone before, essentially letting both capitalism and imperialism off the hook. The Boyle family's destitution, Mary's pregnancy, and Johnny's death are all put down in Juno's last scene to "the stupidity of men," which is then immediately embodied for the audience when Boyle returns to the stage. Adherence to sacrificial politics, like the betrayal of domestic responsibility to which O'Casey connects it, are essentialized through Boyle as deficiencies in the Irish man, innate proclivities that, left to themselves, will reduce the domestic world to "a state o' chassis."

Juno's ending, then, demonstrates some of the dangers of claiming to be a "realist." Simply portraying suffering as accurately as possible will not produce social change if the audience is allowed to read that suffering as "natural," encoded in the bodies of the unfit sufferers. This is something O'Casey might well have learned from the 1913 strike, after which the employers subsidized a book called *Disturbed Dublin,* which argued that the workers' sufferings before, during, or after the strike had nothing to do with the employers' actions. Arnold Wright, the author of this masterpiece of spincraft, describes the conditions of the working poor in language not far from O'Casey's:

> The Dublin slum . . . is a thing apart in the inferno of social degradation. Nowhere can there be found concentrated so many of the evils which are associated with the underworld of our modern civilization. To say that men and women live like beasts of the field is the merest truth. In buildings—old, rotten and permeated with both physical and moral corruption—they crowd in incredible numbers. (qtd. in Fox 18)

Fox comments, when he cites this passage, that "to maintain, on the one hand, that the employers of Dublin were progressively-minded pillars of sweetness and light, while the workers remained sub-human denizens of horrible tenements is . . . a difficult matter" (21–22). Counterintuitive as this proposition may seem, however, it becomes tenable if the reader can be persuaded to accept the first principles of eugenics: that poverty is a biological attribute and that conditions like this are not the creation of a social system but simply the social *expression* of an already innate "physical and moral corruption" that characterizes the urban poor. Simply offering a "photograph" of urban poverty, then, does not make an argument in favor of ending it; in fact, as Wright's bit of sophistry shows, for an audience already so inclined, it can serve as proof of poverty's inevitability, its role in the "natural" order of things.

By invoking essential gender roles in his dramatization of the "hunger-cry of the poor"—by making Juno the good mother and Boyle the bad father; Juno the naturally feminine defender of the home and hearth and children, Boyle the naturally masculine destructive and self-centered force that he is—O'Casey contributes to this naturalization of poverty, the construction of this "reality" as predetermined, essential, unchangeable, biologically based. The Boyles' poverty, like the sacrificial violence that kills Johnny, becomes the "natural" result of the eternal conflict between a mother's natural concern and care for her children and the predator male's natural depravity.

Considering this, it is hardly surprising that even before *The Plough and the Stars,* some Irish critics were beginning to have second thoughts about O'Casey's "realism." In *An Phoblacht,* a year after *Juno*'s Dublin premiere, "Fiach" complains in "Drama and Slavery" that *Juno* is popular with English audiences because it panders to "sensation-hunters," arguing that instead of offering an accurate picture, the play "stress[es] certain abnormalities which pass for realism" (3). The play remained palatable to Dublin audiences, however, because along with these "abnormalities," O'Casey preserves some of the conventions that his predecessors have used to keep audience anxieties at bay. Michael's increasingly abject failure is still recuperated by an invincible Cathleen; Volunteer masculinity becomes a shadow, but the substance of that patriotism is preserved in Juno. The same gender construction that helps undermine O'Casey's socialist agenda also prevents him from completely disabling the sacrificial paradigm.

In *The Plough and the Stars*—O'Casey's final assault on Irish sacrificial politics—we can see him making an effort to complicate these gender roles in order both to debunk the sacrificial mythos once and for all and to avoid letting audiences explain poverty with the Boyle excuse. Bessie is no Juno; and while Nora is still playing Minnie's role, her character is both more complex and more compromised. Fluther's alcoholism is not allowed to cancel out his courage and compassion, and Mrs. Gogan's neglect of her two children suggests that motherhood is not necessarily transformative or transcendent. The same sentiments that are enshrined in *Gunman* and *Juno* as potentially redemptive—heterosexual attraction and maternal love—are still naturalized through Nora, but they are now as impotent as

Davoren's "patriotism." In *Plough* it is made devastatingly clear that when Michael goes down, he drags Delia and Bridget with him. By incapacitating Cathleen without changing the argument he makes about the failure of sacrificial politics, O'Casey moves his audience to anger and sparks, finally, an open debate about who has the right to the body of truth.

The Figure in the Window: Pearse, *Plough*, and the Republican Legacy

The Dubliners who protested at *Plough* responded to it primarily as an attack on Pearse and the Volunteers—and indeed, it would be hard to argue that it was not. Pearse appears in Act II as a shadowy character listed in the cast as "The Figure in the Window," and although he is never named, audiences would have had little trouble recognizing him.[22] All of the Figure's dialogue is lifted almost verbatim from some of Pearse's most famous pieces—"The Coming Revolution," "Peace and the Gael," the graveside panegyric on O'Donovan Rossa—and O'Casey's use of him in this act is a more explicit version of the attack on Volunteer rhetoric and Volunteer masculinity in *Gunman*. But if *Plough* is intended solely as a swipe at Pearse, why is Clitheroe a commandant in the Irish Citizen Army instead of the Volunteers? If O'Casey wants to critique sacrificial politics, why does he do it by attacking the one organization that *did* stand by the striking workers of 1913?[23]

The title, and Clitheroe's affiliations, suggest that what is really being attacked here is not so much sacrificial politics themselves as the pernicious effect they have had on the labor movement. This argument is made most explicitly through the character of the Young Covey, who on the one hand chides members of nationalist organizations for being duped into fighting the wrong battle, and on the other is as unable as they are to resist the infighting and brawling of the pub scene in Act II.[24] The Covey claims the Plough and the Stars is "a Labour flag, an' was never meant for politics" (181), but the play shows the sacrificial "politics" of the Volunteers taking over labor, casting Pearse as the cad who seduces and then betrays the Irish Citizen Army. And the construction of Act II, in which Pearse's oratory is juxtaposed with Rosie Redmond's attempts to find herself a client, argues that "seduction" here is not just a metaphor. Continuing the theme started in Act I, in which Clitheroe's narcissistic interest in honors, ritual, and uniform is opposed to his attraction to Nora in the same way Davoren's romance with Minnie is thwarted by his supposed involvement in the IRA, Act II shows sacrificial rhetoric competing with heterosexual attraction for the attention of the Irish man—and winning.

Higher Things Than a Girl's Garters

Rosie's character is certainly intended in part as a satire on political expediency—she alters her rhetoric to match the taste of her prospective customers and is as willing to repeat the Covey's line as she is to parrot sacrificial rhetoric back to its users. It is probably not a coincidence that she shares a last name with John Redmond, a prominent Irish member of Parliament and a Home Rule advocate. Redmond's involvement with the Volunteers—which led to the split that decimated their organization months before the uprising—was one of the main reasons labor was wary of joining forces with them, and Redmond's declaration of support for England during World War I proved them right. If her name identifies her with Irish politicians, however, her female body is more likely to identify her with Ireland itself; and Rosie's fickleness could just as easily be a representation of Ireland's famous inconstancy regarding its political leaders. Given that her last name is mentioned only once on stage (usually she is addressed as, and calls herself, "Rosie"), while her body is prominently displayed, Rosie-as-Ireland would seem to be the dominant metaphor—at least the one recognized by the protesters, who objected to Rosie as a "realistic" part of O'Casey's Ireland. (Had they seen her as a figure for Redmond, they would have been more likely to applaud and throw flowers.)

Like Minnie in *Gunman,* Rosie stands for the material, "real" Ireland—but whereas Minnie is allowed to retain idealized characteristics and the illusion of romance, the facts of the matter are put much more bluntly here: Rosie's economic survival is directly dependent on her ability to use her body to remind Irish men that they have bodies too. Her job—literally—is to pull Irish men out of "th' glorious company of th' saints, an' th' noble army of martyrs," to convince them to abandon the illusory "sthreets of paradise" for more corporeal pleasures (193). O'Casey's now-familiar argument—that the patriot's real duty is to recognize and struggle to change the material conditions oppressing the Irish poor—is cast again in terms of the Irish man's willingness or refusal to respond to the body of the Irish woman. The only difference—and one reason this argument sets off his audiences here, whereas in *Gunman* and *Juno* it did not—is that the sexual economics underpinning that argument are presented as baldly as possible. In *Gunman,* Davoren's duty is to fall in love with Minnie; in *Juno,* Boyle's duty is to provide for his family; in *Plough,* the transaction is revealed as, at bottom, crassly material: Irish men discharge their responsibilities by first accepting their "natural" heterosexual desires and then paying women for satisfying them. Rosie herself sets this out in terms that are almost a parody of the Griffithian home-and-hearth argument:

> It's no joke thrying' to make up fifty-five shillin's a week for your keep an' laundhry, an' then taxin' you a quid for your own room if you bring home a friend for th' night. . . . If I could only put by a couple of quid for a swankier outfit, everythin' in th' garden ud look lovely (193)

In other words, for Rosie to keep her home together, she needs more clients; the labor of the Irish woman will go for naught without a little help from the Irish man. The division of labor remains the same—the woman works on keeping the man engaged, the man invests his material assets in the home over which she presides—but it is not camouflaged by ideals like motherhood or romantic love.

The fact that Pearse and Rosie are in direct competition for the attentions of the pub's customers, then, suggests that sacrificial rhetoric interferes with the Irish man's fulfillment of his responsibilities toward the "real" Ireland—and that it does so *by* diverting that "natural" heterosexual attraction toward this shadowy, unreal, and "unnatural" object. Listening to Pearse's most famous formula—"Bloodshed is a cleansing and a sanctifying thing, and a nation that regards it as the final horror has lost its manhood"—Fluther feels "th' spirit of a man . . . pulsin'" in his veins, "his feet thremblin'" and "his ears tinglin'" as he contemplates the prospect of death in battle (194). Uncle Peter, whose wizened, desiccated little form is a visible rebuttal of the image of that ideal Volunteer, finds "every nerve in [his] body . . . quiverin'" and reports a "burnin'" urge to "dhraw me sword, an' wave an' wave it" (195).

As Rosie acknowledges, her "thrim little leg" (207) is no match for the power of the shadow's words: "There isn't much notice taken of a pretty petticoat of a night like this" (193). The desires she counts on being able to arouse have already been aroused by Pearse and will seek their fulfillment in the same source. Here, then, O'Casey is using sexuality to make the most direct statement so far of his quarrel with sacrificial rhetoric. Capitalizing on the assumption that heterosexual desire is healthy and "natural"—an assumption that, in 1926, none of his critics will be able to challenge—this scene states in the clearest possible terms that sacrificial rhetoric is destructive of that "natural" instinct, perverting sexual desire so that it attaches to the shadowy and unreal figure of Pearse. O'Casey's construction of both characters emphasizes the contrast between Rosie's "natural" appeal and the artificiality of Pearse's allure.

Rosie is cheerfully down to earth, vividly corporeal (a quality exaggerated by her "obviously suggestive" costume [192]), attractive, and amiable. The Figure in the Window is the first nonnaturalistic stage device Dublin audiences saw O'Casey use, and it is rendered even more jarring and alienating because it is the only such element in a play that is otherwise "realistic." The Figure is mechanized—he appears and disappears without warning at random intervals as if he runs on some kind of clockwork, and the audience recognizes his dialogue as a series of sound bites from familiar speeches, so that he becomes a kind of gramophone. He is disembodied as well—he appears only as a shadow thrown on the window of a pub and the voice that repeats those well-worn passages. O'Casey specifically wanted someone with "a resonant voice" (*LSO* 143) to play this part, indicating that he envisioned a stark contrast between the presence of the speaker's voice and the absence of his body. In every possible way, the Figure in the Window is flagged as artificial—cobbled together from other texts, insubstantial, a vision or hallucination, but not flesh and blood. When Clitheroe and colleagues declare their allegiance to him, they are quite literally chasing shadows—abandoning material reality and the "natural" life of the body for this highly artificial construct.

When Yeats defends Rosie's inclusion on the grounds that "O'Casey is contrasting the ideal dream with the normal grossness of life" and that she is "an essential part" (*LSO* 146) of that life, he is more perceptive than he realizes and yet also sadly mistaken. Rosie is indeed "essential"—her female body, like those of Minnie and Juno, *is* "real life"; and the same trends that prompt Yeats to make that unstated link between female sexuality and the "grossness of life" also make her useful to O'Casey as a figure for the material reality that Clitheroe is about to abandon. What Yeats seems not to realize is that the point of the Figure in the Window is to make it clear that the "ideal dream" is a nightmare—a delusion that, like Nora's psychosis in Act IV, will ultimately wreak destruction and death on the "real" people of Dublin. If audiences objected to Rosie, it was not simply because she is an unflattering commentary on "real" life in Dublin, but because she is valorized, while the "ideal dream" is not.

If that shift in values explains why protesters chose Rosie as their point of attack despite their more basic concerns about O'Casey's depiction of the Rising, it can also help explain the hysteria about the appearance of the tricolor at the end of the act. Accepting Yeats's construction, it would seem that the reason given is sufficient: when Langon carries the tricolor into the same bar that Rosie is working, the "ideal dream" meets the "normal grossness of life," undoing the idealism/materialism split so central to sacrificial politics. In maintaining that no republican would disgrace the flag by bringing it into a pub, protesters are defending the disjunction between the "ideal dream" and the world of mortals; and by suggesting that in "reality" that division is blurry, O'Casey gives mortal offense. However, it is perhaps equally important that when the tricolor is brought into the pub, the Plough and the Stars is brought in too, and that their real purpose is to help solemnize the oath that Brennan, Langon, and Clitheroe drink beneath them. That scene represents something besides the meeting of real and ideal, something that perhaps was as disturbing to O'Casey's former comrades as the sight of Rosie practicing her trade: the subordination of labor concerns to those of the republican movement.

They're Bringin' Nice Disgrace on That Banner Now

As much as Rosie complains about her lack of customers, the only client who explicitly turns her down is the Young Covey, the one character who professes himself untouched by Pearse's rhetoric. Deriding the Figure's call to arms as "dope," the Covey rejects the importance of national struggle in favor of the primacy of economic freedom: "There's only one war worth havin': th' war for th' economic emancipation of th' proletariat" (203). The form this objection takes, however, suggests that instead of rejecting the faulty premise of sacrificial politics—allegiance to the ideal conception rather than material reality—he has simply applied it to socialism, which has the effect of spreading rather than containing the contamination. The Covey's interactions with Rosie and Fluther—the two other proletarians present—demonstrate the corrosive effect of this idealism on socialist practice and argue that Labor politics have stopped resisting Pearse's siren song.

The Covey's first action, once Rosie begins chatting him up, is to offer her a copy of "Jenersky's *Thesis on the Origin, Development, an' Consolidation of the Evolutionary Idea of the Proletariat*" (197). The title alone suggests that this volume may have an unfavorable verbiage-to-meaning ratio, a suspicion supported by the fact that when the Covey quotes it, he does so not to build solidarity with fellow-workers but to prove his superiority to them. During an argument with Fluther—in which, ironically, he is trying to convince Fluther to steel himself against the power of empty rhetoric ("th' sort o' thing that workers are fed on be th' Boorzwazee" [208])—the Covey commits the republican movement's original sin, insisting on the primacy of theory and dogma over the worker's bodily experience of pain. Fluther claims to have been as active in the Labor movement as the Covey, offering as evidence a scar left on his head by "a skelp from a bobby's baton at a Labour meetin' in th' Phoenix Park" (208). Instead of hailing Fluther as a brother in arms, the Covey uses Marxist terminology to assert his dominance, arguing that he is the only "real" socialist because only he understands economic theory:

> THE COVEY. Well, let us put it to th' test, then, an' see what you know about th' Labour movement: what's the mechanism of exchange?
>
> FLUTHER [roaring, because he feels he is beaten]. How th' hell do I know what it is? There's nothin' about that in th' rules of our Thrades Union!
>
> BARMAN. For God's sake, thry to speak easy, Fluther.
>
> THE COVEY. What does Karl Marx say about th' Relation of Value to th' Cost o' Production?
>
> FLUTHER [angrily]. What th' hell do I care what he says? I'm Irishman enough not to lose me head be follyin' foreigners!
>
> BARMAN. Speak easy, Fluther.
>
> THE COVEY. It's only waste o' time talkin' to you, comrade. (209)

Not surprisingly, this exchange convinces Fluther that in fact the Covey is not his natural ally: "Don't be comradin' me, mate. I'd be on me last legs if I wanted you for a comrade" (209). In the Covey's hands Marxism becomes a barrier that discourages activism instead of encouraging it, because he uses it the same way Pearse is using sacrificial rhetoric: to claim for himself an intellectual, idealized form of existence that allows him to transcend his material circumstances and rise above his more lumpen comrades.

This betrayal of the cause in favor of his personal vanity is then made explicit in his treatment of Rosie, who taunts him for "swingin' heavy words about he doesn't know th' meanin' of" (209). The Covey disables her by attacking her profession: "Nobody's askin' you to be buttin' in with your prate. . . . I have you well taped, me lassie. . . . Just you keep your opinions for your own place. . . . It'll be a long time before th' Covey takes any insthructions or reprimandin' from a prostitute!" (209–10). Because Rosie is a sex worker, the Covey denies her the right to an opinion; her transgression of bourgeois social and sexual mores disqualifies her from participation in this dialogue.

The Covey's horror of corporeality—expressed earlier when Rosie's advances terrify him so much that he flees the bar—leads him to repeat the same mistake being made by the Figure in the Window. This betrayal draws labor politics into the same fruitless and destructive conflict in which the republicans are locked: his argument with Fluther degenerates into classic masculine chest-thumping ("I'd beat two o' you before me breakfast" / "You're startin' to take a little risk when you commence to paw the Covey" [210–11]) and finally into a fistfight, which is forestalled only because the barman ejects the Covey from the pub.

Like Jerry Devine, the Covey proves that the "stupidity of men" has infected the labor movement. His primary motivation for becoming a socialist appears to be to assert his dominance over other men; and like his rivals, he is tempted by the "ideal dream"—in his case, Marxist dogma rather than the sacrificial narrative—because it allows him to feed his narcissism and to distance himself from his physical surroundings. Aside from making him, as Act II demonstrates, an inefficient recruiter or organizer, his intellectual snobbery makes him too revolted by Rosie's "gross" materiality to establish a connection with her.

The Covey's failure is amplified for the audience when, almost immediately after his exit, Clitheroe enters with the banner of the Labor movement and in the company of Langon, who is a lieutenant in the Volunteers and is carrying the tricolor. What happens in "reality" when the Covey turns on Rosie is repeated symbolically by Clitheroe, who has been "mesmerized by the fervency of the speeches" and wrought up to a state of sexualized arousal, delivering his first line "almost pantingly," while his face is "flushed" and his "eyes sparkle" (213). Under both flags, Clitheroe renounces his familial responsibilities and corporeal desires: "You have a wife, Clitheroe." / "Ireland is greater than a wife" (213). Langon's call to arms, which parrots the *Volunteer*'s many "now or never" articles ("Th' time for Ireland's battle is now—th' place for Ireland's battle is here" [213]) magically conjures up the Figure in the Window for his final appearance.

The Figure then delivers the last paragraph of Pearse's most famous oration—the graveside panegyric for O'Donovan Rossa. As we have seen, Connolly's tribute to Rossa on the ICA's behalf echoes Pearse's emphasis on the value of heroic resistance and blood sacrifice: Rossa's life is inspiring because he embodied the idea that "no blood-letting could be so disastrous as a cowardly acceptance of the rule of the conqueror" (qtd. in Fox 123). As Rossa's funeral showed Labor willing to adopt Pearsian rhetoric, this last paragraph becomes the inspiration for an impromptu oath of allegiance:

> CAPT. BRENNAN [*catching up the Plough and the Stars*]. Imprisonment for th' Independence of Ireland!
>
> LIEUT. LANGON [*catching up the Tri-colour*]. Wounds for th' Independence of Ireland!
>
> CLITHEROE: Death for th' Independence of Ireland!
>
> THE THREE [*together*] So help us God! [*They drink.*] (213–14)

These two organizations, having previously been anything but friendly, are now joined in the bonds of brotherhood through their common allegiance to an insubstantial illusion—the Figure in the Window. Clitheroe and Brennan have sworn fidelity to Langon's cause—the independence of Ireland, not Ireland itself or the Irish people, let alone the Irish worker—and the Plough and the Stars is now subordinated to the tricolor. The seduction of the ICA is complete. Pearse has lured the labor movement away from their rightful goals; and he has done it by luring Irish men away from their wives.

O'Casey underscores this by paralleling the exit of the three officers with the exit of Fluther and Rosie. As the sacrificial patriots run back to their meeting, Rosie emerges triumphant with Fluther, the one man in the pub who has been willing to consort with her. Rosie's cajoling shows that O'Casey is still making the connection between heterosexual desire and the health of the Irish home: "Come on home, ower o' that, man. Are you afraid or what? Are you goin' to come home, or are you not?" (214). Rosie has finally found an Irish man who can be enticed back "home" instead of onto the battlefield, and Fluther suggests that this is the only sensible and "natural" thing for an Irish man to do: "Of course I'm goin' home. What ud ail me that I wouldn't go?" (214). As an added touch—one which was cut during rehearsal as being simply too provocative to include—Rosie celebrates Fluther's capitulation with a song:

> I once had a lover, a tailor, but he could do nothin' for me,
> An' then I fell in with a sailor as strong an' as wild as th' sea.
> We cuddled an' kissed with devotion, till th'night from th' mornin' had
> fled,
> An' there, to our joy, a bright bouncin' boy
> Was dancin' a jig in th' bed! (214)

This, then, is an alliance that has a chance of bearing fruit, illegitimate though it might be. Fluther is going "home" to something that bears absolutely no outward resemblance to Griffith's home, but in which O'Casey invests the same kind of significance: home to his own body, home to Rosie's, and home to the desire that engenders life instead of death. No matter how "gross" that vision of home becomes—and certainly, O'Casey makes an effort to present the least idealized version possible—it compares favorably to Clitheroe's desertion of his home. As Fluther and Rosie leave, two orders are shouted offstage, one from an officer mobilizing the Volunteers, and one from Clitheroe ordering his battalion of the ICA to follow them.

This is not a new argument. As we have seen, O'Casey's use of sexual attraction as a "natural" check to the idealism of Irish political discourse begins in *Gunman,* and his argument that this same idealism is destructive of the Irish home and family is familiar from *Juno.* Why, then, do audiences riot only now—three years after the republican cease-fire officially ended the civil war? In part, certainly, because this act suggests that the violence Irish audiences have been living through is not the result of one side's perversion of Pearse's purpose, but the fault of Pearse himself—the logical conclusion of that first act of seduction, the most recent link in a chain of betrayal that begins with him. The presence of those flags is troubling, perhaps, as much because they are used to symbolize that betrayal as because they are introduced into this "gross" milieu. And in that sense, they suggest that both the play itself and the protests are as much about the civil war as they are about the Rising. As *An Phoblacht* demonstrates by devoting so much of its space to Labor concerns, in

1926 the Labor/republican alliance is still in force, and by presenting it as this kind of betrayal, O'Casey is casting aspersions on contemporary politicians as well as on Pearse.

But that sudden shift in opinion has, perhaps, another explanation—one which has more to do with Bessie Burgess than with Rosie. Where O'Casey's early reviewers praised his scientific, photographic accuracy about tenement life as his greatest achievement, now his critics call into question not only that accuracy but the merits of "realism" in general. In "Muck-Raking in the Abbey," the writer complains that O'Casey has forgotten that "there is a distinction between the dissecting table and the salon" and that "to mix these is to pander to the lowest instincts of morbid curiosity" (3). This anonymous republican's use of the dissecting table is echoed in Sheehy-Skeffington's complaint that instead of the promised "body of truth," O'Casey delivers "a leprous corpse."

This persistence in calling O'Casey's perspective "morbid" reflects, on the one hand, the lingering persistence of that association between sexuality and disease that we saw in chapter 2; but on the other hand, it may also reflect some of the changes O'Casey has made in his approach to female characterization. What this play does not have, as "Nurse Maguire" points out in her review, is a Juno—a representative of "the grand mothers of the slums" (1) in whose strength and invincibility the dignity and worth of the tenement poor could be preserved. If, for O'Casey, Bessie's dead body is the body of truth, for his critics it becomes the unacknowledged referent for their charges of "morbid perversity."

Bessie's Body and the Death of the Republic

Act II is, essentially, one long festival of degeneracy; the bar is populated with carriers of every social disease that eugenist medicine ever associated with the poor or with the Irish, from venereal disease to tuberculosis to alcoholism. One of its high (or rather low) points is the brawl between Bessie and Mrs. Gogan, during which Mrs. Gogan abandons her baby in the pub while running outside to settle Bessie's hash. This is a clear indication that we are no longer in *Juno*'s universe: the women are at least as aggressive as the men and just as distracted by petty interpersonal conflict. While once again highlighting male refusal to accept responsibility—the baby ends up on the floor of the pub because none of the men are willing to hold it—this scene also suggests that motherhood, in and of itself, is no longer capable of redeeming or transforming even the mothers themselves, let alone their sons and husbands.

Nora's and Bessie's characters, and especially their relationship in Act IV, show both how drastically O'Casey has renovated his female characters and how consistently he has preserved some of the foundational premises that originally shaped them. Nora, for instance, by virtue of her femininity, is still the voice of that essential and undeniable human emotion that must take precedence over sacrificial politics: "An' there's no woman gives a son or a husband to be killed—if they say it, they're lyin', lyin', against God, Nature, an' against themselves!" (220). At the same time, she combines this sensitivity with Johnny's self-centeredness. She says herself that she "can think only of [her] own self" (220), and the bourgeois tendencies that were latent in Juno become "notions of upperosity" (163) that make Nora extremely unpopular in the tenement. While Nora's attachment to her husband remains an essential trait embodied in the baby she is carrying and then in the havoc the miscarriage wreaks on her health, and is therefore more "real" than Clitheroe's devotion to Langon and Brennan, the circumstances of the Rising have rendered it destructive rather than redemptive.

Instead of remaining unconquered and untainted by the carnage around her, Nora has been violated and broken by it; and the play holds Clitheroe's absorption into Volunteer politics directly responsible for that. Bessie suggests that Nora goes into labor early because of the "fright" (238) she suffers on Clitheroe's behalf, but this is certainly helped along by the way Clitheroe throws Nora "roughly" (236) away from him as she is trying to hold him back. Clitheroe does this because Langon, the Volunteer, is dying from the "wounds for th'Independence of Ireland" that he swore to bear bravely during the oath in Act II. Under the Volunteer code of masculinity, Clitheroe's first duty is to help his male colleagues—even though Langon's failure to suffer gladly or stoically has already demonstrated the bankruptcy of that code, as will Brennan's abandonment of Clitheroe in the Imperial Hotel.[25]

Never one to risk underemphasizing a point, O'Casey stages a final confrontation between Nora and Captain Brennan, the only one of the three oath-takers to survive the Rising. Brennan has arrived with a last message for Nora from the dying Clitheroe, which shows him faithful to the end to the sacrificial gospel: "Tell Nora to be brave; that I'm ready to meet my God, an' that I'm proud to die for Ireland" (244). Brennan's claim that "Mrs. Clitheroe's grief will be a joy when she realizes that she has had a hero for a husband" (244) is immediately shot down when Nora appears for her mad scene. Here, Nora demonstrates that her mind has been irrevocably shattered by the loss of her baby and by Clitheroe's betrayal, and that she puts the blame squarely on Clitheroe's comrades:

> Where's my baby? Tell me where you've put it, where've you hidden it? . . . Give him to me, give me my husband! . . . I won't go away for you; I won't. Not till you give me back my husband. [*Screaming*] Murderers, that's what yous are; murderers, murderers! (245–46)

Instead of using Nora to preserve that essential Ireland beyond the reach of British infiltration, O'Casey shows the death of the male martyr causing the destruction of both the female body and what it stands for. The Rising destroys Nora's mind and kills her unborn baby, breaking up the home she has been trying to make and foreclosing any possibility of regeneration through rebirth.

After violating her physically, mentally, and emotionally, the violence that claims Clitheroe also compromises Nora ethically, drawing her out of the morally pure space inhabited by Juno and Minnie and into the morass of delusion and vanity that has assimilated her husband. Bessie's death scene paints Nora's madness as the ultimate in bourgeois self-indulgence; she alternates between fantasies about domestic bliss with Clitheroe and fits of hysteria in which she screams for her husband and baby. During one of these fits, she runs to the window, ignoring the soldiers' warnings to move away from it. When Bessie throws her away from the window, she bumps up against it herself and is shot by British soldiers who think she is a sniper. Bessie's dying soliloquy is both a complete rejection of the sacrificial-martyr role and an indictment of Nora:

> Merciful God, I'm shot, I'm shot, I'm shot! . . . Th' life's pourin' out o' me! [To Nora] I've got this through . . . through you, you bitch, you! . . . O God, have mercy on me! . . . [To Nora] You wouldn't stop quiet, no, you wouldn't, blast you! Look at what I'm afther gettin', look at what I'm afther gettin'. . . . I'm bleedin' to death, and no one's here to stop th' flowin' blood! (258)

Bessie's death is an ugly and drawn-out process during which she screams, curses, collapses, crawls on her hands and knees, moans, and finally dies prone on the floor, "feebly" singing a hymn (258–59). O'Casey makes sure that whatever the director does, this death has to be graphic, painful, and unpleasant. Bessie describes her physical sensations, and the stage directions are very specific about her movements. The stage directions also support Bessie's indictment of Nora; she watches Bessie die without doing anything to help her. Instead, Nora repeats the rejection and denial of the body and its suffering that O'Casey has been attacking since *Gunman:* her response to Bessie's pleas for aid is to back away and cry for Jack. Once Bessie is dead, Nora's only emotion is an overpowering fear of the corpse: "Hide it, hide it, cover it up, cover it up!" (260) Having forced Bessie to die on her behalf, Nora refuses to confront the evidence of her guilt, and she screams for the others to do what sacrificial writers have been doing since *Cathleen ni Houlihan:* hide the sacrificed body so that she will not have to be "lookin' an' lookin' at it" (260).

Brennan's description of the "gleam of glory" that was the end of Clitheroe, the sacrificial patriot, is thus displaced by the affective power of the death of this alcoholic, unrepentantly pro-British Protestant Irish woman. *Plough* closes, then, with a scene that is the photographic negative of the traditional sacrificial tableau. O'Casey deliberately violates all the rules that govern the Pearsian treatment of the martyr's death. The marks of violence have been made visible in the "shock o'sudden agony" that is "written" on Bessie's face; the body is palpably a corpse, "stiffenin' out as hard as she can" (260); and she has not gone either willingly or quietly. Instead of the soil of Ireland, Bessie's blood pours out onto the floorboards of a tenement attic. The maternal body usually charged with transforming this sacrifice through the symbolism of fertility has miscarried the baby that would make that regeneration real; and instead of gathering the victim into her lap pietà-style, Nora refuses to have anything to do with the body. The female body becomes the sign, not of Ireland's invincibility, but of its vulnerability; it is not the ideal Ireland triumphant but the real Ireland—broken, bleeding, and dead.

Especially given the timing of the play's premiere, it is not surprising that republican audiences reproduced Nora's reaction to Bessie's death and demanded that O'Casey be punished for dragging that "leprous corpse" into public view. 1926 was a particularly dangerous year to produce a play about the Easter Rising. For one thing, it was the tenth anniversary year, and commemorations were being planned on both sides of the political divide. Any attempt to represent this event would be read in light of the ongoing battle over who was *really* acting out Pearse's wishes and would necessarily be controversial.

But there is another, more specific reason why February of 1926 was not a good time for *Plough* to premiere. Article 12 of the treaty that created the Free State specified that "the boundaries between Northern Ireland and the rest of Ireland" would be determined by a boundary commission consisting of one representative from each government and a chairman appointed by Britain" (Lee 51). The boundary was to be drawn "in accordance with the wishes of the inhabitants, so far as may be compatible with economic and geographic conditions" (qtd. in Lee 51). The vagueness of Article 12—it did not specify, for instance, who these inhabitants were, how their wishes were to be determined, or even when the commission would be established—meant that until that commission met, the Free State could plausibly claim that the Treaty would let them take back a fairly substantial chunk of territory. In January of 1923, for instance, the Free State North Eastern Boundary Bureau submitted a report recommending that they demand, as an irreducible "minimum," the transfer of "all of Fermanagh, two-thirds of Tyrone, one-third of Londonderry, one-third of Armagh, and a quarter of Down" (Lee 142).[26]

But this vagueness also left Britain and the Unionists plenty of room to maneuver. The Free State delayed the establishment of the commission until after the civil war in order to prevent Britain from using civil disorder as an excuse to refuse to give the Free State more territory. When the commission was finally established, the two British-appointed representatives decided that "geographic considerations" would be given more weight than popular opinion. The Free State representative was Eoin MacNeill, who appears to have been selected, not because he had any special talent for negotiation, but because he was willing to commit political suicide. MacNeill turned out to be no match for his opponents. In November of 1925 it was leaked to the press that the commission's report recommended, as the only substantial change, giving the Free State southern Armagh in exchange for part of eastern Donegal. The Free State government decided that this was worse than no change at all, and negotiated with Britain to suppress the report and keep the existing border (Lee 145).

Thus, although partition had been a threat since Sir Edward Carson's emergence in 1913 and a virtual certainty since 1922, it was not until the final months of 1925 that it became reality. The finalization of the border, on terms that were as unfavorable as they could have been, was in a sense the death of the Republic—or at least the end of any pretense that it and the Free State would ever be coextensive.[27] What happened in the wake of this discovery was that republican rhetoric, as represented by *An Phoblacht,* became less concerned with promoting the speedy establishment of an actual republican government—a less than realistic goal now that the republican cease-fire was two years old—than with mourning the republic's death and bringing its killers to justice. The first step in that process was to establish that a death had occurred—that the Republic did have some sort of "real" existence and was not merely an "abstract formula." And, as it was for *An t-Oglach,* the human body became valuable as a figure for this alternative body politic, a trope through which republicans could speak for the "real" Ireland.

From the beginning of *An Phoblacht*'s run, its contributors worked the body/politic connection, primarily through Maud Gonne's writing on the Free State's treatment of republican prisoners. While her primary purpose was always and obviously to evoke sympathy for, and outrage on behalf of, the prisoner by dramatizing his physical and mental suffering the same way O'Casey dramatizes Johnny's, she also made more wide-ranging claims about the pernicious effect that the Free State government was having on Ireland. In *An Phoblacht*'s premier issue she published an "Invitation to American Doctors," asking them to use "the authority of science to help these victims" by supporting her claim that the Free State government's treatment of republican soldiers was systematically turning out "hopeless numbers of prison-made lunatics" (6). By providing "an authoritative medical expression of opinion as to the danger to the human mind of solitary confinement and of the shocking practice of military interrogation," she argued, American medical science (more trustworthy than either British or Irish medicine since it is theoretically not under imperial control) would help in "shaming" the Free State into treating its prisoners better—but perhaps more important, it would establish that the Free State's anti-republican policies were a real threat to Irish public health (6).

Gonne returned to this theme in "Maryboro Jail—The Same Old Tyranny." Remarking that the location of a "lunatic asylum" just across the street from Maryboro Jail is "appropriate and very typical of the Anglo-Irish town," she discovers that the connection between prison and hospital is stronger than this accident of location suggests:

> I was curious why the latest finished products of Maryboro Jail were being sent to Dundrum Asylum instead of across the road and I

> learned that Dundrum was specially arranged to receive these prison-made lunatics of the Free State because, on grounds of economy . . . the county asylums refused to be burdened with them. (3)

Her message, clearly, is that the Free State treatment of republican prisoners is bad not only for the health of the individual prisoner but also for the health of the state; the Free State prison is the source of an epidemic of mental illness that is spreading faster than hospitals can contain it. The only cure for this epidemic is to stop creating these "lunatics" by torturing republican prisoners.

In Gonne's writing, then, we see her using the political prisoner's body to counteract the Free State's insistence that the Republic is "an abstract formula" with no basis in reality and that republicans are pointlessly preserving a futile and "sterile" fidelity to an unachievable fantasy. In *An Phoblacht,* on the contrary, the Republic is the "real" Ireland—a living, breathing, organic entity being slowly done to death by the machinations of the Free State government, cast first as a disease eating away at the health of that body and later, once the border is finalized, as a demonic doctor bent on dismembering it. "Fingan," writing in June of 1925, uses the disease metaphor to describe the effect of the Treaty on Irish health—the oath of allegiance becomes "the sepsis which poisons our public life"—and blames the "mephitic odour of the Free State" (5) for the passage of the Treason Bill that will result in the execution of republican prisoners.

Once partition is finalized, the disease metaphor gives way to dissection. In "His Excellency the Fatalist—Dismemberment at the Royal College of Surgeons," "Clann Chonchobhair" emphasizes the appropriateness of the fact that "Mr. Tim Healy's first banquet in dissected Ireland was at the Royal College of Surgeons," a "stronghold of dissection" in which this writer suggests Healy is taking an ominous interest (2).

This use of the body is at its most graphic when republicans first register the shock of the boundary commission fiasco. The December 18, 1925, issue—printed as Cosgrave is negotiating the final acceptance of the existing boundary—includes a cartoon called "To the Guillotine" that shows a politician leading a woman labeled "Eire" up a hill toward a guillotine, the blade of which is labeled "Partition" (Fig. 3). The cartoon for the first issue of 1926 features Baby New Year, depicted as a naked toddler carrying a suitcase labeled "1926," staring in consternation at a woman in a gown and cloak with a Celtic brooch (Fig. 4). The woman is sitting on the edge

Figure 3. "To the Guillotine." *An Phoblacht,* December 18, 1925, page 5.

of a tomb with the inscription "Here lie unity, liberty, and justice." She is also holding her own severed head in her lap. Against the tomb leans her shield, which is emblazoned with a harp and labeled "Ireland." Part of the harp and the word are obscured by a bloodstain labeled "Partition." Baby New Year's dismay is conveyed in the caption: "So this is Ireland!" Cathleen is no longer invincible; the female body whose job it has always been to preserve all that is Irish has finally and definitively been destroyed—not just invaded or mutilated, but decapitated.

Thus, in the republicans' own newspaper—to which Hannah Sheehy-Skeffington contributed an article on Free State prisoners and insanity that demonstrates her familiarity with Gonne's arguments—the female corpse that O'Casey displays in *Plough* has already come to symbolize the pain of defeat and the violation of partition, the execution of the "real" Ireland by her faithless sons. It would seem strange, then, that republicans should react so negatively to a play that suggests, just as *An Phoblacht* does, that the Free State is the illusion and the "real" Ireland is this outraged body—that the Republic *is* flesh and blood, but that it can no longer survive under these conditions.

One explanation, certainly, is that a movement dedicated to fighting for this Republic cannot allow itself to mourn its death for very long; if their struggle is to mean anything, they must believe and

1926: "So this is Ireland!"

Figure 4. "So This Is Ireland." *An Phoblacht,* January 8, 1926, page 4.

maintain that this corpse can live again. Thus, even in the pessimistic "So This Is Ireland," the decapitated woman is still sitting upright instead of lying dead on the ground. *An Phoblacht* uses this female body to symbolize the dead Republic but also demonstrates that this is an image too painful to contemplate. On the same page as "To the Guillotine" is a ballad called "The Partition of the Green," which closes with a defiant rejection of Britain's attempt to make partition real: "You may cut a line as deep as hell through stone and soil and sod, / But Ireland knows no other bound than that set out by God."

In "Easter," a later cartoon, "Eire" appears whole again, her head on her shoulders, weeping for the martyrs of 1916 above the caption "Their names shall be remembered forever" (Fig. 5). Cathleen is used to symbolize both the death of the Republic and its immortality, the same way Gonne's descriptions of the broken and decrepit bodies of actual republican prisoners are juxtaposed with the "immortal" Terence MacSwiney, whose death in 1920 on hunger strike is "a national triumph" (Gallagher 3) that allows Ireland to remain undefeated. The corporeal body symbolizes the trauma of partition, but that body must be balanced with a corresponding representation of the vanished ideal; and O'Casey refuses to provide that counterbalance.

Figure 5. "Easter." *An Phoblacht,* April 2, 1926, page 4.

But a much larger problem is that Gonne, Sheehy-Skeffington, and the other *An Phoblacht* writers, while agreeing with O'Casey that the Free State is a miscarriage, differ violently as to exactly what brought it on. As in *Juno,* O'Casey's fidelity to "realism" results in an ideological collapse that drops out some of the links in the causal chain and holds the Irish responsible for their own subjugation. Intent on dramatizing the betrayal of socialism by Irish nationalism and on doing so by providing another spectacular demonstration of "the stupidity of men," O'Casey identifies Pearse, and not the regime he was rising up against, as the ultimate cause of all this death and destruction. The root of Irish suffering is the Irish male's failure to deal with material reality: "British soldiers take over the Clitheroe home because Jack has not kept his home fires burning" (Watt 179). O'Casey's dissection of the corpse of the Republic might have been less problematic if he had not concluded in the inquest that she was killed by Pearse.

Although O'Casey may never have accepted Sheehy-Skeffington's reading of *Plough,* his subsequent career shows that he did ultimately agree with her on one point: that "realism" was an inadequate medium for a revolutionary message. The exchange of letters to the editor between O'Casey and Sheehy-Skeffington over *Plough* eventually led to a live debate in which she challenged him to defend his version of realism in front of a republican audience. Despite his truculence in print, O'Casey turned in a disappointing performance in person. After his opponent put her case, he stood up, "uttered a few sentences," and "was overcome by a temporary weakness and had to sit down for a short period" (*LSO* 179). The debate appears to have changed his relationship with Sheehy-Skeffington. According to her son, at least, after this experience O'Casey had only "appreciation and admiration" for her, despite having called her shrill, hysterical, and a hypocrite beforehand. Similarly, in Owen Sheehy-Skeffington's account, his mother responded to O'Casey's "weakness" with "genuine sympathy," realizing that he "was under great emotional stress before an unfriendly audience" (*LSO* 179).

During the debate, Sheehy-Skeffington describes O'Casey's "realism" as "the art of the photographer rather than the art of the dramatist," an appraisal certainly familiar to him but one that had up to that point been intended as a compliment. What this means, according to her, is that when these "scenes are all put together," the "natural conclusion is that this is a typical picture of the men of 1916" (*LSO* 178). In other words, because of his claim to documentary realism, audiences will assume that O'Casey's depiction is both comprehensive and representative—that he is telling the truth and the whole truth. Whatever is not included in the "photograph" is presumed not to exist at all. As Una Chaudhuri argues, one of the foundational elements of modern naturalism is a "logic of *total visibility*" (xii) that forces spectators to assume that what they can see on the stage is all that there is. For Sheehy-Skeffington this is a problem because "the heroism that did produce Easter Week" (*LSO* 178) is conspicuously absent. But for O'Casey it is a problem because his trilogy dramatizes the effect much more vividly than it suggests a cause: the "spots of disease, of hunger, hardship" (*LSO* 180) that he wants to represent are not linked back to the system that has caused them. The Covey may fume about "th' system we're livin' undher" (249), but the exigencies of naturalism make it much harder to represent the operations of that "system" than to show the death and disease it creates.

When O'Casey left Dublin and realism behind, he was acknowledging the need to represent those extrahuman, institutional causes through expressionist devices like the Figure in the Window. And he was acknowledging too that in order to do so he would have to escape not only from the inside of that camera, but from the Irish audiences who wanted to keep him there.

5
Misbirth of a Nation: Yeats and the Irish Free State

THE 1930S WERE NOT A GOOD DECADE FOR IRISH DRAMA. IN 1928 THE National Theatre lost its most commercially successful playwright when Sean O'Casey's *The Silver Tassie* was rejected by the board of directors.[1] O'Casey, already living in London, declined to return and spent the rest of his life in England. Meanwhile Yeats, who after the Easter Rising moved out of the theater into the drawing room with his Noh-inspired plays for dancers, began turning out a string of esoteric and impenetrable plays based on the mythological system he articulated in *A Vision,* which he had developed over the course of several years based on messages that he believed had been relayed to him from the spirit world through his wife George Hyde Lees.[2] After the republican cease-fire and the consolidation of the Free State, the dramatic movement that had grown up with the struggle for independence settled down into comfortable and respectable middle age, depriving the Dublin theatergoing public of so much as a decent riot.

Irish politics, meanwhile, was characterized by a strange combination of turbulence and stagnation. The wounds inflicted by partition and the civil war continued to fester as debate in the Dáil degenerated into an inconclusive battle between two opposing camps. One was led by William Cosgrave and the Cumann na nGaedheal party (later renamed Fine Gael), which represented those who had originally supported the 1922 treaty and the Free State; the other was led by Eamonn De Valera and the Fianna Fáil party, which represented that segment of the republican movement which could bring itself to participate in a government whose legitimacy they still rejected. In 1932 Cosgrave, whose party had administered the Free State for the first decade of its existence, was defeated by De Valera. Rancor toward Fianna Fáil—and frustration at Cumann na nGaedheal's inability to defeat them electorally—fed the growth of the Blueshirt movement, a right-wing organization influenced by Italian fascism and led by former police chief Eamonn O'Duffy. Each party was now equipped with its own paramilitary organization—the IRA on Fianna Fáil's side, the Blueshirts on Cosgrave's. While violence never returned to civil war levels, the presence of two organizations that flirted with ideas of military revolt helped ensure that Irish politics remained oppositional.

Although Yeats's literary output during this period suggests an increasing immersion in the occult and immaterial, it was accompanied by what has proved to be the most controversial development of Yeats's political career. Yeats's dalliance with fascism has already inspired a number of critical inquiries, as has his championship of eugenist science in *On the Boiler*.[3] That Yeats was at one point involved with the Blueshirts is verifiable historically. Whether this makes him a fascist is a more difficult question. Historians and Yeatsians differ on two major points: to what extent the Blueshirts can be considered a "truly" fascist organization, and how serious Yeats was about endorsing them. What certainly became evident, when Yeats published *On the Boiler* in 1939, was that he was a firm believer in eugenist science and had accepted some of its more repellent implications as necessary and right. *On the Boiler* and *Purgatory*—the political pamphlet and its companion play—remain the two most damning pieces of evidence against Yeats in this respect, since Nazi atrocities have irrevocably identified eugenist science with fascism in its most horrendous form.

As we have seen, however, eugenist science was part of the British imperial arsenal, and as a result it was a formative influence on Irish nationalist discourse long before Hitler or Mussolini rose to power. The fact that eugenist science was not actually invented by Nazis does not make it any less sinister, but it does mean that Yeats's fuming about "limiting the families of the unintelligent classes" (*On the Boiler* 19) is not necessarily evidence of his support for Hitler. In fact, in *On the Boiler* Yeats criticizes European fascists for misunderstanding and misapplying the basic principles of eugenics. Rather than reading Yeats's eugenist phase as the influence of his involvement with the Blueshirts, it makes more sense to read Yeats's interest in the Blueshirts as symptomatic of his longtime obsession with degeneration.

Yeats's preoccupation with good breeding has its roots in his well-established class prejudice, but it also reflects his disillusionment with the progress of Irish politics. By 1932 it was clear that sacrificial violence had given birth, not to a hale and healthy Irish Republic, but to a truncated compromise. And while Yeats, Fine Gael (the new improved version of Cosgrave's Cumann na nGaedheal party), and the Blueshirts were united in their decision to abandon that lost ideal and embrace the imperfect reality represented by the Irish Free State, nostalgia for that lost republic drove their politics as surely as it influenced De Valera and Fianna Fáil. If Yeats's eugenist tendencies become more marked and more obnoxious near the end of his life, this is perhaps because eugenics seems to offer a way to reclaim that ideal without reopening the "poisoned wound" of partition.[4] And if opposition to De Valera's social and economic policies takes the form of a fascist movement, that may be partly because the organicism that is one of fascism's trademarks seemed to make it possible to recover the republic without espousing republican ideology or republican methods.

If, as we have seen, Irish political discourse already had a tradition of identifying the body politic with the human body and a tradition of cementing that identification through the conflation of the Irish wife/mother's body with the Irish home, the Irish economy, and the Irish population, it is not surprising that Irish nationalists would embrace the fascist conception of the state as "a living organism which transcends the sum of its parts," a conception that implies "the subordination of the parts to the whole" (Cullingford, *Yeats, Ireland and Fascism* 154). And if fascism promised—as it seemed to—that by regenerating the race one birth at a time patriotic women could restore the state to health, it makes equal sense that a nationalist community already concerned about the health of the Irish race and the vulnerability of the Irish body would see in fascism the answer to some of its prayers. At the same time, given the realities of post-partition Ireland, it is also not surprising that pursuing this political solution led to contradiction and conflict—or that the Irish woman, assigned once again the task of embodying the impossible, was caught in the crossfire. The trap that sprang shut on the female Irish subject is represented most literally, perhaps, in the 1937 constitution that "protected" her status as unemployed mother and wife. But the violence inherent in that attempt to "protect" the Irish mother is represented more troublingly in Yeats's later work, especially in his little-read 1936 play *The Herne's Egg*.

HORROR HENCEFORTH: EUGENICS AND *The Herne's Egg*

Dublin was denied the chance to make a third *Playboy* of *The Herne's Egg*. Yeats submitted the play to the Abbey board in 1936 but professed himself relieved when the board rejected it: "I am no longer fit for riots, & I thought a bad riot almost certain" (qtd. in Armstrong xxv). Yeats's "almost" seems naively optimistic—in terms of violence and sexuality, *The Herne's Egg* makes *Playboy* look like *Brigadoon*. To expect that, even twenty years after the *Playboy* riots, Dublin audiences might sit still for a play in which one king beats another to death, seven drunken soldiers gang-rape a virginal priestess, a village idiot disembowels the hero, and the heroine orders a donkey-boy to copulate with her would be unrealistic even for Yeats. The only way the play could possibly *not* have caused a riot would be if it had proved "so obscure that no one would notice it was obscene" (O'Connor, qtd. in Armstrong, xxv).

The plot certainly provides some camouflage for the obscenity. The play is loosely based on Sir Samuel Ferguson's epic poem *Congal,* which brings together a number of ancient Celtic myths and legends that would have been familiar to a nationalist audience; but Yeats has altered the story so radically that it is unrecognizable. In the first scene of Yeats's play, we meet Congal and Aedh, two adversaries who, after fifty "perfect battles" (*VPl* 1013), have finally decided to call a truce. They plan a banquet to celebrate. Congal wants to banquet on herne's eggs, which brings him in conflict with Attracta, a priestess who believes herself to be the divinely appointed bride of the Great Herne.[5] Congal steals the eggs without her permission. Cursing him, Attracta prophesies that Congal will become a fool and die by the hand of a fool. At the banquet, Congal is served a hen's egg instead of a herne's egg. Thinking that Aedh has insulted him, Congal declares war. Congal discovers only after killing Aedh that it was Attracta who switched the eggs. As punishment for "changing one egg for another" (*VPl* 1027), Congal and six soldiers rape Attracta. When Congal later encounters her, Attracta refuses to believe that the rape took place and calls on the Great Herne to "declare her pure" (1032), which he does. Congal tries to thwart the Great Herne's curse by killing himself. As he dies, he asks Attracta to keep the Great Herne from reincarnating him as a "brute beast" (1039). Attracta, believing that the first thing to be conceived after Congal dies will become his reincarnation, tries to get Corney the donkey-boy to impregnate her so that Congal will be reborn as her child. Unfortunately, before Corney can comply, his donkey breaks loose and mounts another donkey. Congal will thus be reborn as a donkey.[6]

If ever a plot begged for exegesis, it is this one. Thus, it is not surprising that scholars who take on *The Herne's Egg* generally discuss it in terms of the mythological system Yeats developed in *A Vision,* or in terms of his well-documented interest in "Oriental" mysticism. Vendler, for instance, treats the play as an instance of "Yeats's 'philosophy' confirmed by Indian symbols" (160); Taylor detects the influence of the Noh in Attracta's character; Moore reads it as an attempt to combine earlier uses of myth and ritual with humor and parody. The events that form the play's plot are explained in terms of mythic universalities—the relationship between the poet and the muse, between man and daimon, between creation and destruction. Swimming bravely against the tide, Bernard Krimm, in *W. B. Yeats and the Irish Free State,* appears to be alone in suggesting that the play is a political satire, with Congal standing for De Valera and Attracta playing the role of the Irish electorate (178–84).

This hardy band of *Herne's Egg* scholars is tiny, however, compared to the number of Yeatsians who have declined to notice the play at all. There are, after all, excellent reasons not to—chief among them the play's aesthetic limitations. Even for a contemporary audience used to the techniques and forms of the avant-garde, the play's plot fails to make sense. Because conventional critical wisdom has it that *The Herne's Egg* is comprehensible only insofar as it enacts Yeats's private symbolic system, reading the play means tangling with *A Vision,* a complicated and frustrating text evocatively described by Vendler as "a great dragon lying folded at the entrance to all of Yeats's later work" (viii). All in all, reading *The Herne's Egg* seems to most scholars like a lot of trouble for nothing.

But perhaps more discouraging than these formal considerations is an intensely unpleasant critical problem that *The Herne's Egg* poses: what to make of Attracta's rape. If the plot is not to be taken literally, then the rape must have a symbolic meaning; and to suggest that gang-rape is a metaphor for anything can only lead to trouble. For the Abbey board, the problem was that the signified was presumed to be sullied by the obscene signifier. O'Connor's account, for instance, suggests that the play was rejected because Yeats had indicated that the seven rapists were intended to stand for the seven sacraments; the rape was unacceptable for them, not because it was a rape, but because it was blasphemy.[7] For twenty-first-century critics the problem is reversed—positing a universal signified requires us to elide, trivialize, or glorify the violence done to the victim during rape. Admittedly, many contemporary treatments of *The Herne's Egg* do not seem to acknowledge this second problem, continuing to read the rape symbolically without any apparent awareness that such a reading might be problematic.[8] Attracta's rape, like the similar rape narrated in Yeats's "Leda and the Swan," is assimilated into the mythic category occupied by the divine rapes of Ovid's *Metamorphoses* and treated accordingly.[9]

The play's aggressively antinaturalist presentation of the rape and of Attracta as a character certainly discourages a too-literal reading. But part of the appeal of the allegorical reading is that it allows critics to justify Yeats's presentation of the rape as not only necessary but fortunate. Unless we translate these characters and events into symbol and metaphor, it becomes rather troubling that *The Herne's Egg* suggests that a good raping is exactly what Attracta needs.[10] This message becomes more palatable if we see the rape as a metaphor, Attracta as an allegorical figure rather than a flesh-and-blood woman, Congal as an irresistible creative force rather than a rapist, and the other six soldiers as a symbolic representation of "the septenary nature of man" (Taylor 182) rather than as a gang of assailants whose participation will multiply the cruelty and pain of their victim's torture.

The need to read the rape symbolically affects readings of the eggs that motivate it. In Ferguson's poem, what catalyzes the violence is not the substitution of one egg for another—Congal is served the same kind of egg that everyone else gets—but the fact that it is served on an ignoble wooden platter rather than on a silver dish. Ferguson also makes it clear that this is the last in a series of insults heaped upon Congal's head by the high king Domnal, and that when Congal declares war, it is not really about the egg; it is about the long history of broken promises, failed alliances, and territorial disputes that led up to this incident.[11] Yeats removes that context and alters the insult so that the violence that follows has to be about the egg. Critics have generally responded by reading universal significance onto the egg, making it the lost egg of Leda, "the cosmic egg" (Taylor 183), or "the completed poem" (Vendler 159). Even Krimm, ordinarily so literal-minded, reaches for a vaster meaning: "Well, the eggs surely hold out some notion of future promise, future generations, the future of a country perhaps" (181). If the rape is not a rape, and Attracta is not a woman, then the egg cannot possibly be just an egg.

But if, as I have been arguing, the female body works as symbol or allegory *because* it is also visible as material and human—if Cathleen ni Houlihan does her job *because* Maud Gonne's body is visible underneath that costume, if Juno embodies all that is good and transcendent *because* she refuses to deny the pain of her maternal body—then whatever the rape means in that symbolic register, that meaning becomes real only when it is embodied. Attracta, allegorical figure though she may be, is valuable also as a female body, a woman through whom Yeats can incarnate the "horror" that animates his later work. And if to do her job, Attracta must remain a woman, then the rape works because it remains a rape.

So with *A Vision* glowering over my shoulder and the history of Yeats's involvement with Celtic mythology, Japanese Noh theater, and Indian spirituality spread out before me, I still want to ask: What happens if we take this literally? What if we read this play as having some reference to flesh, blood, and the material world? What if Attracta is a woman, Congal is a man, the rape is a rape, and her eggs are—well—her eggs? What if Attracta's crime, while serious enough to warrant this brutal punishment, is still no more and no less than "changing one egg for another?" What do we gain if we insist on materiality, if we refuse to let these disturbing bodies become those more comforting abstractions?

For one thing, it makes *The Herne's Egg* useful as a highly instructive, if highly disturbing commentary on the way national politics shaped reproductive and sexual politics in post-partition Ireland. But more important, it gives us some insight into how this putatively allegorical use of the female body depends on, and continues to support, the manipulation of actual female bodies. In *The Herne's Egg,* the two elements we have been tracing through the Abbey movement—sexuality and violence—finally come together in rape. My primary intention in unraveling the twisted logic that makes that moment of fusion inevitable is not to explicate a deservedly forgotten text but to shed some light on the cultural forces that shaped this plot—and that continue, in the political sphere, to produce similar fusions, each with its own appearance of inevitability.

The double bind in which *The Herne's Egg* traps Attracta—in which she is first required to embody purity, virginity, and incorruptibility, and then forced by the rape to become carnal, mortal, and violated—is an expression of the same need that created Cathleen ni Houlihan, whose damaged, human shell concealed that radiant ideal essence. The fact that in 1936 the poles are reversed, and Attracta's purity and invincibility must be stripped away to reveal her vulnerable, "womanly" nature, reflects the post-partition transformation of Griffith's gender politics.

Politics and Parody after Partition

By the time Yeats was writing the play, many of the elements that became hallmarks of *The Herne's Egg*—its parodic approach to deeply serious topics, its preoccupation with the increasingly conflicted relationship between the material and the ideal worlds, and even its obsession with eggs—already featured in the Irish political discourse of the 1930s. As we have seen, mainstream nationalist thought had long been structured by a binary opposition between British materialism and Irish idealism. With De Valera's ascension in 1932, the contradictions at the heart of that opposition became obvious. As evidenced by *United Ireland,* Fine Gael's official party newspaper, conservative political thought now rejected that opposition while struggling to remain faithful to the nationalist icons who originally subscribed to it. The desire to do both built an irresolvable tension into Fine Gael rhetoric—one that Fine Gael ultimately tried to resolve through its representation of Irish womanhood.

Having led the fight against the 1922 treaty and refused for years to run for office because to do so would have required him to swear allegiance to the king, De Valera decided in 1932 to take the oath and enter the Dáil. His change of heart was an admission that as far as he was concerned there was no longer a republic to remain loyal to. Thus, the same election that established De Valera as a political threat also established that the Free State per se was no longer in immediate danger of military overthrow. Both parties nevertheless clung to the ideologies that had served them in earlier battles; and as a result, political rhetoric on both sides collapsed into a mess of inversion, contradiction, and irony. Ultimately, at least as far as Fine Gael was concerned, the 1930s became a cynical and bitter parody of the 1900s, in which the act of sacrifice repeated itself with nightmarish persistence but regeneration never occurred.

De Valera continued to appeal to sacrifice during his administration, but this appeal was confined solely to the domestic realm. As military conflict was superseded by the economic war, the Ultimate Sacrifice took the form of self-denial rather than self-immolation. Soon after he and Fianna Fáil displaced Cosgrave's government in 1932, De Valera stopped payment of the land annuities guaranteed to

England by the terms of the 1922 treaty. England retaliated by closing its markets to Irish products, and the Dáil responded with punitive tariffs on English imports. Thus began an economic war that conclusively demonstrated that Ireland was producing both too much and too little to make protectionism work. De Valera attempted to solve this problem through a combination of aggressive legislation and even more aggressive propaganda, the latter drawing heavily on Griffith's ideology of self-sufficiency.

Although, as we have seen, the material/ideal opposition was always unstable, Griffith's colleagues had been able preserve the appearance of stability by describing his economic policies in terms of the idealistic self-denial associated with male martyrs: women who gave up the joy of being "in fashion" and wore Irish-made were sacrificing the pleasures of the flesh for the spiritual satisfaction of knowing they were serving the cause of Irish liberty. But in fact, in Griffith's paradigm, it was not the act of self-denial that served the cause but the act of consumption; insofar as these women were serving the ideal of Irish freedom, they were doing so by making a material contribution to the Irish economy. In 1903 sacrificial rhetoric could still successfully obscure the materialist basis of this economic policy; however, when De Valera tried to put Griffith's ideas into practice in 1932, this rhetorical sublimation no longer worked. It was obvious that simply renouncing the pleasures offered by British imports accomplished nothing unless the Irish consumer could savor in their stead the equally worldly pleasures afforded by Irish products. Thus, although De Valera tried to use the opposition between the "narrow materialists" (159) who opposed protectionism and the idealistic patriots who were willing to buy Irish, he was ultimately forced to become as materialistic as his opponents.[12]

For instance, while reiterating the dress-materials argument—"It is the duty of a woman to go out and boast that from head to foot she is clothed in Irish manufacture" (253)—De Valera admits that it is difficult for the Irish woman to discharge that duty because Ireland does not manufacture the necessary articles. Thus, he finds himself talking about boots and shoes in the same rhetorical vein in which his predecessors spoke of the Ultimate Sacrifice:

> We will not be satisfied until every boot and shoe is made in this country. We want to have boots and shoes made here, and there is no rea son why the hides should not be tanned into leather. I have told you how much the value of imported clothing has fallen, and again we are not satisfied. (252)

Similarly, De Valera acknowledges that the loss of the English market has created a huge beef surplus. His solution is to tell farmers that it is their patriotic duty to move out of livestock and into wheat:

> Yes, grow more wheat. Let us not merely have the paltry increase that was shown last year. We want that proportion to go up. We will not be satisfied, and the farmers are not wise, and our organisation is not doing its duty, and the community is not doing its duty, unless it gets after and stops the import of that wheat. (252)

Any punch this speech may be packing is gone by the time De Valera addresses the fact that this scheme may not always be practical: "The West cannot grow [wheat], but they have got a beet factory, and we will see that they can get a market for their oats. . . . That is all on animal products and on cereals" (252).

It was this kind of reductio ad absurdam combined with appeals to the grand old ideals of the pre-partition era that formed the basis for much of the commentary in Fine Gael's newspaper *United Ireland.*[13] For instance, De Valera's attempt to revive the dress-materials argument is attacked in an article addressing "The Hitherto Unsuspected Heinousness of Heliotrope":

> One of [a Fianna Fáil columnist's] two suggestions for achieving their Ethos was that they should avoid making "one of the greatest mistakes of the last Government. Women in heliotrope got themselves described in the Press at dress parades of all sorts. I gave the advice to abstain from such practices to the Fianna Fáil Party when in Opposition—it was to them I mainly addressed myself. I venture to repeat it now at the beginning of their reign." His words fell on fertile soil. The wearing of heliotrope is in distinct political disfavour. It is recognised to be entirely foreign to Fianna Fáil's Ethos and its perverse addicts are considered proper victims for the rigours of the Revenue Commissioners. ("Top Hats" 5)

Heliotrope was not being produced by Irish textile manufacturers; thus, a woman wearing heliotrope was advertising her willingness to "buy shoddy and pay the duty" ("Top Hats" 5) instead of supporting the economic war effort. For satirical purposes, the author refuses to acknowledge the underlying motive and instead professes bewilderment at this irrational hatred of a perfectly harmless color. This basic tactic—identifying a concrete policy that appears to have displaced the ideal it supposedly serves, and exaggerating that contrast—is repeated in articles mocking, for instance, the government's attempt to regulate tomato consumption.[14] The general thrust is usually to present Fianna Fáil as being both materialistic and fantastic at the same time—driven by theories that have nothing to do with "reality" to meddle obsessively with the minutiae of everyday life.

The figure who most clearly embodies this combination of "narrow materialism" and outlandish fantasy is Dr. Ryan, the minister of agriculture. Along with its regular printed attacks on Ryan as unqualified for the job, *United Ireland* invokes deeper anxieties about the dangers of materialism in a front-page cartoon attacking the "grow more wheat" campaign (Fig. 6). The image shows "the Irish farmer" lying in De Valera's lap while Ryan, in a doctor's coat and stethoscope, force-feeds him wheat through a funnel as a cabinet member in a nurse's uniform tries to wrest a toy cow from the farmer's desperate grasp. De Valera is wearing a dress and cap, and the caption reads, "Mother Knows Best." The implications of this depiction are expanded on in "That Bedside Manner," in which Ryan attempts to "relieve [the Free State] from the pain she is enduring" by "prescrib[ing] the kind of food that must be eaten" but only succeeds in hurrying the "patient" into her "sad sepulture" (7). The wheat scheme, far from keeping Ireland safe from external influence, requires the Irish government to take over Britain's role as imperial doctor, cramming an unwanted prescription down the farmer's throat.

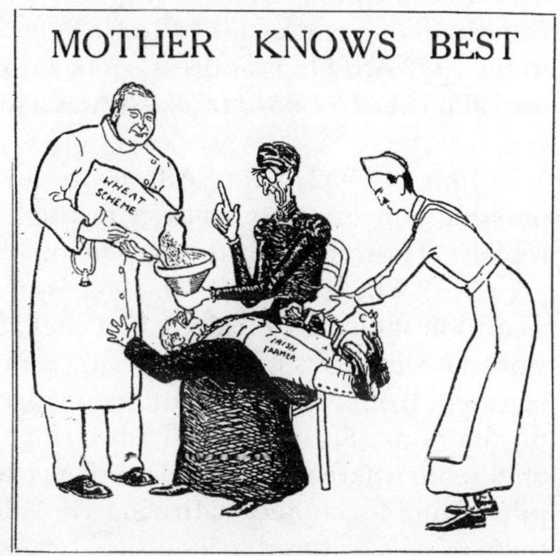

Figure 6.
"Mother Knows Best."
Front page of *United Ireland,*
August 27, 1932.

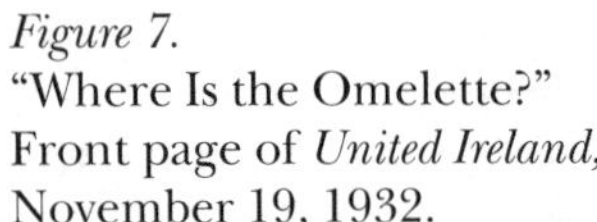

Figure 7.
"Where Is the Omelette?"
Front page of *United Ireland,*
November 19, 1932.

To Fine Gael, De Valera's protectionism was the central irony invalidating his administration: in an attempt to protect the domestic economy, Fianna Fáil was in fact laying it waste. This irony was trenchantly summed up for them when De Valera observed, in defense of his economic policy, that "if [the Irish] wanted omelettes, they must be prepared to crack eggs."[15] To De Valera, this comment—attributed to his 1932 Ard-Fheis address—may have seemed like a shrewd rhetorical move. To *United Ireland,* it was a joke that only got better with age.

In June of 1932, "More Adventures in Blunderland" has Alice expressing concern about noises in the kitchen, to which De Valera replies, "Those are only the eggs being broken for our Omelette Surprise" (5). The November 19, 1932, issue of *United Ireland* opens with a cartoon showing De Valera, in a chef's hat and apron, in front of a stove on which sits an empty frying pan. De Valera holds a broken eggshell, from which yolk and white are dripping toward a puddle on the floor (Fig. 7). "The Irish farmer" complains, "I see the Egg Shells, but where is the Omelette?" A year later the omelet joke is the punch line for a piece satirizing De Valera's policies by describing them as skits featured in a musical revue:

> This was followed by an uproariously funny sketch entitled *Making Omelettes,* the part of the chef being played by a world-famous clown, secured only at great cost. Shrieks of laughter filled the auditorium as egg after egg crashed to the stage, making an unholy mess. The climax is reached when the chef, standing knee-high in egg shells, informs the shrieking audience, without as much as a semblance of a smile, that you can't make omelettes without breaking eggs. ("All-Laugh Show" 3)

De Valera's eggs stand synecdochically for Ireland's agricultural output, which is being literally thrown away.

It is interesting, then, that after *United Ireland* spends a year satirizing De Valera's egg joke, Yeats completes a play that lampoons one man's determination to make what he considers the ultimate omelet. And, especially given the way we have seen Irish nationalist discourse conflate the integrity of the female body and the integrity of the Irish economy, it is interesting that he is opposed in this desire by a woman who insists that he has no right even to look at the eggs he covets. If Yeats was in on the omelet joke, his decision to create a virgin heroine obsessed with protecting a group of eggs from spoliation and defilement suddenly makes more sense. Attracta, like other women before her, has been assigned the task of protecting Ireland's economy by protecting her own body.

But, since protectionism is now the disease instead of the cure, Attracta's job has become much more complicated. The eggs must be broken, Attracta must lose her virginity, and Ireland must give up its determination to be nothing but Irish. Having been compelled to incarnate the dream of purity, she must now be compelled to abandon it. Instead of being allowed to follow her "mad" ideas about keeping herself and the eggs pure, she must allow herself and the eggs to be put to productive use. Instead of continuing to devote herself to abstractions and to believe that "there is no reality but the Great Herne" (*VPl* 1016), she must be brought back to corporeality by her rapists so that "being free from all obsession" she can "live as every woman should" (1028). Now that protectionism has become dangerous, the Irish woman's duty is to open her ports, and it is a crime punishable by Congal's "Court of Law" to unreasonably seek to close them.

Here, then, we have another potential source for Yeats's plot: Attracta's attachment to her virginity mirrors De Valera's devotion to a superseded and dangerous ideal that she must, for the good of the nation, be persuaded to abandon.[16] But *The Herne's Egg* complicates the omelet joke by suggesting a more sinister but no less material meaning for the egg, and thus a more twisted motivation for the rape.

Congal, after all, does not have to rape Attracta just to break the eggs; they are boiled and eaten before she enters the hall. The rape is her punishment, not for denying them the eggs, but for "changing one egg for another"—for giving Congal, instead of the herne's egg, "an egg dropped in the dirty straw / And crowed for by a cross-bred gangling cock" (*VPl* 1024).

Congal's use of the term "gangling" recalls Yeats's poem "A Bronze Head," whose final stanza offers what Stanfield calls "the plainest evocation of degeneration anywhere in Yeats's poetry" (174):

> As though a sterner eye looked through her eye
> On this foul world in its decline and fall;
> On gangling stocks grown great, great stocks run dry,
> Ancestral pearls all pitched into a sty,
> Heroic reverie mocked by clown and knave,
> And wondered what was left for massacre to save.

The fact that the cock is "cross-bred" confirms the eugenist implications of "gangling": Congal's problem with the hen's egg is that it is genetically polluted. With the eugenist vocabulary encouraging us to see this transaction in terms of human reproduction, these become human eggs rather than bird eggs; and Attracta's crime becomes the very serious one of abusing her reproductive powers. She might have gotten away with protesting Congal's theft of the eggs if she had allowed him to use them; but by switching the eggs, she has thwarted the hero's attempted intercourse with a noble stock and substituted a degenerate "gangling" one. In the eugenist universe, when a man of Congal's lineage and rank is offered "an egg that some half-witted slattern / Spat upon and wiped on her apron" (*VPl* 1024), it's more than an insult; it's an injury.

The fact that in "A Bronze Head" Yeats uses racial degeneration to explain Maud Gonne's persistence in selecting lovers less genetically qualified than himself speaks to some of the personal reasons he might have had for finding the eugenist worldview convincing. His consistency, however, in linking Gonne's political activism with a penchant for misbreeding—a connection represented most painfully to him by her marriage to John MacBride—cannot wholly be ascribed to modern literature's most celebrated case of unrequited love. One of the major goals of the Blueshirts was to organize Irish women in a political movement that, instead of turning them into the "Wild, Wild Women" of republicanism, would make them better wives and mothers.[17] Perhaps the most significant effect of eugenist science is the fact that private reproductive behavior becomes a public-policy issue. The Irish woman's actions in the home become a matter of national concern, and her domestic and political activities are conflated.

By now, this should be starting to sound familiar. The Blueshirt take on women's patriotism is similar to Griffith's in that the woman patriot's primary duty is to create the ideal Irish home. However, just as protectionism has been rejected as a viable economic strategy, the ideal home is no longer a hermetically sealed fortress of pure Irishness. Indeed, it is the woman's duty to bring in outside influences, to incorporate technology and the principles of eugenics into her domestic interior, to set up study groups to learn the best way of discharging her duties. She must represent, in her approach to domestic duty, the "right" economic policy, welcoming imported innovations and accepting the proposition that she cannot find all she needs by searching her own heart. She must accept progress, embrace modernity, and be willing to be taught a lesson.

Electricity and Domesticity

The May 21, 1932, issue of *United Ireland* (known, at that point, as *The United Irishman*) carried an advertisement from the Electricity Supply Board urging the Irish to start consuming electricity. As usual, the copywriter assumes that his audience is primarily Irish housekeepers:

> Straight from the Shannon into your home. Immense reserves of energy—enormous supplies of power. Energy and power that you can direct in the performance of your housework. Energy and power that enable you to conserve your own energy and time, to produce better housekeeping results and to reduce housekeeping costs. USE ELECTRICITY for every Household Task. (2)

This was the first in a run of similar advertisements directed at the Irish woman and aimed at persuading her to use electric appliances because this will make her domestic life easier, more efficient, and healthier. After the "Straight from the Shannon" ad comes a series featuring cartoons of rotund, aproned, disgruntled women who appear to be trying to browbeat readers into buying electricity in order to appease their wrath. "They've tried them all," says one ad, "and now they want Electricity because it is cleaner, safer and cheaper than any of the old ways" (11 March 1933: 8). By 1935, the appeal has become more sophisticated, involving the narrative of a domestic servant who feels compelled to quit because her mistress's antiquated kitchen "would kill any girl." Her mistress installs electric appliances; the maid is "glad she took back her notice and stayed on" (21 September 1935: 8).

The message is clear: to refuse to let these "enormous supplies of power" come "straight from the Shannon into your home"—and to materially support the Electricity Supply Board, one of the Cosgrave government's first and most ambitious attempts to modernize post-revolutionary Ireland (Brown 16)—is to court premature aging, trouble with the help, and, in general, waste, fatigue, and entropy. To preserve the bourgeois household, the mother must relinquish her attachment to the old ways and install modern appliances.

The same story is repeated in a less strictly material vein in the columns devoted to women's role in the Blueshirt movement, which began appearing in 1934. "Finola," counseling Blueshirt women to promote "really feminine" activities, suggests that they begin studying "social sciences," since this will prepare them to be efficient wives and mothers. She concludes by demanding that Irish schools teach the business of motherhood:

> Will they start some real practical courses that will result in raising the standard of family life, that will make every woman more efficient, more content, more healthy and more fitted to face life, something that will deal with practical every-day happenings and not occupy precious years in learning "trimmings" that may be ornamental but not at all useful? (5)

Homemaking has become a science and must be taught like one. It is the Irish woman's job to learn skills that will make her "more efficient" in the home. While it is still presumed that this is her "natural" place, her role must be managed by outside experts.

The message that homemaking is skilled, full-time labor that requires special training redefines homemaking not only as a career but as *the* career. "Unit Leader," while claiming that she is not advocating a "return to the hearth," nevertheless makes it clear that her purpose in proposing that the Blueshirts attach "more importance . . . to careers for girls" is to promote "a more natural attitude towards the ultimate job of home-building":

> If instead of tapping typewriters, feeding machines, and standing behind counters, girls could, in the interval between school and mar-

> riage, follow pursuits in which such things as housewifery, cooking, sewing and home-crafts, gardening, social work, etc., were made interesting and gave them some return, surely it would be much better. (5)

This redefinition of the Irish woman's career would enable what "Unit Leader" sees as the "real solution" to Ireland's social problems—an economy in which "men can normally earn enough to keep a decent home" without relying on their wives' wages (5).

So if, in order to keep women in the home, that home has to be opened up to technology and modernity—if, in order to keep Ireland capitalist and healthy, Griffithian protectionism has to be abandoned along with Mary Butler's ideal Irish home—what explains the appearance, in a December 1934 issue of *United Ireland,* of "Roisin Dubh"'s paean to practical patriotism, in which she describes the Irish woman's duty in terms that are virtually indistinguishable from either Griffith or De Valera's rhetoric?

> The woman who, sedulously and consistently, supports home industries, who buys only Irish wools for her knitting, Irish tweeds for her own and her children's clothes, and who in every matter of expenditure on food and goods chooses Irish first, is surely a practical patriot. (5)

Even after Fine Gael has abandoned protectionism, and even after constant enticements to displace the "spinning wheel" (5) of which "Roisin Dubh" speaks fondly with modern sewing machines, the ideal of purity and integrity continues to be viable when kept narrowly attached to the image of the Irish woman. Despite its contention that this vision of the Irish home is outdated, *United Ireland* prints an article that upholds it as the highest goal for which an Irish woman can strive. Mary Butler's model refuses to die, even within the pages of a newspaper that is trying to kill it.

What the appearance of this article suggests is that while in the "real" world of economics purity is a noxious concept upheld by irrational people, it continues, paradoxically, to be part of the Fine Gael vision of Ireland. If economic and cultural purity cannot, except in "Roisin Dubh's" nostalgic trip to the Griffithian past, be realized in the Irish home by the Irish woman, there is one other kind of purity that is not only encouraged but absolutely prescribed, and that is biological purity. The timing of "Unit Leader's" appearance as a columnist and the related surge in columns relating to women's issues suggest that the Blueshirts saw their women's movement as their best chance to protect the last form of "pure" Irishness to which they were still able to cling.

Racism and Blueshirt Policy

Maurice Manning argues that the Blueshirt movement was fascist only in appearance, asserting that anti-Semitism does not appear to have been part of their platform (239–40). It is true that the Blueshirts took their inspiration more from Mussolini than from Hitler and that O'Duffy reiterated in speeches that the Blueshirts did not have a racial axe to grind. Indeed, *The Blueshirt,* their newspaper, is relatively devoid of references that could be read as anti-Semitic. However, in *United Ireland,* the advent of the weekly reports on Blueshirt women's groups is preceded by increasing attention to racial purity.

In February 1934 *United Ireland* printed a piece by "Onlooker" (probably Ernest Blythe) on the "Definition of an Irish National." "Nationality is bred in the home," says "Onlooker"; and he seems to be taking "bred" literally, locating authenticity in the Irish subject's biological relationships to other Irish subjects:

> A Japanese, for example, cannot by any force of will, by any course of study, by any exercise of imagination or any resort to prayer become a good and typical Irishman or a good and typical Englishman. There is an affection and a mercy that can only be found with certainty in relationship. That fact was at the basis of Solomon's judgment when he discovered the true mother of the child by ordering it to be cut in two. (3)

Nationalism is once again naturalized through the mother's relationship to her child. But "Onlooker's" justification of this biological model suggests that it was attractive to Fine Gael for a very specific reason: it allowed them to protect the idea of a unified, identifiable, organic Irish people sharing a "pure" Irishness even as their own policies mitigated against that idea.

"Onlooker" asserts that, although when Ireland was still under occupation anyone willing to aid the struggle could and should be considered Irish, things have changed now that the Free State is here to stay: "Once, however, national sovereignty is re-established things are totally different. In that case the precious gift of national freedom has to be safeguarded; the people have before them a hope of progress which may not be put in jeopardy" (3).

If "Onlooker" feels that the need to "safeguard" national freedom has actually *increased* since the establishment of the Free State, this perhaps speaks to his unacknowledged sense that the economic policies Fine Gael advocates—opening the Irish market to British exports, incorporating technology into the home—are, like the partition that created the Free State, threatening that sense of the Irish as a unique and indivisible "people." If, in "Onlooker's" eyes, it is the supposed *disappearance* of that imperial threat that puts the Irish as a "people" in jeopardy, this is perhaps because the Fine Gael vision of an economically viable Ireland is starting to look too much like any other European nation.

This reading is confirmed when "Onlooker" outlines the benefits of a biological conception of Irishness as opposed to one defined by political commitment:

> The real problem is to decide what will give a reasonable guarantee that any man appointed to the highest offices of national trust and responsibility will have Irish Nationalism not merely as a theory or a creed but as something ingrained in his whole being, something which he can never lose, which will be a perpetual guide to him in all situations of public perplexity. (3)

The true-born Irishman knows in his bones what is best for Ireland, and will "never think that some ideal of nationality is greater than the material and moral interests of the Irish people" (3). In other words, regardless of his ideological position, a "real" Irishman's biological relationship to other Irishmen functions as a "perpetual guide" that prompts him to make the right decisions, even if those decisions appear to endanger Ireland's cultural or political autonomy. This model is useful for Fine Gael because it allows them to abandon policies that supported the separatist model of Irish identity used by their political predecessors without losing their claim to authenticity. Their racial consciousness of their Irishness, "ingrained into [their] whole being," ensures that no matter what their policies are, they are sure to be serving the interests of the Irish people.

"Onlooker's" main point in formulating this race-based conception of Irishness is to support his contention that De Valera, despite his appeal to nationalist ideals, is not a true Irishman. He is instead "the very sort of man who would sacrifice the true interests of the whole people rather than depart from his own ideal conception of what they ought to be" (3). That ideal conception—which Fine Gael now wishes to abandon—is invalidated because it does not spring

Figure 8.
"What! No Jazz?"
Front page of *United Ireland,*
January 27, 1934.

organically from the body and soul of a true-born and purebred Irishman but is instead fabricated by a man whose own Irishness a fabrication.

Other writers help construct De Valera as a foreign influence thwarting the "natural" progress of the Irish state. His inveighing against "jazz dances" as un-Irish inspires a cartoon asking, "What! No jazz? But what about 'The Kid From Spain?'" (Fig. 8). De Valera is shown in what the cartoonist evidently believes to be Spanish dress, shaking a tambourine. This exaggeration of De Valera's Spanish connections goes beyond making fun of an un-Irish name. *United Ireland* notes that in early 1934 De Valera felt it necessary to "occupy Parliamentary time on Friday [March] 2nd with an interminable statement, the main object of which seemed to be . . . to show that he himself was what the Germans would presumably call an 'Aryan,' born in wedlock" ("Notes and Comments" 1).

Only two weeks earlier *United Ireland* had printed a speech in which O'Duffy attacked De Valera's "Shylock dictatorship": "Like the Jew in the celebrated *Merchant of Venice,* the present Government clings to the letter of the law precisely in order that it may violate the spirit. But, like Shylock, if it doesn't take care, it will come to a bad end" (7). Thinly veiled as this appeal to anti-Semitism may be, it is nevertheless more subtle than this contribution, which appeared in the same article that castigated De Valera for wasting the Dail's time with a discussion of his pedigree:

> A correspondent writes that in stating last week that he had, so far as he knew, no Jewish blood in his veins, Mr. de Valera seems to have forgotten one of the cardinal facts of Spanish history. During the Moorish occupation enormous numbers of Jews settled in Spain, where they multiplied so that at the end of the successful wars of Ferdinand and Isabella they numbered something like one-fourth of the population. ("Notes and Comments" 1)

This use of anti-Semitism against De Valera suggests that resemblances between Blueshirt and Nazi fascisms may have been more than superficial. But it also shows that an organic, biologically based conception of Irishness becomes, in the 1930s, an essential element of the Fine Gael party platform. Racial purity is invoked in place of the other forms of purity that Fine Gael has repudiated and stands as their main claim to be representing the interests of the real Irish people. And as the concept of racial purity becomes more important, it becomes equally vital to ensure that Irish women understand their responsibilities as breeders and reproduce that biological Irishness in as pure a state as possible.

The Irish woman, in 1934 and 1935, is thus compelled more forcefully than before to incarnate biological purity, to pass on Irishness from mother to child. But since she cannot discharge that duty without embracing science, technology, and her role as genetic and domestic engineer, she can no longer be allowed to occupy the protected domestic space that has until now symbolized that purity. She must be pure and uncorrupted, but she cannot be unapproachable or impregnable. She must confine herself to the home, but she cannot refuse herself to the forces of progress. She has to protect her eggs, but she must also allow the state to use them. The formulation of, and insistence on, an organic and biologically based conception of Irishness thus puts Irish women in an impossible position. The contradictions inherent in that Griffithian use of the chaste female body finally fracture the female subject position beyond repair. *The Herne's Egg* enacts that fragmentation, translating the "epistemic violence" done by this double interpellation into the violence done on the body of its heroine.[18]

Changing One Egg for Another

Attracta's relationship with the Great Herne is riven by contradiction even before Congal tries to triangulate it. Attracta's bestiality is Yeats's unstable compromise between a fascination with the ideal of purity and a simultaneous conviction that this purity was a dream from which Ireland could not afford not to awaken. Yeats had experimented with this deployment of bestiality in 1922 with *The Player Queen,* whose young queen is obsessed with the story of a virgin martyr named St. Octema who seems to have been a little too close to her favorite unicorn. But whereas in *The Player Queen* purity and carnality are still separated—purity in the Queen, who in her actual life remains a virgin ascetic; and carnality in Decima, whose production number is a dance during which she chooses a lover from a group of players dressed up as animals—Yeats fuses them in Attracta. She is convinced that the Great Herne is both an ideal presence she will feel, "not in the flesh but in the mind" (*VPl* 1020), and a real bird with a real "shaft" that will "shoot" her "into [her] joy" (1017).

Her devotion to the Great Herne combines spiritual purity and sensual depravity, creating as its object an entity that is both divinely ideal and grossly material. Yeats's hope of honoring and preserving that desired purity while attending to the urgent material demands of reality rides on the wings of the Great Herne, who is both a powerful and thunder-wielding god and an actual bird. Congal's speech suggests that this miraculous being exists only because Attracta has been compelled to incarnate two mutually contradictory sexualities. It is her attempt to resolve that enforced conflict that creates the Great Herne:

> Women thrown into despair
> By the winter of their virginity
> Take its abominable snow,
> As boys take common snow, and make
> An image of god or bird or beast
> To feed their sensuality;
> Ovid had a literal mind,
> And though he sang it neither knew
> What lonely lust dragged down the gold
> That crept on Danae's lap, nor knew
> What rose against the moony feathers
> When Leda lay upon the grass. (1016)

In Congal's version, Attracta and her predecessors, trapped between the moral injunction to remain pure and the biological imperative of sexual desire, not only invite but create their divine rapists. It is their conflicted desire that "drag[s]" divinity "down" into material form.

Congal's interpretation is, of course, highly self-interested. But just as the play's treatment of the rape will later support the accuracy of his prescription for Attracta's madness, its treatment of the Great Herne confirms Congal's conclusion that he is the creation of Attracta's own desires. The Great Herne manifests himself through Attracta's body; Corney asks Attracta to "bring the god out of [her] gut" (1017). Up to and including the rape scene, the Herne remains explicable as a hysterical symptom; the only evidence of his existence is Attracta's trance, during which she "move[s] . . . As though her god were there" (1021). The rape is what makes the Great Herne "real": when Attracta calls on the Great Herne to "declare her pure" (1032), he answers with thunder, the first suggestion (to Congal and to the audience) that he is a real god with real powers. The Herne comes into existence because Attracta desires him—because she takes her imagined responsibilities seriously enough to bring that hen's egg down to Tara and exact the vengeance that invites her punishment.

That solution, then—the beast/god whose existence fuses the material and the ideal—can only be produced through the operation of his mate's internally divided sexual desire, which can be produced only by using that double injunction to fracture Attracta's character. The conflict between Attracta's obsession with purity and the sexual desire underlying her talk about shafts and arrowsmiths may render her "mad," but that madness has the power to force the Herne's incarnation. If the Great Herne is to reunite the ideal with the real, Attracta must be both virgin and whore, pure and bestial, at one and the same time.

What that means is that although Attracta's role requires her to desire a sexual union, it also requires her to resist that union. If she does not desire, she is not a real, "sensible woman" (1031); if she consents, she is not pure. For this reason, Attracta can only be entered by a partner willing and able to use enough violence to overcome the resistance she is bound to put up—but whose attentions, violence and all, she has nevertheless invited. Thus, in order to bring the Great Herne into being, Yeats has to engineer an encounter that both is and is not a rape.

What the soldiers do to Attracta is a rape in that Congal intends it as an assault on the Great Herne—"through his betrothed, his bride, / I have the power to make him suffer"—and clearly conceives of it as aggressive and violating: he and his accomplices will "handle, penetrate, and possess" Attracta (1027–28). The fact that Congal recruits his six followers multiplies the violence inherent in that description. This multiplication is necessary because the violence about to be inflicted on Attracta must be unmistakably punitive. The rape is her sentence for offering Congal a "common" egg in place of the rarer ones she guards: "By changing one egg for another / She has brought bloodshed on us all" (1027).

By introducing the specter of degeneration, Attracta forces Aedh and Congal out of the heroic idiom in which their first war was fought and into one "much bloodier" (1026). It is also much more material; instead of becoming "immortal," Aedh is bludgeoned to death with a table leg and "die[s] of a broken head, die[s] drunk" (1025–26). Congal suggests that the egg triggered this abrupt descent to corporeality by showing the combatants what is really at stake:

> They had, we had
> Forgotten what we fought about,
> So fought like gentlemen, but now
> Knowing the truth must fight like the beasts. (1026)

The "truth" is that the real fight is not over land or position but over the egg. The real fight is over the need to ensure that like mates with like and that degeneration is stopped. And the real fight, because it is about real bodies, is a dirty one.

The more bestial nature of this new war is evident from Congal's first maneuver, which is to organize the rape. Now that he knows the "truth," Congal recognizes that the prize is Attracta's egg, and it is his duty as king of Tara to take it. The logic of eugenics makes Congal the closest thing Attracta will find to an ideal partner. But before he can take the egg, he is interrupted by Mike, a soldier given to cryptic monosyllabic pronouncements that Congal interprets. Mike reminds him that because Attracta is "The Great Herne's Bride" (1027)—because she has rejected human sexuality, denying her eggs to any man—Attracta must be made an example of. Her dysgenic behavior amounts to a capital crime: "All that have done what she did must die" (1027). Because killing her would exacerbate the problem by letting her eggs go to waste, however, that sentence is commuted:

> MIKE: Seven men.
> [*He begins to count, seeming to strike the table with the table-leg, but table and table-leg must not meet, the blow is represented by the sound of the drum.*]
> One, two, three four,
> Five, six, seven men. (1027–28)

The blows Mike strikes as he metes out the sentence underscore the fact that this encounter will be brutal, and that he and Congal see Attracta's suffering as part of her sentence.

This rape is not a rape, however, in that Yeats makes Attracta desire it. Violent as this assault is shaping up to be, Attracta's song indicates that it will in fact be the "marriage" Attracta has long been awaiting:

> Where is he gone, where is that other,
> He that shall take my maidenhead?
> *Sang the bride of the Herne, and the Great Herne's bride,*
> Out of the moon came my pale brother,
> The blue-black midnight is my mother.
> Who will turn down the sheets of the bed?
>
> When beak and claw their work begin
> Shall horror stir in the roots of my hair?
> *Sang the bride of the Herne, and the Great Herne's bride,*
> And who will lie there in that cold dawn
> When all that terror has come and gone?
> Shall I be the woman lying there? (1029–30)

Attracta recognizes the violence of the rape to come; the "beak and claw" she "must endure" emphasize the cruelty of the penetration she is about to experience (1029). At the same time, she contemplates this intensely unpleasant encounter with a "joyful breast" (1029) and envisions it taking place between the sheets of a nuptial couch. While Yeats goes to extremes to make sure that this encounter *must* be read as violent, brutal, punitive, and nonconsensual—in other words, that it fits the criteria usually used to define rape—he goes to the same extremes to show that Attracta consents, not to this specific act, but to the act that he intends it to stand for. She desires, but doesn't; consents, but doesn't; defends her fidelity to the divine Herne, but prepares to accept his crude earthly substitute. By using this assault as a metaphor for divine consummation, Yeats theoretically creates the impossible: a rape that is not a rape, a violation that leaves its victim pure, that breaches her boundaries without corrupting what they contain. This is the only kind of sex a woman in Attracta's position can have: an encounter both desired and resisted, consented to at the level of metaphor but refused on the literal plane.

But Yeats's impossible construction incorporates such blatant contradictions that ultimately it can only be untenable. Just as Blueshirt logic invests so much in the Irish woman's reproductive function that any attempt on her part to deviate from the state's prescribed use for it justifies drastic intervention, that logic generates such intense panic about purity and contamination that the very punishment designed to force Attracta to fulfill her duties pollutes her to the point where she can no longer do so. In the end, Yeats cannot have it both ways: by forcing Attracta to use her body to try to bridge the widening divide between materialism and idealism, he only manages to destroy her, Congal, and the universe they inhabit. Not only is her sacrifice in vain, but it renders her incapable of giving Congal's sacrifice the regenerative meaning that is the foundation of *Cathleen ni Houlihan*'s paradigm.

The representational problems Yeats encounters in *The Herne's Egg* demonstrate that the contradiction at the heart of the sacrificial narrative has finally become extreme enough to destroy both the paradigm and the female figure trapped inside it. As we have seen, in order for Attracta to do the job Yeats has assigned her, she must both desire and resist her defloration; that crucial encounter must be *both* a rape *and* consensual. But by the end of the scene that leads up to it, it is already getting hard to read the rape both ways. Congal and his men are steeling themselves to vanquish a resistance that remains hypothetical; Attracta never actually defends herself, allowing Congal to take the egg and standing by patiently while her rapists determine their order of entry. As the element that makes or breaks the definition of rape, the question of Attracta's consent has to stay unresolved if the ambiguity is to be preserved. Any attempt to represent the rape could only destroy that ambiguity. If Yeats showed them attacking her, and she continued to put up no resistance, the audience would cease to read this encounter as rape. On the other hand, if Yeats showed Attracta resisting and being overpowered, this scene would certainly become not only a rape, but one too horrifying to be recuperated. Even if the audience believed that despite her protests Attracta might cherish a secret desire for Congal, by the time Pat, Malachi, Mike, John, James, and "that coarse hulk of clay, Mathias" (1028) had had their turns to subdue and violate her, the audience would have a hard time seeing that banquet-hall floor as the Great Herne's bridal bed.

Yeats therefore declines to represent the rape itself. Since the audience does not know whether Attracta consented to the actual penetration, they do not know whether she was raped or she wasn't. Just as Schroedinger's cat is half alive and half dead, this sexual act is half a violation and half a consummation. However, just as Schroedinger's formula makes sense mathematically but not intuitively, Yeats's dodge may work semiotically but destroys the integrity of his characters and his universe.[19]

The first thing we see Attracta doing, after the inferred rape, is packing up "the uneaten or unbroken eggs" (1030). She is still performing her function as guardian, despite the fact that these eggs have been permanently contaminated by Congal, who has "had them all boiled soft" (1030). Though they are now useless for reproduction, Attracta insists that "such eggs are holy" and fears offending the "country-people," who would "shudder if herne's eggs were left / For foul-tongued, bloody-minded men" (1030). Her concern for these "pure souls" and the reference to "country-people" evoke Synge and Griffith; to avoid making the pure-minded "shudder," Attracta is bound to preserve the *appearance* of purity, no matter how badly reality may have violated her. The rape would appear not to have gone very far in making her "free from all obsession" (1028); she carries out her imagined duties even after they have been emptied of meaning.

Congal, however, reads this gesture as proof of success; her concern for these soft-boiled eggs proves her "a sensible woman" with her mind where it should be, "upon the cupboard and the larder" (1030). As far as he is concerned, Attracta, no longer distracted by her "lonely lust," can now do her *real* job—which is to look after the pantry and "look for a man" (1031). Her pragmatic decision to take the eggs home with her even though his touch has tainted them ratifies her transformation from a "crazed loony / Waiting to be trodden by a bird" (1031) into the good housewife, willing and able to put her body and her money to work for the public good.

In order for the rape to be the solution Yeats wants, both things have to be true. On the one hand, Congal's vision of her as the "sensible woman" whose decisions are based on her "natural" material needs rather than on ideas or abstractions must, according to Blueshirt logic, be realized if Ireland is to survive as a modern European nation. On the other hand, according to the same logic, she must retain that connection with the ideal, incorporating an imagined purity and power that Congal's hardheaded heroism rejects; she must link material prosperity with occult mystery. But these two things are still in irresolvable tension.

If Congal and his accomplices were simply the earthly tools through which the Herne consummated his marriage to Attracta, then Attracta should emerge from it both chaste and fruitful, having undergone the sexual contact that will make her eggs useful but remaining pure in her devotion to her divine mate. But the more Yeats works at creating that resolution, the more impossible it becomes. Although on the level of literary analysis it might be possible to read the rape as the corporeal approximation of a spiritual union, the realities of sexual politics mean that if Attracta wants to claim that she is the Herne's "pure bride," she cannot concede that the rape actually happened. Congal responds to her claim with incredulity: "Pure in the embrace of seven men?" (1031). From Congal's perspective, no woman who has been used by seven men—especially these seven, six of whom are cut from coarse cloth—can remain "pure." Those extra assailants have polluted her genetically; if she were to conceive as a result of this experience, there would be no way to tell whose seed had taken root. Like the soft-boiled eggs, Attracta—if any of this really happened—is a write-off.

Congal's insistence that Attracta cannot still be "pure" points out that just as the violence of this encounter forecloses ambiguity in one direction—by making it impossible for me to read this as anything other than a rape, Attracta's trance-induced consent notwithstanding—patriarchal sexual mores foreclose it in the other direction, making it impossible for Congal to believe that her physical violation has not contaminated her morally, Attracta's trance-induced paralysis notwithstanding. To him, Attracta has been defiled simply because she has been violated; the success of the assault implies the complicity of the victim. If Attracta admits that this encounter happened—whether she consented or not—the purity that Yeats's compromise was supposed to protect has been destroyed.

Attracta therefore has to deny the rape; and to make this lie true, she summons the Great Herne and asks him to "declare her pure." He does, through the thunder that terrifies the soldiers into disavowing their testimony:

> JAMES: Great Herne, I swear that she is pure;
> I never laid a hand on her.
>
> MATHIAS: I was a fool to believe myself
> When everybody knows that I am a liar.

PAT: Even when it seemed that I covered her
I swear that I knew it was the drink. (1032)

These extorted denials contain embedded contradictions; Mathias and Pat admit that they "covered her" even as they recant. Congal refuses to recant at all, insisting that "we seven held you in our arms" (1033). Congal's defiance is necessary because the play's entire structure will collapse if the audience has no sexual encounter to read; they must believe that it took place, even as they are forbidden to interpret it as evidence of Attracta's impurity.

In order to make her denial credible, Yeats has to explain why Attracta does not remember the rape. Congal provides an explanation: "Though I thought / Because I took the egg out of her hand / That she awoke, she did not wake" (1031). Attracta "slept" through the entire encounter, assuming when she awoke that during her blackout she had been with the Great Herne. This, one can only say, would have to be one hell of a trance. Even admitting that this play leaves the world of verisimilitude behind on page one, it is significant that Attracta's consciousness has to lapse this totally before she can fulfill those contradictory injunctions. At the moment when she is supposedly realizing her destiny, Attracta ceases to exist as a sentient being.

Vendler and others agree that the answer to Attracta's anticipatory question—"Shall I be the woman lying there?"—is no, but fail to grasp how total that negation is. Attracta is not "changed" by her brush with godhead; she is obliterated. At the moment of impact, the war between those two competing injunctions becomes so intense that it destroys her ability to function either as a subject in her own world or as a character in our reading. Nobody could "be" the woman lying there; she is an impossibility, a self-negating contradiction in terms. If Attracta were present, her agency or lack of it would resolve that contradiction. To bring those disparate worlds together, Attracta has to disappear.

The fragmentation she experiences proves so extreme that after the rape Attracta cannot pull herself together. In order to believe that "my husband came to me in the night" (1031), Attracta has to either deny the physical evidence of her rape or drastically misread it. In either case, her interpretation of events requires her to dissociate her consciousness from her body, intensifying the split between ideal and material that her rape was supposed to heal. Instead of defining a third position between materiality and spirituality, she must reject the testimony of her corporeal body and put her faith in her original assertion that only abstraction and purity matters, that "there is no reality but the Great Herne" (1016).

Yeats tries to support Attracta's definition of reality through his staging, rendering the violence that we see so stylized and mannered that the violence we don't see can be assumed to be equally unreal. During the two battle scenes—the choreographed battle that opens the play, and the fight at Tara that precedes the rape—Yeats specifies that there is no physical contact between assailants; the clash of weapons is represented musically, and "sword and sword, sword and shield, never meet" (1012). Violence is represented, but as far as the audience is concerned, it does not *happen*. There is no physical evidence of violence on the bodies of the characters; Aedh and Congal talk about their wounds, but we do not see them. Since Attracta's rape is not represented, the audience can analogize from the play's other treatments of violence and perhaps believe that it happened, but didn't; that despite submitting to violence, she remains inviolate.

But by requiring Attracta and the audience to dissociate themselves so extremely from physical reality—by requiring her to read her gang-rape as a divine visitation and by creating a universe in which the rules of representation are distorted enough to make that plausible—Yeats rejects the claims of the body so completely that he undoes his own compromise. Destroying Attracta's "human life" so that she becomes "a doll upon a wire" (1021), Yeats also destroys his hero in a sacrifice that conclusively demonstrates the impossibility of rejuvenating Cathleen.

The Herne orders Congal's death as proof that he alone has the power to determine what "really" happened; that Congal, though he believes he acted on his own desires, was "under the curse in all / [he] did, in all [he] seemed to do" (1033). But by asserting that power, the Herne drives the wedge further between the spirit world and the material one. Attracta's triumph forces Congal to act out Yeats's eugenist nightmares. Now that Attracta has failed to bridge the gulf between the ideal and the real, Congal's sacrifice becomes an empty gesture—an exercise in futility that functions only as proof of the inevitable degeneration of the material world.

After accepting the Herne's existence, Congal repairs to the scene of his original crime to meet the punishment outlined in the Herne's initial curse:

> He that a herne's egg dare steal
> Shall be changed to a fool. . . .
> . . . .

And to end his fool breath
At a fool's hand meet his death. (1018)

Congal wonders why the Great Herne could not come up with a better curse: "That I shall . . . die upon some battlefield / At some fool's hand, is but natural" (1018). What he does not understand—yet—is that Yeats and the Herne have a very specific definition of "fool" in mind.

While the fools of *On Baile's Strand* and *The Hour-Glass* are patterned after Shakespeare's wise fools, the fool who arrives to kill Congal conforms more closely to the eugenist idea of a mental defective. Tom Fool is a village idiot, egged on to his task by the peasants who mock him. Instead of being fascinated with stories of the Shape-Changers and other such tales, as *Baile*'s fool is, Tom remains myopically focused on his pennies and his reputation, repeating his determination to kill Congal and eclipse his rival, Johnny of Meath.[20] The one subject on which the Fool speaks with authority is the definition of "fool": to Congal's "Am I myself a fool?" he responds, "You are King of Connacht. If you were a fool / They would have chased you with their dogs" (1038).

The Fool's assertion that Congal cannot be a fool because he is a king is an indication that social and biological hierarchies are still aligned. Congal's lineage will prevent him from becoming the kind of "fool" that Tom is; he is not the stuff that idiots are made of. But although this mitigates against Congal's being "changed into a fool," it cannot save him from the progress of degeneration he envisions as he looks forward to a slow and miserable death:

Here I must sit through the full moon,
And he will send up Fools against me,
Meandering, roaring, yelling,
Whispering Fools, then chattering Fools,
And after that morose, melancholy,
Sluggish, fat silent Fools;
And I, moon-crazed, moon-blind,
Fighting and wounded, wounded and fighting. (1037)

Even if Congal is not himself a fool, he cannot prevail against this endless tide. His own superiority has become irrelevant; the only way to avoid being pulled down by this army of the degenerate is to kill himself, falling on his own sword in the manner of the ancient Romans.

As the substitution of Tom Fool's cooking spit for Congal's sword indicates, however, even self-immolation has come down in the world. The Herne's curse is forcing him into the fool's role in spite of his lineage. His final defiant gesture, the best evidence Congal has furnished so far of anything heroic in his nature, will be invalidated by the Great Herne, who will reincarnate him as "a brute beast" (1039). Congal's self-sacrifice only accelerates the threat of degeneration. The sooner Congal dies, the sooner the Herne can "push [him] down a step or two" (1033) on the evolutionary ladder.

Congal appeals to Attracta to save him from this fate, and she agrees. By any rules of characterization we may be familiar with, this decision makes no sense. Having already denied Congal's claim to have raped her, called down vengeance upon his head as punishment for what supposedly did not happen, and stood idly by as Congal fatally impaled himself, Attracta should logically allow the Herne to complete the curse and change Congal into a "fool." Instead, a woman who has hitherto defended her purity at tremendous cost to herself agrees to copulate with a peasant in order to conceive and give birth to the reincarnation of her chief rapist and thus save him from the righteous vengeance of her beloved Herne.

The only way to read this decision is as the final and most disruptive manifestation of the contradiction at the heart of this play. Attracta's decision to help Congal acknowledges Congal's rape—and the testimony that challenges her self-declaration as "pure"—as necessary; without his actions, her union with the Great Herne would have been impossible. Just as Yeats's logic dictates that Attracta must be punished for defending the sexual purity she is strictly enjoined to defend, it also dictates that Congal must be punished for violating the purity that he is strictly enjoined to violate. Just as her imagined-yet-real union with the Great Herne is Attracta's reward for undergoing this necessary violation, Attracta's decision to help Congal is his reward for doing his duty and violating her. In order to show the audience that the rape really was necessary, Attracta has to see that Congal gets his reward. Yeats's decision to force Attracta to reward her rapist is not a departure from the play's logic; it is the inevitable outcome of the double injunction that drives the plot. The fact that this decision makes Attracta's character so incoherent as to be unreadable points out how impossible, self-subverting, and damaging the double injunction is.

That attempt also demonstrates, once and for all, the impotence of the sacrificial narrative when faced with the challenges of post-revolutionary Ireland. By seducing Corney, Attracta is attempting to engineer the traditional ending of the sacrificial narrative—to use her reproductive function to turn Congal's sacrifice into regeneration and rebirth. But the opposition between the material and the ideal has become so extreme that this act of recuperation is no longer possible. In addition to causing Attracta to disintegrate as a character, Yeats's fusion of those two contradictory premises—that purity is imperative, and that violation is necessary—makes the disintegration of his world inevitable. The same eugenist prescriptions that made Attracta's violation necessary also make Congal's regeneration impossible.

The insistence on valuing purity has already led Yeats to make one eugenist faux pas: by using seven assailants rather than one, Yeats does effectively convince the audience of Attracta's commitment to sexual purity, but he also defeats his own purpose. Attracta's failed attempt to save Congal from degeneration is the logical result of that initial catastrophe. By actively seeking copulation with an inferior partner—Corney, who although a pleasant and loyal lad is no rocket scientist—Attracta accelerates degeneration by being willing to conceive one of those "cross-bred, gangling" creatures that inhabit Yeats's nightmares. Even as she shows that she has learned her lesson and is willing to put her womb to work, she also shows that the initial pollution that happened during the rape will inevitably spread and worsen.

About to violate genetic codes of conduct, Attracta also violates moral codes:

> ATTRACTA: Come lie with me upon the ground,
> Come quickly into my arms, come quickly, come
> Before his body has had time to cool.
>
> CORNEY: What? Lie with you?
>
> ATTRACTA: Lie and beget. (1039)

Attracta points out that this copulation will take place in public and that it will happen before the "body" of her most recent sexual partner has had "time to cool"; she also repeats the imperative "come" with an insistence that can hardly be accidental. Attracta's eagerness to be useful has transformed her; any vestiges of purity she may still be clinging to disappear as utility becomes her driving motivation. But even utility is now an unattainable goal; their attempt is foiled by Corney's donkey, whose animal lust proves more efficient than man's.

To say, then, that by the end of this play things have fallen apart would be an understatement. Congal's death cannot redeem anything, and the sacrifice that once enabled Ireland's regeneration now accelerates its degeneration. Even Attracta's more painful and protracted sacrifice proves useless: she has lost that dangerous purity but has lost along with it any chance of putting her reproductive power to work. The rape and all the trauma, destruction, and pain it involved is finally all for nothing; violence fails to "beget" anything of value, and Congal's attempt to teach Attracta her lesson ends in futility. Musing on the thirteen-month gestational period of the species to which Congal now belongs, Corney sums up the outcome both of the play and of the ideological battles it reflects: "All that trouble and nothing to show for it, / Nothing but just another donkey" (1040).

The Herne's Egg, then, finally dramatizes the danger at the heart of the sacrificial paradigm—the consequences of insisting both on an impassable divide between the material and the ideal, and on using the Irish woman to embody both. The cost is, in the end, terribly high—not only for Congal and the kingdom he leaves in chaos and disarray, but for Attracta, who cannot fulfill her contradictory roles without coming apart at the seams. The physical and sexual violence she undergoes in that missing scene register in the psychic violence that destroys her consciousness and her character. Yeats's attempt to insist on Attracta's inviolability and purity even as he violates and pollutes her renders her irretrievably broken—shattered more completely than any of the other female figures we have seen. Yeats's attempt to use the reproductive power of the Irish woman to remedy the failures of Irish politics thus proves to be ineffective, irresponsible, and tremendously destructive—both to the male patriot whose sacrifice is compelled and then nullified, and to the female figure who breaks under the strain of trying to occupy a subject position that has become untenable.

The Harlot and the Beggar Man: Cuchulain's Legacy

Although *The Herne's Egg* ranks among Yeats's least important plays in terms of literary reputation (being generally unadmired and infrequently performed), it is nevertheless significant as the first example of a transformation that shapes Yeats's late work. The obvious application of Yeats's interest in eugenics to *Purgatory* has been investigated thoroughly elsewhere. But if we understand how Yeats's eugenist phase relates to the anxieties about gender, sexuality, and reproduction that drive his earlier work, then this reading of *The Herne's Egg* also helps us understand what happens when Yeats revisits the heroic universe in the 1939 *Death of Cuchulain.*

The dramatis personae of that play reads like the invitation list for a Cuchulain Cycle cast party: the Blind Man from *On Baile's Strand;* Emer and Eithne Inguba from *The Only Jealousy of Emer;* and Aoife, who "appears" (but is never on stage) in *On Baile's Strand* and *At the Hawk's Well.* But although the play is presented, primarily, as a sequel to *On Baile's Strand,* it is also an attempt to rewrite *The Herne's Egg* with something closer to a happy ending. Like Congal, Cuchulain is killed by a kitchen utensil wielded by a "defective" whose motive is the "pennies" he expects to get in return. Like Congal, Cuchulain is forced into this position by a bird-god adversary, this time the Morrigu, who foretells and then engineers his death. But if he occupies Congal's position, Cuchulain also seems to have taken on some of the powers and attributes of the Great Herne, in particular the ability to "make the truth"—especially about women.

Eithne, one of Cuchulain's lovers, arrives at the beginning of the play to tell him that his only hope for safety is to "ride out and fight" (*VPl* 1053). Cuchulain then discovers a letter in her hand from Emer, Cuchulain's wife, which tells him that if he moves from his present position he "must face odds no man can face and live" (1053). Eithne is intensely confused about how she came to be bearing two such contradictory messages, but we should not be; we have seen this before. Like Attracta, Eithne is being asked to personify two contradictory opposites. Like Attracta, she can only do this because she has been put in a trance by Maeve. And, like Attracta, Eithne becomes incoherent in her attempt to live up to both meanings. First she insists that she never intended Cuchulain harm—"Who can have put that letter in my hand?" (1054)—but then she refuses to accept his forgiveness for what she claims not to have done: "You're not the man I loved, / That violent man forgave no treachery" (1055). In fact, she promises to exact from Cuchulain's followers the punishment that he refuses to mete out:

> When you are gone
> I shall denounce myself to all your cooks,
> Scullions, armourers, bed-makers and messengers,
> Until they hammer me with a ladle, cut me with a knife,
> Impale me upon a spit, put me to death
> By what foul way best please their fancy,
> So that my shade can stand among the shades
> And greet your shade and prove it is no traitor. (1055–56)

The imagery recalls both Attracta's rape and Congal's death: Eithne imagines herself being purified by this combination of rape and murder, and emerging clean enough to once again become Cuchulain's right and fitting partner.

Cuchulain prevents her from doing this by "mak[ing] the truth"—preempting her story so that no matter what she says, the army of cooks and scullions will not believe her. "This woman, wild with grief, declares that she / Out of pure treachery has told me lies. . . . How can I save her from her own wild words?" (1056) The servant offers to help by pushing Eithne back into that convenient trance: "What if I make her swallow poppy-juice?" Eithne is bundled off the stage to wait out Cuchulain's sacrifice in her opiated state and then to be given "to Conall Caernach because the women / Have called him a good lover" (1056). Cuchulain's reconstruction of the "truth," which wipes out her "treachery" and recreates her as suicidally loyal to him, collapses that deadly opposition and puts Eithne into a stable and livable position.

Cuchulain, then, saves Eithne from making Attracta's sacrifice. However, in the process, Eithne's agency is negated as completely as Attracta's. Cuchulain can only "save" her by overwriting her "wild words"—words that in fact originated from him. Eithne accuses herself of treachery only after becoming convinced that he believes she betrayed him. She is no longer asked to commit the suicide that would prove her devotion; but she is still being forced into the sacrificial position by the playwright who shoves her on stage with the letter in her hand, and by the hero who claims the right to interpret those authorial intentions.

Eithne is replaced by Aoife, who appears on stage for the first time. In *On Baile's Strand* the much-discussed but never-represented Aoife embodied the possibility of mediation, a third position between the material world of domesticity and the occult world of the Shape-Changers—the position that Conchubar shuts down by forcing Cuchulain to fight and kill Aoife's emissary, the son that she and Cuchulain conceived after their first battle. As the unfortunate Attracta demonstrates, this third position is no more part of *The Herne's Egg*'s universe than Conchubar wanted it to be part of his: Attracta is enjoined not to mediate between these two positions but to occupy both simultaneously. Aoife's appearance on stage recalls that third position as a possible alternative—a different end to the story, one that might not involve the violence and death that ended *Baile's Strand* and *The Herne's Egg*.

The fact that Aoife can now be represented on stage with Yeats's other characters, instead of remaining outside the polarities set up by the sacrificial paradigm, indicates that she has lost that power to mediate. Her dialogue reinforces the idea that the window of opportunity she represented is closed. After Cuchulain evokes their sexual encounter, the "brief forgiveness between opposites" he spoke of in *On Baile's Strand,* Aoife dismisses it: "That time was long ago, / And now it is my time. I have come to kill you" (*VPl* 1057). Instead of integration and mediation, Aoife represents defeat and overthrow. Aoife speaks wistfully of lost opportunities, recalling both Cuchulain's attempt to befriend their son and her own decision to abandon—willingly—the "invulnerable" purity that Attracta is forced to cling to:

> I seemed invulnerable; you took my sword,
> You threw me on the ground and left me there.
> I searched the mountains for your sleeping-place
> And laid my virgin body at your side,
> And yet, because you had left me, hated you,
> And thought that I would kill you in your sleep,
> And yet begot a son that night between
> Two black thorn-trees. (1059)

This memory of their son's conception is offered as a vanished alternative, in which the female body becomes fertile without requiring either the violence of rape or the irrigation of the martyr's blood. This is the alternative Cuchulain killed when he killed their son, and the one that he has now moved so far away from, as he stands on the threshold of his own sacrificial death, that he "cannot understand" it (1059).

Aoife withdraws as the Blind Man approaches, and Yeats replaces the death he might have had at Aoife's hands with this more pedestrian demise. Like Attracta, Cuchulain is forced to submit his body to the depredations of the degenerate while insisting that his soul is thereby transformed and glorified. As the Blind Man begins "feeling Cuchulain's body," looking for a spot to insert the knife, Cuchulain has a vision of the "soft feathery shape" that he will assume after death, which is "about to sing" as the Blind Man stabs him (1060–61). Cuchulain will be reborn as a bird, not a donkey; degeneration may claim his body, but it no longer has the rights to his soul.

But the scene that ratifies that transformation—in which Emer dances before a painted parallelogram intended to represent Cuchulain's head, or rather to represent the transformation of Cuchulain from fleshly creature into abstract symbol—is interrupted by the Street-Singer. At the moment of Cuchulain's apotheosis, the play abruptly descends to corporeality, as the harlot—the paradigmatic exponent of degeneration—speaks through the Street-Singer's ballad, complaining that a man without a body is no use to her:

> I meet them face to face,
> Conall, Cuchulain, Usna's boys,
> All that most ancient race;
> Maeve had three in an hour, they say.
> I adore those clever eyes,
> Those muscular bodies, but can get
> No grip upon their thighs. (1062)

The problem of the body is not something Yeats can escape, no matter how thickly he piles on the heroic accoutrements. The insertion of this ballad is his admission that the harlot and the beggar-man stand for something necessary and real: the "flesh" that resists glorification, the flesh that the harlot professes to both "adore and loathe," the "imperfection of a man" that Attracta realizes is necessary. And as Yeats finally admits, the vision of sacrifice that he and his fellow-playwrights "adore" is inseparable from the violence, pain, and destruction that accompanies its incarnation—from the trauma inflicted on that "loathed" body. His long career as the visionary, the intellectual, the midwife of the Irish renaissance is not, and cannot be, distinguished from the messy consequences that the sacrificial paradigm has engendered in the material world. His work as a playwright has only become part of political "reality" because it meddled with that "adore[d] and loathe[d]" (*VPl* 1063) flesh, because it drew on the same material, corporeal desires and anxieties that it tried for so long to deny and reject.

Through the harlot, Yeats admits the inseparability of mind and body, and the commerce that imagination necessarily has with physical reality:

> Are those things that men adore and loathe
> Their sole reality?
> What stood in the Post Office
> With Pearse and Connolly?
> What comes out of the mountain
> Where men first shed their blood?
> Who thought Cuchulain till it seemed
> He stood where they had stood? (1063)

If that adored and loathed "flesh my flesh has gripped" really is man's sole reality, the answers to the next two questions become doubtful. The Yeats who wrote "Easter 1916" knew the answers: what came out of that mountain was the "terrible beauty" of transfiguration, a power that, while moving momentarily in the material world, was not *of* the material world. Here, the verse still suggests the operation of a transformative power. If it was Pearse, Connolly, and the other men and women of 1916 who "thought Cuchulain" into being, then perhaps there really was something in the Post Office with them. But if, as that "who" insinuates, it was Yeats who did the thinking, then Cuchulain was never there; he only "seemed" to be standing there because this self-created strain of sacrificial rhetoric had taught them to look for him. And if Yeats is confronting the possibility that the otherworld in which he has long been immersed is not the "sole reality," then he must also confront the possibility that the answer to the second question—"What stood in the Post Office / With Pearse and Connolly?"—is "Nothing." Or rather, the "[statue] there to mark the place" (1063)—the inadequate, inanimate, lumpenly concrete representation of that wished-for transcendent and immaterial being.

Admitting the importance of the flesh and the necessity of embodiment, Yeats nevertheless pushes that admission as far away as possible, putting this tale in the mouth of a whore and closing the song with another evocation of degeneration that separates Cuchulain from the corruption of modernity:

> No body like his body
> Has modern woman borne,
> But an old man looking on life
> Imagines it in scorn. (1063)

To be valuable, even the flesh must be idealized; it must belong to that irrecoverable heroic past where heroes never bleed, hunger never corrupts, and rape does no damage. Cuchulain's adored body can never enter the modern world where our flesh is so corrupted and polluted that it can only be loathed. Eugenics becomes Yeats's last defense against the body, the only way to maintain plausible deniability, to acknowledge the power of the flesh while at the same time denying and despising it.

In his final play, then, we see Yeats still unable to create that moment of perfect transcendence, even through the ultimate hero's ultimate sacrifice. The problem of the body remains unresolved and—as this play acknowledges, perhaps for the first time—irresolvable. If it ever is solved, it will have to be by the harlot and the beggar man, the diminished corporeal counterparts of Aoife and Cuchulain. Now that the last sacrificial hero is gone, the world will belong, not to the heroic dead, but to the walking wounded, the mortal survivors of this cataclysmic period and all of its terrible beauty.

Afterword

About a year after *The Herne's Egg* was rejected by the Abbey board, Ireland's new constitution was ratified in a 1937 plebiscite. There is, of course, no direct connection, except inasmuch as the new constitution was the brainchild of De Valera and Fianna Fáil, whom Yeats had very much in mind when he wrote *The Herne's Egg*. But the creation and ratification of that constitution was the material counterpart of the symbolic misbirth that Yeats represented in *The Herne's Egg, Purgatory,* and *Death of Cuchulain.* As the last word on the central question we have been investigating—the question of how sexual and national politics relate and what their intercourse can engender—I want to briefly examine the moment of that constitution's birth. By looking at that foundational document in light of the discursive trends we have discussed here, I hope to suggest why, in concrete terms, the reading that I have been trying to articulate matters.

Despite the fact that De Valera's ideologies and motivations were radically opposed to those legible in Yeats's later work, some of his methods turned out to be curiously similar. Just as Yeats attempted to use Attracta to reconcile the necessity of violation with the desire for purity, the constitution used the Irish woman to negotiate a compromise between the conflicting ideals driving De Valera's attempt to make a united Ireland possible. As we saw in O'Casey's trilogy, the sanctity of motherhood became attractive in the post-civil-war era as a way of transcending political divisions; but more than that, appealing to this ideal enabled De Valera to legislate an "Irish Ireland" without having to insist on provisions that would make reunification difficult.

De Valera's main objective in proposing the new constitution was to accelerate the Free State's transformation into a "republic in fact," a process that began with the passage of the Removal of Oath Bill.

The bill both removed any mention of the king from the constitution and did away with the oath of allegiance that had prevented republicans from holding public office. At the same time, De Valera wanted to maintain Ireland's membership in the Commonwealth, partly because he feared that severing ties would create opposition in the North and decrease the chances of reunification. Thus the Removal of Oath Bill was accompanied by the External Relations Act, which provided for Ireland's continued connection to the Commonwealth as regarded foreign policy.[1] As this example illustrates, Fianna Fáil's logic made compromise and contradiction an inevitable part of their platform. On the one hand, since their ultimate goal was the creation of an autonomous Irish republic, Fianna Fáil was committed to separation from, and hostility toward, England; on the other, unification was part of that goal, and conventional wisdom had it that this would only be possible if the twenty-six-county state made enough concessions to render the republic a hospitable place for the Unionists in the northeast corner.

Aside from giving the appearance of hypocrisy, this need to compromise endangered one of Fianna Fáil's main objectives, which was the establishment of a "really Irish Ireland" (De Valera 372). The more concessions were made to Protestant/Unionist wishes, the more contaminated and adulterated that implicitly Catholic/republican "Irishness" appeared to be. Thus, to compensate for the concessions De Valera made to Unionist desires, the constitution included language declaring that despite these concessions and the imposition of partition, the new Ireland was nevertheless "a sovereign, independent, democratic, Gaelic, and Catholic country" (A. Ward, *Irish Constitutional Tradition* 240). Because most of these articles were "not enforceable in law" (Pakenham 295), they would not erect legal barriers to reunification; but they would, nevertheless, preserve Ireland as the kind of nationalist construct to which Fianna Fáil and its supporters could pledge their allegiance.

De Valera's position, however, limited the extent to which he could declare those intentions, even in an "unenforceable article." Had De Valera not anticipated the eventual incorporation of a sizable Protestant/Unionist minority, he might have attempted to include language explicitly declaring Catholicism Ireland's national religion. As it was, the 1937 constitution did recognize the "special position" of the Catholic Church in Irish society, but that was the result of compromise. De Valera rejected several versions of this declaration, including one that identified the Catholic Church as representing

93 percent of Ireland's population and one giving "special recognition" to the Catholic Church while pledging to "simply tolerate" other churches, because he felt they would make reunification problematic (Pakenham 296). The final version follows the declaration of the Catholic Church's "special position" by recognizing all "other religious denominations existing in Ireland at the date of the coming into operation of this constitution" (qtd. in Pakenham 297). The fact that some Catholic groups rejected this language as weak-kneed indicates that by some that article was seen as a concession—one that caused De Valera "more anxiety than anything else in the Constitution" (Pakenham 297).

But if any attempt to write Catholicism explicitly into the constitution was bound to create trouble, De Valera could still maintain that "Irish Ireland" through a more indirect route—by making the constitution Gaelic and Catholic in *spirit* if not in letter. To this end, De Valera based the document as much as possible on ideas from Catholic traditions of political science. De Valera's "social programme"—the part of the constitution that deals with motherhood, marriage, and the family—was very much a part of his attempt to instill that Catholic spirit (Pakenham 297) Besides protecting the patriarchal family unit so dear to the hearts of the Church hierarchy, the constitution's "social programme" protected all the national ideals that we have seen associated with that family—economic independence, cultural integrity, purity, power, and productivity. While he worked toward the creation of an Ireland that would have to be hybrid—Catholic and Protestant, Commonwealth and republican—De Valera, like the Blueshirts, used the construct of the Irish woman to preserve the ideals that material circumstances were forcing him to abandon.

De Valera's defense of these provisions shows him still making that old equation between the integrity of the home and economic prosperity. He claims that Ireland can cure the "economic evils" that have resulted from the trade war by keeping women in the home, which conversely will get the men into the workplace:

> But the present social system, inasmuch as it compels mothers to leave their natural duties as mothers and go out and become breadwinners when their husbands are idle and cannot get work, is a system which we ought to try to reform. One of the reforms should be in the direction of enabling a man, if it is a man, to earn sufficient to cover all his domestic needs; and, if it is a widow who has young children, to enable the State to come to her aid and contribute to such an extent as will not necessitate her leaving her duties as a mother and engaging in

> outside labour. I do not mind being a whole-burnt offering in working for that. (325)

The reference to "idle" husbands tacitly acknowledges the unemployment created by the economic war and offers Article 41 as a solution: keeping the wife and mother in the home is the first step toward "enabling a man . . . to earn sufficient to cover all his domestic needs." Where the Blueshirts sought to solve Ireland's economic problems by opening up the home to external products, technologies, and ideologies, De Valera seeks to solve them by sealing the home off and trapping the Irish woman inside. By "protecting" the home and the captive mother, De Valera still believes he is protecting Ireland's economy.

De Valera's appeal to motherhood is also part of a more complicated strategy related specifically to the problem of legitimacy. Part of De Valera's reason for proposing a new constitution was to establish a government that would not owe its existence directly to the contested Treaty. Instead of an artificial and unsatisfying compromise rigged up in a hurry by diplomats with suspect motives, the new constitution was to be an authentic expression of Irish popular opinion—a "natural" thing emanating directly from Ireland and incorporating the true and sincere patriotism of "the Irish people, or the section of the Irish people we can consult on the matter" (qtd. in Pakenham 299). As De Valera's qualifier indicates, this return to authenticity was possible only in the realm of wishful thinking. After 1922, determining who "the Irish people" were became impossible, never mind figuring out what they wanted. Taking a leaf from O'Casey's book, De Valera tries to make this fantasy real by embodying it in his social legislation—which is based on that most natural thing in the world, a woman's desire to care for her children. By legislating traditional family structures and gender roles, the constitution seeks to reach beyond the conflicts created by partition to the bedrock of moral certainty, authenticating itself and the government it legitimates by recognizing and enforcing these "natural" and self-evident gender constructions.

Despite objections raised by feminist groups, the Dáil discussions of these articles show that De Valera's political opponents were unable or unwilling to challenge the premises on which the "social programme" was based. The only challenge they *can* make, in fact, is that these provisions are so self-evident that to restate them is a waste of space:

> We say, therefore, that the inadequate strength of women or the tender age of children should not be abused. We also say that women and children ought not to be forced by the necessity of the economic compulsion driving women into avocations unsuited to their sex or strength or age. What is wrong about that, I should like to know?
>
> *Mr. J. I. McGuire:* Why not put in the Book of Proverbs? We all agree with it.
>
> *The President:* If you do all agree, is it not a good thing to have it here as a headline?
>
> *Mr. McGuire:* Why not put in the Book of Proverbs? (De Valera 326)

De Valera, true to form, takes the question seriously and actually tries to answer it, missing McGuire's point: that as long as De Valera is restating the obvious, he should throw in the Bible while he's at it. But Article 41 is valuable to De Valera precisely because it *is* obvious, because it is something "we all agree with." If the constitution legitimates traditional family and gender structures, then through these provisions those structures also legitimate the constitution.

The 1937 constitution, then, leaves the Irish woman where *The Herne's Egg* left her—still under that double injunction, still required to reproduce the ideal that her male counterparts have found it necessary or expedient to depart from, still asked to use her body to create the "natural," authentic, pure, whole, and healthy Ireland that partition and its politics are making increasingly impossible. Whatever differences separate Fianna Fáil and Cumann na nGaedheal, there is one thing they can "all agree with"—the need to keep the Irish woman in this position, to put on her shoulders the responsibility of making the impossible possible and giving material being to the ideals that are becoming more illusory as partition gets older and the wound gets deeper.

De Valera, basking in the afterglow of the successful referendum, is confident that his tactics have done no permanent damage to Ireland or its women:

> I am sure you will be amused in recalling . . . the supposed 'discrimination' which was to be exercised against women and their loss of status and 'degradation' as a result, as well as the 'encroachment upon the rightful liberty of the individual' and 'attack upon the freedom of the press', not to mention the all-embracing assertion that 'the new Constitution was not, from the national point of view, nearly as good as the old.' Now that these contentions have passed into history, I am

> sure you find it difficult to believe that they could have been taken seriously. (363)

History, alas, has not been so kind. In fact, Ireland's recent history—a history that includes the Kerry babies, the X case, and several bitterly divisive referenda on abortion and divorce—suggests that De Valera's "unenforceable" articles did produce the discrimination, degradation, and "loss of status" his feminist critics feared. It has also, ironically, frustrated the process that De Valera was hoping the constitution would facilitate: the Republic of Ireland's repressive policies regarding divorce, contraception, and reproductive freedom ultimately became part of the argument against reunification. By underwriting the conflation of family and nation to this extent in the foundational document of the Republic of Ireland, De Valera's attempt to drain the poisoned wound of partition simply ensured that it would continue to fester.

If that poisoned wound ever does heal, it will be interesting to see how the successful completion of the peace process—whatever form that ultimately takes—changes the situation of Irish women. For now, all we know is that Irish women are still grappling with the material consequences of the discursive trends we have been discussing—on both sides of that partition.

Notes

Introduction

1. Any attempt to summarize the chain of events that led to the dirty protests is necessarily an oversimplification. Without detailing the many individual steps in the escalating conflict between prisoner resistance and the authorities' attempts to enforce compliance, it is very difficult to give an accurate explanation of how and why the prisoners came to be living under these conditions. Indeed, any explanation involves interpretation and is therefore subject to challenge.

2. Tim Pat Coogan notes that "the protest received curiously little publicity" until Cardinal O'Fiach visited the prison in 1978, after the dirty protest had been going on for two years (224).

3. As Mary Karen Dahl points out in her introduction, contemporary dramatists continue to revisit and revise the Aristotelian model (1–4).

4. There are exceptions, of course, but often the exceptions prove the rule. In Friel's *Freedom of the City,* for instance, one of the three victims is a woman, but symbolically she functions more as a displaced figure for Mother Ireland than as a victim. Her suffering is persistently described in terms of the suffering of her children; and the Balladeer, after assimilating her under the rubric of "the lads inside the guildhall" (118) in his first song about the incident, represents her simply as "a mother" (148) in the corrective version in the second act.

5. James provides a summary of the standard anthropological take on this in his chapter on vegetative rituals (49–77).

6. Poovey discusses Petty's leadership of the 1653 Down Survey of lands seized in the Cromwellian invasion (120–22).

7. On Petty's responsibility for the "idea that national wealth derived from domestic production, and thus from labor," see Poovey 127.

8. See Poovey 122–26.

9. Derek Attridge and Marjorie Howes's introduction to their collection *Semicolonial Joyce* provides one of the most comprehensive and coherent statements of some of the difficulties involved in reading Irish literature from a postcolonial perspective.

10. See, for instance, L. Perry Curtis Jr.'s *Apes and Angels,* Noel Ignatiev's *How the Irish Became White,* or Theodore W. Allen's *The Invention of the White Race.*

11. For a more comprehensive discussion of family planning in post-independence India, see Marika Vicziany's two-part series "Coercion in a Soft State: The Family Planning Program of India," *Pacific Affairs* 55 (1982): 395–97, 557–92.

12. See Ornella Moscucci's *The Science of Woman: Gynaecology and Gender in England, 1800–1929;* Jo Murphy-Lawless's *Reading Birth and Death;* and Terri Kapsalis's

Public Privates for examples of scholarship that investigates the masculinist bias of obstetric medicine.

13. For more on the "federation" structure of science within the Empire, see Roy Macleod's "On Visiting the 'Moving Metropolis.'"

1. Body and Soul

1. To what extent Yeats can take credit for *Cathleen ni Houlihan* is a question that has not yet been definitively answered. Elizabeth Coxhead, in her 1961 *Lady Gregory: A Literary Portrait,* advanced the theory that Lady Gregory was responsible for the Gillane family's scenes, while Yeats provided the overall concept. Daniel J. Murphy's "Lady Gregory, Co-Author and Sometimes Author of the Plays of W. B. Yeats" (1972) asserts that "all the evidence clearly indicates that Lady Gregory wrote the play in its entirety" (47). James Pethica (1988) argues for a "greater degree of mutuality" (5) in their collaboration and suggests, based on his reading of the Berg notebook manuscript, that Lady Gregory wrote the part leading up to Cathleen's entrance alone and continued to write most of the Gillane family dialogue but that thereafter Yeats took "responsibility for the central symbolic character of Cathleen" (9). Based on both the quality of the various arguments and my own reading of the play, I believe Pethica's description is the more accurate.

2. "Republican" in the Irish context refers to a person or organization dedicated to securing an independent and unified Irish republic, a politically autonomous entity that would include what is now known as Northern Ireland and would have no administrative ties to England. The Irish Free State was created in 1922 when, after three years of guerilla warfare in Ireland, a treaty was signed dividing the island into two political units, Northern Ireland and the Irish Free State, which was later renamed the Republic of Ireland.

3. On the contributions of the Gaelic League to nationalist theater at the turn of the century, see Trotter 3–6.

4. For analysis of much earlier imperial attempts to control the Irish subject through gender construction, see Jones and Stallybrass's discussion of Spenserian tropes in "Dismantling Irena" and Elizabeth Butler Cullingford's examination of the history of the Irish-Carthaginian connection in "British Romans and Irish Carthaginians."

5. Frazier discusses the characterization of the peasants in contrast to that of the countess on 6–17.

6. The destruction of the shrine was suppressed during the initial production, probably as a response to F. H. O'Donnell's attack on the play.

7. Kinealy's *This Great Calamity: The Irish Famine 1845–52* details the British government's relief policies as well as the laissez-faire economic philosophy used to justify them; Turner's study of the famine's effect on agriculture documents the importance of the landlord/tenant system in creating the subsistence farming system that made the famine as much of a disaster as it was, a view borne out by John Killen's introduction to his collection of contemporary coverage of the famine. Although denying that "the extirpation of the Irish race" was one of the conscious goals of British policymakers, O Grada attributes the devastation caused by the potato blight to "an ideology ill geared to saving lives" on the part of Britain's administrators and to the "mass poverty" created by the colonial land ownership

system (122). Joel Mokyr's *Why Ireland Starved* also makes the argument that the famine was created as much by the weakness of the Irish economy as by the blight itself.

8. Yeats revised this play extensively several times. I am citing the first revised version of 1899, which is the one that O'Donnell would have been reading. Most of this version is to be found in the notes at the bottom of the pages in the *Variorum Plays*. It is indexed as "5" in the annotations, and most of the lines cited will be at the bottom of the recto page under the dividing line that separates the main text from the variants. For stories about people dying with their mouths stained green from eating grass, dock, and dandelion in post-famine folklore, see Poirteir 59, 66–67, 88–89, 90, 95.

9. Poirteir's collection of folklore includes accounts of famine victims killed by animal bites (60) and eaten by rats (60, 192), foxes (61), and dogs (64, 106). Killen's anthology of contemporary reports of the famine includes several accounts that dwell on the fact that people are dying too fast to be given burial, including, in addition to the *Vindicator* report of M'Manus's inquest, a piece from the *Weekly Freeman's Journal* (17 July 1847) that shows corpses "devoured by dogs" (Killen 148).

10. See Howes 48, where she traces the development of the "souls for gold" barter as a metaphor in nationalist discourse for "Irish complicity in colonization."

11. The citations here are drawn from the *Irish Times* review of *The Heather Field* (10 May 1899: 5). The same criticisms, couched in slightly different language, appeared a day earlier in the *Irish Times* review of *The Countess Cathleen* (9 May 1899: 5).

12. At the beginning of Act III, Tyrrell tells Ussher that "since those evictions" he can no longer go out without police protection: "I should be shot at otherwise" (*Heather Field* 255).

13. The 1912 revisions suppress Shemus's destruction of the shrine (*VPl* 31); the First Merchant's line, "No curses injure the immortal demons" (*VPl* 47); Shemus's line, "God and the mother of God have dropped asleep" (*VPl* 29); and the story of Father John (*VPl* 93)—all singled out by O'Donnell for special comment. The only passage O'Donnell objects to that is not omitted on revision is the angel's speech exonerating Cathleen.

14. Coleman's survey of responses to the original production shows that Yeats and Martyn were dismayed by the audience's laughter during the opening scene, which they felt detracted from the tragic impact of Cathleen. Later on, Yeats wrote to Gregory that the audience now understood the play and had no trouble making the transition from comedy to tragedy.

15. Since most Irish peasants could not actually own the land they worked, "inheriting" in this context means taking over the lease.

16. Turner concludes that the 1841 census data indicate that 40 to 45 percent of all farms were smaller than ten acres and that the famine demonstrated the "precariousness of peasant survival" at "these remarkably low acreages" (69).

17. Concern about emigration is evident, for instance, in Maud Gonne's "Ireland and the Children" (7 June 1902: 3); Mary E. L. Butler's "Womanhood and Nationhood III" (17 January 1903: 6); "Brigid"'s "How to Popularize Irish Dress Materials" (1 April 1903: 5); and Lasairfhiona Ni Shamhraidhin's "Irish Shoddy" (11 February 1905: 6 and 4 March 1905: 3) and "A Paper for Irishwomen" (8 April 1905: 6).

18. Trotter suggests that Gonne may have been fully aware of the ways in which theatrical performance might limit the scope and impact of her political perfor-

mance but that she agreed to do *Cathleen ni Houlihan* because she recognized its enormous potential as a political catalyst. In that sense, Gonne's performance of the role is in itself a sacrifice. See Trotter, *Ireland's National Theaters* 93–94.

2. Under Siege

1. Griffith's review of *Shadow* appeared October 17, 1903; Yeats's "The Irish National Theatre and Three Sorts of Ignorance" appeared a week later along with Griffith's response. The Petronius question was debated in a series of editorials and letters to the editor during October of 1903 and January–February 1905. Griffith initially confused the issue by stating that the play was "no more English than the Decameron," implying that he thought Synge was basing *Shadow* on Boccaccio's work. As Yeats later points out in 1905, the *Decameron* does not contain a version of the Ephesus story. Griffith then denies having claimed that the play had anything to do with the *Decameron* and states firmly that *Shadow* is based on the version of the Ephesus story that appears in Petronius. The *Satyricon* is one of the earliest surviving Roman novels and was written/circulated during Nero's reign.

2. Crucifixion was a method of execution for convicted criminals in the Roman Empire, and the continued display of the victim's decomposing body was considered part of his sentence.

3. The Widow of Ephesus story takes up chapters 111–13 of the *Satyricon* and appears on pages 95–98 of Sage and Gilleland's Latin edition. Sage's supplementary note provides a useful summary of the story's subsequent history in European literature (229).

4. See Yeats's letters to the editor, published January 28 and February 4, 1905.

5. Griffith claims in his original review of *Shadow* that the Ephesus story was brought into Ireland via "hedge-schoolmasters," who taught classical languages in rural Ireland during the nineteenth century. Yeats reminds Griffith of this in his letter published in the January 28, 1905 issue of *United Irishman.*

6. I base this assumption on the fact that many of these articles are signed with feminine Gaelic pseudonyms. Since each member of Inghinidhe na hEireann was required to adopt a Gaelic name, and since Gonne herself was a frequent contributor to the *United Irishman,* it is likely that some of these pseudonyms belong to Inghinidhe writing under their *noms de guerre.* On Inghinidhe na hEireann's contribution to nationalist drama during this period, see Trotter 73–100.

7. "Irish Shoddy" appears in the February 11, 1905, issue with two letters to Griffith from Synge and Yeats, and Griffith's response, all referring to the February 4 issue's treatment of the Petronius controversy. The same author published another piece with the same title in the March 4 issue.

8. Like many of the *United Irishman*'s contributors, this author writes under a Gaelic pseudonym. I have so far been unable to identify her, but the "Ni" (daughter of) indicates that she is a woman (or at least that she is presenting as a woman).

9. The source story for *Shadow* appears in Synge, *The Aran Islands,* 58–60.

10. The play is coy about whether Nora and Michael have been committing adultery prior to the events depicted; but once Michael enters, he and Nora are in view of the audience the entire time.

11. For a discussion of the effect of the famine on marriage and fertility patterns, and the role British imperialism played in same, see the previous chapter.

12. Maire Nic Shiubhlaigh originated the role of Nora and played Cathleen during the company's May 1903 tour of London and the December 27, 1904, opening of the Abbey Theatre. The logical assumption is that Nic Shiubhlaigh stepped into the role after Gonne stepped out of it. In her memoir, Nic Shiubhlaigh does not mention playing Cathleen the night of *Shadow*'s premiere; but her account of that period focuses almost entirely on *Shadow* and on Griffith's reaction to it.

13. On the formal importance of the oath, see Skene 42; on the 1904 staging, see Holloway 50; on Yeats's lighting techniques, see Flannery 253.

14. For readings that make this equation, see Moore's *Masks of Love and Death* 114; Good 22; Skene 42–43.

15. Scolnicov substantiates this claim in her close reading of *Lysistrata,* 29–40.

16. According to several accounts, audience restlessness reached its flash point during Act III when Christy said the word "shift," referring to a woman's nightgown.

17. Synge was directly attacked by the *Irish Times* for doing exactly this in reference to *Riders of the Sea,* in which the corpse of the drowned Bartley is brought on stage (Kiely 125).

18. "Morbid variation from an original type" was incorporated by Morel into the definition of "degeneration" in 1857 (Soloway 38); the belief that genetic degeneration would ultimately destroy the human population was one of the tenets of eugenicist science. The eugenicist association of disease and genetic "defects" with urban poverty meant that "squalid" had pathological as well as sociological connotations.

19. On the effect of Boer War hysteria on the public health movement, see Hopkins 245–47; Soloway 13, 38–41.

20. For a basic overview of the eugenicist movement and its theoretical premises, see Pauline Mazumdar's *Eugenics, Human Genetics and Human Failings: The Eugenics Society, Its Sources and Its Critics in Britain* (London: Routledge, 1992).

21. On the doctrine of differential fertility, see Mazumdar 35–38.

22. It is probable that the vagina was not included for the same reason that the anus is referred to as "the digestive tube"—the *Dublin Evening Mail's* readers were not ready to hear such a private part of the body named in such a public forum. Whatever the reason, its absence means that the list as it stands suggests a male rather than a female body.

23. Zam-Buk ran this ad in the *Dublin Evening Mail* over a period of several weeks in two versions, one text-only and one accompanied by an illustration. The text was consistent throughout, and the same illustration was always used.

24. By "state-sponsored" I am referring to the public health administration set up in Ireland as part of the colonial government, which concerned itself primarily with sanitation, institutionalization, and epidemiology. From the Famine onward, medicine in Ireland became increasingly regulated by other government bodies, a trend that many individual Irish doctors resisted to the best of their ability. For instance, in the *Dublin Evening Mail,* an October 21, 1903, article reports on clashes between the Poor Law Guardians and the Irish Medical Board over the administration of state-sponsored dispensaries; the January 4, 1904, issue reports on the role the Dublin workhouse system has played in the recent measles epidemic; a January 31, 1905, item addresses compulsory vaccination; a February 1, 1905, piece discusses the institutionalization of lunatics in workhouses; the January 15, 1907, issue includes a report on smallpox in Belfast; February 1, 1907, covers the spotted fever outbreak in Belfast; a column on February 7, 1907, announces a plan to build a public sanatorium for tuberculosis victims in Dublin; articles in February 12 and 13,

1907, document medical efforts to contain a spotted fever outbreak in Dublin. The practice of medicine in Ireland was also "state-sponsored" in a more abstract sense in that medical teaching and resultant medical practice within the British Empire was shaped by what was going on at medical universities in London. For more on this more insidious version of state control, see Macleod's discussion of the administrative/institutional structures of imperial science, 232–42.

25. Vaccination paranoia has recently reappeared in contemporary American popular culture, loaded with many of the same implications. Chris Carter, producer of *The X-Files,* incorporated into the show's "mythology" a plot suggesting that the U.S. government used smallpox vaccines to identify and monitor immunized Americans. Carter's use of this motif both references his country's colonial history—the smallpox plot was obscurely related to the fate of the now-lost Anasazi tribe—and sketches out a futuristic "colonization" story line in which an unspecified alien race, with the collaboration of a select group of powerful humans, uses smallpox vaccination to prepare the ground for its eventual conquest of Earth.

26. Yeats expounds on this idea of aesthetics/eugenics in his poem "The Statues."

27. Greene and Stephens endorse this reading in *J. M. Synge: 1871–1909;* Kiberd incorporates it into his treatment of Christy as a parodic Cuchulain (*Synge* 113–14); Kiely reads *Playboy* as an allegory about the rise and fall of the Irish nationalist leader Charles Stuart Parnell (177–79).

28. I read Quin's "maiming ewes" as part of the agrarian campaigns of the nineteenth century in which tenants vandalized landlord property and livestock in retaliation for evictions. In doing so, I contradict Declan Kiberd's reading, which treats Quin's ewe-maiming as an expression of the cruelty to animals that Synge commented on in *The Aran Islands.* However, given that Kiberd also lumps together many details that I see as distinct (for instance, he sees Daneen Sullivan and the Mad Mulrannies as equivalent), and the implication that Quin was jailed for this offense, I feel justified in challenging this interpretation.

29. The word "shift" occurs twice before the third act, which is when the initial rioting began.

30. Weldon Thornton has done the most thorough treatment of this theme in *J. M. Synge and the Western Mind.*

31. Greene's "A Reappraisal" credits Masefield with starting this trend. Although Greene challenges the prevailing view of Synge as a sickly invalid, he feels bound to accept the agreement on Synge's "morbidity," attributing it to a hereditary tendency toward gloom and seriousness in Synge's family (17–18).

3. Excess of Love

1. The Irish Volunteers will be discussed in more detail below. The Irish Citizen Army (ICA) was a volunteer militia organized for the purpose of protecting Irish workers from police violence during the great strike of 1913. It was led by James Connolly, who along with Jim Larkin was one of the major leaders of the trade union movement in Dublin.

2. Roger Casement, whose fascinating life and career have furnished material for a number of biographies, was apprehended shortly before the appointed date of the attack while trying to bring a shipment of arms from Germany to Ireland. After news of his arrest reached Dublin, there was some disagreement about whether to

call the attack off or go ahead as planned. In the end, confusion about whether and/or when the attack would actually take place meant that there was almost no activity outside of Dublin itself. This greatly limited the effect that the Rising could possibly have, although the prevailing opinion among Irish historians has always been that the Rising could never have been practically successful under any circumstances.

3. The revisionist argument, in brief, runs thus: if, instead of staging the Easter 1916 uprising, Pearse and his colleagues had either allowed Home Rule to pass (Fr. Francis Shaw's perspective) or waited until Britain's strength was depleted by the Great War (O'Brien's argument in "The Embers of Easter," 225–27), Irish independence could have been achieved with much less bloodshed and perhaps without partition. This argument, as Alan Ward points out, downplays the problem of militant Unionist opposition to Home Rule even with partition (see *Easter Rising: Revolution for Irish Nationalism*).

4. Sheehy-Skeffington's husband, Francis Sheehy-Skeffington, was shot and killed by a British officer during the Rising despite the fact that as a pacifist he was not actually participating in the rebellion. Many of the other protestors had also lost loved ones in the Rising. O'Casey did not participate in the Rising, a fact that no doubt helped fuel resentment.

5. For a typical use of this formula, see Richard Kearney's "Myth and Motherland"; for an especially crude deployment of it, see Padraig O'Malley's introduction to *Biting at the Grave.*

6. For more on the European context of Pearse's celebration of bloodshed, see Declan Kiberd's *Inventing Ireland,* Sean Farrell Moran's *Padraig Pearse and the Politics of Redemption* 177–82, and Fr. Francis Shaw's "The Canon of Irish History: A Challenge," 150. Edwards, *Patrick Pearse and the Triumph of Failure,* specifically discusses the "hysteria of British Army recruitment propaganda" (179).

7. For examples of contemporary commentators citing Pearsian rhetoric as a major or contributing cause of political violence in Ireland, see Conor Cruise O'Brien's *States of Ireland* (89), Father Francis Shaw's "The Canon of Irish History: A Challenge," Richard Kearney's "Myth and Motherland," and Padraig O'Malley's *Biting at the Grave.*

8. The terms "republican" and "nationalist" are by no means interchangeable, but during the period under discussion the distinction often became blurry. In general, republicans advocated complete separation from England and absolute political autonomy, whereas nationalists favored Irish self-determination but were more likely to accept Home Rule (which would mean limited political autonomy within Great Britain) as a valid compromise. Republicans were more likely to advocate the use of physical force to achieve their goal, whereas nationalists tended to be more constitutionally minded. However, republican publications sometimes used "nationalist" to mean "republican," since some contributors felt that no one who would accept Home Rule had the right to call himself a nationalist. In this chapter, "republican" will refer to advocates of physical force and/or complete separation; "nationalist" will refer to proponents of cultural nationalism and/or constitutional reform.

9. While the desire for inclusivity is certainly apparent, the Volunteers' claim to be a nonpartisan organization is highly debatable. From its earliest beginnings the leadership of the Volunteers included a "disproportionate number of IRB members" (Edwards 209), who were all by definition physical-force republicans; and the *Irish Volunteer* reflects their convictions. For this reason, despite the fact that

the Volunteers were supposedly not "political," I will be including the *Irish Volunteer* in the category of "republican" discourse.

10. John Redmond was a member of Parliament and one of the original founders of the Volunteers. He was a major figure in the constitutional nationalist movement, which favored achieving Home Rule through legal means instead of achieving independence through military revolt (which was the physical-force republican position). It was Redmond's decision to endorse the British Army's attempt to recruit in Ireland during the First World War that precipitated the final schism in the Volunteers between the constitutionalists and the militant republicans.

11. "Lucan" is citing John Mitchel's earlier *Jail Journal.* "Lucan" is the name of a historian of the Roman silver age, primarily remembered for his account of civil violence in the late Roman republic.

12. Seamus Deane's "Civilians and Barbarians" provides an overview of the process whereby England's invasion and occupation of Ireland was transformed into a conflict between the benign and enlightened forces of "English civilization, based on laws," and the darkness of "Irish barbarism" (35); and of the discursive history that makes that construction so difficult to challenge.

13. In 1915, probably because Redmond's defection depleted the Volunteers' coffers, the paper's layout and content are drastically revised, and the graphic disappears.

14. "From the Outpost" always appeared on the front page. It was anonymous and was divided into several individually titled sections.

15. This anonymous admonition appears by itself in a box at the end of a column on page 4 of the September 5, 1914, issue.

16. The *Irish Volunteer* took ballads seriously, devoting several column inches per issue to them. However, this enthusiasm seems to have been outdone by that of their contributors. The editors suggest to their readers more than once that they should spend their energy on drilling instead of writing, and that if they *must* pour out their revolutionary souls on paper, they should consider doing it in prose. See "From the Outpost," 23 May 1914; "Ricochets," 28 November 1914: 16.

17. "Ode to a Rifle" may have been intended as a militant and aggressive response to Terence MacSwiney's "An Ode to a Bullet" (*Irish Volunteer* 1 August 1914: 14), in which the narrator eagerly anticipates being shot in the head for the greater glory of Ireland: "Sweet Messenger of Death, your kiss of pain / Lay on my brow, before dishonour base / Shall once again drag down our ancient race."

18. During the sentencing phase of Roger Casement's trial, his personal diaries, in which he recorded his desires for, and sexual encounters with, other men, were shown to various British officials in order to convince them to insist on the death penalty. After Casement's execution they were used to prevent him from becoming a republican martyr. One of the first newspaper accounts of the diary scandal was headlined "Diaries of a Degenerate." The genuineness of the diaries has been a subject of controversy since they were first leaked to the press; but even if they were forgeries, the point I am making here—that the British authorities encouraged an equation between homosexuality and degeneracy—is still valid.

19. Deane's "Civilians and Barbarians" discusses the use of criminology to pathologize and criminalize Irish resistance during the nineteenth century (38–40).

20. "Steady, Volunteers," "Seaghan O'Neill," and "Forgive and Forget" were all published under the alias "Rory of the Hill," who is also responsible for "The Recruiting Sergeant."

21. "O'Kelly's Bride" was published in the *Irish Volunteer* in two installments, 1 August 1914: 12 and 8 August 1914: 2–3, 6.

22. Mary Trotter's discussion of Pearse's productions in *Ireland's National Theaters* is one of the few serious critical treatments of Pearse as a dramatist, and even she gives more consideration to Pearse's pageants than to his plays (157–66).

23. For an example of this approach, see Brian P. Murphy's *Patrick Pearse and the Lost Republican Ideal,* 41–42.

24. Treatments of Roger Casement show both how powerful those cultural forces were in 1916 and how their grip on the European and American imaginations has weakened (somewhat). When Casement's diaries first came out, nobody tried to defend him by arguing that homosexuality was not in fact disgusting and degenerate. Instead, his supporters were forced to explain the diaries as British forgeries. In 1956, biographer Rene MacColl felt a need to assure readers of his own "lack of understanding of what makes perverts behave in the way that they do," but he was also able to admit that the diaries are genuine because he could now suggest that "not all [homosexuals] are monsters" (285). In 1976, B. L. Reid argued that "Casement was not a pervert: he was an invert; and he was not a degenerate: he was a homosexual" (465), still using pathologizing terminology but arguing that "nothing . . . entitles us to call 'the other love' . . . sinful or even shameful" (465). In 1984, Roger Sawyer finally asserts that "the disjunction 'Saintly Patriot or Treacherous Pervert' is a bogus one" (135).

25. While Moran does not deny that Pearse "found boys attractive in a physical sense" or that this emerges in Pearse's writing, he also clearly sees this writing as proof that Pearse had "severe psychological limitations," suffered from "sexual backwardness" and "sexual immaturity," and was "unprepared for an autonomous adulthood" (Moran 197). Moran's analysis nicely supports the connection between homophobia and the delegitimization of Irish political violence; this gratuitous pathologization of Pearse's sexuality is brought in to support his argument that the Rising was "not . . . the result of some rational process," but "the manifestation of deep-seated psychological and emotional conflicts, arising from the failures of cultural and constitutional nationalism" (177).

26. Lewis Carroll was the pen name of Charles Dodgson; I will be referring to him as Dodgson since I am talking about the individual rather than the author-function.

27. As Mary Trotter's examination of the St. Enda's productions in *Ireland's National Theaters* demonstrates, the nationalist press took the St. Enda's productions as seriously as they took the Irish Literary Theater or the Abbey. See Trotter 137–66 for a fuller account of the St. Enda's boys' reception.

28. Most of the more explicit expressions of desire in Pearse's writing appear in Irish-language texts. This would seem to suggest either that Pearse was to some extent aware of what he was doing and therefore only allowed himself this much room for expression in texts that he knew could only be read by a limited audience, or that Irish somehow allowed him to express this desire more directly. However, Pearse did publish *The King,* "Little Lad of the Tricks," and *The Master* in English. The translations I am citing are his own.

29. The alternate version of this scene is printed in the Appendix to *Plays, Stories and Poems* (iii–v). Although the editor's preface says that it is difficult to tell which version was intended as the final one, it seems highly probable that the version in the Appendix is an abandoned first draft. The appendix version includes not only Sighle but also Colm, who in the final version of *The Singer* has already gone out to

the battle by the time this scene takes place. To integrate the alternate version into the play itself would have required a number of changes in the play's structure and would have decreased the impact of this scene. In the version printed in the text, the kiss scene takes place moments before MacDara's final rush toward death; whereas in the fragment preserved in the Appendix, it leads into what looks like the beginning of a fairly long oration in the style of Pearse's political speeches. It is much more likely, therefore, that the appendix version represents an earlier draft that was discarded after Pearse reworked MacDara's final speech to make it more dramatic and less rhetorical.

30. For instance, in the Catholic Mass, once the host is consecrated, it becomes sacred in and of itself and is treated accordingly. The miraculous nature of transubstantiation makes communion more central to Catholic practice than it is in many other Christian traditions and partially explains the importance invested in going to weekly mass and receiving communion.

4. The Body of Truth

1. Krause's edition of O'Casey's letters, *The Letters of Sean O'Casey (LSO),* includes letters written to him by other people and letters to the editor published by his sparring opponents, including Sheehy-Skeffington.

2. My summary of melodramatic conventions is adapted from Michael Booth's discussion in *English Melodrama* (13–39).

3. Hogan and Burnham make this argument, for instance, in *The Years of Sean O'Casey,* 147.

4. The ballad Fox cites is a socialist reworking of the popular nationalist anthem "Who Fears to Speak of '98?"

5. The Auxiliaries, also known from their uniforms as the Black and Tans, were a supplemental police force used by the British government against the Irish Republican Army during the Anglo-Irish war.

6. IRA stands for Irish Republican Army and refers in this context to the military organization that defended the Dáil Éireann and enforced its attempts at government. There were other names for this organization, as there are several terms for most of the political or military groups O'Casey represents in his trilogy. I will use O'Casey's terms for the sake of clarity and consistency.

7. Bernard Benstock credits Frank O'Connor with having coined this pejorative term for O'Casey's tendency to glorify and exalt his maternal figures (67).

8. Most of these flow from the pen of "Fiach," who also appears to have been *An Phoblacht*'s drama critic. See "Demoralizing Irish Amusements" (20 June 1925: 4), "Where Are Our Amusements?" (26 June 1925: 4), and "Irish and Foreign Dances" (12 November 1925: 4).

9. The Irish-language title of the *Irish Volunteer* is "oglac na h-eireann," and *An t-Oglach* clearly wants its readers to see it as carrying on the *Irish Volunteer*'s mission.

10. What to call the army defending the Free State, once the civil war starts, is a difficult question. After July 1922, the first issue of the "War Series," the term "Volunteers" disappears from *An t-Oglach*'s masthead; and the army defending the Free State, when mentioned in the text, is simply referred to as "the Army." When discussing the civil war period, I will be referring to it as "the Free State army."

11. Articles about republicans headlined "Military Tyranny" and "The New Dictatorship" appear in *An t-Oglach*'s April 22 and April 25 issues of 1922; in the same issue a piece on the Free State army has the subhead "The People's Army."

12. Fallon originated the role of Charles Bentham, the English schoolteacher who seduces and then abandons Mary Boyle.

13. Theosophy is a form of spiritualism that was promoted in Britain by Madame Blavatsky and was closely associated with W. B. Yeats. Making Bentham a theosophist is, of course, a dig at Yeats; but it is also a statement about the importance of materialism. As expounded by Bentham, the central tenet of theosophy is that materiality is an illusion, and the only "reality" is the life-breath of the spirit, or "prawna." The joke is that Bentham not only reveals himself to be crassly materialistic, but he refuses to accept responsibility for the material consequences of his actions (the botched will, Mary's pregnancy).

14. I refer to these characters as "Irregulars" because O'Casey does. "Irregular" was a Free State term for soldiers who were fighting against the Free State and for the republic; they are also sometimes referred to in the play as Die-Hards.

15. The Alfred Hitchcock film of *Juno and the Paycock,* while awful in almost all conceivable respects, does demonstrate how conspicuous Johnny's presence can become.

16. The Abbey stage was notoriously difficult to work with, and one of the main problems was a lack of space in which to store sets. This helps explain why so many early Abbey plays take place on a single set. Since O'Casey had written Johnny's execution scene to take place outside on a deserted road, staging the execution would have necessitated two set changes toward the end of Act III. This may have played as large a part in the directors' decision to cut the scene as the aesthetic considerations Fallon cites. Staging Minnie's death, since it has to occur outside, would have created the same problem. As soon as O'Casey has the opportunity to stage a death indoors—which comes in *Plough* because Bessie is killed by snipers—he takes it. See Clarke 35–38.

17. Father Farrell's interest in placing Captain Boyle derives from his admiration for Johnny's service as a republican, so Devine's offer is further proof of labor's entanglement with sacrificial politics.

18. Since Mrs. Madigan does not speak after Juno starts her final lament, it is possible to get her off stage so that Juno is alone with Mary when she delivers it.

19. In Act I of *Shadow of a Gunman,* Gallogher presents a petition to Davoren on behalf of his family, indicating that he identifies Davoren as a representative of the Dáil court system.

20. It is possible that the will is intended to stand, not just for the Treaty, but for Article 12, the clause that provides for the establishment of the actual border. The wording of Article 12 was so vague as to make it nearly meaningless when it came to establishing the actual border. The will has the same problem—because Bentham does not include the proper names of the legatees, the will is too vague to be executed.

21. Upon hearing the news, Boyle speaks Irish (badly) for the first time; during Act II he disclaims any connection to the political violence that has killed Tancred: "That's enough about them things; they don't affect us, and we needn't give a damn" (124).

22. Sheehy-Skeffington reports that the actor playing Pearse made an effort to reproduce Pearse's distinctive speaking style (*LSO* 172).

23. O'Casey served as the Irish Citizen Army's secretary but quit over Countess Marciewicz. He forced a vote on whether she should be forced to resign her membership in the Volunteers, and he lost. He later wrote a history of the ICA.

24. The OED defines "Covey" as a synonym for "chap" or "buddy."

25. During the Easter Rising, James Connolly sent the Labor flag to the Imperial Hotel as soon as it was taken, to be flown as a symbol that Labor had finally triumphed "over Martin Murphy and his kind." Murphy, who owned the Imperial Hotel, was the employer whose intransigence made the 1913 strike as brutal as it was; and the hotel itself was the site of a battle in which at least five hundred striking workers were assaulted and wounded by the police. Clitheroe thus dies as a result of Connolly's failed attempt to use Volunteer symbolism to achieve Labor's concrete goals.

26. This would have made a significant difference to contemporary Irish history. If the Free State had been able to insist on this "minimum" demand, Northern Ireland would have consisted, essentially, of the county Antrim and a corridor around Lough Neagh comprised of portions of Derry, Tyrone, Armagh, and Down. The city of Derry would be part of the Republic of Ireland, as would Enniskillen.

27. I am not arguing that the imposition of the border made partition an irrevocable and eternal fact. It did, however, mean that until republicans could achieve reunification, the Ireland to which they were loyal would never exist as a political entity.

5. Misbirth of a Nation

1. This rejection sparked a violent paper war between O'Casey and Yeats that eventually included Lennox Robinson, Lady Gregory, and several national newspapers. The *Tassie* controversy is well documented in Krause's *Letters of Sean O'Casey* (chapter 4, "The *Tassie* Scorned," 225–327).

2. While on their honeymoon in 1917, George began automatic writing, which was one of the methods used by mediums to relay messages from the spirits that were believed to be communicating with them. Yeats responded with tremendous enthusiasm, and he and George worked together for years gathering messages from the beyond and shaping them into a coherent (if not necessarily intelligible) mythology, which influenced almost all of Yeats's later writing.

3. Although Conor Cruise O'Brien is credited with being one of the first to raise the issue (in his 1965 *Writers and Politics*), Elizabeth Butler Cullingford's *Yeats, Ireland and Fascism* will probably remain the definitive scholarly treatment of this question. At any rate, it supersedes O'Brien's argument, which Edward Said describes as "hopelessly inadequate" in comparison with Cullingford's work (87). Paul Stanfield's *Yeats and Politics in the 1930s* and Marjorie Howes's *Yeats's Nations* both provide useful treatments of Yeats's fascination with degeneration and eugenics.

4. A July 27, 1935, *United Ireland* editorial about partition and its evils is headlined "A Poisoned Wound" (1).

5. "Herne" is a variant form of "heron," a large wading bird that lives in wetlands.

6. Ferguson's poem provided Yeats with the quarrel over the eggs, the curse, and Congal's ignominious idiot-inflicted death; but Yeats invented almost everything else. In Ferguson's poem, the eggs are wild goose eggs being guarded by a

Christian hermit named Erc, and it is king Domnal and not Congal who steals them from him. There is no Great Herne, no Attracta, no rape, and no reincarnation.

7. According to O'Connor, the Abbey board maintained that Yeats had told them something to this effect. Yeats later denied ever having said "anything so silly," which O'Connor believes because to him it is transparently clear that the seven rapists represent "the seven sciences' assault on revealed religion" (O'Connor, qtd. in Armstrong, xxv).

8. Sydney Poger's "Ritual and Parody in *The Herne's Egg*" is particularly egregious in this regard, but he is not alone. John Moore, while recognizing the brutality involved in what he terms a "rapture," views Congal's act as a generous-hearted attempt to "make a normal woman of [Attracta]" ("Cold Passion" 295). Richard Taylor's reading of the rapists as "the septenary nature of man" leads him to call the rape "natural and necessary" and argue that Attracta is "elevated" by it (183–84). And lest we be tempted to attribute this insensitivity to biology alone, Helen Vendler opines that "the most appealing thing about the play is that Yeats leaves us suspecting that perhaps it was the sevenfold rape, and not the Great Herne, that changed Attracta" (163).

9. The scholarly tradition of treating Ovid's divine rapes as "love stories" results from the same desire to save the author from the unpleasant implications of his artistic choices. However, Nancy Elizabeth Reynolds suggests in *Narrative Metamorphoses of Rape in Ovid* that in fact Ovid is deliberately representing these encounters as rapes. According to Reynolds's reading of the *Metamorphoses,* Ovid's narrators often attempt to present divine rape as either love or prostitution when they tell the stories, but Ovid undercuts these narrators by making it clear that they have ulterior motives for engaging in this kind of interpretive cover-up.

10. See Poger 43.

11. See Ferguson 255–81.

12. All quotations from De Valera's speeches are taken from Moynihan's collection unless otherwise indicated.

13. When first published in 1932, the paper was titled *The United Irishman* in a deliberate homage to Arthur Griffith. Later it changed to *United Ireland.* I will be using the second title throughout to avoid confusion with Arthur Griffith's *United Irishman.*

14. See S.O.S's "A Plaint Against Bureaucracy," *United Ireland* 12 October 1935: 5.

15. I have been unable to locate the speech in which De Valera first made this remark. It is first quoted in *United Ireland* as part of the caption for "Where Is the Omelette?" (19 November 1932: 1).

16. Counterintuitive as it might at first seem to figure De Valera as female, there is some precedent for this in *United Ireland,* where in cartoons he is frequently pictured in a dress or an apron.

17. This is stated most explicitly in "For the Female of the Species Is More Deadly Than the Male," which inveighs against the "Wild, Wild Women" in question (4), but is reiterated in most of the articles by Blueshirt women printed in *United Ireland.*

18. I borrow the phrase "epistemic violence" from Foucault via Spivak's "Can the Subaltern Speak?" (Spivak 281).

19. Schroedinger's Cat is one of the few problems of theoretical physics that has crossed into popular culture. In Schroedinger's example, you put a cat in a closed box and then explode a charge that has a 50 percent chance of killing the cat. Since you can't see the cat, you don't know whether it's dead. As far as you are concerned,

the cat now exists in a "probabilistic state" where it is 50 percent dead and 50 percent alive. While this cannot possibly be what actually happened (since the cat either is dead or it isn't), this is the most accurate way to describe the cat's situation, given the available data.

20. Tom Fool's motivation represents a significant revision of Ferguson's treatment of this incident, in which the fool who kills Congal is the "idiot son" of one of the kings Congal has slain in battle and is driven by revenge rather than a desire for fame and fortune. See Ferguson 360–61.

Afterword

1. Since all of Ireland's ambassadors at the time were authorized through their connection to the King of England, completely dropping out of the Commonwealth would have created recognition problems. See Pakenham 293.

Works Cited

"The All-Laugh Show. Mystery Playlet." *United Ireland* 18 November 1933: 3.

Alarcon, Norma. "Traddutora, Traditora: A Paradigmatic Figure of Chicana Feminism." *Scattered Hegemonies: Postmodernity and Transnational Feminist Practices.* Ed. Inderpal Grewal and Caren Kaplan. Minneapolis: University of Minnesota Press, 1994. 110–33.

Allen, Theodore W. *The Invention of the White Race.* London: Verso, 1995.

Anderson, Benedict. *Imagined Communities.* London: Verso, 1983.

Aretxaga, Begona. *Shattering Silence: Women, Nationalism, and Political Subjectivity in Northern Ireland.* Princeton: Princeton University Press, 1997.

Armstrong, Alison. Introduction. *The Herne's Egg: Manuscript Materials.* Ithaca: Cornell University Press, 1993. i–xxxi.

"The Army." *An t-Oglach* 3 July 1922: 1.

Arnold, David. *Colonizing the Body: State Medicine and Epidemic Disease in Nineteenth-Century India.* Berkeley: University of California Press, 1993.

Attridge, Derek, and Marjorie Howes, eds. *Semicolonial Joyce.* Cambridge: Cambridge University Press, 2000.

Beaslai, Piaras. "The Irish Volunteers." *An t-Oglach* 10 December 1918: 1.

Beers, William. *Women and Sacrifice: Male Narcissism and the Psychology of Religion.* Detroit: Wayne State University Press, 1992.

Benstock, Bernard. *Paycocks and Others: Sean O'Casey's World.* Dublin: Gill and Macmillan, 1976.

Beresford, David. *Ten Men Dead: The Story of the 1981 Hunger Strike.* New York: Atlantic Monthly Press, 1987.

Berrow, Hillary. "Eight Nights in the Abbey." *J. M. Synge Centenary Papers.* Ed. Maurice Harmon. Dublin: Dolmen Press, 1972. 75–87.

Booth, Michael. *English Melodrama.* London: H. Jenkins, 1965.

Brennan, James. "Types of Irishmen. I.—The Imperialist." *Irish Freedom* 15 August 1911: 2.

Brigid. "How to Popularise Irish Dress Materials." *United Irishman* 1 April 1903: 5.

Brown, Terence. *Ireland: A Social and Cultural History, 1922 to the Present.* Ithaca: Cornell University Press, 1985.

Butler, Judith. *Bodies that Matter.* New York: Routledge, 1993.

Butler, Mary E. L. "Womanhood and Nationhood." *United Irishman* 17 January 1903: 6; 24 January 1903: 6; 31 January 1903: 6.

"Carry On!" *An t-Oglach* 2 September 1922: 1.

Ceannt, Eamonn. "The Volunteer Giant." *Irish Volunteer* 7 February 1914: 3.

Chaudhuri, Una. *Staging Place: The Geography of Modern Drama.* Ann Arbor: University of Michigan Press, 1995.

"Clann Chonchobhair." "'His Excellency the Fatalist'—Dismemberment at the Royal College of Surgeons." *An Phoblacht* 2 April 1926: 2.

Clarke, Brenna Katz. *The Emergence of the Irish Peasant Play at the Abbey Theatre.* UMI Research Press: Ann Arbor, 1982.

Cohen, Morton. "Lewis Carroll and Victorian Morality." *Sexuality and Victorian Literature.* Ed. Don Richard Cox. Knoxville: University of Tennessee Press, 1984. 3–19.

Coleman, Antony. "A Calendar for the Production and Reception of *Cathleen ni Houlihan.*" *Modern Drama* 18 (1975): 127–40.

Coogan, Tim Pat. *The Troubles.* Boulder: Robert Rinehart, 1996.

Cullingford, Elizabeth Butler. "British Romans and Irish Carthaginians: Anticolonial Metaphor in Heaney, Friel, and McGuinnes," *PMLA* 111 (1996): 222–39.

———. *Gender and History in Yeats's Love Poetry.* Cambridge: Cambridge University Press, 1993.

———. *Yeats, Ireland and Fascism.* New York: New York University Press, 1980.

Curtis Jr., L. Perry. *Apes and Angels: The Irishman in Victorian Caricature.* Washington, D.C.: Smithsonian Institution Press, 1996.

Cvetkovich, Ann. *Mixed Feelings: Feminism, Mass Culture, and Victorian Sensationalism.* New Brunswick: Rutgers University Press, 1992.

Dahl, Mary Karen. *Political Violence in Drama: Classical Models, Contemporary Variations.* Ann Arbor: UMI Research Press, 1987.

"Deadly Tram Rides: How Public Vehicles Cause Disease." *Dublin Evening Mail* 12 January 1907: 2.

Deane, Seamus. "Civilians and Barbarians." *Ireland's Field Day.* Ed. Field Day Theatre Company. London: Hutchison, 1985. 33–44.

"Desecration." *An t-Oglach* 22 July 1922: 1.

De Valera, Eamon. *Speeches and Statements by Eamon De Valera 1917–1973.* Ed. Maurice Moynihan. Dublin: Gill and MacMillan, 1980.

"Dublin Honors the Brave." *An t-Oglach* 12 August 1922: 1.

Eakin, David B., and Michael Case, eds. Introduction. *Selected plays of George Moore and Edward Martyn.* Washington, D.C.: Catholic University of America Press, 1995. i–xxi.

Edwards, Ruth Dudley. *Patrick Pearse and the Triumph of Failure.* London: Victor Gollancz, 1977.

Eglinton, John. "The Place of Synthesis." *United Irishman* 9 May 1903: 2.

Fay, W. E. "A Note on National Games." *Sinn Fein* 12 January 1907: 4.

Ferguson, Sir Samuel. *Poems of Sir Samuel Ferguson.* Ed. Alfred Percival Graves et al. Dublin: Talbot Press, [1916?].

"Fiach." "Demoralizing Irish Amusements." *An Phoblacht* 20 June 1925: 4.

———. "Drama and Slavery." *An Phoblacht* 27 November 1925: 3.

———. "Irish and Foreign Dances." *An Phoblacht* 12 November 1925: 4.

———. "Where Are Our Amusements?" *An Phoblacht* 26 June 1925: 4.

"Fingan." "Who Stands for Ireland a Nation?" *An Phoblacht* 26 June 1925: 5.

"Finola." "A Word to the Women." *United Ireland* 24 March 1934: 5.

Flannery, James W. *W. B. Yeats and the Idea of a Theatre.* New Haven: Yale University Press, 1976.

Fleetwood, John F. *The Irish Body Snatchers: A History of Body Snatching in Ireland.* Dublin: Tomar Publishing, 1988.

"For the Female of the Species Is More Deadly Than the Male." *United Ireland* 2 July 1932: 4.

Fox, Richard M. *The History of the Irish Citizen Army.* James Duffy and Co.: Dublin, 1943.

Frazier, Adrian. *Behind the Scenes: Yeats, Horniman, and the Struggle for the Abbey Theatre.* Berkeley: University of California Press, 1990.

Friel, Brian. *Selected Plays.* London: Faber and Faber, 1984.

"Futility." *An t-Oglach* 22 July 1922: 4.

Gallagher, Frank. "Terence MacSwiney." *An Phoblacht* 23 October 1925: 3.

Good, Maeve. *W. B. Yeats and the Creation of a Tragic Universe.* London: Macmillan, 1987.

Gonne, Maud. "Invitation to American Doctors." *An Phoblacht* 20 June 1925: 6.

———. "Ireland and the Children." *United Irishman* 7 June 1902: 3.

———. "Maryboro Jail—The Same Old Tyranny." *An Phoblacht* 23 October 1925: 3.

Greene, David H. "J. M. Synge—A Centenary Appraisal." *J. M. Synge Centenary Papers.* Ed. Maurice Harmon. Dublin: Dolmen Press, 1972. 180–96.

Greene, David H., and Edward M. Stephens. *J. M. Synge, 1871–1909.* New York: New York University Press, 1989.

Gregory, Augusta. *Our Irish Theatre: A Chapter of Autobiography.* Gerrards Cross: Colin Smythe, 1972.

Griffith, Arthur. "The Abbey Theatre." *Sinn Fein* 2 February 1907: 2.

———. "Constitutionalism. Lecture by Mr. F. H. O'Donnell." *United Irishman* 15 April 1899: 3.

———. "The 'Economics' of Irish Famine." *United Irishman* 6 December 1902: 5.

———. Editorial. *United Irishman* 18 March 1899: 1.

———. Editorial. *United Irishman* 13 May 1899: 2.

———. Editorial. *United Irishman* 20 May 1899: 1.

———. Editorial. *United Irishman* 18 April 1903: 1.

———. Editorial. *United Irishman* 17 October 1903: 1.

———. Editorial. *United Irishman* 24 October 1903: 2.

———. Editorial. *United Irishman* 21 January 1905: 1.

———. Editorial. *United Irishman* 28 January 1905: 1.

———. Editorial. *United Irishman* 4 February 1905: 1.

———. Editorial. *United Irishman* 11 February 1905: 1.

———. *How Ireland Has 'Prospered' Under English Rule* and *The Slave Mind.* New York: Irish Progressive League (Donnelly Press), n.d.

———. "The Immorality of the British Army." *Sinn Fein* 9 February 1907: 2.

Grosz, Elizabeth. *Volatile Bodies: Toward a Corporeal Feminism.* Bloomington: Indiana University Press, 1994.

Harrington, John P., ed. *Modern Irish Drama.* New York: Norton, 1991.

Harris, Jose. *Private Lives, Public Spirit: A Social History of Britain, 1870–1914.* Oxford: Oxford University Press, 1993.

Hassett, Joseph M. *Yeats and the Poetics of Hate.* New York: St. Martin's Press, 1986.

Herr, Cheryl. *For The Land They Loved: Irish Political Melodramas, 1890–1925.* Syracuse: Syracuse University Press, 1991.

Hewson, Thomas. Letter to the Editor. *Irish Times* 29 January 1907: 8.

Hogan, Robert, and Richard Burnham. *The Years of O'Casey, 1921–1926: A Documentary History.* Gerrards Cross: Colin Smythe, 1992.

Holland, D. "O'Kelly's Bride." *Irish Volunteer* 1 August 1914: 12; 8 August 1914: 2–3, 6.

Holloway, Joseph. *Joseph Holloway's* Abbey Theatre: *A Selection from His Unpublished Journal "Impressions of a Dublin Playgoer."* Ed. Robert Hogan and Michael J. O'Neill. Carbondale: Southern Illinois University Press, 1967.

Hopkins, Eric. *Childhood Transformed: Working-Class Children in Nineteenth-Century England.* Manchester: Manchester University Press, 1994.

"How Smallpox Is Spread." *Irish Times* 31 January 1904: 5.

Howes, Marjorie. *Yeats's Nations: Gender, Class and Irishness.* Cambridge: Cambridge University Press, 1996.

H.S.D. "A Dramatic Freak. First Night at the Abbey Theatre. Paris Ideas and Parricides." *Dublin Evening Mail* 28 January 1907: 2.

Hubert, Henri, and Mauss, Marcel. *Sacrifice: Its Nature and Function.* Chicago: University of Chicago Press, 1964 (1898).

Hunter, A. S. "Health and Nationality." *Sinn Fein* 5 January 1907: 1.

"I Don't Care a Rap: Mr. Synge's Defence." *Dublin Evening Mail* 29 January 1907: 2.

Ignatiev, Noel. *How The Irish Became White.* New York: Routledge, 1995.

"Irial" [Fred Ryan]. "Revolution and Hysteria." *United Irishman* 31 January 1903: 3.

"Irish Literary Theatre." *Irish Times* 9 May 1899: 5.

"Irish Literary Theatre." *Irish Times* 10 May 1899: 5.

James, E. O. *Origins of Sacrifice: A Study in Comparative Religion.* London: John Murray, 1933.

Jones, Ann Rosalind, and Peter Stallybrass. "Dismantling Irena: The Sexualizing of Ireland in Early Modern England." *Nationalisms and Sexualities.* Ed. Andrew Parker et al. New York: Routledge, 1992.

Joy, Maurice C. "Mr. Yeats and the Freedom of the Theatre." *United Irishman* 29 November 1902: 3.

Judge, M. J. "To the Trenches: The Mother Calls." *Irish Volunteer* 14 February 1914: 13.

Kapsalis, Terri. *Public Privates: Performing Gynecology from Both Ends of the Speculum.* Durham: Duke University Press, 1997.

Kearney, Richard. "Myth and Motherland." *Ireland's Field Day.* Ed. Field Day Theatre Company. Notre Dame: University of Notre Dame Press, 1986. 61–82.

Kennedy, Robert E. *The Irish: Emigration, Marriage, and Fertility.* Berkeley: University of California Press, 1973.

[Kenny, P. D.] "That Dreadful Play." *Irish Times* 30 January 1907: 9.

Kiberd, Declan. *Inventing Ireland: The Literature of the Modern Nation.* Cambridge: Harvard University Press, 1996.

———. *Synge and the Irish Language.* London: Macmillan, 1979.

Kiely, David M. *John Millington Synge: A Biography.* Dublin: Gill and Macmillan, 1994.

Killen, John. *The Famine Decade: Contemporary Accounts, 1841–1851.* Belfast: Blackstaff Press, 1995.

Kinealy, Christine. *This Great Calamity: The Irish Famine 1845–52.* Dublin: Gill and Macmillan, 1994.

Kittson, E. Creagh. "The Citizen and the State: What Is Nationality? The Need for Self-Reliance." *Irish Volunteer* 7 February 1914: 13.

Krimm, Bernard G. *W. B. Yeats and the Emergence of the Irish Free State 1918–1939: Living in the Explosion.* Troy, N.Y.: Whitston Publishing Co., 1981.

Landen. "The Arming of Ulster." *Irish Freedom* 15 December 1910: 5.

"Lasairfhiona ni Shamhraidhin." "Irish Shoddy." *United Irishman* 11 February 1905: 6.

———. "Irish Shoddy." *United Irishman* 4 March 1905: 3.

———. "A Paper for Irishwomen." *United Irishman* 8 April 1905: 6.

Lee, J. J. *Ireland 1912–1985: Politics and Society.* Cambridge: Cambridge University Press, 1989.

"Lucan." "Not Peace but a Sword." *Irish Freedom* 15 September 1911: 5.

Macalister, A. "A Sketch of the History of Anatomy in Ireland." *Dublin Journal of Medical Science* 77 (1884): 1–19.

MacBride, John. "Major Macbride on Emmett." *Irish Freedom* 15 March 1911: 2–3.

MacColl, Rene. *Roger Casement: A New Judgment.* London: Hamish Hamilton, 1956.

Macleod, Roy. "On Visiting the 'Moving Metropolis': Reflections on the Architecture of Imperial Science." *Scientific Colonialism: A Cross-Cultural Comparison.* Ed. N. Reingold and M. Rothenberg. Washington, D.C.: Smithsonian Institution Press, 1987. 229–42.

MacSwiney, T. "Principles of Freedom—Brothers and Enemies." *Irish Freedom* 15 June 1911: 6.

———. "Principles of Freedom.—Womanhood." *Irish Freedom* 15 November 1911: 10.

Manning, Maurice. *The Blueshirts.* Toronto: University of Toronto Press, 1971.

Martyn, Edward. *The Heather Field: Selected Plays of George Moore and Edward Martyn.* Ed. David B. Eakin and Michael Case. Washington, D.C.: Catholic University of America Press, 1995. 217–68.

Mazumdar, Pauline M. H. *Eugenics, Human Genetics and Human Failings: The Eugenics Society, Its Sources and Its Critics in Britain.* London: Routledge, 1992.

McClintock, Alfred, and Samuel Hardy. *Practical Observations on Midwifery, and the Diseases Incident to the Puerperal State.* Dublin: Hodges and Smith, 1848.

"Microbes and Their Doings: The Curious Tricks They Play." *Dublin Evening Mail* 3 October 1907: 7.

Mokyr, Joel. *Why Ireland Starved: A Quantitative and Analytical History of the Irish Economy, 1800–1850.* London, Boston: Allen and Unwin, 1983.

Moore, John Rees. "Cold Passion: A Study of *The Herne's Egg.*" *Modern Drama* 7 (1964): 287–98.

———. *Masks of Love and Death: Yeats as Dramatist.* Ithaca: Cornell University Press, 1971.

"Morality and Patriotism: How an Irishman Should Feel." *Irish Volunteer* 4 April 1914: 10.

Moran, D. P. "The Gaelic and the Other Movement." *An Claidheamh Soluis* 8 July 1899: 260–62.

Moran, Sean Farrell. *Patrick Pearse and the Politics of Redemption.* Washington, D.C.: Catholic University Press, 1994.

"More Adventures in Blunderland." *United Ireland* 18 June 1932: 5.

Moscucci, Ornella. *The Science of Woman: Gynaecology and Gender in England, 1800–1929.* Cambridge: Cambridge University Press, 1990.

Moses, Marcus Tertius. Letter to the editor. *Irish Times* 28 January 1907: 6.

"Mr. Synge's Secret." *Dublin Evening Mail* 5 February 1907: 2.

"Muck-Raking in the Abbey." *An Phoblacht* 19 February 1926: 3.

Murphy, Brian P. *Patrick Pearse and the Lost Republican Ideal.* Dublin: James Duffy and Co., 1991.

Murphy, Daniel J. "Lady Gregory, Co-author and Sometimes Author of the Plays of W. B. Yeats." *Modern Irish Literature: Essays in Honor of William York Tindall.* Ed. Raymond J. Porter and James D. Brophy. New York: Iona College Press, 1972. 43–52.

Murphy-Lawless, Jo. *Reading Birth and Death: A History of Obstetric Thinking.* Cork: Cork University Press, 1998.

Nathan, Leonard E. *The Tragic Drama of William Butler Yeats.* New York: Columbia University Press, 1965.

Newman, A. "How National Degenerates Are Made." *Irish Volunteer* 14 November 1914: 9.

———. "National Degeneration." *Irish Volunteer* 11 November 1914: 2.

Nic Shiubhlaigh, Maire, and Edward Kenny. *The Splendid Years: Recollections of Marie Nic Shiubhlaigh as told to Edward Kenny.* Dublin: James Duffy and Co., 1955.

"Notes and Comments." *United Ireland* 10 March 1934: 1.

"Nurse Maguire." "What I Saw at the Abbey." *An Phoblacht* 19 February 1926: 1.

O'Brien, Conor Cruise. "The Embers of Easter 1916–1966." *The Easter Rising.* Ed. O. Dudley Edwards and Fergus Pyle. London: Macgibbon and Kee, 1968. 223–40.

———. *States of Ireland.* New York: Pantheon Books, 1972.

———. *Writers and Politics.* New York: Pantheon Books, 1965.

O'Casey, Sean. *The Letters of Sean O'Casey. 1910–1941.* Ed. David Krause. Vol. 1. New York: Macmillan, 1975.

———. *Selected Plays of Sean O'Casey.* New York: George Braziller, 1954.

O'Connor, Emmet. *A Labour History of Ireland, 1824–1960.* London: Gill and Macmillan, 1992.

O'Donnell, Frank Hugh. "Souls for Gold: Pseudo-Celtic Drama in Dublin." *Our Irish Theatre: A Chapter of Autobiography.* Gerards Cross: Colin Smythe, 1972. 261–70.

O'Duffy, Eoin. "An Irish Corporate System the National Need To-Day." *United Ireland* 24 February 1934: 3, 7.

O hEaluigh, Seamus. "Ode to the Rifle." *Irish Volunteer* 18 July 1914: 11.

O hUiathne, F. "Health, Nationality, and Vaccinations." *Sinn Fein* 12 January 1907: 3.

O Grada, Cormac. *Ireland Before and After the Famine: Explorations in Economic History, 1800–1925.* New York: St. Martin's Press, 1988.

O'Malley, Padraig. *Biting at the Grave: The Irish Hunger Strikes and the Politics of Despair.* Boston: Beacon Press, 1990.

"Onlooker" [Ernest Blythe]. "Definition of an Irish National. Do Emigrants Abandon National Status? Birthplace Not Sole Factor. Children of Mixed Parentage." *United Ireland* 10 February 1934: 3

Ould, Fielding. *A Treatise on Midwifery in Three Parts.* Dublin: Oli. Nelson, 1742.

"Our Purpose." *An t-Oglach* 7 July 1922: 1.

Pakenham, Frank. *Eamonn de Valera.* London: Hutchison, 1970.

"The Partition of the Green." *An Phoblacht* 18 December 1925: 5.

"The Patriot's Grave." *Irish Volunteer* 25 July 1914: 13.

Pearse, Padraig. "By Way of Comment." *An Macaomh* 1.1 (1909): 7–16.

———. "By Way of Comment." *An Macaomh* 2.3 (1910): 1–18.

———. *Plays, Stories, Poems.* Dublin: Phoenix Publishing Company, n.d.

———. *Political Writings and Speeches.* Dublin: Phoenix Publishing Company, n.d.

Pethica, James. "'Our Kathleen': Yeats's Collaboration with Lady Gregory in the Writing of *Cathleen ni Houlihan.*" *Yeats Annual* 6 (1988): 3–31.

Plunkett, Joseph. "Civilized Nationhood: Reached through the Volunteers." *Irish Volunteer* 7 February 1914: 4.

"P.M.E.K." "A Plea for the Playboy." *Sinn Fein* 9 February 1907: 3.

Poger, Sydney. "Ritual and Parody in *The Herne's Egg.*" *Canadian Journal of Irish Studies* 4 (1978): 37–44.

Poirteir, Cathal. *Famine Echoes.* Dublin: Gill and Macmillan, 1995.

"A Poisoned Wound." *United Ireland* 27 July 1935: 1.

Poovey, Mary. *A History of the Modern Fact: Problems of Knowledge in the Sciences of Wealth and Society.* Chicago: University of Chicago Press, 1998.

Radhakrishnan, R. "Nationalism, Gender, and Narrative." *Nationalisms and Sexualities.* Ed. Andrew Parker et al. New York: Routledge, 1992. 77–95.

Redmond, P. J. "The Volunteers." *Irish Volunteer* 14 September 1914: 8.

Reid, B. L. *The Lives of Roger Casement.* New Haven: Yale University Press, 1976.

Reynolds, Nancy Elizabeth. "Narrative Metamorphoses of Rape in Ovid." Thesis. University of North Carolina at Chapel Hill, 1994.

"Ricochets." *Irish Volunteer* 28 November 1914: 16.

Roche, Anthony. Letter to the Editor. *Irish Times* 29 January 1907: 8.

"Roisin Dubh." "What Is Practical Patriotism? Real Qualities Often Obscured by False Glamour. The Moral for Irishwomen." *United Ireland* 15 December 1934: 5.

de Roiste, Liam. "Now or Never." *Irish Volunteer* 14 February 1914: 7.

"Rory of the Hill." "Forgive and Forget." *Irish Volunteer* 26 September 1914: 3.

———. "The Recruiting Sergeant." *Irish Volunteer* 19 September 1914: 2.

———. "Seaghan O'Neil." *Irish Volunteer* 17 October 1914: 15.

———. "Steady, Volunteers." *Irish Volunteer* 4 July 1914: 15.

Said, Edward. "Yeats and Decolonization." *Nationalism, Colonialism, and Literature.* Ed. Seamus Deane. Minneapolis: University of Minnesota Press, 1990. 69–95.

Sage, Evan T., and Brady B. Gilleland, eds. *Petronius: The Satyricon.* New York: Irvington Publishers, 1982.

Sawyer, Roger. *Casement: The Flawed Hero.* London: Routledge and Kegan Paul, 1984.

Scolnicov, Hannah. *Woman's Theatrical Space.* Cambridge: Cambridge University Press, 1994.

Shaw, Fr. Francis. "The Canon of Irish History: A Challenge." *Studies* 6 (1972): 113–53.

Skene, Reg. *The Cuchulain Plays of W. B. Yeats: A Study.* London: Macmillan, 1974.

Smellie, William. *A Treatise on the Theory and Practice of Midwifery.* Dublin: 1764.

"Social Order." *An t-Oglach* 3 February 1922: 1.

Soloway. *Demography and Degeneration: Eugenics and the Declining Birthrate in Twentieth-Century Britain.* Chapel Hill: University of North Carolina Press, 1990.

"A Song for the Irish Militia." *Irish Volunteer* 14 February 1914: 7.

"S.O.S." "A Plaint Against Bureaucracy. Is the Tomato Muddle Clear—or a Bit Thick? 'Hunt the Slipper' Now an Outdoor Game." *United Ireland* 12 October 1935: 5.

Spivak, Gayatri. "Can the Subaltern Speak?" *Marxism and the Interpretation of Culture.* Eds. Cary Nelson and Laurence Grossberg. Champaign: University of Illinois Press, 1988. 271–313.

Stanfield, Paul. *Yeats and Politics in the 1930s.* New York: St. Martin's Press, 1988.

"The Study of Cancer. Treatment and Remedy." *Dublin Evening Mail* 2 January 1907.

Swift, Jonathan. *A Modest Proposal. Swift's Irish Pamphlets: An Introductory Selection.* Ed. Joseph McMinn. Gerards Cross: Colin Smythe, 1991. 447–51.

Synge, J. M. *The Aran Islands.* Boston: John W. Luce and Co., 1928.

———. *The Complete Plays of J. M. Synge.* New York: Vintage, 1960.

———. Letter to the editor. *Irish Times* 31 January 1907: 5.

———. Letter to the editor. *United Irishman* 11 February 1905: 1.

Rev. of *A System of Clinical Medicine,* Robert James Graves. *Dublin Quarterly Journal of Medical Science* 23 (1843): 122–52.

Taylor, Richard. *The Drama of W. B. Yeats: Irish Myth and the Japanese No.* New Haven: Yale University Press, 1976.

"That Bedside Manner." *United Ireland* 10 December 1932: 7.

"The Third Oireachtas." *An Claidheamh Soluis* 10 June 1899: 200.

Thornton, Weldon. *J. M. Synge and the Western Mind.* Gerrards Cross: Colin Smythe, 1979.

Tifft, Stephen. "The Parricidal Phantasm: Irish Nationalism and the Playboy Riots." Ed. Andrew Parker et al. *Nationalisms and Sexualities.* Routledge: New York, 1992. 313–32.

"Top Hats Versus White Waistcoats—Democracy and Colour Prejudice. The Hitherto Unsuspected Heinousness of Heliotrope." *United Ireland* 28 May 1932: 5.

Trotter, Mary. *Ireland's National Theaters: Political Performance and the Origins of the Irish Dramatic Movement.* Syracuse: Syracuse University Press, 2001.

Turner, Michael. *After the Famine: Irish Agriculture, 1850–1914.* Cambridge: Cambridge University Press, 1996.

"Ultach." "Don't Play the Enemy's Game." *Irish Volunteer* 14 July 1914: 8.

"Unit Leader." "The Employment of Women in the New Ireland. A Suggested Change. Cutting Out Blind Alley Jobs." *United Ireland* 14 April 1934: 5.

Vendler, Helen Hennessey. *Yeats's* Vision *and the Later Plays.* Cambridge: Harvard University Press, 1963.

Vicziany, Marika. "Coercion in a Soft State: The Family-Planning Program of India." *Pacific Affairs* 55 (1982): 385–97, 557–92.

Ward, Alan. *The Easter Rising: Revolution and Irish Nationalism.* Arlington Heights, Ill.: AHM Publishing Corp., 1980.

———. *The Irish Constitutional Tradition: Responsible Government and Modern Ireland, 1782–1992.* Washington, D.C.: Catholic University of America Press, 1994.

Ward, Margaret. *Unmanageable Revolutionaries: Women and Irish Nationalism.* London: Pluto Press, 1983.

Watt, Stephen. *Joyce, O'Casey, and the Irish Popular Theater.* Syracuse: Syracuse University Press, 1991.

Watts, Sheldon. *Epidemics and History: Disease, Power, and Imperialism.* New Haven: Yale University Press, 1997.

"What Is Irish National Literature?" *An Claidheamh Soluis* 1 July 1899: 248–49.

Wolveridge, James. *Speculum Matricis: Or, the Irish Midwives' Hand-Maid.* London: E. Oakes, 1670.

Worth, Katharine. *The Irish Drama of Europe from Yeats to Beckett.* Atlantic Highlands, N.J.: Humanities Press, 1978.

Yeats, W. B. *The Collected Letters of W. B. Yeats.* Ed. John Kelly. Vol. 1. Oxford: Clarendon Press, 1986.

———. "The Freedom of the Theatre." *United Irishman* 1 November 1902: 5.

———. "The Irish National Theatre and Three Sorts of Ignorance." *United Irishman* 24 October 1903: 2.

———. Letter to the editor. *United Irishman* 28 January 1905: 1.

———. Letter to the editor. *United Irishman* 4 February 1905: 1.

———. *On the Boiler.* Dublin: Cuala Press, 1938.

———. "The Theatre, the Pulpit, and the Newspapers." *United Irishman* 17 October 1903: 2.

———. *The Variorum Edition of the Plays of W. B. Yeats.* Ed. Russell K. Alspach and Catharine C. Alspach. New York: Macmillan, 1966.

———. *A Vision.* London: Macmillan, 1961.

Index

Susan Cannon Harris is Assistant Professor in the Department of English and the Keough Institute for Irish Studies at the University of Notre Dame. She has published articles on Brian Friel, James Joyce, Frank McGuiness, J. M. Synge, and W. B. Yeats and is writing a book about theater and culture in eighteenth-century Dublin.